Vāda in Theory and Practice

Vāda in Theory and Practice

Studies in Debates, Dialogues and Discussions in Indian Intellectual Discourses

Radhavallabh Tripathi

INDIAN INSTITUTE OF ADVANCED STUDY
Shimla

PRINTWORLD
Publishers of Indian Traditions

Cataloging in Publication Data — DK
[Courtesy: D.K. Agencies (P) Ltd. <docinfo@dkagencies.com>]

Tripathi, Radhavallabh, 1949- author.
Vāda in theory and practice : studies in debates, dialogues and discussions in Indian intellectual discourses / Radhavallabh Tripathi.
pages cm
Includes bibliographical references.
ISBN: 9788124608562

1. Knowledge, Theory of — India — History. 2. Debates and debating — India — History. 3. Debates and debating in literature. 4. Sanskrit literature — History and criticism. 5. Sanskrit drama — History and criticism. 6. Theater — India — History. I. Indian Institute of Advanced Study.publisher. II. Title.

B132.K6T75 2016 DDC 121.0954 23

ISBN: 978-81-246-0856-2
First published in India in 2016

Published by:
The Secretary
Indian Institute of Advanced Study
Rashtrapati Nivas, Summerhill, Shimla - 171 005
Phones: (0177) 283 1379; Fax: 283 1389
e-mail: proiias@gmail.com
Website: www.iias.org

and

D.K. Printworld (P) Ltd.
Regd. Office: *Vedaśrī*, F-395, Sudarshan Park
(Metro Station: Ramesh Nagar), New Delhi – 110 015
Phones: (011) 2545 3975, 2546 6019
e-mail: indology@dkprintworld.com
Website: www.dkprintworld.com

Printed by: D.K. Printworld (P) Ltd., New Delhi

अनुपश्य यथा पूर्वे प्रतिपश्य तथाऽपरे।
सस्यमिव मर्त्यः पच्यते सस्यमिवाजायते पुनः॥

— *Kaṭhopaniṣad* I.i.6

Look back and see — even as the men of old, — look around! — even so are they that have come after. Mortal may wither like the fruits of the field and like the fruits of the field he is born again.

— Tr. Sri Aurobindo[1]

A man may spend his life studying the Kāvyas, he may cross the vast sea of Śāstras, but look at his pathetic condition if he has not studied the Nyāyaśāstra! His tongue would become still when he tries to say something in the assembly where a *vāda* is going on! Away with these scholars who have not made inquiries into the Pramāṇaśāstra, have not considered the categories and have not delved deep into the logics, and have not studied the *Tarkavidyā*!

— Veṅkaṭādhvarin in *Viśvaguṇādarśacampūḥ*[2]

पक्षयुगलोज्ज्वलो जल्पकेलीमरालो विमलमवगाहते मानसं सुमनसाम्।

— *Jalpakalpalatā*

The swan of debate, with both its *pakṣas* (the prima facie view and its rejoinder/the two wings of the bird) takes dip in the *mānasa* (mind/Mānasarovara) of good-hearted persons.

. . . we need a sort of continuous dialogue between persons who do not treat knowledge as power, who want to use knowledge as process of understanding, a process of becoming, that can bring together all living beings. It is a process of love and a process of discovering what has been universal across cultures.

— Rafael Argullol[3]

1 Sri Aurobindo, 2001, *The Upanishads*, Part II, *Kena and other Upanishads*, p. 102.

2 See Chapter 6 of this work.

3 Ibid.

Prologue

THIS monograph is mainly the result of studies conducted by me as a Fellow at the Indian Institute of Advanced Study, Shimla; during the year 2014-15. My areas of study were Sāhityaśāstra (Literary Theory) and Nāṭyaśāstra (Theory of Drama and Theatre). But as a teacher and researcher, I have always remained conscious of the vitality of *vāda* — which is roughly translated for the purpose of this work as a category involving theory and practice of intellectual debates, dialogues and discussions. Traditional knowledge systems in India thrived because of *vāda*. These traditional systems have been subjected to a general negligence during the last two centuries or have been largely misrepresented. There has been an over-emphasis on spirituality and religion in the recent studies on the ancient Indian knowledge systems, and the disciplines having a focus with logic and arguments remained sidetracked. Ānvīkṣikī (logic and investigation) was a major discipline which was highly valued in BCE era. K. Satchidananda Murty rightly points out that "the study of classical philosophy in India has been dominated by *darśana*-concept, ignoring the Ānvīkṣikī-concept of philosophy".[1] A revisit to the theories and practices of *vāda* will hopefully lead to viewing these knowledge systems in their right perspective.

Vāda subsists on diversity. No *vāda* is possible if there is only one point of view. Also, *vāda* does not happen in singularity, it always is a prerequisite to the other and mostly promotes the presence of many others. India's history of ideas and debates presents a

---

1 K. Satchidananda Murty, 1985, *Philosophy in India: Traditions, Teaching and Research*, p. 194.

multilinear view. The tradition of *vāda* envisages pluralism. The learned editors of *Isibhāsiyāin*, a neglected work, but immensely valuable for understanding the Indian *vāda*, tell us that during the days of Mahāvīra there were as many as 363 theories discussed under four well-known sects. *Vāda* vitalized intellectual life and the seers, monks and intellectuals residing in the *āśrama*s, *vihāra*s and *saṁgha*s.

I have used the Sanskrit term *vāda* in a broad sense here and have given its nearest approximation — "debate" in bracket where *vāda* is used to denote a restricted sense. The seven chapters of this book deal with various aspects of the theory and practice of *vāda*. Since no comprehensive study in this field has so far been made (the works by Amartya Sen and A. Raghuramaraju merely touch its fringes, and the work by Esher Solomon mostly takes up the dialectic divergences) and the present study is intended to be a groundwork only, it was not possible for me to go deep into so many versatile aspects of study on *vāda*. The use of the word "Indian" in the subtitle may be termed as a misnomer. Owing to my limitations, I have mostly used Sanskrit sources for the treatment of *vāda* in theory and practice. But the intention was not to keep this work confined only to Sanskrit traditions of *vāda*; I have tried to include alternate or parallel traditions. Reference to Naryosang, Al-Beruni, Dara Shikoh or the works like *Dabistān-e-mazahib*, how so ever insufficient and scanty they may be, do indicate a broad framework for a study like this.

I hope that this book will prove how vital and important *vāda* — comprising theories and practices of debate, dialogue and discussion — has been, not only for the growth of our knowledge systems and ideologies, but also for our socio-political fabrics. *Vāda* was cultivated in India's intellectual discourses to project the distinct nature and uniqueness of each concept. This was possible through the frank admittance of both the agreements and the disagreements. *Saṁvāda* (correspondence) and *vivāda* (difference) are two faces of *vāda*. Texts like *Isibhāsiyāin* and *Śāstravārtāsamuccaya* of Haribhadra Sūri could be composed because of the first, whereas the second inspired a vast mass of philosophical literature. But then, there are inherent correspondences in the differences and the differences loom large when correspondences are being sought out. Gauḍapāda categorically said in *Māṇḍūkyakārikā* IV.99 that he has not borrowed from Buddha, but his concept of *vijñāna* or consciousness as the Ultimate Reality and the world appearing due to the diverse nature of *vijñāna* together with the examples he has given to illustrate his thesis are derived from Buddhism. A little intriguing example of such correspondence is Śaṅkarācārya himself. He vehemently criticized Buddhist philosophies, but beneath a very intense tussle and difference of outlook, there is an inherent acceptance of the Vijñānavādin for which he is also labelled as a Buddhist in disguise (*pracchannabaudha*), not by a section of modern scholars alone, but by some of the adherents of classical non-dualist philosophers like Vedāntadeśika, an extraordinary philosopher-poet of thirteenth century CE and a nephew of Rāmānuja. F. Stcherbatsky and Dhirendra Sharma have shown that by begging to differ with his *guru* Kumārila on the nature of *abhāva* (non-existence), Prabhākara denied the status of a *pramāṇa* to *abhāva* and thus followed the path of Dharmakīrti, a well-known Buddhist logician; and hence he was decried as "a friend of the Buddhists" (*bauddhabandhuḥ*).

It is true that we find a lot of manoeuvring in *vāda*s. But this has contributed to maturing a particular system of ideas. The search for truth led the seeker to traverse on diverse paths.

> During the days of the Pallava Renaissance, there was a close interconnection between the learned brāhmaṇas of Kerala and the Pallava court at Kāñcī. It is worth noting that Cheramān Perumāḷ, who could have been a contemporary of Śaṅkara or of his disciples, is said to have taken an interest in diverse religious faiths including Christianity and Islam. A story even relates to his conversion to Islam and pilgrimage to Mecca. He is also said to

have partitioned Kerala in deference to Śaṅkara's prescriptions.[2]

Intellectual discourses in India have remained so much argumentative that most of the works written in Sanskrit under diverse knowledge systems are structured in the techniques of debate. This applies not only to philosophical writings but to works belonging to medical sciences (Āyurveda) or works related to the management of society and life like *Arthaśāstra* of Kauṭilya or *Kāmasūtra* of Vātsyāyana. There are texts that have been thoroughly structured through *vāda*.

Some of the issues that have repeatedly surfaced in *vāda*s are concerned with the conflict between *karma* (action) and *jñāna* (knowledge), choice between violence and non-violence, the clash between two ideologies — *pravṛtti* (empiricism) and *nivṛtti* (renunciation) and these still persist in modern India in some form or the other. The doctrine of cumulative pursuit of *karma* and *jñāna* continued till Śaṅkara vehemently discarded it.

Even though marginalized to a large extent in the textual tradition of philosophical literature and surviving in thin numbers, the *lokāyatas* — materialists — have always remained assertive. Due to their skills in *vāda*, they actually commanded respect and were given prominence in socio-political life. There are epigraphic records to prove that they flourished in Karnataka and continued to practically debate with Vedāntins and other philosophers till fourteenth-fifteenth centuries.[3] The Cārvāka philosophy has remained a contentious issue with almost all the philosophical schools for more than two millennia. The modern scholars have vehemently debated on various perspectives of the Cārvākas.[4] The

---

[2] K. Satchidananda Murty, 1985, *Philosophy in India*, p. 77.

[3] Ibid., p. 17.

[4] Sadashiv Athawale in the Preface to the third edition of his Marathi book *Cārvāka: Itihāsa āṇi Tattavajñāna* (1997) gives a brief resume of these debates, referring to the divergence of opinions between A.H. Salunkhe and Shrinivas Dikshit.

present work repositions Cārvākas and their postulations in the light of *vāda*s and the *vāda* texts.

That *vāda* could transform society, could bring changes in the lifestyles, and quite often could also result in conversions of faith or religion are evidenced through numerous examples in this work. The concepts and categories related to *vāda* not only shaped up the course of discussions in the areas of philosophy or religion, they cast everlasting impact on the milieu and traditions of arts and aesthetics also. In Chap. 6, I have discussed some well-known masterpieces from Sanskrit literature in which *vāda* forms the structural or narrative design. There are literary pieces in which the debate becomes a major theme, whereas in others, debates are employed as a device to enrich the narrative. *Āgamaḍambaraprahasana*, *Dhuttakkhāṇa* (*Dhūrtākhyāna*), *Mudritakumudacandra*, etc. are works by philosophers composed with the intention of projecting *vāda*. *Mahiṣaśatakam* by Vāñchānātha is a poem penned with fervour and intensity by a *puṇḍit-kavi* (scholar poet). It is a poetic statement in protest in which the author enters into *vāda* with social institutions and oppressive systems.

At the surface level, the culture of *vāda* involves verbal duals, attacks and even violence of speech — debates on the propriety of such ramifications of *vāda* have been noticed in this monograph. But at the deeper levels, the *vāda* culture imbibes values and harmony. Al-Beruni, whom I have viewed as a source of inspiration for this work, had closely watched the people of our country and our habits of debate 1,000 years ago. His remarks on the Hindus are noteworthy:

> . . . at the utmost they fight with words, but they will never stake their soul, or body or their property on religious controversy.[5]

The *vāda* traditions have not simply subsisted on refutation. They evolved methods for critiques of reasoning. Each system

[5] *Albiruni's India*, ed. Edward C. Sachan, 2005, p. 19.

established its uniqueness through *vāda*. Prashant Dave rightly pointed out during the discussions with the present author that *vāda* led to revitalizing each theory, and each system got further developed by undergoing a series of *vāda*s with other systems. In fact, history of Indian philosophy should be rewritten from the point of view of *vāda* which led to culling out the essentialities of a system and assumption of its precise nature.[6] *Vāda*s were taken up to reinvigorate a thought system and also to sharpen one's own intellect. Mahima Bhaṭṭa, a logician wanted to prove the applicability of *anumiti* in the field of *belless lettress* and for this he composed an extensive text — *Vyaktiviveka* — with a twofold purpose, i.e. to establish the theory of poetic inference (*kāvyānumiti*) and also to earn instant recognition by the way of posing a potent challenge to as great a stalwart as Ānandavardhana.[7] Texts such as *Vyaktiviveka* are created in deep structures of agreement with surface structures in sharp disagreements.

Finally it is intended to search the resonances and percolations of the *vāda* traditions in modern times, to investigate how this tradition still continues to enrich our intellectual life and can contribute to create better stands and harmony in our society. Some of the spiritual or religious *guru*s like Ramana Maharshi, J. Krishnamurti and Vinoba Bhave have served as men of dialogues. Of these, Vinoba Bhave, remains most misunderstood, yet most versatile and learned *bhāṣyakāra* of ancient wisdom. His *āśrama* at

---

[6] Narmada Shankar Mehta in his Gujarati work *Hind Tattvajñāna no Itihāsa* made such an attempt.

[7] Cf. his prefatory remarks — "युक्तोऽयमात्मसदृशान् प्रति मे प्रयत्नो, नास्त्येव तज्जगति सर्वमनोहरं यत्। केचिज्ज्वलन्ति विकसन्त्यपरे निमीलन्त्यन्ये यदभ्युदयभाजि जगत्प्रदीपे।। इह सम्प्रतिपत्तितोऽन्यथा वा ध्वनिकारस्य वचोविवेचनं नः। नियतं यशसे प्रपत्स्यते यन्महतां संस्तव एव गौरवाय।।" (I am appropriately making an effort for those who are like me, everything is not agreeable in this world. When the lamp of the world (the Sun) rises in the horizon, some start burning, some are blooming, while others wither out. The propositions of the author of *dhvani* theory by agreements or disagreements are being taken up here for fame, because acquaintance with great theories leads to glory.)

Paunar, Wardha functioned as a vibrant place for discussions on social, moral and religious issues, and continued to be frequently visited by persons from diverse walks of life. Vinoba Bhave strived to create conciliations in a society torn by strife. Texts like *Samaṇasutta, Svarājyaśāstra*, commentaries on *Gītā* and *Japujī*, as well as the institutions like Ācāryakula and Sarvasevāsaṅgha were created due to his efforts. The idea of giving up the fight (*raṇachoḍanīti*), Sakalāyatanapaddhati and silence mooted by him are fresh manifestations of the potential nature of *vāda*.

Vāda has manifested in our responses to the opinions on Indian traditions of intellectual discourse by Western philosophers. S. Radhakrishnan gave a critique of Albert Switzer's view which he had expressed in *Indian Thought and Its Development* in 1939. Switzer had opined that Indian philosophy has been escapist. Radhakrishnan challenged his views in his *Eastern Religion and Western Thought* in the year 1939 itself. In another work he also presented a critique of Burgsan.

In the last chapter, I have tried to present the manifestations of *vāda* on a vast canvas during the nineteenth and twentieth centuries. India was facing the onslaught of modernity and social reforms as well as the ethics evolved through its contact with Christianity during these two centuries, drawing sharp reactions from fundamentalists or puritans. "Modern Indian thought finds itself in a historical context created by Europe, and it has difficulties speaking for itself. Even in its self-representation and self-assertion, it speaks to a large extent in a European idioms. This does not however mean that the dialogue between India and Europe has been decided in favour of Europe, or that India has been superseded by Europe. The power of the Indian tradition has not exhausted itself in self-representation and self-interpretation of modern India. The dialogic situation is still open."[8] At the backdrop of these remarks by

---

[8] Extract from the Preface to the German edition of *India and Europe: An Essay in Understanding,* Wilhelm Halbfass, 1988, p. xiii.

Wilhelm Halbfass, this chapter raises several questions, i.e. whether with the anthropocentric self-confidence of the West remains an overpowering force; whether the relationship between Orient and Occident is a relationship of subordination of India and subjugation by the West; or there are possibilities in the *paṇḍit*'s tradition for rejuvenating itself. Ananda K. Coomarswamy says that India would come out unscathed from the colonial onslaught though its body was badly damaged.[9] Sri Aurobindo would view the scenario as a mere surface deterioration.

One of the issues that consistently came up in all the knowledge texts is related to freedom. The concept of salvation in *darśana*s seeks individual liberation linked to social aspirations. The last criterion of *dharma* defined by Manu is *svasya ca priyam ātmanaḥ* (that which pleases the self). There is a continuity of search for the liberation in Smṛti texts, philosophical discourses, texts on aesthetics and literary theory through logics and reasoning, and this has continued to the twentieth century.

Due to the nature of this work and my own limitations, I have profusely used original terms from Sanskrit sources. I have also tried to limit myself to the original sources following the model set by Mallinātha, the great commentator of Sanskrit classics. In the preface to his commentary on *Kirātārjunīyam*, an epic by the poet Bhāravi, he said:

> इहान्वयमुखेनैव सर्वं व्याख्यायते मया।
> नामूलं लिख्यते किञ्चिन्नानपेक्षितमुच्यते।।
>
> Here I have explained everything just by paraphrasing, have not written anything without the base of the original and have not said anything unwanted.

Giving the final touches to this work, the memories of Pratapchandra and Bachchulal Awasthi have been flooding in my mind. The informal sittings (chitchats) in their homes at Gournagar, Sagar

[9] A. Raghuramaraju, 2006, *Debates in Indian Philosophy: Classical, Colonial and Contemporary*, p. 6.

during 1973-83 were the best practical demonstrations of *vāda* for me and they also represent two faces of *vāda* which I have talked about.

I could access the two volumes of *Indian Dialectics* by Esther Solomon after I had finalized the preliminary draft of this work. In fact, Solomon has already covered some of the topics dealt with here in a more comprehensive way. The last three chapters of my work, however, make a departure from the line adopted by her. In the earlier chapters I have tried to substantiate or to avoid repetition by referring to Solomon's work.

Vāda has been within and without me over these years and hopefully it will continue to grow.

Radhavallabh Tripathi

Contents

	Prologue	vii
	Acknowledgements	xxiii
1.	**The Nature of Vāda**	1
	Vāda, Saṁvāda and Vivāda	5
	Vāda, Protests and Dissents	9
	Reverting the Gaze	13
	Concept of Sabhā	13
	Appreciating a Conversation	16
	Ethics of Debate	17
	Violence of Speech	20
	Sandhi: Agreement with Disagreements	23
	Language and Stylistics	23
	The Ego, Prides and Prejudices	28
	Types of Debates, Dialogues and Discussions	29
	Vāda as a Digvijaya	31
	Vāda Internalized	32
	Vāda in Texts	33
	Texts on the Theory of Vāda	34
	Manuals on Vāda	36
	Documenting Vādas	37
	History of Vāda	38
	Genres	38

2. A Brief History of Vāda 40

I. Mantra-kāla (The Age of Revelation) 42

Upaniṣadic Debates 47

Debates, Dialogues and Discussions in Rāmāyaṇa 55

Debates in Mahābhārata 66

Nirukta as a Documentation of Debates 77

II. Tarka-kāla (The Age of Arguments) 78

The Continuance of Ānvīkṣikī 83

Buddha's Dialectical Method of Discourse 83

Mahāvīra and the Tradition of Debate 86

Arthaśāstra as a Text of Debates 88

Other Knowledge Texts 90

Buddhist Councils, Debates and Split 90

Kuṇḍalakeśī: The Lady Debater 94

Milindapañho 94

Aśvaghoṣa: His Debates with Buddhists and Non-Buddhists 96

Debates within Buddhist Schools 97

Debates between Buddhist Logicians and Naiyāyikas 98

Debates within Orthodox Systems of Philosophy 101

Debates between Buddhists and Naiyāyikas 107

Vādas after Dharmakīrti 109

Return of Cārvāka 112

Debates on Philosophy of Language 114

Śaṅkara's Conquests 115

Udayana 118

III. Vistāra-kāla (The Age of Diversification) 121

Challenges to Śaṅkara's Advaitavāda 126

Vādirāja 132

Creating Bridge through Vāda 138

The Reconciliation 146

3. Vādaśāstra: The Theories of Debate, Dialogues and Discussions 152

Theory of Vāda in Mahābhārata 152

Vāda and Nyāyadarśana 156

Caraka on the Theory of Vāda 166

Asaṅga on the Types of Vāda 178

Debate on the Debate: Buddhist Critique of Naiyāyika 180

Codes for Conducting the Debate 184

4. Vāda in Darśana: Philosophical Debates 188

Tussle between Action, Knowledge and Devotion 188

Revisionism 189

Debates between Idealism and Materialism 190

Critique of Cārvāka Philosophies 195

Debates on the Nature of Reality 196

Debates on Scriptural Authority 208

Debates on the Theory of Knowledge 209

Debates on the Theory of Causality 212

Debates on the Absolute and God as Creator 213

Debates on the Concept of Mokṣa 219

5. Vāda in Dharma: Socio-Political and Legal Debates 221

Debates on Polity and Governance 225

Vajrasūcī and the Debate on the Caste System 226

Debates in Dharmaśāstras 227

Debates on Rights of Women 229

Openness for Debate 236

6. Vāda in Literary Theory and Literature 239

Nāṭyaśāstra as a Saṁvāda Text 239

Vāda Reflected in the Conceptual Framework of Nāṭyaśāstra 241

Concepts and Categories of Vāda in Literary Theory 245
Major Debates in Literary Theory 246
Kāvyamīmāṁsā as a Vāda Text 247
Rasa Discourse: Debates and Diversities 248
Debates on the Theory of Alaṁkāra 256
Naṭāṅkuśa: A Vāda with the Cākyārs 257
Vādas in Kāvya Literature 259
Kālidāsa's Kāvyas as Debates 259
Bhavabhūti's Plays as Vāda Texts 262
Bṛhattrayī: As a Vāda Discourse 266
Dhuttakkhāṇa (Dhūrtākhyāna): Debates by Rogues 269
Āgamaḍambaraprahasana of Jayanta Bhaṭṭa 269
Vāda in Kāvya and Kāvya in Vāda 271

7. Vāda in Modern Age 282

Debates on India's Identity: Relocating Her Global Image 284
The Role of the Paṇḍit: Vāda Reformulated 286
The Shift in the Debates 291
Orientalism 295
Romantic Shifts in the Debate 300
Theological and Religious Debates 303
The Debates by Roy 305
The Vilification and Its Aftermath 307
Debates on Social Issues 310
Debates of Arya Samaj 314
Satyārthaprakāśa: A Text on Debate 314
Refutations of Satyārthaprakāśa and Rejoinders 319
Dayānanda's Debates on Public Platforms 321
Ramabai 324

The Śāstrārtha Continues 326
Paramārthadarśanam 327
Creating Hermeneutics 329
The Dialogue Renewed 331
Epilogue 336
Appendix : Selected List of Vādas Referred in This Work 338
Bibliography 345
Index 361

Acknowledgements

I AM thankful to the authorities of the Indian Institute of Advanced Study (IIAS), Shimla, specially its Director, Chetan Singh and Secretary Sunil Verma for their generous support during my stay at Shimla; to Premchand, the Librarian of IIAS and its efficient staff for taking care to make the reference material for this work available to me. My friend Manabendu Banerjee, one of the senior most Sanskrit scholars in the country today, has been immensely helpful as the General Secretary of the Asiatic Society, Kolkata by providing valuable source material. The shocking news of his sudden demise came after I had already gone through the final proofs of this work. A tremendous loss indeed. J.B. Shah readily provided me some important Jaina texts on *vāda* from his institution — the L.D. Institute of Indology. I am indebted to Uma Maheshwari for drawing my attention to *Nīlakeśī* (*Neelakesi*) — the Tamil text and providing me her copy of its abridged English version; to Arindam Chakravarti for providing me with a copy of Waymann's paper on *The Rules of Debate According to Asaṅga*; to Madhav M. Deshpande for kindly sending me the copies of two of his papers which have been useful for my work; for Lala Lajpat Rai's assessment of Dayanand I have consulted Kundan Tuteja; Balram Shukla has been my only source for the treatises in Persian and Urdu, he read and explained to me the relevant passages from *Dabistan-e-Mazahib* and *Mubahisa-e-Hudusa-e-duniya*. Thanks to Vasant Kumar M. Bhatta for drawing my attention to Esther Solomon's work on Indian dialectics and to Harsha Dev Madhav for arranging to send me the two volumes of her work. Rajendra Nanavati, Prashanta Dave and Pravin Pandya went through the rough draft and discussed some of the issues emerging out of this work. Prof. B.K. Bhattacharya not only drew my attention to the *Hindu-Turk-Saṁvāda* of Eknātha, he also made me available the copy of the paper by Elleanor Zellior on this poem. I have no words to thank Shatavadhani R. Ganesh. He pointed out various lacunae in my monograph after going through it carefully, and also gave a number of suggestions. I am also benefited by some positive suggestions by Prof. Shashiprabha Kumar.

Finally, I owe this work to the person who stands behind all my endeavours and who has carried *vāda* with me for the last forty years — my wife Satya. She allowed me to stay at Shimla, which was neither easy for her, nor me. The present work, with all its shortcomings and drawbacks, together with some of the breakthroughs that it could make, was possible because of her magnanimity.

1

The Nature of Vāda

Right from a hoary past, debates and discussions have helped Indian society to develop democratic values. As long as there was a scope for logic and reasoning, the possibilities of overthrowing authoritarian tendencies remained. S. Radhakrishnan says:

> Helped by natural conditions, and provided with the intellectual scope to think out the implications of things, the Indian escaped the doom which Plato pronounced to be the worst of all, viz. the hatred of reason." [1]

A country where debates do not happen is "a place without gestation". Authoritarian regimes do not allow debates to happen. The lack of *vāda* (debate, dialogue and discussion) leaves a society in a morbid state. *Vāda* envisages a culture of pluralism and democratic values.

B.K. Matilal recognizes two distinct traditions of Indian logic – one is the tradition of *vāda* (debates, dialogues and discussions) and the other is the *pramāṇa* tradition. The former is concerned with dialectical tricks, arguments and sophistry, whereas the latter with criteria for empirical knowledge.[2] However, Matilal does not define the interconnections between these two traditions. In fact, the *vāda* tradition does not simply subside in sophistry and tricks, it very much effects and enriches the other tradition concerned with epistemology, providing a critique of diverse schools of

---

1 S. Radhakrishnan, 2013, *Indian Philosophy*, vol. I, p. 2.

2 B.K. Matilal, 2005, *Epistemology, Logic and Grammar in Indian Philosophical Analysis*, p. 96.

philosophy. *Vāda* leads to true knowledge which would culminate in salvation (*mokṣa*).[3] In fact *pramāṇa* is invariably linked to both *vāda* and *darśana*. There is a popular saying amongst Sanskrit *paṇdits* —*vāde vāde jāyate tattvabodhaḥ* (after going through the series of *vādas*, true knowledge is acquired). In fact, it is this idea of *tattvabodha* — arriving at the very essence and ultimate truth — that distinguishes the Indian tradition of *vāda* from Western dialecticism. Greek philosophers like Aristotle have given the idea of dialectics primarily in the sense of "the art of discussion, debate, controversy, a method of argument or disputation, the process of discursive or conversational thinking".[4]

Speech can liberate. Words are illuminators and are capable of enlightening. Creating a theory and purging out the unacceptable theories through *vāda* (proper debate, discussions and dialogue) settles disputes and purifies the self.

In some of the orthodox Indian philosophies where the Word was viewed as the world, and the Ultimate Reality (*Brahman*) as well, *vāda* assumed utmost importance. Proper employment of words is equated to spiritual pursuit and would emancipate. *Ānvīkṣikī*, the earliest form of Indian logic, subsisted in *vāda*. It was an amalgam of three philosophies — Sāṁkhya, Yoga and Cārvāka. In fact, *Ānvīkṣikī* is the science of reviewing. Kauṭilya therefore holds that *ānvīkṣikī* reviews and investigates upon the contents of the other three disciplines (see Chap. 2).

---

[3] The first aphorism of *Nyāyasūtra* by Gautama says that by the true knowledge of sixteen categories of this discipline, *niḥśreyasa* (liberation) is acquired. Diṅnāga in his *Nyāyapraveśakasūtram* says:

सम्यङ् न्यायपरिज्ञानाध्धेयोपायदेयवेदिनः।
उपादेयमुपादाय गच्छन्ति परमां गतिम् ।। — p. 10

After acquiring a comprehensive knowledge of Nyāya, one knows the despicable and the acceptable, and acquisitioning the acceptable, one gets salvation.

[4] Esther Solomon, 1976, *Indian Dialectics*, vol. 1, p. 4.

In the course of time, the concept of *ānvīkṣikī* underwent a change. *Nyāyadarśana* rightly made a claim on it and Gautama in his *Nyāyasūtra* treated his philosophy at par with the Ānvīkṣikī. Rājaśekhara (tenth century CE), in his *Kāvyamīmāṁsā,* revisited the concepts of *vidyās* (branches of learning) and the Ānvikṣikī. According to him:

> The Ānvīkṣikī is divided into two parts — *pūrva-pakṣa* (the prima facie view) and *uttara-pakṣa* (the rejoinder). Buddhism, Jainism and Cārvāka philosophies are included in *pūrva-pakṣa* and Sāṁkhya as well as Nyāya and Vaiśeṣika in *uttara-pakṣa.* Taken together, they form six argumentative systems.[5]

Ānvīkṣikī or Nyāya[6] has been singularly devoted to arguments and logic. Vijñāneśvara in his *Mitākṣarā* commentary on *Yājñavalkyasmṛti* (I.3) defines Nyāya as *tarkavidyā* (the system of learning based on arguments). But the tradition of *Nyāyadarśana* does not simply regard this *darśana* confined to logic and arguments only. It has been defined as a Pramāṇaśāstra as well as *adhyātmavidyā* both. Rightly does Udayana, one of the greatest Naiyāyikas or experts in *Nyāyadarśana*, give the title to his magnum opus as *Ātmatattvaviveka* (true knowledge of the Self) even though his treatise is mainly devoted to *vāda* (debate) with Buddhists.

On the other hand, the systems said to have emphasized over self-realization and pursuing the path of salvation do recognize the importance of critical examination and reasoning. *Bṛhadāraṇyaka Upaniṣad* says: *ātmā vā are śrotavyo mantavyaḥ* (the Self must be listened to, must be contemplated upon with reasoning). Here *manana* stands for reasoning and rational thinking.

---

5 *Kāvyamīmāṁsā*, chap. II, p. 24.

6 The term *nyāya* was also adopted by Gautama from the social institutions that preferred reasoning. Yājñavalkya says that in case of divergence of opinions or difference in prescriptions, decision should be taken by *nyāya*. *Nyāya* here comprises three facets — the practices of the elders who are reliable, the prevalence and the precedence.

A *śāstra* (an authoritative documentation of the theory and practice of any knowledge system) is normally written in the style of debate, discussion and dialogue. There is an imaginary interlocutor, raising objections, demanding clarifications and asking questions. A debate within the mind of the author constantly goes on during the course of the creation of a treatise. A section of a *śāstra* is termed as *adhikaraṇa* or *adhikāra*. Jaimini's *Mīmāṁsāsūtra* is the first authentic text on the Mīmāṁsā philosophy. The sections of *Mīmāṁsāsūtra* are called *adhikaraṇas* and each *adhikaraṇa* has a fivefold structure involving — *viṣaya* (theme), *saṁśaya* (doubt), *pūrva-pakṣa* (the prima facie view), *uttara-pakṣa* (the rejoinder) and *nirṇaya* (conclusion).[7] It is true that Mīmāṁsā comprises an exegesis of Vedic rituals. Paul Deussen rightly says that Jaimini's text is "a methodical handbook treating the various questions arising out of the complicated Vedic ritual".[8] But it is also true that Jaimini has designed his aphorisms to form a text in debate and he was able to create a powerful discourse for debate. Veṅkaṭādhvarin in his *Viśvaguṇādarśacampū* (564) goes to the extent of saying that the proponents of all other Śāstras suffer debacles when a battle of debate is carried out by Jaimini's disciples.

The *adhikaraṇa* structure applies more or less to most of the śāstric texts and it invariably invests the texts with a dialogic nature — rooted in some kind of debate.

The practice of debating percolated various levels of Indian social life. Royal courts, assemblies of *paṇḍits* and even marriages[9]

---

[7] विषयो विशयश्चैव पूर्वपक्षस्तथोत्तरम्।
निर्णयश्चेति पञ्चाङ्गं शास्त्रेऽधिकरणं स्मृतम्।
— quoted in *Svarūpaprakāśa*, p. 27

[8] Quoted by K. Satchidananda Murty, 2007, *Evolution of Indian Philosophy*, p. 60.

[9] There was a tradition of holding a *śāstrārtha* (intellectual debate) between the *paṇḍits* representing *vara-pakṣa* (bridegroom's party) and the *kanyā-pakṣa* (bride's party) on the occasion of a marriage amongst brāhmaṇa families. Unfortunately *śāstrārthas* in marriage have now become extinct, and none of those that were held earlier is known to →

provided occasions for debates on issues pertaining to philosophy, ethics, polity, etc.

There is some debate on the question whether debate lies at the genesis of Indian world-view. The myth of the Sanakādi brothers brings out the tussle between two tendencies — *karma* (action) and *vāda*. The four boys — Sanaka, Sanandana, Sanātana and Sanatkumāra — were asked to cooperate in the act of creation by Prajāpati (the Lord of Creation), immediately after they were born. They asked why they should employ themselves in the act of creating; first the Prajāpati should reply to their questions. They were banished from the *brahmaloka* immediately because of this questioning spirit.[10] But they are held as great seers and authorities in Āgamas. Interestingly, almost all the Āgama texts are structured in *vāda* as dialogues between two persons, a *guru* and a *śiṣya*, or a Śiva and a Pārvatī; and the text unfolds in resolution to the doubts and replies to the queries of the *jijñāsu* (the seeker of knowledge).

Vāda, Saṁvāda and Vivāda

The term *vāda* is derived from the root *vad-* (to speak). The dictionary by Monier-Williams gives the following meanings of *vāda* — speaking of or about, causing a sound, playing, advice, council, speech, discourse, talk, utterance, statement, a thesis, proposition, argument, doctrine, discussion, controversy, dispute, contest, quarrel, etc. The term *śāstrārtha* came in vogue during nineteenth and twentieth centuries for *vāda* in a limited sense

← have been recorded. Prof. Ramesh Kumar Pandey, Vice-Chancellor of the Lal Bahadur Shastri Rashtriya Sanskrit Vidyapeeth, New Delhi, told me that he had represented the bridegroom's party in a *śāstrārtha* during a marriage, and his opponent representing the other party was no less than Pundit Badrinath Shukla, one of the greatest Naiyāyikas of Kāśī. Mostly such *śāstrārthas* were not taken seriously, the victory of the *paṇḍit* representing the *vara-pakṣa* being a foregone conclusion.

[10] This episode is described in *Viṣṇu Purāṇa* I.76.6, cf. *Prācīnacaritrakośa*, ed. Siddheshwar Chitrav, Pune, 1964, p. 1016.

(scholastic debate). It is mostly used for debates on public platforms or sometimes debates through the print media. *Vāda* has a wider connotation. It is accepted as a type of *kathā* (discussion) involving debates, dialogues and discussions on a philosophical, religious, social or ethical issue.

During Vedic period (before 600 BCE) the term *brahmodya* was used in the sense of *vāda*. K. Satchidananda Murty rightly suggests that "the oldest word used in the Vedic literature for the discussion of philosophical/ theological problems is *brahmodya*".[11] *Brahmodya*[12] is the technical name for the assemblies for holding discussions, debates and dialogues on ontological or epistemological issues.[13]

Brahmodya is not debate in the modern sense of the term, as the answers given by the respondent are known to the disputant and they are not challenged and questioned.

The dialogues involving heated discussions and rejoinders were called *vākovākya*. Yājñavalkya includes *vākovākya* in his list of subjects for study.[14] A *vākovākya* is treated sometimes synonymous to *brahmodya*. K.F. Geldner "sees in the *vākovākya* as an essential part of the Itihāsa-Purāṇa, the dialogue or dramatic element as opposed to narrative portion".[15]

---

[11] K. Satchidananda Murty, 1985, *Philosophy in India*, p. 3.

[12] The word *brahmodya* is formed by *brahma* + *ut* + √*yam*. *ut* + √*yam* would yield the sense of raising one's voice. Monier-Williams (p. 741) explains *brahmodya* as rivalry in sacred knowledge, playful discussion on theological questions or problems.

[13] *Bṛhadāraṇyaka Up.* III.8.1.12. The term *brahmavādin* has been used for the debaters in a *brahmodya* (*Chhāndogya Up.* II.24.1, *Śvetāśvatara Up.* I.1, II.41 and *brahmavādinī* is the lady debater (*Bṛhadāraṇyaka Up.* IV.5.1).

[14] वाकोवाक्यं पुराणं च नाराशंसीश्च गाथिकाः।
इतिहासास्तथा विद्याः शक्त्याऽधीते हि योऽन्वहम् ।। — *Yājñavalkyasmṛti* 45

[15] Cited in A.A. Macdonell and A.B. Keith, 1995, *Vedic Index of Names and Subjects*, vol. II, p. 279.

The assembly for a *brahmodya* was called *brahma-saṁsad*.[16] The term *vāda* came to be used subsequently with the emergence of systems of philosophy. *Milindapañho,* a Pāli text of second century BCE, uses the term *saddhi* for *vāda*. The term *brahma-sabhā* was also used for the assembly were debates or discussions on philosophical issues were organized. Rājaśekhara in the tenth chapter of his *Kāvyamīmāṁsā* directs the king to organize *brahma-sabhā*s in his capital to identify and honour the best of the philosophers and scholars. A special vehicle called *brahma-ratha* was arranged for the best debaters of the *brahmodyas*. Rājaśekhara has also informed that *śāstra-parīkṣā*s (examinations of the scholars through debate and discussion) used to be organized in the city of Pāṭaliputra (see Chap. 2). The kings presided over the *śāstra-sabhā*s in different disciplines. In addition to these, there were institutions in later period organizing *śāstra-sabhā*s. The Tripunithura court organized *vākyārtha-sabhā*s. In several towns of Kerala *śāstra-sabhā*s were held.[17]

Indian debate has a rich history of three millennia. There have been debates with a view to find out the truth, for a search of harmony and inherent unity of divergent theories. There have also been debates with sharp differences emphasizing the distinctions.

Isibhāsiyāin (Ṛṣibhāṣitāni), a collection of discourses by seers belonging to the Vedic, Ājīvaka, Cārvāka, Buddhist and Jaina traditions, is a unique text building up bridges and creating dialogues between diverse sects and traditions. Compiled around the fourth-third centuries BCE,[18] the text is immensely valuable for understanding the Indian traditions of sharing knowledge systems.

---

16 य इमं परमं गुह्यं श्रावयेद् ब्रह्मसंसदि। — *Kaṭhopaniṣad* I.17

17 "Intellectual Discourses in Medieval India: Historical Tracts of Śāstrasabhās", paper presented by K. Rajesh in the 47th session of All India Oriental Conference (AIOC), Guwahati, 2-4 January 2015, summaries of papers, p. 324.

18 *Isibhāsiyāin*, Preface, p. 11.

Amongst the seers included, twelve belong to Nirgrantha sect or Jainism, five to Buddhist philosophy and as many as seventeen to Vedic tradition. Amongst the remaining seers, Maṅkhali Ghosāla is known as the founder of Ājīvaka sect and while the affiliations of nine others are unknown. The 20th chapter named Utkala Adhyayana does not give the name of any sage, but it discusses the materialist philosophy through very interesting illustrations. The 21st chapter cites the *gāthās* of Gāthāpatiputra Taruṇa propounding Ajñānavāda, the philosophy of ignorance.

The whole process of *vāda* should lead to conclusion and theory building. Therefore the word *vāda* also came to be used in the sense of theory. Some of the well-known theories in the philosophical systems were named as *vādas*, viz. Ārambhavāda, Prāmāṇyavāda, etc. Some of the treatises dealing with specific theories were named as *vāda granthas*. Gadādhara Bhaṭṭācārya, a well-known Naiyāyika of seventeenth century CE, has written several *vāda* texts, viz. *Vyutpattivāda*, *Śaktivāda*, *Viṣayatāvāda*, *Muktivāda*, *Vidhivāda*, etc.[19] Madhva's works are also known as *vāda granthas.*

The word *saṁvāda* is used in *Mahābhārata* in the sense of a highly-profound discussion between two intellectuals that was carried out in past and lives in the collective memory of a race. This kind of *saṁvāda* becomes *itihāsa*. Many such *saṁvādas* are cited in *Mahābhārata.*

In Gautama's system of Nyāya, the term *kathā* is used for all kinds of discussions, conversations, debates and dialogues. *Vāda* is understood as a type of *kathā.* Caraka, the savant of Āyurveda, understands the term *vāda* in the sense of a formal or proper debate, where one party differs with the other and each adopts a position as per their system of thought or discipline. Instead of grouping *jalpa* (wrangling) and *vitaṇḍā* (cavil) as types of *kathā* (as Gautama, the author of *Nyāyasūtra* has done) Caraka defines these two as types of *vāda* (for details see Chap. 3).

---

[19] Nine such texts by Bhaṭṭācārya were published in a volume entitled *Vādavāridhi.*

Vāda, Protests and Dissents

Śvetaketu, who is being discussed in the next chapter here, is the first person to have raised a voice of protest against sexual exploitation of women. He also introduced a revolutionary change in the social practices. The Cārvākas always served as a protestant group that questions the prevailing norms and lifestyles (see Chaps. 2 and 4).

The question as to what extent protests and dissents are possible in a society, which has glorified *vāda* to a great extent, needs consideration. To a certain extent, a vigorous tradition of *vāda* has served as an outlet for the release of violence and has helped in keeping the voices of protests and dissents muffled. Pratap Chandra says:

> Terms like protest, dissent, heterodoxy (in a generalized sense), deviation from the mainstream, etc. are irrelevant in the Indian context. Ideological divergence obtaining in a plural context cannot be expressed in a terminology clearly implying a non-linear situation. It is indeed a pity that a modern scholar has been obliged to point out chinks in a non-existent monolith. But such are the consequences of a failure to critically evaluate the historical model before putting it into use.[20]

But then the dynamics of *vāda* themselves provided occasions for meaningful protests and raising the voices of protests. Śvetaketu, had protested against men's oppression of women and had told his father: "I raise my voice of dissent against such law. Henceforth no man will forcefully take any woman." The story of Sulabhā from *Mahābhārata* (see next chapter) brings out a woman's fight against man's pretensions and arrogance.

It is interesting to note that voices of dissent were raised in the very tradition of Vedānta against the caste system. While Śaṅkara,

---

[20] Pratapchandra, 1977, "Study of Ideological Discord in Ancient India: Search for a Suitable Model" in *Dissent, Protest and Reform in Indian Civilization*, p. 97.

Rāmānuja and even Madhva in their *bhāṣyas* agreed with the injunctions of Bādarāyaṇa in *Apaśūdrādhikaraṇa*[21] on denying the knowledge of *Brahman* to the lower castes, Rāmānuja, Rāmānanda and several medieval saints, preaching their philosophy, stood against the caste system.

The Lokāyatikas, Ājīvakas, the Sikh *gurus*, Kabīr (1398–1448), Vasava and B.R. Ambedkar raised the voices of protest against the system. They fought against hierarchies, feudalism and tyranny also. It is in the literary traditions — poetry, drama and fiction — that we find *vāda* reverberating with notes of dissent and protests. Chap. 6 of this work is devoted to documenting some of the literary pieces voicing such notes. Poets like Bhartṛhari, Bhavabhūti and Bilhaṇa have raised their voices of protest against the kings, as well as social and political institutions. *Mahiṣaśatakam* of Vāñchānātha (also known as Vāñcheśvara, and a descendant of Govinda Dīkṣita) is a powerful text against a ruler, the oppressive system and exploitation.[22]

Vāda worked for erasing boundaries and watertight compartments. Max Weber says:

> Without becoming a non-Hindu, a Hindu could accept highly important, most characteristic doctrines which every denominational Christian would consider *exclusively* his own. In Hindutva a teaching may be *orthodox* without being blindly valid, indeed the doctrinal fluidity of Hinduism is not incidental, but rather, the central, the central issue of religion, as we conceive it.[23]

The atmosphere conducive to free dialogues led to equilibrium. *Vādas* also served as platforms for purging the violence in various groups and thus served as catalysts for bringing harmony and peace. Jainism, Buddhism and Ājīvakas arose parallel to the

[21] *Brahmasūtra* I.3.34-38.

[22] For details see *Mahiṣaśatakam*, Preface.

[23] Quoted in Pratapchandra, 1977, op. cit., p. 95.

orthodox priestly systems. It could be possible in this system that the *gṛhasthas* (householders) who paid the priests for rituals also gave alms to the Buddhist monks.

Suppression of debates and resistance to them leads to the erosion of democratic systems and values. There are standpoints. Sticking to any one of them, may lead to clashes. Truth may emerge from them out of constant dialogues and conversations.

The royal courts served as academies and provided a platform for exchange of thoughts and ideas between diverse sects and philosophical schools. The spirit of *vāda* in the broad sense of the term is reflected in the edicts of King Aśoka, which give the message of harmony:

> King Priyadarśī Devānam Priya, wishes that all [religious] sects should live [harmoniously] everywhere in [his dominions], for all of them want self-control and purity of thought; . . . there is no person who is not devoted to a particular religious sect; [the King] honours all sects. . . .
>
> . . . there should be no extolment of one's own sect or disparagement of other sects . . . other sects should be honoured in every way on all occasions.
>
> . . . whosoever extols his own sect and disparages other sects . . . injures his own sect severely. . . .
>
> . . . this indeed is the desire of King Priyadarśī Devānam Priya that followers of all sects should be well informed [about others] and acquire benevolent thoughts. . . .
>
> . . . all the religious sects have been honoured by me with various kinds of honours.
>
> . . . The *dharma-mahāmātras* are occupied with all the religious sects — the brāhmaṇas, the Ājīvakas, Nirgranthas — with these and other sects.
>
> — From the Edicts of Aśoka: R.E. VII Shahbazgarhi, R.E. XII, XIII, XI and VII

On the other hand, the people belonging to the establishment were afraid of those who indulged in *vādas*. The philosophers like the Lokāyatikas or Cārvākas were also regarded dangerous because they constantly raised questions and debates. The kings were advised not to pay attention to them. When Bharata visits Rāma in Citrakūṭa the later asks him — "O dear one! do you keep away from the brāhmaṇas who are Lokāyatikas? They are skilled in creating disasters, foolhardy and think themselves as very knowledgeable!" (see Chap. 2).

So much importance was attached to *vāda* that Kṛṣṇa while enumerating his glorious forms (*vibhūtis*) describes *vāda* as one of his *vibhūtis*: *vādaḥ pravadatām aham* (*Gītā* X.32) — I am *vāda* amongst the disputants. Śaṅkarācārya in his *Bhāṣya* talks about *pravadatām* as implying three forms of *kathā* (discussion) — *vāda, jalpa* and *vitaṇḍā*. Amongst these, *vāda* is the best as it leads to the truth.

The tradition therefore respected the *paṇḍits* who promoted *vāda* tradition. This tradition could also carry the spirit of challenge to the highest limits. Udayana a tenth-century philosopher came to be worshipped for having proved the existence of God. But Udayana could also challenge the Lord of Jagannātha when denied access to the temple at Purī. Myths and legends came to be woven around the great practitioners of *vāda*. Śrīharṣa, a well-known philosopher and poet, is said to have entered into debate even with the goddess of learning (Sarasvatī) and ultimately defeated her. Owing to their debating skills, some of the scholars are better known by the titles such as *vādībhasiṁhasūrin* (lion for the elephant-contenders in *vāda*), *prativādibhayaṁkara* (terrific for the respondents) and *vādirāja* (king amongst debaters), and their real names have sunk into oblivion. Siddhasena Divākara is eulogized in the following terms in *Ādipurāṇa*: "He was lion for the opponents in debate who were like elephants before him. He was lion of the theories."[24] Varadācārya alias Alagiya Maṇavala, who flourished in thirteenth century CE was a reputed author in philosophy and Tantra, was

---

[24] प्रवादिकरियूथानां केसरी नयकेसरी।
सिद्धसेनकविर्जीयात् विकल्पनखराङ्कुरः।। — *Ādipurāṇa*

known as *vādikesarin* (lion among the debaters).[25] Aṇṇagarācārya (14th-15th century CE) was called *prativādibhayaṁkara* (frightful to the opponents in debate). Vedāntadeśika (Veṅkaṭanātha) was given the title of *Kavitārkikacakravartī* (sovereign of poets and logicians).

Reverting the Gaze

A thorough understanding of the *pūrva-pakṣa* (the prima facie view) is required to start a *vāda*.[26] There are philosophers who could present the opponent's view with such exact comprehension that we can restore some of the lost philosophical systems only through the debate that was carried on in their refutation.

For a real *vāda*, the argument should be meaningful. It is true that there were debates in which facts were distorted, reasoning were mutilated, and arguments were not properly utilized. Kālidāsa had perhaps witnessed debates with meaningless arguments. Duṣyanta in *Abhijñānaśākuntala* says: *kiṁ vṛthā tarkeṇa anviṣyate* (what is to be sought by futile arguments?). Dharmakīrti, a renowned Buddhist philosopher has given an account of futile debates (see Chap. 3). In *Milindapañho*, cited here as an example of one of the most intense and profound debates (see Chap. 2), there are many presumptuous statements by Nāgasena, the great preceptor, with reference to geography and history. In one of his illustrations, Nāgasena describes several rivers like Sarayū and Vetravatī as having streamed from Himalayas (p. 141). Sometimes beliefs into supernatural phenomena are also aired (p. 148). But for more than two millennia, Indian culture has thrived because of real good debates.

Concept of Sabhā

Asaṅga has described six types of court rooms for holding the *vādas*: (i) *rājakula* — the royal palace, (ii) *yuktakula* — the residence

[25] C.S. Sundaram, 1999, *Contribution of Tamilnadu to Sanskrit*, pp. 102-03.

[26] "A defeated argument that refuses to be obliterated can remain very alive." — Amartya Sen, 2005, *The Argumentative Indian*, p. 6

of some officer, (iii) *parṣatsattvā* — assembly, (iv) *dharmārthakuśala-śramaṇabrāhmaṇa-vāsa* — the places where the śramaṇas are available, (v) residence of brāhmaṇas adept in *dharma* or brāhmaṇas adept in *dharma* are available, (vi) *dharmārthakarmasattvā* — places where persons desirous of learning *dharma* are present.

Rājaśekhara has described the assembly hall, arrangements for seats, etc. in it for holding *kāvyakāra-parīkṣās* (examination of poets) and *śāstrakāra-parikṣās* (examination of scholars). The assembly hall should have sixteen pillars, for doors and eight *mattavāraṇīs*, with one platform with the royal seat for the king (he is supposed to preside in all the *parīkṣās*). The poets, scholars of diverse knowledge systems, artists, etc. are assigned places in the assembly hall. This assembly hall served the purpose for holding all sorts of *vāda*s — *vāda*s for judging the quality of a new poet or the acquisitions of an emerging scholar. Even when speaking as an *ācārya* of Alaṁkāraśāstra (literary theory) and making recommendations to a poet-king, Rājaśekhara wants the *śāstrakāra-parikṣās* to be held in between the poets meets, as "wine alone does not taste good, it required some snacks to be combined with".[27]

---

[27] राजा कविः कविसमाजं विदधीत। राजनि कवौ सर्वो लोकः कविः स्यात्। स काव्यपरीक्षायै सभां कारयेत्। सा षोडशभिः स्तम्भैश्चतुर्भिर्द्वारैरष्टभिर्मत्तवारणीभिरुपेता स्यात् तदनुलग्नं राज्ञः केलिगृहम् मध्येसभं चतुःस्तम्भान्तरा हस्तमात्रोत्सेधा समणिभूमिकावेदिका। तस्यां राजासनम्। तस्य चोत्तरतः संस्कृताः कवयो निविशेरन्। बहुभाषाकवित्वे यो यत्राधिकं प्रवीणः स तेन व्यपदिश्यते। यस्त्वनेकत्र प्रवीणः, स सङ्क्रम्य तत्र तत्रोपविशेत्। ततः परं वेदविद्याविदः प्रामाणिकाः पौराणिकाः स्मार्ता भिषजो मौहूर्तिका अन्येऽपि तथाविधाः। पूर्वेण प्राकृताः कवयः। ततः परं नटनर्तकगायनवादकवाग्जीवनकुशीलवतालापचरा अन्येऽपि तथाविधाः। पश्चिमेनापभ्रंशिनः कवयः, ततः परं चित्रलेप्यकृतो माणिक्यबन्धका वैकटिकाः स्वर्णकारवर्धकिलौहकारा अन्येऽपि तथाविधाः। दक्षिणतो भूतभाषाकवयः, ततः परं भुजङ्गगणिकाः प्लवकशौभिकजम्भकमल्लाः शस्त्रोपजीविनो अन्येऽपि तथाविधाः।

तत्र यथासुखमासीनः काव्यगोष्ठीं प्रवर्तयेत् भावयेत् परीक्षेत च। वासुदेवसातवाहनशूद्रक-साहसाङ्कादीन् सकलान् सभापतीन् दानमानाभ्यामनुकुर्यात् । तुष्टपुष्टाश्चास्य सभ्या भवेयुः स्थाने पारितोषिकं लभेरन् । लोकोत्तरस्य काव्यस्य च यथार्हा पूजा कवेर्वा। अन्तरान्तरा च काव्यगोष्ठीं शास्त्रवादाननुजानीयात्। मध्वपि नानवदंशं स्वदते। काव्यशास्त्रविरतौ विज्ञानिष्वभिरमेत। देशान्तरागतानां च विदुषामन्यद्वारा सङ्गं कारयेदौचित्याद्यवस्थितिपूजां →

Vādin (proponent/disputant), *prativādin* (respondent), *prāśnika* (jury) and *sabhya* (member of the assembly) — these are said to be the four pillars of *vāda*.[28] A king should employ only those as the members of the *sabhā* who are religious, well tested, and can bear the *dhūḥ* (brunt) of *vyavahāra* (issues for debate/petitions) like good bulls. They should be adept in Dharmaśāstras, should come from good families, should always speak truth, and should consider a friend or a foe as equal.[29]

In fact, *sabhā* came to be known as an institution for the progress of *vāda*-tradition. There is a floating verse about the *sabhā* which says:

> There is no *sabhā*, if elders are not there. They are not elders if they do not give ruling according to *dharma*. *Dharma* is not *dharma* if it is without truth, and *truth* is not *truth* if it is mingled with cheating.

In *Mahābhārata*, Draupadī before initiating her debate, which is being discussed in the next chapter, recites this verse. Nārada in his Smṛti repeats it in the context of a judicial court (see Chap. 5).

← च। वृत्तिकामांश्चोपजपेत् सङ्गृह्णीयाच्च। पुरुषरत्नानामेक एव ह्यसावुपकारो यद्राजोपजीविनां संस्कारः।

महानगरेषु काव्यशास्त्रपरीक्षार्थं ब्रह्मसभाः कारयेत्। तत्र परीक्षोत्तीर्णानां ब्रह्मरथयानं पट्टबन्धाश्च। श्रूयते चोज्जयिन्यां काव्यकारपरीक्षा —

इह कालिदासमेण्ठावत्रामरूपसूरभारवयः।
हरिशचन्द्रचन्द्रगुप्तौ परीक्षिताविह विशालायाम्।।

श्रूयते च पाटलिपुत्रे शास्त्रकारपरीक्षा —

अत्रोपवर्षाविहपाणिनिपिङ्गाविह व्याडिः।
वररुचिपतञ्जली इह परीक्षिताः ख्यातिमुपजग्मुः।
— *Kāvyamīmāṁsā*, chap. X, pp. 174-78

[28] *Nyāyapraveśakasūtram*, Preface, p. 20.

[29] राजा तु धार्मिकान् सभ्यान् नियुञ्ज्यात् सुपरीक्षितान्।
व्यवहारधुरं वोढुं ये शक्ताः सद्गवा इव।।
धर्मशास्त्रार्थकुशलाः कुलीनाः सत्यवादिनः।
समाः शत्रौ च मित्रे च नृपतेः स्युः सभासदः। — *Nāradasmṛti* III.4-5

Appreciating a Conversation

Bhāravi in his *Kirātārjunīyam* has presented a debate between Draupadī, Bhīma and Yudhiṣṭhira involving perennial questions of polity and war. He has also described the qualities of speech for any conversation. They are — brilliance, perspicuity, grace and defined import (*sauṣṭhvodāryaviśeṣaśālinīṁ viniścitārthāṁ* — I.3), reasoning and radiance (*upapattimadūrjitāśrayam* — II.1), free from vagueness, pure, concise but heavily loaded with meanings (*...garīyasi... bahur alpīyasi dṛṣyate guṇaḥ* — II.4) charming in sense (*rucirārthā* — II.5).

Bhīma delivers a discourse on the necessity of quick action against Duryodhana. Yudhiṣṭhira praises Bhīma:

> Your pure intention is clearly reflected in your speech, which is free from arguments going against reasoning and proof, it is elegant, attractive for the heart as the image reflected in a mirror free from any coating of dust, transparent and charming to the mind and auspicious. (*apavarjitaviplave śucau hṛdayagrahiṇi maṅgalāspade . . . vimalā tava vistare girāṁ matir ādarśa iva abhilakṣyate.*)

He further says:

> Not that perspicuity from the words was removed, not that the depth of meaning was not attended to, distinctness of every section of speech was brought out, and power of expression never overruled.
>
> — II.27

In fact, Yuḍhiṣṭhira in his praise uses the exact terms from Nyāya philosophy to bring out the force of Bhīma's argumentative discourse — *upapatti*, *āgama*, *anumāna* (inference), *āśaya* (implication), etc. "The *āgama* was not mutilated by the deliberate use of *anumāna* in your speech" — he says (II.28). The commentators understand *āgama* as *nīti* (good policy) only. However, *āgama* has a wider connotation in Bhāravi's treatment of the qualities of good discourse. It is a paradigm for life.

In the eleventh canto of *Kirātārjunīyam*, Arjuna is performing rigorous penances and Indra comes to test his resolve. Arjuna lauds his speech as marked with clarity, charm, force, conciseness, open to questions, embracing wide range and undisturbed. It became like the word of scriptures being unshaken, and was like a flooding deep sea that could not be crossed by common men. It had wealth of meanings and grandeur like the tranquil mind of a seer.[30]

Ethics of Debate

Mahābhārata describes one of the greatest debates of our history that occurred when the Kauravas made an attempt to humiliate Draupadī in the presence of her husbands (the Pāṇḍavas). Draupadī raised a question about the legality of staking her in the game of dice. This resulted in a fierce debate involving perennial questions of morality (*dharma*) and also the rights of slaves and women. Vidura, the step-brother of King Dhṛtarāṣṭra, spoke about the norms and ethics of debate in an assembly on this occasion. He said:

> Knowing the rules of *dharma*, and attending an assembly, he who does not answer a query that is put forward, incurs a half of the demerit that is attached to telling a lie. If a person in the assembly knows the rules of *dharma* and speaks and gives a wrong answer, he incurs the sin of telling a lie. [31]

---

30 प्रसादरम्यौजस्वि गरीयो लाघवान्वितम्
साकाङ्क्षमनुपस्कारं विष्वग्गति निराकुलम्।।
न्यायनिर्णीतसारत्वान्निरपेक्षमिवागमे।
अप्रकम्प्यतयाऽन्येषामाम्नायवचनोपमम्।।
अलङ्घ्यत्वाज्जनैरन्यैः क्षुभितोदन्वदूर्जितम्।
औदार्यादर्थसम्पत्तेः शान्तं चित्तमृषेरिव।। — *Kirātārjunīyam* XI.38-40

31 Nārada in his *Smṛti* repeats Vidura's discourse almost verbatim.
यत्र धर्मो ह्यधर्मेण सत्यं यत्रानृतेन च।
हन्यते प्रेक्षमाणानां हतास्तत्र सभासदः।।
विद्धो धर्मो ह्यधर्मेण सभां यत्रोपतिष्ठते।
न चास्य शल्यं क्रन्तन्ति विद्धास्तत्र सभासदः।
सभायां न प्रवेष्टव्यं वक्तव्यं वा समञ्जसम्।
अब्रुवन् विब्रुवन् वाऽपि नरो भवति किल्बिषी।
ये तु सभ्याः सभां प्राप्य तूष्णीं ध्यायन्त आसते।
यथा प्राप्तं न ब्रुवते सर्वे ते ऽनृतवादिनः।। →

In this connection, Vidura recounted the tale of Prahlāda. Prahlāda was made arbitrator in a quarrel between Virocana and Sudhanvan, the former being his son. Facing a dilemma, Prahlāda approached Kaśyapa and asked him:

> What are the other worlds in which a man falls if he chooses not to answer a question in a debate/quarrel or if he gives a wrong answer?

Kaśyapa told him:

> A person who knows but prefers not to give an answer gets himself encaged in a thousand nooses of Varuṇa. If a person called as a witness in a dispute speaks carelessly, he also gets himself encaged in a thousand nooses of Varuṇa. Out of these one thousands nooses, one noose is released annually. Therefore a person should speak truth without concealment (whenever there is a dispute or a debate) in the assembly. If *dharma* is entangled with *adharma* in an assembly, it is the duty of each and every member of the assembly to take off the dart, lest they themselves be entangled with that *adharma*. In an assembly where a sinful act is not condemned, half of the demerit of that sinful act clings to the head of that assembly, one-fourth of it to the guilty, and the remaining fourth to the members of the assembly present there.

In this way Kaśyapa continued to dwell upon the guilt a person is subjected to, in case he utters a lie during the course of a dispute or debate. After hearing Kaśyapa, Prahlāda told his son the truth: "your contender Sudhanvan is superior to you".

In the Śāntiparva of *Mahābhārata*, Bhīṣma establishes *ānṛśaṁsya* (non-cruelty) as a criterion for carrying out a proper discussion. A person hurting the other by his speech is also a cruel person. Using of foul and harsh language is equated with inflicting violence.[32] A good speaker is the one who speaks without going against his own

---

← पादोऽधर्मस्य कर्तारं पादः साक्षिणमृच्छति।
पादः सभासदः सर्वान् पादो राजानमृच्छति।। — *Nāradasmṛti* III.8-12

32 *Mahābhārata,* Śāntiparva, 164.6.

intentions and also against the intentions of the hearer.

Yājñavalkya in his law book gives a list of persons with whom no debate should be taken up. The list includes parents, guests, brothers, married ladies, in-laws, maternal uncle, an old man (above seventy according to Vijñāneśvara), a child, a patient, an *ācārya* (who has given initiation by sacred thread, according to Vijñāneśvara), a *vaidya* (physician), those who are dependents (for their livelihood), relatives (belonging to both the father's and mother's side), *ṛtvik* (the priest), *purohita* (the person who performs rituals), sons, daughters, wife, servants and real brothers.[33]

The efficacy of *vāda* lies in encouraging the others to speak out and to establish communication. Debate for the sake of debate was never appreciated. Buddha has used the words *kalaha* (quarrel) and *vivāda* (verbal combat) to indicate the negative aspects of human personality. What is the genesis of *kalaha, vivāda* (debate), *vilāpa* (lamentation), *śoka* (sorrow), *mātsarya* (jealousy), *māna* (pride), *abhimāna* (ego) and *paiśūnya* (backbiting) — this question is asked to him in *Kalahavivādasutta* of *Suttanipāta.* Buddha says that all these evils are produced by attachment. The question of the propriety of creating controversies through debates is raised again in the next *sutta* (*Cūlavyūhasutta*) of *Suttanipāta*. Buddha is of the view that if a man does not follow the middle path, he gets stuck with a certain view and then he starts declaring that his view alone is right. He has denounced the tendency to enter into debates for creating controversies. Both praise and denouncement are fruits of this tendency. There are persons who would praise their own sects, methods and *dharmas*, and they will just decry the other systems as degraded (*hīna*). In fact, Buddha's discourse on the ethics of debate here is very pertinent:

> A brāhmaṇa does not depend on others, he transcends the quarrels and verbal duals.[34]
>
> It is difficult to pacify or bring a person to senses who out of

---

[33] *Yājñavalkyasmṛti,* Ācārādhyāya, 157-58, p. 52.

[34] *Suttanipāta, Mahāvyūhasutta* 10.

> prejudice regards his own view as right and quarrels with others about it.[35]
>
> Controversies are created by those only who are lacking in true knowledge and understanding. A man who has developed equality of view will not join any debate.[36]
>
> Those who go to an assembly to join the debate with an intention to prove that their opponents are fools, do so to earn public applaud. They shoot arrows at their opponents to earn praise. When they are defeated, they hide themselves, when they are condemned, they are furious and start searching the faults of the others. In *vāda-vivāda*, a man either attacks the other or harms himself. Such debates are of no use except earning praise or abuse. The arrogance that a man develops after emerging victorious in the debates ultimately leads to his downfall. A wise man therefore should avoid indulging in such debates. If the debates do not lead to self-purification, what is the use of nourishing one's own ego through them? A person who is free of ego will not enter into debate with anyone.[37]

On the contrary, many of the followers of Buddha themselves came to regard *vāda* essential for protecting his message. *Upāyahṛdaya*, a text of pre-Diṅnāga period wrongly ascribed to Nāgārjuna, begins with a *vāda* on the utility of *vāda* and the author of this text argues against the view that the debate only "creates bitterness, strife and hard-heartedness, and so should be avoided".[38]

Violence of Speech

The history of debates also comprises narratives of very tense moments and violent designs. The very titles of several works composed as debates are suggestive of the acts of smashing, breaking, uprooting, condemning or crushing.

---

[35] *Suttanipāta, Mahāvyūhasutta* 13.

[36] Buddhacaryā, *Mangādiyasuttanta*, ed. Rahul Sankrityayana.

[37] *Suttanipāta* 51, *Mahāvyūhasutta* 9-12.

[38] Solomon, 1976, op. cit., p. 10.

Stuti (praise) and *nindā* (abuse) are necessary ingredients of the discourses that were delivered in Vedic sacrifices. In Vedic sacrifices such as the Aśvamedha, the priest functions both as an *apagara* (reviler) and *abhigara* (praiser).

Debates involve violence in various ways. In one of the most profound and prolonged debates described in the Upaniṣads, Gārgī challenges Yājñavalkya with an attacking stance. She compares her pair of questions with two fatal arrows. Commenting on the episode relating to the debate between Janaka and Sulabhā (which is being discussed in the next chapter), Nīlakaṇṭha, a commentator par excellence on *Mahābhārata*, also uses the metaphor of a battle, where both discussants (Janaka and Sulabhā) fought with *buddhyastra* (the weapon of intelligence) with each other.

The law books of Manu, Yājñavalkya, Nārada and others define *vāk-pāruṣya* (harshness of speech) as one of the sins and also prescribe punishment for it. The concept of *vāk-pāruṣya* involves shouting, calling names and throwing abuses. According to Nārada, a statement made out of malice towards a country, a nation or a kin makes a person inflicted with the sin of *vāk-pāruṣya*. Both Manu[39] and Yājñavalkya[40] prescribe penalty for a man who uses humiliating terms for physically disabled persons (Manu prescribes only less than a *kārṣāpaṇa* but Yājñavalkya makes it thirteen and a half *paṇas*).[41] There are severe penalties for a man who speaks dirty words for anyone's mother, sister or wife. Kauṭilya defines the following categories of *vāk-pāruṣya* — attributing physical deficiency (calling someone blind, deaf, etc.), use of filthy language and condemnation.[42]

Vātsyāyana in his *Kāmasūtra* has discussed *samāja*, *kathā* and *goṣṭhī*. *Samāja* is a community hall. *Kathā* is a discussion which is

---

[39] *Manusmṛti* VIII.274.

[40] *Yājñavalkyasmṛti*, Vyavahārādhyāya, 204-07, pp. 283-84.

[41] Coins of copper.

[42] *Arthaśāstra* III.18, vol. II, pp. 103-04.

taken up when a *goṣṭhī* (group, circle) meets. *Kathā*s and *goṣṭhī*s could be held in *samāja* or during a trip outside the town. Vātsyāyana has laid down the norms with a view to avoid unsavoury episodes and violence in *kathā*s and *goṣṭhī*s. He says:

> The citizen attains utmost honour in the community by carrying on discussion (on poetry and art) neither very much through Sanskrit nor very much through *deśabhāṣā* (regional language). A wise man should not join circles (*goṣṭhī*s) not liked by the community, and carried on arbitrarily, and which are violent to others. The learned man attains success in the world by joining a circle which is run in accordance with the notions of the community, and which is essentially sportive in nature.[43]

Nāṭyaśāstra of Bharata Muni is a text against violence of speech. The very first performance of the play *Samudramanthana* (churning of the ocean) generated controversy and debates, and was attacked by demons called *vighna*s, who created a pandemonium when his repertoire was giving a show. They alleged that the performance is humiliating to them. But Bharata Muni was able to calm down the protestors and mischief-mongers to their senses and to see reason by carrying out a *vāda* with them.[44]

The devastating nature of the violence of speech is brought in the last chapter of *Nāṭyaśāstra*. Bharata's sons, trained by him in Nāṭyaveda later on began to perform the *śilpaka*s of rustic nature (*grāmyadharmaka*) and presented the life and deeds of the sages residing in the vicinity of Himalayas by the way of *viḍambana* (caricature) and *vyaṅgyakaraṇa* (satire). The sages being laughed

---

[43] नात्यन्तं संस्कृतेनैव नात्यन्तं देशभाषया।
कथां गोष्ठीसु कथयंल्लोके बहुमतो भवेत्।
या गोष्ठी लोकविद्विष्टा या च स्वैरविसर्पिणी।
परहिंसात्मिका या च न तामवतरेद् बुधः।।
लोकचित्तानुवर्तिन्या क्रीडामात्रैककार्यया।
गोष्ठ्या सहचरन् विद्वांल्लोके सिद्धिं नियच्छति।। — *Kāmasūtra* I.IV.37-39

[44] *Nāṭyaśāstra*, chap. I.

at in this way got infuriated and cursed the actors to be expelled from the divine region of the Himalayas and to become śūdras. But again Bharata Muni gets his sons reconciled to their predicament through discussion.

Sandhi: Agreement with Disagreements

Viśvaguṇādarśacampū by Veṅkaṭādhvarin is being discussed as a text of *vāda* in the Chap. 6 of this book. *Viśvaguṇādarśacampū* is a work of fiction. The author makes two *gandharvas*, Kṛśānu and Kṛśāśva, debating with each other on merits and demerits of phenomena. During the course of their debate, Veṅkaṭādhvarin gives dramatic directions like *sārdhāṅgīkāram* (accepting half-heartedly). Veṅkaṭādhvarin also introduces the idea of reaching a compromise by way of agreeing to disagree. He calls it *sandhi*. Viśvāvasu after initial disagreement on the discussion about Rāmānuja and his sect, finally says that he would like to enter into a *sandhi* to felicitate Ramānuja's contribution.[45]

In fact, the whole debate between Kṛśānu and Kṛśāśva in *Viśvaguṇādarśacampū* is an example of agreement on the differences.

Language and Stylistics

With a fully developed theory of *vāda* (see Chap. 3), which was reflected in actual practice in debates held in public or through writings, the interlocutors experimented with language and introduced their own idioms.

Dharmakīrti, a very serious Buddhist philosopher, displays a rare sense of subtle humour, when he chides his opponents — specially the orthodox Naiyāyikas. He then uses some of the finest proverbial expressions for mockery and satire. Here are some examples revealing Dharmakīrti as a philosopher who can also laugh and rejoice by the way of defeating the opponents in the battle

---

[45] अन्यदास्तां नाम तामेव काममन्योन्यं कलहायमानानां नानाविधानां श्रुतीनामविरोधसाधनेन साधुभावं प्रकटयन्तीमखिलगुणाभिरामां रामानुजसरस्वतीमभिनन्दामि। प्रसिद्धं हि सन्धि-मिच्छन्ति साधवः इति। — *Viśvaguṇādarśacampū*, p. 196, prose 99

of arguments. In the discussion of the causal property of *svabhāva hetu* (self-nature kind of probans) Dharmakīrti makes fun of his opponent for the view that a incapable cause is seen to produce its effect, by these remarks:

> Oh how highly powerful is the glance of the highly influential one, that it assigns activities of various kinds to incapable things. Our minds are pained by the worry that when this glance of your stops falling, alas, things will be rendered as having a non-productive character and will be removed from a causal series![46]

Taking into consideration the opponent's contention that the self-nature characterized by the uninterrupted action remains with the cause even before the final state, Dharmakīrti again finds an occasion to be mused by the absurdity of this argument and laughs at him by saying:

> [If this is the case], then how is it that someone is a mother and is also a barren lady? Or what is the meaning of this saying — that a thing by its nature possesses uninterrupted action, but does not perform the action?[47]

Refuting the opponent's view of the six characteristics of sound probans, Dharmakīrti says: "why does this poor fellow seek a son after marrying a eunuch?".[48]

Sometimes he is rather harsh on his opponents and hurls accusations on them with remarks such as:

> They do not deserve any attention, since they are simply crying in distress, their vitals being pierced with the spear of envy (on

---

[46] अहो महाप्रभावं महाप्रभावस्य दर्शनं यस्मादतत्स्वभावान् अपि भावान् स्वभावमात्रेण नानाप्रकारेषु नियुङ्क्ते। यदि नाम किञ्चित् कथञ्चिदत्रभवतो दर्शनविषयताम् अतिक्रामेत्, हन्त, अप्रसवधर्मकमपेतसन्तानं स्यादितीयं चिन्ता चित्तं दुनोति। — *Hetubindu* II.17

[47] तत् किमिदानीं माता च वन्ध्या च अस्ति? को वास्य भाषितस्यार्थः — अक्षेपक्रियास्वभावः कार्यं च न करोतीति? — *Hetubindu* II.18

[48] तत् किमयं तपस्वी षण्ढमुद्वाह्य पुत्रं मृगयते? — *Hetubindu* V.1

account of my victory in the arguments)![49]

He calls the followers of Sāṁkhya system as animals.

Dharmakīrti rejoices in teasing his opponents and at times becomes quite dramatic in his attacks. This tendency specially surfaces when he enters into an argument with the Sāṁkhya philosophers. In *Vādanyāya*, he refutes their idea of *anupalabdhi*. His acquaintance with the use of the figure of speeches like *vakrokti* and *ukta-pratyukta* in the poetic fancies of his times must have led him to make remarks such as:

> Wherefrom your honour has learnt this magic without *mantra* and *auṣadha* (herbs) that the same object, with no excess in its nature being generated or destroyed (remaining intact in the same form), sometimes becomes an object of perception, sometimes not, sometimes it is apprehended through inference, and again through perception and by verbal testimony at the same time without any change in its excess of its form and without having any change nature and not having getting any kind of excess?[50]

His satires and sarcastic remarks also reveal repulsion against the tenets of Brāhmanism. Dharmakīrti has used some rare idioms, phrases and expressions when laughing at his enemies. In one such context, he has used the term *parvakārin*. A *parvakārin* is a brāhmaṇa performing rites on the occasion of a *parva*, i.e. the 8th, 14th and 15th days of *śukla-pakṣa* (the full moon half month). From *parvakārin* comes the term *parvabrāhmaṇa* which Dharmakīrti has used for a greedy brāhmaṇa demanding more fees after having free food in a *śrāddha* ritual. Dharmakīrti has equated his opponents — the orthodox Naiyāyikas to this *parvabrāhmaṇa* in the context

---

49 तदयमीर्ष्याशल्यवितुद्यमानमर्मा विक्लवं विक्रोशतीत्युपेक्षामेवार्हति। — *Hetubindu* II.20

50 कुत इदममन्त्रौषधिजालं भावेन शिक्षितम् यदयमजातानष्टरूपातिशयोऽ व्यवधानिदूरस्थानस्तस्यैव तदवस्थेन्द्रियादेरेव पुरुषस्य कदाचित् प्रत्यक्षः, अप्रत्यक्षश्च। येन कदाचिदस्यामनुमानमुपलब्धिः, कदाचित् प्रत्यक्षम्, कदाचिदागमः। एकस्मिन्नैवातिशये अमीषां प्रकाराणां विरोधात्। — *Vādanyāya*, p. 28

of their insistence on the inclusion of *pratijñā* (statement) in the *pañcāvayava-vākya* (fivefold statement).[51] *Amūlyadānakrayin* (a person trying to purchase things without paying their price) is another such term used by Dharmakīrti in the context of Naiyāyikas and the Vaiśeṣikas imputing the difference between the pot and its form.[52] *Bhaṇḍālekhyanyāya* and *ḍiṇḍikarāga* are other interesting phrases which Dharmakīrti uses to rebuke his opponents. *Ḍiṇḍikarāga* is cited as an instance for the Naiyāyikas who are making argument for the sake of argument only. *Ḍiṇḍika*s are supposed to be the naked Jaina monks. They were known for their habit of writing their names again and again.[53] *Bhaṇḍālekhyanyāya* must have been a popular maxim, but it is not listed in the *laukika nyāyas* (popular maxims) in the lexicons and grammar manuals. Dharmakīrti has used this *nyāya* as an illustration for the buffoonery of his opponents[54] (a *bhaṇḍa* is a buffoon and *ālekhya* is painting.)

Jayarāśī was a follower of Cārvāka system (see next chapter). In his *Tattvopaplavasiṁha* he has critiqued all the systems of philosophy and spares none of them from making a fun. He has chided the Buddhists philosophers like Dharmakīrti by using such phrases as — *tad bālavilasitam* (acting like a child, p. 29), *jadaviteṣṭitaṁ* (acting like a fool, p. 32), *tadetan mugdhābhidhānaṁ dunoti mānasaṁ* (this kind of saying like that of a simpleton really hurts our mind, p. 39), *tad bālavalgitaṁ* (that was the chattering of a child, p. 39), *tan mugdhavilasitaṁ* (that was the act by a fool, p. 53), etc. He is still more harsh and sarcastic for the Jaina monks.[55]

Śrīharṣa is well known for his wit and sharpness in attacking his

---

[51] *Hetubindu* II.3.

[52] *Vādanyāya*, p. 21.

[53] *Hetubindu* II.4.

[54] *Vādanyāya*, pp. 87, 146.

[55] इमामेव मूर्खतां दिगम्बराणामङ्गीक्रत्य उक्तं सूत्रकारेण यथा
नग्न श्रणणक दुर्बुद्धे कायक्लेशपरायण।
जीविकार्थेऽपि चारम्भे केन त्वमसि शिक्षित:।। — *Tattvopaplavasiṁha*, p. 79

opponents in debates. In the discussion on Asatkāraṇavāda (effect being produced without a cause) he remonstrates his opponent by saying:

> Even this stretching of feet by the way of saying that there are infinite universals will not be for your relief.[56]

He further adds on his discussion on *sattā* according to Sadvāda and Asadvāda:

> This is like the sentry awakening after the thieves have already taken away the loot![57]

The Jaina philosophers theoretically upheld non-violence as the highest virtue, but did not leg behind in indulging in the violence of speech in most sarcastic ways. Nor did they lack in the capacity of boasting about their debating skills. Devasūrin (CE 1186–1269) in his *Syādvādamañjarī* says:

> I have the power to drown the elephants like Udayana in the sea of my arguments; O Jayanta! Where do you count there — you are just an insect![58]

In the Mīmāṁsakas are laughed at with this interjection on behalf of the followers of Rāmānuja:

> Who can make such remarks if he leans on the arms of Prabhākara or if Kumārila Bhaṭṭa has extended him his hand?[59]

Mudritakumudacandra, a play portraying debate between two Jaina monks, gives interesting account on the gusto and airs with which

---

[56] न च सत्ताभेदानन्त्यमस्त्येवेत्यपि पादप्रसारिका न निस्ताराय।
— *Khaṇḍanakhaṇḍakhādya*, chap. I, p. 30

[57] प्रयोजनानुपयुक्ते काले तस्य स्वरूपतोऽवस्थानं पाटच्चरलुण्ठिते वेश्मनि यामिकजागरण-वृत्तान्तमनुहरति। — *Khaṇḍanakhaṇḍakhādya*, chap. I, p. 30

[58] यदत्र शक्तिसंसिद्धौ मज्जन्त्युदयनद्विपाः।
जयन्त हन्त का तत्र गणना त्वयि कीटके।। — *Syādvādamañjarī*, chap. II

[59] को ह्येव ब्रूयात् प्रभाकरकरावलम्बी भट्टदत्तहस्तो वा। — *Sarvadarśanasaṁgraha*, Rāmānuja systems, p. 129

the challenges are given for the debate and accusations are made (see Chap. 6).

The Ego, Prides and Prejudices

It is difficult to judge the subtle levels of ego and prejudices that percolate any debate. In *Kāmagītā* of *Mahābhārata*, Kāma (desire) is made to say:

> No living being can defeat me without any appropriate method, though some try hard to kill me with a weapon they know to be powerful. For them, I emerge anew in that very weapon.
>
> When for example some people try to destroy me by means of sacrificial rituals, ceremoniously giving away various kinds of precious gifts, I, Kāma, appear in their minds again, in the form of craving for heaven or reputation, like a pious soul reborn as a living moving sentient creature.
>
> When some people try to destroy me by constant contemplation of Veda and Vedānta, I reappear in their philosophical egos, imperceptibly as the elemental soul is present in a subtle form even in immobile plants.
>
> . . . The learned one exerts himself to get rid of me by striving to attain liberation (*mokṣa*). I dance and laugh at him, because he sits right in the middle of his burning desire for freedom.
>
> Thus I am one Perennial force, never to be killed by any embodied being, unless he adopts appropriate technique.[60]

Śaṅkarācārya initially refused to enter into a debate with Bhāratī, the wife of Maṇḍana Miśra, with a male chauvinistic attitude, which was softened when Bhāratī convinced him that debating with her will not be below his dignity — though she is a woman.[61]

---

[60] *Kāmagītā* (sermon of desire) in Aśvamedhaparva of 13.12-18: A. Chakrabarti and S. Bandhyopadhyaya (eds.), 2014, *Mahābhārata Now*, p. 260.

[61] Shatavadhani R. Ganesh has informed me that this aspersion of Śaṅkara is just an inference validated only by one reference in *Śaṅkaradigvijayam* →

Types of Debates, Dialogues and Discussions

There can be several types of *kathā*, a generic term for all types of debates, dialogues and discussions in the Sanskrit intellectual discourse. While they have been classified into two types according to their nature — friendly or hostile — there can be other norms for classification. Depending on the subject or theme of discussion, debate or dialogue, *kathā* can be philosophical, legal, social or religious. In respect of the occasion and venue, it can be occasioned, pre-planned or impromptu. It may be held on a public platform, in an institution like royal court, a temple or a monastery. There are occasioned debates — a *kathā* may ensue out of a challenge by a person desirous of entering into a scholastic combat or discussion. It may be arranged in an institutionalized form, held regularly in a selected place, or it can be started by a sudden and unexpected turn of a situation.

Sometimes out of strange circumstances, a person is forced to enter into the debate. Carried out spontaneously in an instant reaction the debate in such cases presents a human drama. A person is helplessly thrown into a debate out of sheer compulsion of the situation and is either forced to stand for an issue.

One such debate occurred when Draupadī in a most humiliating way was dragged into the court of Duryodhana and was asked to become a slave, she started pleading her case. As per the original version, Kṛṣṇa does not appear to supply the chain of *sari*es, neither there is an actual attempt to disrobe her. She is teased and molested. She makes an appeal to the elders in the assembly and raises a question — whether her husband was authorized to make her a bet when after putting himself on stake, he had lost and become a slave himself. Draupadī not only pleads her own case, she is able to generate a public opinion in her favour. This whole unsavoury happening was conceived by the authors of *Mahābhārata* as an

← of Mādhava (IX.59), whereas rest of the narrative by Mādhava himself does not seem to support this contention.

impromptu debate. The court of Duryodhana became an assembly for debate; Draupadī was the petitioner (*vādin*). Duryodhana and his accomplices became the respondents. This debate is being further discussed in the next chapter.

One more instance of a debate having started unexpectedly was the dialogue between Śaṅkarācārya and a *cāṇḍāla* (scavenger, sweeper). It has been described by Mādhava in his *Śaṅkaradigvijaya,* and in several other works like *Bhagavatpādābhyudaya* and *Bṛhacchaṅkaravijaya.*[62] Going on the way of Varanasi, Śaṅkarācārya with his entourage is confronted by the scavenger. When asked to move away, he points out that ascetic does not practise what he preaches and there is a contradiction between the Vedāntic idea of spiritual unity and the caste notion of untouchability. The sweeper asked him:

> Do you want to remove the *annamaya* from the *annamaya*, the consciousness from the consciousness by asking me to move away? Are you forsaking the body or the soul by asking me to move away? Does the Sun reflect in the waters of Ganges or in a pond used by the sweepers differ? What is this confusion of difference between a *vipra* and a *śvapaca* (scavenger) in the vast *sea* of bliss?[63]

Śaṅkarācārya had to concede to his admonitions. G.C. Pande has referred to this incidence. *Manīṣāpañcakam* of Śaṅkarācārya was the result of this encounter. Pande says:

> The incidence could hardly be a fabrication of later times when such a repudiation of untouchability or caste inequality was unthinkable within orthodoxy.[64]

The incidence therefore has a historical basis being "too

---

[62] *Śaṅkaravijayamakaranda*, pp. 88-90.

[63] Ibid., p. 88.

[64] G.C. Pande, 1998, *Life and Thought of Śaṅkarācārya*, p. 87.

untraditional to have been fabricated in later times".[65]

Vāda as a Digvijaya

With the growth of religion in the organized forms, the abbots and heads of diverse sects assumed political power and started behaving like kings and masters. Debates came to be conducted on war-footing basis. Veṅkaṭādhvarin in his *Viśvaguṇādarśacampū* (564) uses the metaphor *vādāhava* (debate as a battle). A man engaging himself in a series of scholastic debates at different places was projected as a warrior set out for *digvijaya* — a journey for victory throughout the country. The word has been used in the context of *vāda* perhaps for the first time by Śrīharṣa in his *Khaṇḍanakhaṇḍakhādya* — a text on refutation of all philosophical systems.[66] In many of the biographies of Śaṅkarācārya, which were written after twelfth century CE, the series of his conquests in debates are described as his *digvijaya*.

Swami Dayananda also began his *digvijaya* — the great journey for intellectual victory, and again in hundreds of Caritakāvyas that were composed after him in Sanskrit as well as in vernaculars, this great journey for the intellectual victory has been termed as *Dayānandadigvijaya*.

In the Sanskrit play *Mudrārākṣasa* of Viśākhadatta (around fifth century CE), Rākṣasa, the antagonist, compares his fight with his adversary, the great Cāṇakya, to the fight of a disputant with his rival in a debate:

> That *sādhana* (army, the probans in the debate) alone leads to success (victory of the warrior/debater) which has the *sādhya* (aim, probandum), established, which has *anvaya* (unity, perfection in five-member syllogism), which has *sapakṣa*

---

[65] G.C. Pande, 1998, op. cit., p. 89.

[66] शब्दार्थनिर्वचनखण्डनया नयन्तः
सर्वत्रनिर्वचनभावमखर्वगर्वान्।
धीराः यथोक्तमपि कीरवदेतदुक्त्वा
लोकेषु दिग्विजयकौतुकमातनुध्वम्।। — *Khaṇḍanakhaṇḍakhādya* I.3

(supporters, thesis case/homologue), and is turned away from *vipakṣa* (the rival armies, dissimilar case/heterologue). By accepting a *sādhya* which is common to both and is opposite to the *pakṣa* (armies revolting, thesis case, i.e. which is fallacious) a king will be routed like a disputant in a debate.[67]

Vāda Internalized

A person debates with himself, the debates and ideological conflicts going on in the society are reflected in his psyche. He/she creates an opponent and a respondent within and his/her mind becomes a locale of debate. Hanumān's contemplations during his search for Sītā in Laṅkā bring out the queries and the dichotomies that the society of his times was undergoing through, so that he appears to be debating with himself. Rāma in *Uttararāmacaritam* of Bhavabhūti debates with himself and his inner conflicts present premonition of Hamlet's speculations in Shakespeare. Presenting an analysis of the debate between Janaka and Sulabhā (see Chap. 2), Arindam Chakrabarti points out that "even public dialogues happen simultaneously inside each interlocutor's body". This may be the body of a particular "cultural ethos" as well as a "conversation of cultures"[68] so that the account of the debates that have occurred in the practical world could be viewed as a dramatized narrative of an internal event.

Mādhava in his *Śaṅkaradigvijaya* describes a debate between Bādarāyaṇa and Śaṅkarācārya. The former wants to test the scholarship of the *bhāṣyakāra* and comes to discuss the interpretations of various aphorisms of his own text with Śaṅkara in disguise. The legend seems to have its genesis in *Śāṅkarabhāṣya* itself, as in some of the places, Śaṅkarācārya argues with the author of *Brahmasūtra*.

---

[67] साध्ये निश्चितमन्वयेन घटितं बिभ्रत्सपक्षे स्थितिं
व्यावृत्तं च विपक्षतो भवति यत् तत् साधनं सिद्धये।
यत् साध्यं स्वयमेव तुल्यमुभयोः पक्षे विरुद्धं च यत्
तस्याङ्गीकरणेन वादिन इव स्यात् स्वामिनो निग्रहः।। — *Mudrārākṣasa* V.10

[68] Chakrabarti and Bandhyopadhyaya (eds.), 2014, op. cit., p. 325.

Nyāyakusumāñjali of Udayana is a text on debate about the existence of God. At the outset of his brilliant exposition, Udayana proceeds with the basic premise that the existence of a God in some form or the other is accepted in all philosophical schools and faiths. Then what is the need for a debate? Udayana says that *vāda* on God after considerations of the doubts and counter-arguments will lead to *manana* (contemplation) and this *manana* will become an *upāsanā* (worship of God) for me.[69]

Vāda in Texts

While the texts like *Nyāyasūtra* of Gautama and *Brahmasūtra* of Bādarāyaṇa take into account the rival systems for critiquing, the authors of *bhāṣyas* on these *sūtra* texts specially entered into debates with their opponents. *Brahmasūtra* itself is a *vāda* text, almost all the aphorisms are structured in giving a reasoning and argument to refute the prima facie view. The use of *apādāna kāraka* (ablative case) in many of the aphorisms (like *tattu samanvayāt*) indicates a proban and argumentative design.

In fact, during the past two millennia, all adherents of the orthodox or the non-orthodox Indian philosophical systems confronted their rival systems, attacked them by sharp weapon of arguments and reasoned against them in their texts. On the other hand some authors specially wrote texts in refutation. *Tattvopaplavasiṁha* of Jayarāśibhaṭṭa (eighth century CE) is a marvellous exercise in *vitaṇḍā* (cavil). *Khaṇḍanakhaṇḍakhādya* of

---

69 इह यद्यपि यं कमपि पुरुषार्थमर्थमानाः शुद्धबुद्धस्वभाव इत्यौपनिषदाः, आदिविद्वान् सिद्ध इति कापिलाः, क्लेशकर्मविपाकाशयैरपरामृष्टो निर्माणकायामधिष्ठाय सम्प्रदायप्रद्योतकोऽनुग्राहकश्चेति पातञ्जलाः, लोकवेदविरुदैरपि निर्लेपः स्वतन्त्रश्चेति महापाशुपताः, शिव इति शैवाः, पुरुषोत्तम इति वैष्णवाः, निरावरण इति दिगम्बराः, उपास्यत्वेन देशित इति मीमांसकाः, लोकव्यवहारसिद्ध इति चार्वाकाः, यावदुक्तोपपन्न इति नैयायिकाः, किं बहुना यं कारवोऽपि विश्वकर्मेत्युपासते तस्मिन्नेव जातिगोत्रप्रवरचरणकुल धर्मादिवदासंसारं सुप्रसिद्धानुभावे भगवति भवे सन्देह एव कुतः किं निरूपणीयं तथापि —

न्यायचर्चेयमीशस्य मननव्यपदेशभाक्।
उपासनैव क्रियते श्रवणानन्तरागता।।

— *Nyāyakusumāñjali*, chap. I, p. 15

Śrīharṣa (twelfth century CE) also employs all the tactics of *vitaṇḍā*. Śrīharṣa demolishes all the theories with a view to uphold Advaita Vedānta. Some of the texts of Jaina tradition of *khaṇḍana* have been discussed by Muni Sukhalalji Sanghavi,[70] viz. *Syādvādaratnākara* of Devasūrin and *Jalpakalpalatā* of Ratnamaṇḍana.

There are a few texts in other languages on the theory of *vāda*. Zalāluddin Dāvānī (CE 1426–1502) wrote a text on the theory of debate entitled *Akhlaque Nāsirī*. It is basically a didactic work, but also incorporates general instruction on how to behave during a debate. *Dabistān-e-mazahib*,[71] a Persian text by unknown author, presents debates and dialogues between various faiths. It was written in seventeenth century under the patronage of Akbar. It begins with an account of Zoroastrianism and describes various faiths like *Sarvadarśanasaṁgraha*. It has 12 *tālīms* on various faiths including those of Parsis, Christians, Hindus, Muslims and Sufis. It also describes living practices and discussion in the court of Akbar.[72]

Mubahisa-e-Hudusa-e-duniya (Debate on the Antiquity of Creation) comprises debate between Maulawi Sanaullah of Amritsar and Vazirchandra, editor of *Arya Musafir* magazine published from Haridwar in the form of question and answers presenting Islamic perspective.[73]

Texts on the Theory of Vāda

The profundity of the debates in the areas of philosophy, *dharma* (ethics and law) and Āyurveda, etc. led to the theoretical discussion on *vāda*, and a conceptual framework for Vādaśāstra was thus

---

[70] *Tattvopaplavasiṁha*, Preface by Sukhalalji Singhavi, p. 20.

[71] *Dabistan-e-mazahib*, ascribed to Kaikhusrow Isfandiyar and edited by Rahim Rezazade Malik, was published in original Persian by Kitabkhana- e-Tahoori, Tehran in 1362 Hizri.

[72] An Urdu translation of this work by Shraddharam Phullori was published by Mitra Vilas Press, Lahore, in 1898.

[73] Published in 1910 from Maktaba-e-Ahale-Hadis, Amritsar.

created. Independent texts on the theory of *vāda* were written in Sanskrit. Perhaps no other language and no other culture has such a rich tradition of having consistent dialogues on the concept of dialogue, discussions on the discussion, debates on the debate and conversations on the conversation. There are independent treatises exclusively or partly composed for the exposition of the theory of *vāda*. Vasubandhu's *Vādavidhi*, Dharmakīrti's *Vādanyāya* are treatises exclusively devoted to *vāda* theory. The theory of *vāda* is taken up in some of the works of Asaṅga and Udayana. Dharmakīrti in his *Nyāyabindu* has devoted the section on the *parārthānumāna* to the theoretical aspects of *vāda*. *Pramāṇapaddhati* on the epistemology of Mādhva school[74] has discussion on debates. Vasubandhu's *Vādavidhi* was not available to me. For discussions on debate by Asaṅga, I have depended on Alex Wayman.

Mahābhārata presents the first authentic exposition on the theory of debate through the discourse of Sulabhā. Even though the tradition of intellectual discourses, debates and discussions was assiduously pursued for more than a millennium in the philosophical discourses, it was the Nyāya philosophy that made it a part of an epistemology within the system. *Nyāyasūtra* of Gautama (sixth-fifth century BCE) discusses the theory of debate in detail. Out of the sixteen *padārtha*s (categories) that are supposed to be essential for the discipline of Nyāya, the following fourteen are directly related to debate — *saṁśaya* (doubt), *prayojana* (purpose/motive), *dṛṣṭānta* (illustration), *siddhānta* (theory/tenet), *tarka* (argument/hypothetical reasoning), *avayava* (members of a syllogism, parts of sentence presenting the thesis), *nirṇaya* (conclusion), *vāda* (discussion), *jalpa* (debate/wrangling), *vitaṇḍā* (cavil), *hetvābhāsa* (fallacy), *chala* (trick/quibbling), *jāti* (rejoinder)[75] and *nigrahasthāna* (clinchers/checks); and the remaining two — *pramāṇa* and *prameya* are indirectly linked with debate.

---

[74] Shrinivas Verkhedy has translated this work.

[75] *Jāti* has been translated by different terms. Esther Solomon has used words *sophistical refutation* and *futile rejoinder* for it.

Hetuviḍambanopāya by an unknown author and *Jalpakalpalatā* of Ratnamaṇḍana follow Jayarāśi's design, i.e. demolishing all systems. *Hetuviḍambanopāya* however is limited to the discussion of the theories of *anumāna*.[76]

Vādavidhi by Vasubandhu, *Nyāyapariśuddhi* of Veṅkaṭanātha, *Vādivinoda* of Śaṅkara Miśra and *Jainatattavaślokavārttika* by Vidyānanda are some other texts dealing with the theory of *vāda*.

Śāstrārthavicārapaddhati by Mahamahopadhyaya Rajeshwar Shastri Dravid (twentieth century) is a proof of the continuity of the practice of *vāda* and revisits to its theory amongst the traditional pundits in modern times.

Manuals on Vāda

Some of the texts cited here were written for a dual purpose, i.e. they deal with the theory of *vāda* and also aim at teaching the novices how to carry on a *vāda*. In *Khaṇḍanakhaṇḍakhādya* Śrīharṣa not only demolishes all the theories with a view to uphold Advaita Vedānta, he also visualizes his text as a manual for training in debate. He claims that even if the novices aspiring to learn the skills of *vāda* memorize some of the clichés as given in this text, they can confound the opponents in the debate.[77] He advises such aspirants to memorize the expressions and arguments from his texts and repeat them in the debate like a parrot. In Jaina tradition, texts like *Vādadvātriṁśikā, Syādvādaratnākara* of Devasūrin and *Syādvādamañjarī* are also manuals for the practitioners of *vāda*.

---

[76] *Tattvopaplavasiṁha*, Preface by Sukhalalji Singhavi, p. 20.

[77] एवं प्रकाराणि तल्लक्षणेषु खण्डनान्यूहनीयानि। तदेतासु खण्डनयुक्तिषु कामपि स्थानान्तरस्थां केनापि प्रकारेणानीय तत्सदृशीमन्यां वा स्वयमूहित्वा परैर्विविच्यमानानि पदार्थान्तराण्यपि बुद्धिमता बाधनीयानि। अत्र चास्माभिर्दूषयितुं शङ्कितेभ्यः परपक्षप्रकारेभ्यो यदि प्रकारान्तरं कोऽपि स्वयमूहति उक्तानां बाधकानां मध्ये क्वचित् प्रज्ञया समाधानमभिदध्यात् तत्र खण्डनवादिनः प्रस्तुता प्रतिक्रिया न स्फुरेत् तदा परेण प्रयुज्यमाने वाक्ये बहुपदात्मके कस्यचित् पदस्यार्थं खण्डयितुं खण्डनान्तरमवतारणीयम्। एवं तत्रापि परेण प्रज्ञाषोषणे पुनस्तथैव शाखान्तरेषु सङ्क्रमणीयमिति प्रकारेण खण्डनमये चक्रे सम्यगवधेयम्। — *Khaṇḍanakhaṇḍakhādya*, chap. IV, p. 753

Hetuviḍambanopāya displays skills in the employment of *hetu* (cause) as per the theory of *anumāna* for defeating an adversary in arguments. The methods for refutation as adopted by authors like Jayarāśi actually served as guidelines for later authors aspiring to contest with their opponents.[78]

Documenting Vādas

One of the most comprehensive works on *vāda* in practice is *Nīlakeśī* (*Neelakesi*) — a Tamil text giving account of the debates of Nīlakeśī, a Jaina nun around fourth-fifth centuries. The biographies of philosophers like Śaṅkarācārya in Sanskrit written between fourteenth and eighteenth centuries, and accounts of the life and deeds of Diṅnāga and Dharmakīrti from Chinese and Tibetan sources provide detailed accounts of the public debates these philosophers entered with their rivals. These biographical accounts sometimes tend to become mythical and over-exaggerated.

There are some Saṁgraha texts that put various systems of philosophy with a view to present the debates amongst them. *Ṣaḍdarśanasamuccaya* of Haribhadra and *Sarvadarśanasaṁgraha* of Mādhavācārya are examples of such attempts.[79] Mādhavācārya presents the systems in an ascending order of their acceptability according to him. The least acceptable ones are treated in the beginning and the systems like Pātañjala Yoga and Śāṅkara-Vedānta are discussed in the last chapters to suggest that they are the most perfect ones. Mādhavācārya takes up the main contention of each system, then refutation of the other systems according to it, and then the arguments that have been advanced therein for possible doubts and objects that may be raised by other systems.

---

[78] *Tattvopaplavasiṁha*, Preface by Sukhalalji Singhavi, p. 13.

[79] In addition to these, Vishweshwari Amma (1985: 91) has referred to a text *Sarvamatasaṁgraha* by Nārāyaṇabhaṭṭa, published from Oriental Research Institute and Manuscript Library, Trivandrum, 1977.

History of Vāda

Right from the inception of Indian civilization, the art of debating was taken up seriously and cultivated assiduously. The debates have been diverse and shifting; many a times very complex and competitive; or enduring and lasting in agreements and understanding also.

There are situations of debate described in the Vedic Saṁhitās. The Upaniṣads use the term *brahmodya* for *vāda* and give a number of specimens it — great debates revealing with insights of seers and intellectuals.

I have presented the history of debates in India in four successive stages (see next chapter). They can be named as *mantra kāla, tarka kāla, prasāra kāla* and *ādhunika kāla*. Intrinsic and intensive debates were carried during the second and third phases between the Realists and Idealists, between the Realists and Realists, between the Idealists and Realists and between the Idealists and Idealists. Vigorous interactions and encounters led to revisions and corrections in the systems. Dharmaśāstra offered wider and more potential field for oppositions and providing alternate systems.

Genres

During this second phase in the history of *vāda*, several genres of creating a *vāda*-text or any śāstric treatise were developed. They are — *sūtra, vṛtti, paddhati, bhāṣya, samīkṣā, cūrṇi, ṭīkā, pañjikā, kārikā* and *vārttika*.[80] A *bhāṣya* provides new interpretations, takes note of the diverse views and offers their critique. A *vārttika* examines a *sūtra* (aphorism) from the express point of view of what is stated

---

[80] सूत्रदिभिश्चैषां प्रणयनम्। तत्र सूत्रणात् सूत्रम्। यदाहुः —

अल्पाक्षरमसन्दिग्धं सारवद्विश्वतोमुखम्।
अस्तोभमनवद्यं च सूत्रं सूत्रकृतो विदुः।।

सूत्राणां सकलसारविवरणं वृत्तिः। सूत्रवृत्तिविवेचनं पद्धतिः। आक्षिप्य भाषणाद् भाष्यम्। अन्तर्भाष्यं समीक्षा। अवान्तरार्थविच्छेदश्च सा। यथासम्भवमर्थस्य टीकनं टीका। विषमपदभञ्जिका पञ्जिका। अर्थप्रदर्शनकारिका कारिका। उक्तानुक्तदुरुक्तचिन्ता वार्तिकमिति शास्त्रभेदाः — *Kāvyamīmāṁsā*, chap. II, pp. 26-27 (*ukta*) by a rule, what is not stated (*anukta*) by a rule, and what has been restated, or poorly stated (*durukta*) by a rule (*uktānuktadurukta-cintakatvam vārttikatvam*). A fairly substantial number of *vārttikas* formulated by Kātyāyana on the *sūtras* of Pāṇini are cited in the *Vyākaraṇa-Mahābhāṣya* of Patañjali. *Samīkṣā, ṭīkā* (commentary) and *mahābhāṣya* (detailed exposition) were other genres promoting diverse traditions of debate. *Samīkṣā* presents the critique of *bhāṣya; ṭīkās* basically paraphrased and explained a text but also took notice of the debatable issues. Patañjali presented such outstanding example of a *mahābhāṣya* that his name has become synonymous with this genre. He structured his arguments in a unique style of a dialogue with questions (*praśnas*), illustrations (*dṛṣṭāntas*), examples (*udāharaṇas*), counterexamples (*pratyudāharaṇas*), answers (*uttaras*), objections (*ākṣepas*), doubts (*sandehas*) and resolutions of doubts (*samādhānas*), carefully leading the reader towards the final view (*siddhānta*).[81]

Rājaśekhara (tenth century CE) rightly views a *śāstra* as the flow of rivers, which at its source appears in a subtle form, but assumes multifarious proportions and multiple streams.[82]

The tradition of *vāda* has developed through centuries. It manifested in multifarious channels of textual corpus, public debates and various platforms. It vitalized knowledge systems.

---

[81] Commentator Madhusudan Mishra has pointed out lacunae in the readings here, and he suggests अवान्तरार्थविच्छेदश्चूर्णिः। तथा च चूर्णिः महाभाष्यम्। चूर्णतिखण्डयति निखिलपण्डितानां तर्कमिति घृणिपृश्निपार्ष्णिचूर्णिभूर्णि इत्युणादि सूत्रेण निपात्यते। चूर्णिः पातञ्जलं व्याकरणमिति लिङ्गादिसङ्ग्रहटीकायां भरतः। चूर्णिं भाष्यं करोतीति चूर्णिकृत् भाष्यकारः गोनर्दीयः पतञ्जलिः इति त्रिकाण्डशेषः। — Ibid., p. 27

[82] सरितामिव प्रवाहास्तुच्छाः प्रथमं यथोत्तरं विपुलाः।
ये शास्त्रसमारम्भा भवन्ति लोकस्य ते वन्द्याः॥ — *Kāvyamīmāṁsā*, chap. II, p. 26

2

A Brief History of Vāda

Right from the inception of Indian civilization, the art of debating was taken up seriously and cultivated assiduously. There are situations of debate described in the Vedic Saṁhitās. The Upaniṣads use the term *brahmodya* for *vāda* and give a number of specimens — great debates revealing with insights of seers and intellectuals.

The history of debates in India can be classified into four successive ages:

- The Age of Revelation (around 3000 BCE to 500 BCE): was the period when *mantras* were revealed to the seers through their vision.
- The Age of Argument (around 500 BCE to CE 1000): was the most fertile period for the development of concepts related to *vāda* and it was also marked with most serious debates.
- The Age of Diversification (around CE 1000 to CE 1800): sectarian debates and debates between diverse philosophical schools were intensely carried on in this age.
- The Modern Age (around CE 1800 onwards).

The divide between first two is very aptly suggested by Yāska in his *Nirukta* (700 BCE) through the following mythical narrative:

> The seers were departing from this world for ever. The human beings asked them — "who will be our seer if you are leaving us?" The seers replied — "henceforth *tarka* (argument) will be your seer".

Yāska rightly concludes this story by stating that the age of *mantras* is over, now by exploring the *mantras* through *tarka* (argument), *ūha* (confutation) and *abhyūha* (investigation) one can reclaim the *ārṣa* — the vision of the seers that has been lost by their departure.[1]

Yāska exemplifies both in theory and practice how argument and investigation can be made tools to unravel the meanings of the *mantras*. Every *mantra* unfolds a vision (the *mantradṛṣṭi*) and this *mantradṛṣṭi* embraces high and low contentions, it does not traverse through linear paths.[2]

Yāska also shows that the seers themselves applied the method of *abhyūha* by taking up the example of *Ṛgveda* X.71.8. The word *ohabrahmaṇaḥ* in this passage according to Yāska actually means *ūhabrahmāṇaḥ* (those seers for whom the process of *ūha* {confutation} is *Brahman*).[3]

Nirukta also in a way exemplifies the symbolism of this story by actually presenting debates on interpretation of the *mantras* and referring to various schools of Vedic interpretation — like the *aitihāsikas*, *ākhyānavida,* etc.

Ānvīkṣikī, which can be called the oldest philosophical system, developed at the juncture of the first and the second stage around sixth-fifth centuries BCE. It was known as the foundation of the scientific thinking. Manu has equated it with *ātmavidyā* and Kauṭilya (fourth century BCE) cites Ānvīkṣikī as one of the disciplines to be studied along with Vedas. He defines the group of three — Sāṁkhya, Yoga and Lokāyata as Ānvīkṣikī. Adjusting Ānvīkṣikī as the most important amongst all the disciplines of learning, Kauṭilya says:

---

1 अक्षरं न क्षरति न क्षीयते वाऽक्षयं भवति वाचो अक्ष इति वाक्षो यानस्याञ्जनात् तत्प्रकृतीतरद्वर्तनसामान्यादित्ययं मन्त्रार्थचिन्ताभ्यूढोऽपि श्रुतितोऽपि तर्कतो न तु पृथक्त्वेन मन्त्रा निर्वक्तव्या न ह्येषु प्रत्यक्षमस्त्यनृषेरतपसो वा पारोवर्यवित्सु तु खलु वेदितृषु भूयोविद्यः प्रशस्यो भवतीत्युक्तं पुरस्तान्मनुष्या वा ऋषीसूत्क्रामत्सु देवानब्रुवन् को न ऋषिर्भविष्यतीति तेभ्य एतं तर्कमृषिं प्रायच्छन् मन्त्रार्थचिन्ताभ्यूहमभ्यूढं तस्माद् यदेवं किञ्चानूचानोभ्यूहत्यार्षं तद् भवति। — *Nirukta*, pt. II, p. 1002

2 एवमुच्चावचैरभिप्रायैर्ऋषीणां मन्त्रदृष्टयो भवन्ति। — Ibid., p. 618

3 Ibid., p. 1004.

> Prominence and weakness of these branches of learning are decided by reasons, and examined in this way the Ānvīkṣikī is helpful in this world, it keeps the wisdom in order during calamities and prosperities, brings clarity in intellect and expression. (As it is said that) Ānvīkṣikī is a lamp for all branches of learning, is a solution for all actions, and is a perennial source for all types of *dharmas*.[4]

A few centuries after Kauṭilya, the concept of Ānvīkṣikī had considerably undergone a change. *Nyāyadarśana* made a claim on it, and Gautama in his *Nyāyasūtra* had already treated his philosophy at par with Ānvīkṣikī. After almost a millennium, Rājaśekhara, in his *Kāvyamīmāṁsā* revisits the concepts of *vidyās* (branches of learning) and Ānvikṣikī. According to him:

> Ānvīkṣikī is divided into two parts — *pūrva-pakṣa* and *uttara-pakṣa*. Buddhism, Jainism and Cārvāka philosophies are included in the *pūrva-pakṣa* (the prima facie view) and Sāṁkhya as well as Nyāya and Vaiśeṣika in the *uttara-pakṣa* (acceptable view). Taken together, they form six argumentative systems.[5]

I. Mantra-kāla (The Age of Revelation)

The tendency for making philosophical speculations and enquiring into the truth is reflected in some of the Vedic hymns that were composed possibly before 3000 BCE. Vedic seers have used two terms *sampṛcchā* (inquiry) and *saṁvāda* (dialogue) in the contexts of man's quest for knowledge. Jamadagni Bhārgava attaches a great value to *sampṛcchā* and *saṁvāda*. He requests Mitra and Varuṇa to protect him from such enemies who do not ask questions, do not offer sacrificial oblations and do not rejoice at a conversation.[6] In

---

[4] साङ्ख्यं योगो लोकायतं चेत्यान्वीक्षिकी। . . . बलाबले चैतासां हेतुभिरन्वीक्षमाणान्वीक्षिकी लोकस्योपकरोति, व्यसनेऽभयुदये च बुद्धिमवस्थापयति, प्रज्ञावाक्यवैशारद्यं च करोति।
प्रदीपः सर्वविद्यानामुपायः सर्वकर्मणाम्।
आश्रयः सर्वधर्माणां शश्वदान्वीक्षिकी मता।। — *Arthaśāstra* I.2.1

[5] *Kāvyamīmāṁsā*, chap. II, p. 24.

[6] न यः सम्पृच्छे न पुनर्हवीतवे न संवादाय रमते।

→

this way, inquiry and conversation formed as integral part of the life and culture of Vedic people as sacrificial rituals. Those who did not rejoice at sharing spaces through dialogues were unwelcome.

The very existence of Indra, the supreme deity is questioned by some.[7] There are hymns in which perennial questions regarding life and destiny are raised.[8] In the hymn on the creation of *Ṛgveda*, the seer dares to say that gods do not know how this creation came out, and even if there is a Supreme Being who presides over this creation, we are not sure whether he knows or knows not as to how this creation proceeded. There is *vāda* going on within the poet-seer.

There were democratic institutions in Vedic age, i.e. *sabhā* and *samiti* (like perhaps the lower and upper houses of parliament today), where discussions and debates could materialize. While *Yajurveda* simply mentions *sabhā*,[9] *Atharvaveda* presents a glorified picture of *sabhā* and *samiti*, calling them the two daughters of *prajāpati*. It was expected that the people gathered in a *sabhā* or *samiti* will maintain decorum and will make suitable remarks only. The *sabhā* is called *nariṣṭhā* — attended by best of men, and the members of a *sabhā* are called *sabhāsadas*. They are expected to

---

← तस्मान्नो अद्य समृतेरुरुष्यतं बाहुभ्यां न उरुष्यतम्।। — *Ṛgveda* VIII.101.4

[7] यं स्मा पृच्छन्ति कुह सेति घोरमुतेमाहुर्नैषो अस्तीत्येनम्।
सो अर्यः पुष्टीर्विजइवा मिनाति श्रदस्मै धत्त स जनास इन्द्रः।। — Ibid. II.2.12
(Not seeing him, they ask — "where is he?" Believing that he is no where, they say — "oh, he does not exist". Then like a terror, he slaughters cows, destroys houses and riches of the enemy. Therefore believe that he is.) Sāyaṇa here refers to *Ṛgveda* VIII.100.3 also, which refers to the doubts raised on the existence of Indra — "नेन्द्रो अस्तीति नेम उ त्व आह क ईं ददर्श कमभिष्टवाम".

[8] किं स्विद्वनं क उ स वृक्ष आस
यतो द्या पृथिवी निष्टतक्षुः।। — *Ṛgveda* X.81.8

[9] यद् ग्रामे यदरण्ये यत्सभायां यदिन्द्रिये।
यदेनश्चकृमा वयमिदं तदवयजामहे स्वाहा।। — *Śukla Yajurveda* 3.35, p. 34

bear good will for each other.[10]

The continuity of a *sabhā* and *samiti* was maintained in village *panchayats*. In 1828, Raja Rammohun Roy traced an analogy of "Panchayat" to ancient Hindu law books connecting them to the organization of *sabhā*.[11]

Dīrghatamas, the seer of Asyavāmīyasūkta (*Ṛgveda* I.164) is not only a visionary and a great philosopher, he also makes investigations, enters into dialogue with himself.[12]

The dialogue hymns of *Ṛgveda* have ample elements of debate. In the "Hymn of Yama and Yamī" (X.10), the dialogue between a brother and a sister turn on the propriety of incestuous relations. Yama counters each and every statement of Yamī. In the hymn on Purūravas and Urvaśī (X.95) all the points raised by Purūravas are countered by Urvaśī.

The concept of *brahmodya* is spelled out in the dialogue between Śauceya and Uddālaka Āruṇi. Śauceya approached the Sage Uddālaka and told him that he wants to know about *brahmodya*. He asks many questions about *brahmodya* to the seer, to which the latter replies. After every answer, he goes on saying "now I understand".[13]

Brahmodyas (the assemblies for conducting debates and discussions) were held during the Aśvamedha and Daśarātra *yajñas* also. The scholars giving best performance in a *brahmodya* were honoured with the title of *kavi* and *vipra*.[14]

---

[10] सभा च मा समितिश्चावताम् प्रजापतेर्दुहितरौ संविदाने।
येना सङ्गच्छा उप मा स शिक्षाच्चारु वदामि पितरः सङ्गतेषु।।
वदाम ते सभे नाम नरिष्ठा नाम वा असि
ये ते के चन सभासदस्ते मे सन्तु सव . . . — *Atharvaveda* VII.12.1

[11] C.A. Bayly, 2010, "Rammohun Roy and the Advent of Contributional Liberalism", in *An Intellectual History of India*, p. 28.

[12] न वि जानाम यदि वेदमस्मि निण्यः सन्नद्धो मनसा चरामि।
यदा मागन् प्रथमजा ऋतस्यादिद्वाचो अश्नुवे भागमस्याः।। — *Ṛgveda* I.164.37

[13] *Śatapatha Brāhmaṇa* XI.5.3.1.

[14] *Taittirīya Saṁhitā* II.5.9.1, III.5.3.1; *Śatapatha Brāhmaṇa* III.5.3.2.

Brahmodyas were also comprised of asking riddles and getting them solved. Specimens of such *brahmodyas* are given in *Śatapatha Brāhmaṇa* and other Vedic texts. The following dialogues can be cited as an example:[15]

> "Who is born again?"
>
> "It is the moon that is born again."
>
> "What is the great vessel?"
>
> "The great vessel, undoubtedly, is the world".
>
> "Who was the beautiful one?"
>
> "Śrī (Lakṣmī) was the beauty beyond any doubt."
>
> "What is the remedy for cold?"
>
> "The remedy for cold undoubtedly, is fire."
>
> "Who was the tawny one?"
>
> "Undoubtedly, there are two tawny ones — the day and the night."

In another interesting *brahmodya* described in *Śatapatha Brāhmaṇa* XI.4, Uddālaka Āruṇi, a resident of Kurupāñcāla country is confronted by the brāhmaṇas of north with several complicated questions related to the performance of the ritual of Darśapūrṇamāsa sacrifice. The *yājamāna* had chosen Uddālaka Āruṇi as a priest for the sacrifice and had placed a *niṣka* (coin) in his honour. Unable to resolve the riddles of the brāhmaṇas, Uddālaka placed the *niṣka* offered to him before one Svedāyana, telling that being more knowledgeable, he deserves the coin. The ceremony of the *yajña* being over, Uddālaka went to Svedāyana to learn the answers of the questions asked to him.

Vāda or *brahmodya* formed a part of sacrifices like the Āśvamedha, but there the questions and answers were defined. It was like a demonstration of a prepared debate or discussion. *Brahmodya* organized during the course of Aśvamedha ceremony has been described in *Yajurveda*. Questions proceeded like this. The Hotā

---

[15] *Śatapatha Brāhmaṇa* XIII.2, 6, 10-17.

would ask — "What is the ultimate space for speech?" The Brahmā (one of the four priests for the *yajña*-ritual) would reply — "*Brahman* is the ultimate space for speech". The assembly in a *brahmodya* session became divided in two groups — one asked questions and the other answered them. *Yajurveda* provides specimen of a session of *brahmodya* as under:

> Q : Who is the one that roams alone? Who is the one that is reborn again and again? What is the remedy for ice? What is the great field for sowing?
>
> **A:** The sun roams alone. The moon is the one that is reborn again and again. Fire is the remedy for ice. Earth is the great field for sowing.
>
> Q: What is the radiance equal to the sun? Which is the pond equal to the sea? What is bigger than the earth and what is that which does not have a limit?
>
> A: *Brahman* is the radiance equal to sun. *Dyauh* (orbit) is the pond equal to sea. Indra is bigger than the earth and cow does not have a limit.
>
> Q: In which substance *Puruṣa* gets dissolved? What entities are subsumed within *Puruṣa*?
>
> A: *Puruṣa* gets dissolved in five, the five are subsumed within *Puruṣa*.[16]

The queries made in *brahmodyas* were not necessarily metaphysical. In *Taittirīya Saṁhitā* of *Yajurveda*, a question regarding the centre and the farthest end of the earth is discussed.[17] The answer however reflects the cosmic view of *yajña* — "the alter is the centre as well as the farthest end of the earth" — says the seer.[18]

Kauṣītaki Brāhmaṇa 17.4 and *Taittirīya Saṁhitā* 2.5.8.3 use two

---

[16] *Śukla Yajurveda* 23.9-12, 45-52, pp. 341, 348-49.

[17] पृच्छामि त्वा परमन्तं पृथिव्याः पृच्छामि त्वद् भुवनस्य नाभिम्। — *Taittirīya Saṁhitā* VII.4.10

[18] वेदिमाहुःपरमन्तः पृथिव्याः। — *Taittirīya Saṁhitā* VII.4.10

other terms for *brahmodya* — *brahmavadya* and *brahmavādya.*[19]

Brahmavāda, brahmavādin and *brahmavādinī* — these terms have been used in Vedic literature for the debaters and discussants.[20] Other key terms and concepts related to *brahmodya* are *pṛcchā* (inquiry) and *vicikitsā* (investigation). In *Ṛgveda* I.164, the seer makes *pṛcchā* to *kavis* (the knowledgeable ones) as to where does the ultimate end of this earth lie, and where does reside the *paramavyoma* (the ultimate space) of speech.

Kavi (poet), *vipra* (scholar) and *ṛṣi* (seer) are the titles given to the learned and gifted with vision. Assemblies were held to identify such poets, seers and scholars. They were called *vidatha.*[21]

Upaniṣadic Debates

The Upaniṣads refer to various schools of thought and constant dialogues going on between them. Niyativādins, Kālavādins, Svabhāvavādins and Bhūtavādins were promulgating their ideologies. *Śvetāśvatara Upaniṣad* describes the Niyati School and Pāṇini refers to it as *diṣṭāmati.*

V.S. Aggrawal opines that Prajñāvāda arose in opposition to Niyativāda, offering a rationalistic view of life. Kṛṣṇa was a

---

[19] A.A. Macdonell and A.B. Keith, 1912, *Vedic Index of Names and Subjects*, vol. II, p. 80.

[20] ब्रह्मवादिनो वदन्ति — *Atharvaveda* 11.3.26 and 3.8.8.

[21] "*Vidatha* is a word of obscure sense, confined mainly to *Ṛgveda*. According to Roth, the sense is primarily order, then the concrete body which gives the orders, then 'assembly' for secular or religious ends, or for war. . . . Ludwig thinks that the root idea is an 'assembly' especially of *maghavans* and the brāhmaṇas. Geldner considers that the word primarily means 'knowledge', wisdom', 'priestly lore' and then 'sacrifice' and 'spiritual authority'. Bloomfield on the other hand, insists that *vidatha* refers to the house in the first place (from *vid* — acquire) and then to the sacrifice as connected with the house; this interpretation at any rate appears to suit all passages." — Macdonell and Keith, 1912, op. cit., vol. II, p. 296

Prajñāvādin. He adjusts Vidura as one of the prominent advocates of Prajñāvāda school.[22]

Brahmodya comprised of questions raised by one wing and answers provided from the other wing. This method is followed in the great debate or *brahmodya* between Yājñavalkya and other scholars in the court of Janaka as described in the Upaniṣad. Yājñavalkya, having been challenged by a multitude of the Brahmavādins or scholars in an assembly, suggests that either they confront him with their questions one by one or he confronts them with his questions one by one.[23] In fact, this was one of the biggest debates held in the assembly of King Janaka around 1000 BCE. It has been termed as *brahmodya* in *Bṛhadāraṇyaka Upaniṣad.* Śaṅkarācārya in his *Bhāṣya* has called the whole of its proceedings as *saṁvāda-prakaraṇa*. Amongst hundreds of intellectuals present, Gārgī, a *brahmavādinī* (lady philosopher) alone could stand as a peer to Yājñavalkya. Besides Yājñavalkya, Janaka and Gārgī, several participants — all opponents of Yajñavalkya — the disputants — have been described. The disputants raise questions, counter questions and their resolutions are given by the respondent — Yājñavalkya. The extensive record of the proceedings of this debate in the Upaniṣad is one of the most valuable and authentic documentations of a philosophical debate. Even if the characters of this narrative do not belong to the history in the modern sense of the term, they are very much parts of a larger history of ideas.

Aśvala was first to confront Yajñavalkya with his question:

> By what means, the sacrifice is liberated having overcome the clutches of death?

Yājñavalkya replied:

---

[22] V.S. Aggrawal, 2015, "General President's Address, 22nd Session of AIOC", *Saumārajyotiḥ*, pp. 97-98.

[23] ब्राह्मणाः भगवन्तो यो वः कामयते स मा पृच्छतु। सर्वे वा मा पृच्छत। यो वः कामयते तं वः पृच्छामि। सर्वान् वा वः पृच्छामीति। — *Bṛhadāraṇyaka Up.* 3.9.27

> By speech which is fire in the shape of *hotā*, the first priest. The speech is fire, and fire is *hotā*, this fire of *hotā* is liberation, and this liberation is absolute liberation.

Aśvala again asked:

> Yājñavalkya, all this is pervaded by day and night, all this is subjected by day and night. By what means, the sacrifice is liberated having overcome the clutches of the day and night?

Yājñavalkya replied:

> By the eye, which is Āditya, in the form of the *adhvaryu* priest. Verily, the eye of the sacrifice is *adhvaryu*. This eye is Āditya, this Āditya is *adhvaryu*, and *adhvaryu* is liberation, and this liberation is absolute liberation.

There is a pattern in the questions posed by all challengers. Aśvala's further questions pertain to the means of overcoming the clutches of the light and dark halves of the lunar month.

In reply to Jāratkārava Ārtabhāga, Yājñavalkya described eight fetters and eight auxiliaries. These include all the sense-organs and mind with their subjects as auxiliaries. If all phenomenon is the food of death, then for whom death becomes the food? — Jāratkārava Ārtabhāga questions. Fire is death and it becomes food for water — replied Yājñavalkya. What remains when the man dies? "The name" replies Yājñavalkya.

The questions in this way became sharper and more penetrating. They pertained to the other world, life after death and destiny. Uṣastā asked Yājñavalkya about *Brahman* and soul.

Gārgī declared in *brahmodya* held in the assembly at the royal court of King Janaka: "If Yājñavalkya answers my questions correctly, I swear that none amongst you will be able to win him in this *brahmodya*."[24]

---

[24] *Bṛhadāraṇyaka Up*. 3.8.1.

The questions posed by Gārgī were cleverly formulated and in the terminology of the Nyāya, they were likely to trap the respondent in *nigrahasthānas* (clinchers), which are being described in the next chapter of this work. Gārgī knew that her question pertained to the Ultimate was indescribable. If Yājñavalkya replied it, he would be committing a mistake by saying that which aught not to be said. (Technically that was a *nigrahasthāna* called *avācyavacana*). If he avoided the question, he would be trapped in the *nigrahasthāna* called *apratibhā.*

After receiving satisfactory answers of her questions she made this announcement:

> O knowledgeable ones, it will be the best thing for you all to offer obeisance to Yājñavalkya and free yourselves from him. There is none amongst you who could win over him!

The *ṛṣis* who participated in the debate with Yājñavalkya were intellectuals, seers and thinkers of their own standing. Many of them, though they lost and suffered a defeat because of the quick wit and brilliance of their adversary, had otherwise influenced the milieu by their ideas through *vāda* (debates and discussions). Amongst them Śvetaketu was an eminent ideologist and thinker. The earliest reference to Śvetaketu occurs in *Śatapatha Brāhmaṇa.*[25] He was a descendant of Gautama and grandson of Āruṇa. His father Uddālaka Āruṇi is a well-known seer and thinker in the Upaniṣads and is also referred in *Mahābhārata*. Even great sages like Yājñavalkya, Vājasaneya and Kauṣītaki are said to be his disciples. Uddālaka was a resident of Kurupāñcāla and was a student of Ayoda Dhaumya. He had learnt *brahmavidyā* with King Pravahaṇa Jaivāli. *Kauṣītaki Brāhmaṇa* gives the detailed views of Uddālaka and Śvetaketu on the duties of a priest. Śvetaketu was also a man who could stand against the prevailing notions and customs and change the course of history. *Gopatha Brāhmaṇa* and *Śāṅkhāyana Brāhmaṇa*

---

25 *Śatapatha Brāhmaṇa* XI.2.7.11-12; ref. from A.A. Macdonell and A.B. Keith, *Vedic Index*, 1912, vol. II, p. 409.

(I.33) describe how even as a student he had violated the ban on eating of sweets for *brahmacārins* of the *gurukula.*[26]

Bṛhadāranyaka Upaniṣad also describes his dialogues with the King Pravahaṇa Jaivāli and Janaka. Śvetaketu also disagreed with his own father on the performance of rituals. In *Āpastamba-Dharmasūtra* he is referred as an *avara* type of priest.

Sujātā, his sister, was married to Kahoṭaka, father of Aṣṭāvakra. Aṣṭāvakra was initiated and educated in the hermitage of Uddālaka. He was a dwarf and suffered from physical deformity, but an intellectual giant, he defeated the detractor of his father in a debate.

Śvetaketu must have been somewhat of an irritating, proud and envious nature in his childhood. He did not join his father, when the latter was going to learn *brahmavidyā* (spiritual knowledge).[27] He was also proud of his knowledge of rituals and expressed his dissatisfaction when the kings of Kāśī, Kosala and Videha nominated Jātukarṇya as their priest. The course of the life of Uddālaka by this time had undergone a change, and he advised his son to devote himself to the pursuit of knowledge and spirituality.

That Śvetaketu with his Vedic lineage and Upaniṣadic background continued to be remembered as a thinker during the later centuries is evident from two episodes in *Mahābhārata.* He was the first person to have protested against the violence on women. The episode narrated in *Mahābhārata* is as follows.[28] It so happened that Śvetaketu saw his mother being dragged out of the house by a brāhmaṇa, who was intoxicated. He was declaring that he needs a woman for satiation of his sexual urge and he is therefore taking away this woman with him. "Why don't you stop this man?" – Śvetaketu asked his father. His father said – "Under what law can I stop him? The law in our society gives a man right

---

26 Ref. in Vettam Mani, 1975, *Puranic Encyclopaedia*, p. 780.

27 *Bṛhadāṇyaka Upaniṣad, Īśādidaśopaniṣadaḥ, Śaṅkarācārya-granthāvalī*, pt. I, 1st edn, Delhi, repr., 1978, pp. 986-87.

28 *Mahābhārata,* Śāntiparva, chap. 35.

to take any woman for the satiation of his sexual urge." Śvetaketu said — "I raise my voice of I dissent against such law. Henceforth no man will forcefully take any woman."

Yaśodhara, a well-known commentator on Vātsyāyana's *Kāmasūtra*, also cites this episode. Śvetaketu is said to have composed a text on Kāmaśāstra also and Vātsyāyana in his *Kāmasūtra* refers to him as one of the authorities on Kāmaśāstra.

Another narrative in *Mahābhārata* describes Śvetaketu's marriage with Suvarcalā. Suvarcalā herself chose to marry Śvetaketu because he could prove himself a suitable match by satisfying her queries.[29] Besides fulfilling their responsibilities as householder, the couple frequently had discussions on the perennial questions related to the reality, language and speech. *Mahābhārata* tells that they were spending their life on two levels, at one level they were living a normal life as the husband and the wife, and discharging their duties as householders. But they also soared above in the world of intellectual debates. Suvarcalā, when she felt that they were too much engrossed in the worldly affairs, enticed her husband to join her for a discussion. On one such occasion, she raised the questions of language and reality.

Śvetaketu agrees that the language fails to comprehend reality, but it can become a medium leading to the path of knowing reality. The words actually do not consist of the meaning, the meaning slips and slides on the word, like a drop of water on the petals of a lotus flower.[30] The relationship between the word and its meaning is not *ātyantika* (invariably permanent).

Suvarcalā very pertinently objects here and suggests that the relationship has to be accepted as eternal, otherwise the words of the scriptures would also become fragile (like of drop of water on the petals of a lotus flower). Śvetaketu resolves the dilemma by

---

[29] *Mahābhārata*, Śāntiparva, chap. 220.

[30] शब्दार्थयोर्न चैवास्ति सम्बन्धोऽत्यन्त एव हि।
पुष्करे च यथा तोयं तथाऽस्तीति च वेत्थ तत्।। — Ibid.

the illustration of space holding the world, and also by introducing the concept of *upacāra* (figurative use). The whole discussion, in the words of Śuvarcalā, was to drag Śvetaketu out of the rut of routine activities, as she felt that his knowledge is in the danger of vanishing.[31]

Bhīṣma narrates the story of Sulabhā in *Mahābhārata*.[32] It is a woman's fight against man's pretensions and arrogance. Janaka displays overconfidence in his spiritual attainments and appears to be blind to reason. There is a heated argument from Janaka, who pretends to be a liberated soul, but starts talking in a vulgar and licentious tone. He attributes ulterior motifs to Sulabhā's visit. This is followed by very patient and insightful rejoinder from Sulabhā. She clearly tears away the mask worn by the king. But *Mahābhārata* does not tell us who won this debate. Arindam Chakrabarti points out:

> The indecisiveness of *Mahābhārata* as to who is the winner, Janaka or Sulabhā, narratively draws us nearer to the cognitive – discursive caution of never claiming dogmatically to have "got it right".[33]

Mahābhārata also indicates that this debate is happening in *dharmayuga* (time of morality) inside Janaka, because Bhīṣma, who describes this debate, also says that the debate happened in a single locus.[34]

In the very preceding chapter (319th), *Mahābhārata* depicts Janaka as a liberated soul. Here he is portrayed in all garrulousness

---

31 क्रियाकलापैर्ब्रह्मर्षे ज्ञाननष्टोऽसि सर्वदा।
तन्मे ब्रूहि महाप्राज्ञ यथाऽहं त्वामनुव्रता।। – *Mahābhārata*, Śāntiparva, chap. 220 (Gita Press edn, p. 4992).

32 Ibid., chap. 320.

33 A. Chakrabarti and S. Bandhyopadhyaya (eds.), 2014, *Mahābhārata Now*, p. 247.

34 *Mahābhārata*, Śāntiparva, 320.19.

with his pompous behaviour and manner quite unbecoming of a "saint-king". Perhaps *Mahābhārata* suggests that there are layers of liberation. Janaka himself says — how am I any less liberated than you are?

The questions posed by Yakṣa in *Mahābhārata* and by Karkaṭī (a titan) in *Yogavāsiṣṭha* indicate how the techniques of *vāda* were adopted for meta-discourses.

The Upaniṣads also evolved some simple but very systematic techniques for carrying out *vāda*. They are:

1. *Praśna*: questioning to initiate a dialogue,
2. *Anupraśna*: counter-questions arising out of the discussions on the preliminary query,
3. *Anatipraśnanivāraṇa*: avoiding too much questioning which leads to the sidetracking of the issue itself,
4. *Vyākhyā*: detailed explanation of the theory,
5. *Anuvyākhyā*: further explanations,
6. *Dṛṣṭānta*: illustration,
7. *Ākhyāyikā*: narrating a story as an exposition of the theory, and
8. *Ūrdhvapravacana*: deciphering the extant of learning that has already been acquired by a disciple, so that discussion be carried on after it.

These techniques became the precursors of the concept of *pañcāvayava-vākya* (sentence with five divisions).

That the lady seers (*brahmavādinīs*) used to participate in the debates is exemplified by the narratives related to Gārgī, Maitreyī, Suvarcalā and Sulabhā.

The Cārvākas or Lokāyatikas known for their debating skills, dominated the discussions in *āśramas* (hermitages) or in royal courts. The tale of Śakuntalā in *Mahābhārata* describes that the hermitage of Kaṇva was resounding with the voices of the chief

Lokāyatikas engaged in propounding their theses, raising objections and establishing the theory.[35]

Debates, Dialogues and Discussions in Rāmāyaṇa

Rāmāyaṇa of Vālmīki was written in the age of dialectic of ideologues. The ethical concepts as well as the tenets of major philosophical systems were in the process of their evolution. This is reflected in the scepticisms, discussions, dialogues and debates in which we find the characters of *Rāmāyaṇa* involved. There are sceptics and believers taking positions and counter-positions. Lokāyata and Ānvīkṣikī — these two schools of philosophy — posited challenges and raised questions on the existing practices and norms. The *yajña* ceremony was comprised of a number of performances, including *vādas*. The Putreṣṭiyajña performed by Sage Ṛṣyaśṛṅga for Daśaratha, the *vipras*, adept in oratory and having patience for arguments gathered to hold *hetuvādas*. It is said that all the members of the assembly performing the rites of the *yajña* were adept in debates.[36]

The following debates, dialogues and discussions in *Rāmāyaṇa,* reflecting divergence of ideas, may be mentioned:

1. Discussion and debate between Rāma, Bharata, Jābāli and Vasiṣṭha on nullification of Rāma's banishment.
2. Dialogue between Sītā and Rāma in Daṇḍakāraṇya on the vulnerability of violence and practice of non-violence.
3. Dialogue between Rāma and Sitā before Sitā's *agniparīkṣā* (the fire test).

---

[35] स्थापनाऽऽक्षेपसिद्धान्तपरमार्थज्ञतां गतैः।
लोकायतिकमुख्यैश्च समन्तादनुनादितम्।
— *Mahābhārata* I.64.37

[36] कर्मान्तरे तदा विप्रा हेतुवादान् बहूनपि।
प्राहुः सुवाग्मिनो धीराः परस्परजिगीषया।।
नाषडङ्गविदत्रासीन्नाव्रतो नाबहुश्रुतः।
सदस्यस्तस्य वै राज्ञो नावादकुशलो द्विजः।। — *Rāmāyaṇa* I.13.14, 16

4. Hanumān's debate with his own self during his search for Sītā in Laṅkā.

The first discussion directly pertains to a family matter, it is marked with heated arguments and passionate appeals but it eventually culminates in the discussions on *dharma* (morality) and ethics. It begins with Rāma's questions to Bharata about the welfare of the family and the kingdom of Ayodhyā and through his queries he brings out discordance of ideologies and outlooks. The whole discussion here invokes policies and thought processes.

Rāma asks:

> O dear one, will you confirm that you do not serve the brāhmaṇas who are Lokāyatikas? They are imprudent, adept in bringing disasters and presumptuous to think that they are very wise. Even when the principal Dharmaśāstras are there, they chatter meaninglessly taking recourse to their understanding of the Ānvīkṣikī (logic).[37]

The brāhmaṇas mentioned by Rāma here belong to a protestant group that questions the prevailing norms and lifestyles. It is also clear from Rāma's question that these brāhmaṇas were known for their opposition of the dictates of Dharmaśāstra. On the other hand, there were orthodox brāhmaṇas who cherished the Vedic *dharma* with a catholic spirit and regarded the Veda as their greatest treasure.[38] Being *maryādā puruṣottama* (the noble one who maintains the order), Rāma clearly supports this second category of the brāhmaṇas. Utterly dismayed and feeling helpless at the critical juncture of Rāma's exile, these Vedic brāhmaṇas take a decision to relinquish the city of Ayodhyā and follow their protector to the forest.

---

[37] कच्चिन्न लोकायतिकान् ब्राह्मणांस्तात सेवसे ।
अनर्थकुशला ह्येते बालाः पण्डितमानिनः ।।
धर्मशास्त्रेषु मुख्येषु विद्यमानेषु दुर्बुधाः ।
बुद्धिमान्वीक्षिकीं प्राप्य निरर्थं प्रवदन्ति ते।। — *Rāmāyaṇa* II.94.32-33

[38] हृदयेष्ववतिष्ठन्ते वेदा ये नः परं धनम् ।
वसन्त्यपि चे गृहष्वेव दाराश्चारित्ररक्षिताः ।। — Ibid. II.40.23

"O son! Our intelligence which always follows the *mantras* of the Veda has now become a follower of the path of the forest for you" — they say.[39] Having a soft corner in his heart for such brāhmaṇas, Rāma had earlier ordered bounty of gifts for them before his sojourn to forest. With a tinge of pity and humour, Rāma remarks:

> These brāhmaṇas belonging to the Kaṭha and Kalāpa branches of Vedic learning, do not do anything because they have to study the Vedas constantly, they are lazy and gourmets, but they are held in high esteem by the noble ones" (*nityam svādhyāyaśīlatvāt na anyat kurvanti kiñcana, alasāḥ svādukāmāśca*).[40]

Replying to Bharata's appeal to put an end to his exile and accept the royal throne, Rāma brings in the question of freedom. "A person does not have any control over the course of events and cannot take an action arbitrarily" — he says — "the destiny drags him hither and thither."[41] He also talks of evanescence. Death is inexorable, the companions depart. "Our father Daśaratha gave up his body for *dharma* and therefore we also have to observe *dharma* by acting as per his order."

Reacting to this discourse, Bharata presents his case in more

---

39 ब्राह्मण्यं कृत्स्नमेतत् त्वां ब्राह्मण्यमनुगच्छति ।
द्विजस्कन्धाधिरूढास्त्वामग्नयोऽप्यनुयान्त्यमी ॥
वाजपेयसमुत्थानि छत्राण्येतानि पश्य नः ।
पृष्ठतोऽनुप्रयातानि हंसानीव जलात्यये ॥
अनवाप्तातपत्रस्य रश्मिसन्तापितस्य ते ।
एभिश्छायां करिष्यामः स्वश्छत्रैर्वाजपेयकैः ॥
या हि नः सततं बुद्धिर्वेदमन्त्रनुसारिणी ।
त्वत्कृते सा कृता वत्स वनवासानुसारिणी ॥ — *Rāmāyaṇa* II.40.19-22

40 पशुकाभिश्च सर्वाभिर्गवां दशशतेन च ।
ये चेमे कठकालापा बहवो दण्डमाणवाः॥
नित्यस्वाध्यायशीलत्वान्नान्यत्कुर्वन्ति किञ्चन।
अलसाः स्वादुकामाश्च महतां चापि सम्मताः ॥
तेषामशीतियानानि रत्नपूर्णानि दापय। — *Rāmāyaṇa* II.32.18-20

41 नात्मनः कामकारो हि पुरुषोऽयमनीश्वरः।
इतश्चेतरश्चैनं कृतान्तः परिकर्षति।। — Ibid. II.98.15

logistic framework. The arguments advanced by him can be summarized in the following way:

1. The eternal *dharma* is greater than *rājadharma*, and he (Bharata) should follow this eternal *dharma* by giving up the royal seat in Rāma's favour.
2. King Daśaratha was not in his senses when he was beguiled by Kaikeyī.
3. Even if Rāma wishes to observe the rigour of *dharma*, he can do it better by being a king, thereby nourishing the four *āśramas* and by repaying the three debts as laid down in the scriptures.

In his rejoinder to Bharata's arguments, Rāma says that truth is the greatest *dharma*, our father stood for truth and we have also to follow him.

The passage following after this discussion is an interpolation and has been added to the original *Rāmāyaṇa* as an evidence of the conflict and debates between the followers of Vedic *dharma* on one hand and the followers of Cārvāka and Buddhist systems on the other. Jābāli, a seer and one of the counsellors in the royal court of Ayodhyā, joins this series of arguments and counter-arguments. He says:

> Enough O Rāghava! Do not let thy wisdom be rendered void like a common man, thou who art distinguished for thy intelligence and virtue! Who is man's parent? From whom can be obtain anything? Man is born alone and dies alone. He who clings to another, saying — "this is my father, this is my mother" — should be regarded as one who has lost his wits. O Rāma! There is none who belongs to another!
>
> As one who passes through a strange village, spends the night there, and the next day, leaves that place, and continues his journey, so are father, mother, home and possessions of a man; they are but a resting place, O Kākutstha, and wise do not become attached to them. Thou can't therefore abandon thy father's

> kingdom, O chief of men, in order to dwell in a lonely forest that is gloomy and full of thorny thickets! Come and be crowned in the prosperous city of Ayodhyā, thy locks unbound; the capital awaits thee! Come and taste the royal luxuries worthy of thee, O son of a king! Divert thyself in Ayodhyā as Śakra (Indra) in Triviṣṭapa (heaven)! Daśaratha is nought to thee now, nor thou to Daśaratha! The diseased king was one person and thou another, therefore do whatever is proper for thee to do! The seed is the only father of all beings. It is the seed and the blood from blending of which at the right time in mother's womb that man is born in this world! The king has gone where he had to go, it is the fate of all beings, do not grieve uselessly! I pity those who give themselves up especially to that which is meritorious, disregarding their own interest; I do not pity others; they suffer misery here; and in the end find extinction! Pious men say: "The eighth day should be given up to the sacrifices for the spirits of our ancestors"; the food that is offered is wasted, can the dead eat? If that which is eaten here, could enter the body of another, then let a sacrifice be offered for those who are setting out on a distant journey and they will not need provisions! The *granthas* (texts) were all made by learned men for the sake of including others to give; their doctrine is "distribute gifts, perform sacrifices, consecrate yourselves up to asceticism and renunciation!"
>
> O Exceedingly sagacious Prince! There is no world but this; let this thought be absorbed by thee. Concern thyself with what is evident and turn the back on what is beyond our knowledge! Accept the judgement of the good and regarding that which is approved by all, accept the crown and allow thyself to be swayed by Bharata![42]

Jābāli also speaks in a tone of condemnation for the authors of the Dharmaśāstras, like Medhātithi.

Replying to him, Rāma argues for the righteous path leading to heaven. He then goes to the extent of saying:

---

[42] Hari Prasad Shastri (tr.), 1962, *The Rāmāyaṇa of Vālmīki,* vol. I, pp. 413-14.

> I blame my father for having employed a man of perverse understanding like you (as minister[43]) — swerving from the path of *dharma*, who has turned to frightfully atheistic with this kind of his intellect. As a thief is, so is Buddha, let it be known to you that *tathāgata* is an atheist. A man of righteous understanding should not talk in his terms.[44]

Rāma's rejoinder to Jābāli is believed to be an interpolation by modern scholars. At least the remarks on Buddha do not form a genuine part of the epic. Amartya Sen rightly suggests:

> The problem with invoking the *Rāmāyaṇa* to propagate a reductionist account of Hindu religiosity lies in the way the epic is deployed for this purpose — as a document of supernatural veracity, rather than a "marvellous parable" (as Rabindranath Tagore) describes it and a widely enjoyed part of India's cultural heritage.[45]

Rāma emphasizes over the values of life, sacrifice, renunciation, truth and duty. His prolonged discourse here is a strong refutation of all the arguments advanced by Jābāli. Rāma points out that the apparently honest intention of Jābāli is in fact nefarious. He puts forward the view of the Dharmaśāstra that gives utmost importance to duty. A man is known for his actions. It is his actions which reveal his baseness or nobility. If Jābāli's advice is accepted, people will start acting whimsically, the ignoble would resemble the noble, it will lead to confusion of castes. Just and unjust, evil and good

---

[43] Jābāli is mentioned as one of the ministers of Daśaratha in *Rāmāyaṇa* I.8.6 in its Mumbai edition; but in the critical edition of Vālmīki's *Rāmāyaṇa* published from Vadodara, the list of ministers (I.7.1-3) does not include his name.

[44] निन्दाम्यहं कर्म कृतं पितुस्तद् यस्त्वामगृह्णाद् विषमस्थबुद्धिम्।
बुद्ध्यानयैवंविधया चरन्तं सुनास्तिकं धर्मपथादपेतम्।
यथा हि चौरस्स तथा हि बुद्धस्तथागतं नास्तिकमत्र विद्धि।
यस्माद्धि यः शक्यतमः प्रजानां स नास्तिकेनाभिमुखो बुधाः स्यात्।
— *Rāmāyaṇa* II.109.33-34 (not included in Vadodara edn)

[45] Amartya Sen, 2005, *The Argumentative Indian*, Preface, p. xii.

are discerned only on the basis of scriptures. He (Rāma) will be setting a bad example before the world by following Jābāli's advice. *Dharma* is the soul of governance and the subjects are also guided by *dharma*. Man is not alone, his *dharma* always goes with him. Jābāli's counsel, couched in excellent words, is unworthy for Rāma's noble descent. By forsaking the vow he will incur a sin. Everybody reaps the fruits of his acts.

Seeing Rāma's stern consternation, Jābāli cleverly changes his position "I do not speak the language of unbelievers" he says, "nor am I an atheist. This is not true that there is nothing beyond this world. (I became an atheist and) considering the occasion again turned to be a believer. On other occasion I may become an atheist again. This was an occasion for me to adopt the speech of an atheist just for persuading you to return back and to please you."[46]

Vasiṣṭha joins this discussions and he recites the genealogy of Rāma's line beginning from Brahmā and Vivasvān to Aja and Daśaratha. The purport of citing the names of all great kings of the dynasty is to emphasize over the need of maintaining the tradition of the house of Raghu, to protect the *kula-dharma*, which is *sanātana* (eternal). The requirement of *kula-dharma* (practice in the family line) in this context is that the eldest son receives the royal anointing and also the order of the *guru*. In this case he himself is one of the *gurus* and Rāma's mother, Kausalyā is also his *guru*.

Rāma remains unshaken even over this well-formulated reasoned appeal. His reply to Vasiṣṭha's arguments proceeds from the same position — and the argument of obeying to one's *guru* also does not stand here because to respect the pledge given by his father Daśaratha as per his commitment to Kaikeyī, he has to continue his sojourn in the forest.

---

[46] न नास्तिकानां वचनं ब्रवीम्यहं न नास्तिको ऽहं न च नास्ति किञ्चन।
समीक्ष्य कालं पुनरास्तिकोऽभवं भवेय काले पुनरेव नास्तिकः॥
स चापि कालोऽयमुपागतः शनैर्यथा मया नास्तिकवागुदीरिता।
निवर्तनार्थं तव राम कारणात् प्रसादनार्थं च मयैतदीरितम्। — *Rāmāyaṇa* II.109.38-39

Seeing all his arguments and appeals falling apart, Bharata decides to lie down before Rāma and fast till his death if the later does not concede to his demand. Rāma tells him that this is not the *vidhi* (way of life) for a man belonging to the military class, only a brāhmaṇa is allowed to obstruct persons in this way.

Bharata makes a fervent appeal to the people of Ayodhyā who have accompanied him to dissuade Rāma from his decision to continue his stay in the forest. The people express their helplessness in doing so, they unanimously speak for Rāma, appreciating his adherence to truth and duty. Bharata then decides to return to Ayodhyā as per the advice given by the counsel of *paura-jānapadas* (citizens and dwellers of the provinces) and the sages present there.

The debate in Citrakūṭa regarding the dichotomy between obedience to father and *rājadharma* (duty of a king) is the culmination of the initial expression of Lakṣmaṇa's outrage on Rāma's banishment and his advice to his elder brother to refuse the orders of banishment.

Another episode in *Rāmāyaṇa* reflects the debate on the value of non-violence. How can a person shun violence completely? This is the question Sītā raises to her husband. A person can attain *dharma* by eschewing three evils born out of *kāma* (desire) — false utterance, illicit relationship and vengeance. Sītā says that there is no possibility of the first two in Rāma but the third evil, bearing hostility for others without cause may make a room in him. "Out of love and respect for you, I just want to remind you", she further pleads, "and do not venture to instruct you, that please give up the idea of killing the demons of this forest by bearing this bow. Bearing arms and retirement to the forest do not go together. Practising war and renunciation are in opposition to each other, therefore please follow the *dharma* of *vanavāsa* (forest dwelling). The very association of a weapon would vitiate one's mind making a room for murderous thoughts."[47]

---

[47] *Rāmāyaṇa* III.8.2-29.

In support of her thesis, Sītā also gives an illustration by the way of narrating the predicament of a sage, who fell from his glory just by keeping a weapon even as a trust and just holding it in his hands to avoid its loss, he developed war-like inclinations.

Rāma counters Sītā's argument by reiterating his commitment to *dharma*. "The person of warrior class puts on the bow so that there is no cry from the helpless", he says.[48]

Elsewhere Sitā outmatches Rāma by her skill of debate in one of the most difficult and sensitive situations. After winning the war with Rāvaṇa, she is brought before Rāma at his orders in the presence of the multitude of monkeys and demons. Rāma feels the pressure of the congregation and utters most harsh words to Sītā:

> O illustrious Princess, I have won thee and mine enemy has been defeated on the battlefield; I have accomplished all that fortitude I could do; my wrath is appeased; the insult and the one who offered it have both been obliterated by me. Today my prowess has been manifested; today my exertions have been crowned with success, today I have fulfilled my vow and am free. As ordained by destiny, the stain of thy separation and thine abduction by that fickle-minded titan has been expunged by me, a mortal. Of what use is great strength to the vacillating, who do not with resolve avenge the insult offered to them?

Sītā started weeping hearing these words and looking at her Rāma was torn within himself. Then he was in a rage and said:

> What a man should do in order to wipe out insult, I have done by slaying Rāvaṇa for I guard my honour zealously. Thou were re-won as the southern region, inaccessible to man, was re-gained by the pure souled Agastya through his austerities. Be happy and let it be known that this arduous campaign, so gloriously terminated through the support of my friends, was not undertaken wholly for thy sake. I was careful to wipe out the affront paid me completely and to avenge the insult inflicted on mine illustrious house.

---

[48] क्षत्रियैर्धार्यते चापो नार्तशब्दो भवेदिति। — *Rāmāyaṇa* III.9.3

> A suspicion has arisen, however, with regard to thy conduct, and thy presence is as painful to me as a lamp to one whose eye is diseased. Henceforth go where it best pleaseth thee, I give thee leave, O daughter of Janaka! O lovely one, the ten regions are at thy disposal, I can have nothing more to do with thee! What a man of honour would give reign to his passion so far as to permit himself to take back a woman who has dwelt in the house of another? Thou hast been taken into Rāvaṇa's lap and he has cast lustful glances on thee; how can I reclaim thee, I who boast of belonging to an illustrious house? The end which I sought in re-conquering has been gained; I no longer have any attachment for thee; go where thou desirest! This is the outcome of my reflections, O lovely one! Turn to Lakṣmaṇa or Bharata, Śatrughna, Sugrīva or the titan Vibhīṣaṇa, take thy choice O Sītā, as pleases thee best. Assuredly Rāvaṇa, beholding thy ravishing and celestial beauty, will not have respected thy person during the time that thou didst dwell in his abode.[49]

Confounded by this unexpected unkindness and Rāma's sudden outburst, Sītā summons all her strength to give a passionate, yet befitting rejoinder to the charges inflicted on her. It is a lonely woman's defence in a cruel society of men. Even though on the verge of an emotional breakdown, and being unduly stigmatized, Sītā pleads her case and a summary of her arguments in her own words can be given in the following way:

1. All women cannot be maligned if some of them become sluts.
2. I was helpless and without any defence when Rāvaṇa forcibly carried me away and touched my body.
3. We both (i.e. Rāma and herself) have grown together and lived together for long, and even then you have failed to understand me, which is like a death to me.
4. What was the purpose of sending Hanumān to me with all the message of reassurance? Had you communicated these

---

[49] Hari Prasad Shastri (tr.), 1959, *The Rāmāyaṇa of Vālmīki,* vol. III, pp. 334-36.

feelings for me that time itself, I could have ended this life of mine, and it would have saved you from all the troubles of waging a momentous war and causing such an enormous destruction.

5. Overcome with your anger, it is you who are acting like a degraded person showing the characteristics of a lowly woman in yourself.[50]

A man debates with himself, the debates and ideological conflicts going on in the society are reflected in his psyche. He creates an opponent and a respondent within himself and his/her mind becomes a locale of debate. Hanumān's contemplations during his search for Sītā in Laṅkā bring out questions and dichotomies that the society of his time undergoing through, so that he appears to be debating with himself.

Not finding Sītā anywhere in Laṅkā after continuous search, Hanumān grew pensive and in a mood of melancholy started debating with himself:

> I, not having found Sītā, shall become a hermit, subsisting on fruits and roots. (Otherwise) preparing the funeral pyre on the shores of the sea, in a place abounding in roots, fruits and water, I shall enter the flames or allow myself to die of hunger; or else I will sit with a vow and let the wild beats or crows eat this body of mine. I think this also is the way of giving up this life envisaged by the seers. Or else I will drown myself in the sea if I do not see the daughter of Janaka.[51]

---

[50] *Vālmīki Rāmāyaṇa* 6.104.14.

[51] हस्तादानो मुखादानो नियतो वृक्षमूलिकः ।
वानप्रस्थो भविष्यामि अदृष्ट्वा जनकात्मजाम् ।।

सागरानूपजे देशे बहुमूलफलोदके।
चितिं कृत्वा प्रवेक्ष्यामि समिद्धमरणीसुतम् ।।

उपविष्टस्य वा सम्यग् लिङ्गिनं साधायिष्यतः ।
शरीरं भक्षयिष्यन्ति वायसाः श्वापदानि च ।।

इदमप्यृषिभिर्दृष्टं निर्याणमिति मे मतिः ।

→

The long soliloquy of Hanumān is marked with *ūha* (confutation), *tarka* (argument) and considerations of various possibilities, and he builds up the *pūrva-pakṣa* (prima facie view) and the *siddhānta-pakṣa* (final view). He concludes by considering the other aspect:

> Yet, there are incalculable evils in thus destroying oneself. If I continue to live, I may attain success. Therefore I will uphold my life, if I live the re-union (of Rāma and Sītā) may materialize.[52]

At other place Hanumān argues with himself by saying:

> Perseverance is the root of success, perseverance is the root of prosperity, and perseverance brings supreme facility.[53]

Hanumān's reveries bring out the clash between two ideologies: *pravṛtti* (empiricism) and *nivṛtti* (renunciation).

Debates in Mahābhārata

The tendency to use tricks in scholarly debate must have been in practice during the age of *Mahābhārata*. Śakuni when remonstrated by Yudhiṣṭhira on the use of trick in the game of dice, says: "a scholar surpasses a non-scholar only through his *nikṛti* (trick), but it is not regarded as trick".[54]

Techniques of *vāda* had systematically been developed when this great epic was being compiled. Vyāsa, delivering a discourse on governance before Yudhiṣṭhira and other Pāṇḍavas, recommends that the king should employ ministers who are well-versed in Tarkaśāstra (logic). He also emphasizes over the need for inculcating the Tarkaśātra in life.[55] Ānvīkṣikī is actually mentioned

---

← सम्यगापः प्रवेक्ष्यामि न चेत् पश्यामि जानकीम् ॥ — *Vālmīki Rāmāyaṇa* 5.11.40-43

[52] विनाशे बहवो दोषा जीवन् प्राप्स्यामि भद्रकम् ।
तस्मात् प्राणान् धरिष्यामि ध्रुवो जीवति सङ्गमः ॥ — Ibid. 5.11.47

[53] अनिर्वेदः श्रियो मूलमनिर्वेदः परं सुखम्।
अनिर्वेदो हि सततं सर्वार्थेषु प्रवर्तकः॥ — Ibid. 5.10.10

[54] *Mahābhārata*, Sabhāparva, 53.11.

[55] तर्कशास्त्रकृता बुद्धिर्धर्मशास्त्रकृता च या।

→

here in the enumeration of the four branches of learning.[56] There is a reference to *pañcāvayava-vākya* (five-member syllogism), which is essential for carrying out a debate as per the methodology laid down in *Nyāyadarśana*.[57] *Mahābhārata* also refers to four *pramāṇas*[58] and scholars especially adept in the virtues and flaws of *pañcāvayava-vākya*.[59]

Mahābhārata reflects dilemmas on perennial questions of destiny, life and death to set the ground for debates on crucial issues of human life. Immediately after the great war, Yudhiṣṭhira suffers from a moral dilemma. He is appalled at the devastation the war has caused and bitten with remorse and a persisting sense of guilt; he even declines to accept the throne and expresses his desire to retire to the forest and lead the life of an ascetic.[60] This puts him in bitter debate with Draupadī and Bhīma, who go to the extent of calling Yudhiṣṭhira a mentally deranged person; Draupadī even suggesting that her husband has gone insane and needs to be treated or be sent behind the bars along with the heretics (*nāstikas* or *Ājīvakas*).[61]

Ultimately Vyāsa joins this discussion and resolves the dilemma.[62]

← दण्डनीतिकृता चैव त्रैलोक्यमपि साधयेत्। — Ibid., Śāntiparva, after XXIV.17 in Gita Press edn.

56 Ibid., XXIV.18.

57 See Chap. 2 for details.

58 प्रत्यक्षेणानुमानेन तथौपम्यागमैरपि।
परीक्ष्यास्ते महाराज स्वे परे चैव नित्यशः।।
— *Mahābhārata*, Śāntiparva 56.41 (Gita Press edn)

59 पञ्चावयवयुक्तस्य वाक्यस्य गुणदोषवित् । — *Mahābhārata*, Sabhāparva 5

60 हित्वा ग्राम्यसुखाचारं तप्यमानो महत्तपः।
अरण्ये फलमूलाशी चरिष्यामि मृगैः सह।।
— *Mahābhārata*, Śāntiprvan, IX.4 (Gita Press edn)

61 Ibid. 14.33-35.

62 Ibid. 1.13-18, 7.31-35, 32.10-11, 76.15-17, 77.1-25.

Again, Kausalyā, wife of Janaka, the celebrated patron of philosophy seminars, raises a debate when her husband is ready to leave the royal palace for forest and become a mendicant. She calls the monks as parasites sucking the householders because of their vow of poverty and living on alms.

Thus one of the recurring themes for debate in *Mahābhārata* is the conflict between *karma* (action) and *jñāna* (knowledge). The concept of *bhakti* (devotion) as an alternate vision for life came to be introduced later. The first thirty-five cantos of the Śāntiparva in *Mahābhārata* are devoted to this debate. The theme is again taken up in the dialogue between Suvarcalā and Śvetaketu referred earlier. Vyāsa comes back to the same question of choice between action and knowledge in the cantos 267-70 and also 326, opening the gateway of diverse conflicting views.

Another conflicting issue is the choice between violence and non-violence. How can a king observe his duties and rule over the kingdom without hurting any of the subjects — this is the question Yudhiṣṭhira asks Bhīṣma in the beginning of the canto 267. Bhīṣma narrates the story of the dialogue between Dyumatsena and Satyavān. Even condemnation and censure could sometimes suffice as punishments for severe offences if the offender does not inflict further harm on the society.[63] In the next canto Kapila discusses the question of violence in the rituals. And then he reverts back to the tussle between *pravṛtti* (empiricism) and *nivṛtti* (renunciation).

The royal courts functioned like academies for cultivating debates on issues related to literature, philosophy and arts. In *Mahābhārata*, the court of King Janaka is described in a number of episodes as a flourishing centre for vigorous intellectual discussions and debates. Chapter 266th of Śāntiparva describes the visit of Pañcaśikha, one of the proponents of Sāṁkhya system, to this court to discuss his philosophy.

Besides the royal courts, a hermitage also became a potential

---

[63] *Mahābhārata*, Śāntiparva 267.19 (*mṛdavaḥ satyabhūyiṣṭhā . . .*).

venue for holding live debates. The 222nd chapter of Śāntiparva describes the debates conducted in the assembly of 6,000 sages in the Himalayan region. The debates proceeded on the following questions — 1. what is the nature of this Universe and how was it created?, and 2. what is the nature of *karma*?

Diverse views were propounded in this assembly with regard to this Universe, some said it is eternal, some said it is created by a God, the other would say there is no God, still others would even deny the very existence of this universe.

The brāhmaṇas (the knowledgeable ones) in this debate were armed with hundred kinds of reasoning and they had initiated several types of Śāstras (knowledge systems). In that grand debate, (the assembly came to be divided in two different groups of *vādin*s (the proponents) and *prativādins* (the opponents). But they could not reach any solution to these fundamental problems. The sages were agitated to such an extent that out of fury they tore away cloths and destroyed the pots and sticks.[64] Then they calmed down and approached Sage Vasiṣṭha to resolve their questions with regard to the eternal truth. When Vasiṣṭha expressed his inability to do so, they all went to Nārada. Ultimately a divine voice told them to go to Sanatkumāra. They were finally preached by Sanatkumāra, much on the lines of the Upaniṣadic discourses, incorporating even sentences in prose instead of the usual verse form in which most of the epic is structured.

The word *saṁvāda* is used in *Mahābhārata* in the sense of a highly-profound discussion between two intellectuals that was carried out

---

[64] ततस्तु मूलमुद्भूतं वादिप्रत्यर्थिसंयुतम्। पात्रदण्डविघातं च वल्कलाजिनवाससाम् एके मन्यु समापन्नास्तत: शान्ता द्विजोत्तमा:। — *Mahābhārata*, Śāntiparva 222 (It is not very clear whether the debaters were tearing their own cloths of bark, and destroying their own pots, etc. out of dejection or tearing cloths or destroying the properties of the opponents out of fury. The word *manyu* (vengeance) used here suggests that the scene of debate was transformed into a scene of scuffle.)

in past and lives in the collective memory of a race, constituting an *itihāsa*. Many such *saṁvādas* are cited in *Mahābhārata*. The *saṁvāda* between Kṛṣṇa and Nārada on various questions of diplomacy of polity is cited as something that happened in yore.[65]

It is during the age of *Mahābhārata* that the term *nyāya* came to be used for the proper methodology for discussions and debates involving the style and form that vouch for accuracy of the whole process of a debate or discussion.

The dice game between Duryodhana and Yudhiṣṭhira resulted in one of the most tense and exciting debates in human history. It is an example of impromptu debate as described earlier. This type of debate gets started under compulsion all of a sudden.

Yudhiṣṭhira lost Draupadī on his final bet in the game of dice. Duryodhana sent the messenger (*pratikāmin*) to bring Draupadī. Draupadī asked *pratikāmin* to go and ask the gambler (Yudhiṣṭhira) whether he had lost himself first or her.[66] Then Duryodhana sends his younger brother to bring Draupadī by force. Being forcibly taken to the assembly with her hair dishevelled and half her attire loosened, Draupadī told her tormentor Duḥśāsana:

> My Lord Yudhiṣṭhira is bound by obligations of *dharma*, *dharma* however, is subtle. Only those who are possessed of clarity of vision are able to ascertain *dharma*.

Dragged forcibly by Duḥśāsana in the assembly, an utterly helpless Draupadī dares to confront the elders in the congregation with a question. The question raised by her pertains to *dharma*. She started a debate as a complainant and pleaded her case. Subjected to humiliation in public, she questioned the elders in the assembly and the question was: whether her husband was authorized to bet

---

65 अत्राप्युदाहरन्तीममितिहासं पुरातनम्। संवादं वासुदेवस्य सुरर्षेर्नारदस्य च।।
— *Mahābhārata*, Śāntiparva 81.2

66 गच्छ त्वं कितवं गत्वा सभायां पृच्छ सूतज।
किन्नु पूर्वं पराजैषीरात्मानमथवा नु माम्।। — *Mahābhārata* 2.60.7

on her in the game of dice when after putting himself on stake, he had lost and become a slave himself.

Bhīṣma is perplexed and looks askance. At his wit's end, he hesitates in answering the question of Draupadī, and then somehow manages to say that the *dharma* is very subtle and he is unable to decide on either side, because arguments can be advanced from both sides. It is true that having become a slave, Yudhiṣṭhira had no right to put her on bet, but then it is also true that he continues to be her husband even as a slave, and as a husband he had right to bet on her.[67] Only Vidura and Vikarṇa (the youngest brother of the Kauravas) stand in Draupadī's defence.

One point which Bhīṣma had raised in his reply was that Yudhiṣṭhira chose to play the game of dice on his own, and he staked Draupadī voluntarily. Draupadī refuted this claim. She said:

> The king (Yudhiṣṭhira) was summoned to this assembly, and though possessing no skill of dice, he was forced to play with skilled, wicked, deceitful and desperate gamblers. How can you say then that he staked me voluntarily? The chief of Pāṇḍavas was deprived of his senses by wretches of deceitful conduct and unholy instincts having joined their hands together and defeated him. He could not understand their tricks and he was not his own when he did so (staked me). Here in this assembly there are Kurus who are the lords of their sons and their daughters-in-law. Let all of them consider my statement and duly decide the issue I have raised.

She asked the elders to think of *dharma*, and found that they have been taken aback. Then she condemned them in most unequivocal terms:

---

[67] धर्मस्य सौक्ष्म्यात् सुभगे विवेक्तुं शक्नोमि ते प्रश्नमिमं यथावत्।
अस्वो ह्यशक्तः पणितुं परस्वं स्त्रियश्च भर्तुर्वशतां समीक्ष्य।।
त्यजेत सर्वां पृथिवीं समृद्धां युधिष्ठिरो धर्ममथो न जह्यात्।
उक्तं जितोऽस्मीति च पाण्डवेन तस्मान्न शक्नोमि विवेक्तुमेतत्।।
— *Mahābhārata* 2.60.40-41

> The virtue of the people of Bharata race is gone! The practices of the kṣatriyas have disappeared! Otherwise the Kurus present here would never have silently watched such an act being performed which violates these very practices! Both Droṇa and Bhīṣma have lost their energy, and so has the noble Vidura and also this King (Dhṛtarāṣṭra). Else why are they sitting silently over this crime?[68]

The whole unsavoury episode included a fierce debate between two sides. The court of Duryodhana was immediately converted into a scene of debate and a court for justice, where not only the fate of a woman was to be decided; the destiny of the two races (Kauravas and Pāṇḍavas) was also to be rewritten. This is one of the greatest debates in the history of civilization. It raises serious questions with regard to man's attitude towards women, property rights, values and social norms. Draupadī not only pleads her own case, she is able to generate a public opinion in her favour. After going through the whole agony and ordeal, she wins her case and also successfully gets herself and her five husbands freed from the bond of slavery.

It is only through her debating skill and moral courage to put up a question that Draupadī poses a challenge before an entirely nonchalant and chauvinistic gathering and is able to create a conscience to win the verdict in her favour. The *Mahābhārata* presents this whole episode to be viewed as a scene of debate. Draupadī is therefore made to make a remark about the responsibilities of the members of the assembly. She says:

> An assembly not attended by the elders is not a proper assembly for the debate and men who do not speak *dharma* are not elders. The *dharma* without truth is not *dharma*, and the truth imbued with deception is not truth.[69]

---

68 धिगस्तु नष्टः खलु भारतानां धर्मस्तथा क्षत्रविदां च वृत्तम्।
यत्राभ्यतीतां कुरुधर्मवेलां प्रेक्षन्ति सर्वे कुरवः सभायाम्।।
द्रोणस्य भीष्मस्य च नास्ति सत्त्वं ध्रुवं तथैवास्य महात्मनोऽपि।
राज्ञस्तथा हीममधर्ममुग्रं न लक्षयन्ते कुरुवृद्धमुख्याः।। — *Mahābhārata* II.60.33-34

69 न सा सभा यत्र न सन्ति वृद्धा न ते वृद्धा ये न वदन्ति धर्मम्।

→

Vikarṇa and Vidura also use similar terms to invoke the conscience of the members of the assembly. Vikarṇa gave reasons why Draupadī could not be considered to have been won and why the issue raised by her needs to be considered.[70] He finally made a fervent appeal to decide the case in Draupadī's favour. There was uproar in the assembly. Vikarṇa's fervent appeal was applauded. Karṇa rose to silence Vikarṇa, telling him that he is too immature and young to take a decision in this case while the elders have not spoken a word. He emphatically said that Draupadī, being a possession of Yudhiṣṭhira which has been lost in stake is properly won and acquired rightfully.

Amidst the clamour, people in the assembly started censuring Dhṛtarāṣṭra, who as a king ought to have stopped the heinous act of dishonour to a lady. Vidura then said:

> Draupadī has put up a question and is weeping helplessly. Virtue and *dharma* are being persecuted by such conduct (of Kauravas). When an afflicted person asks an assembly of noble persons about his rights, as sanctioned by *dharma*, members of the assembly should, without being affected by interest and anger, answer his question.

With these words he supported the statement of Vikarṇa.[71] Both Vikarṇa and Vidura expressed their opinion in unequivocal terms that Draupadī cannot be forced to become a slave because putting

---

← नासौ धर्मो यत्र न सत्यमस्ति न तत् सत्यं यच्छलेनानुविद्धम्।
– *Mahābhārata*, Sabhāparva, 2.89.65, Southern edn, pt. II, chap. 101, Delhi: Sri Sadguru Publications

70 *Mahābhārata* (BORI) II.61.12-25.

71 द्रौपदी प्रश्नमुक्त्वैव रौरवीति ह्यनाथवत्।
न च विब्रूत तं प्रश्नं सभ्या धर्मोऽत्र पीड्यते।।
सभां प्रपद्यते ह्यार्तः प्रज्ज्वलन्निव हव्यवाट्।
तं वै सत्येन धर्मेण सभ्याः प्रशमयन्त्युत।।
विद्धो धर्मो ह्यधर्मेण सभां यत्रोपपद्यते।
न चास्य शल्यं कृन्तन्ति विद्धास्तत्र सभासदः।। — *Mahābhārata* (BORI) II.61.69

her on stake by Yudhiṣṭhira was illegal.[72] Vidura was silenced by Duryodhana, calling him a śūdra. But listening to Vikarṇa's fervent appeal, the members of the assembly raised their voices to support him.[73] Again there were arguments and counter-arguments. The debate can be summarized as under.

Draupadī is a property put on the stake.

- She was put on the stake by her husband Yudhiṣṭhira and he lost the bet.
- Whatsoever is put on the stake in the game of dice and lost is to be claimed by the opposite party.
- Therefore the treatment given to Draupadī by the Kauravas is justified.

This was the argument from Duryodhana's side. What Vikarṇa and Vidura were trying to establish can be logistically summarized in the following way:

- Yudhiṣṭhira was not authorized to put Draupadī on stake in the game of dice because he was not in his senses when he started playing the game.
- The stake was also illegal because Yudhiṣṭhira had become a slave, hence he had lost his rights on any property and was not authorized to stake claim on any property.
- Therefore the game he played after having become a slave is illegal.

---

72 दुर्विभाषं भाषितं त्वादृशेन न मन्दं सम्बुध्यसि पाशबद्धः।
प्रपाते त्वं लम्बमानो न वेत्सि व्याधामृगः कोपयसेऽतिवेलम् ।।
न हि दासीत्वमापन्ना कृष्णा भवितुमर्हति।
अनीशेन हि राज्ञैषा पणे न्यस्तेति मे मतिः।। — *Mahābhārata* 2.59.4

73 जितेन पूर्वं चैतेन पाण्डवेन कृतः पणः।
इयं च कीर्तिता कृष्णा सौबलेन पणार्थिना ।
एतत् सर्वं विचार्याहं न मन्ये निर्जितामहम्।
एतच्छ्रुत्वा महान्नादः सभ्यानामुदतिष्ठत।
विकर्णं शंसमानानां सौबलं चापि निन्दताम्। — Ibid. 2.61.21-25

This way, the argumentative design of *vāda* as envisaged through five-member syllogism (see next chapter) was inherent in this debate.

Śākuntalopākhyāna in *Mahābhārata* is comprised of a vigorous debate between a lady and her lover who deliberately refuses to recognize her in public. Duṣṣanta,[74] an emperor of Kuru dynasty, is enchanted by the beauty of Śakuntalā when he visits the hermitage of Kaṇva. Śakuntalā accepts the proposal of a *gāndharva-vivāha* (love marriage) from him on the condition that her son, born from this marriage, will be given the royal throne. After making love with her, the king leaves the forest grove assuring her that a royal entourage will soon be sent to bring her to the capital. The promise was never fulfilled and when, Bharata, the son, born out of this marriage grew up to be young enough, Śakuntalā came to Hastināpura, Duṣṣanta's capital, and met the king with a demand for being accepted as the queen in the royal harem and enthronement of her son. Duṣṣanta's ill-conceited and roguish denial to recognize her resulted in a fierce debate between the two, which involved moral and ethical issues apart from the personal grievance of the lady. Śakuntalā said:

> An imposter is a thief and a sinner. You think that you were alone when you committed a sin, but that is not true. My father, the Sage Kaṇva knows of your evil design because of the power of his penance. A person having committed a sin thinks that no one has seen him, but gods see him doing the evil, and his *antarapuruṣa* (the soul) sees him doing the evil.

Śakuntalā then threatens the traitor that his head will split into hundred pieces if he betrays her in this way:

> A husband having made an intercourse with a lady duly wedded is reborn as his son. By refusing to accept your son therefore, you are denying your own self.

---

[74] It is spelled as "Duṣyanta" in Kālidāsa's well-known play based on this very story from *Mahābhārata*. The name of the king as spelled in the epic of Vyāsa originally was almost forgotten later.

Like the debate started by Draupadī after the game of dice between Yudhiṣṭhira and Duryodhana, the war of words between Śakuntala and Duṣṣanta here is conceived as a debate on morality and human weaknesses. Śakuntalā delivers a discourse on sin, human destiny and relations between the father and the son. The arrogant king behaves in a most outlandish manner and abuses her in filthy language. He laughs at her, calling her an unchaste woman, doting upon her illicit relations. Śakuntalā's remarks on the character of men here bring out a minute study of inner contradictions of a man's character. She is all set to depart with the promise that one day her son, trained to be a mighty warrior, will take her revenge and Duṣṣanta will have to pay for his sins. At this juncture, a divine intervention, as an *ākāśavāṇī* (voice from heaven), forces the king to change his stance and accept her.

The Vanaparva of *Mahābhārata* presents the scene of intriguing debates between Vandin, a courtier of the king on one hand and Kahoḍa on the other. Venue of this debate was a prolonged sacrifice performed by King Janaka of Videha.

Aṣṭāvakra was the son of Kahoḍa, the brother-in-law of Śvetaketu. Even when he was in the womb of his mother, Aṣṭāvakra is said to have raised an objection upon his father's studying in the night, and was cursed to be born with eightfold deformity in his limbs.

Vandin was known as a notorious debater. Defeated by him in a debate, Kahoḍa had to be drowned in waters. When Aṣṭāvakra came to know of this unsavoury episode, he decided to visit the premises of the sacrifice. Upon being told that only elders are allowed to enter the pavilion of the sacrifice, Aṣṭāvakra gave a scholarly discourse defining who is a real elder.

The king himself entered into a debate with Aṣṭāvakra. Being satisfied he allowed the boy to debate with his protege — Vandin. Aṣṭāvakra debated with Vandin on numbers and cosmology. Vandin was silenced when they reached number thirteen. Aṣṭāvakra had his revenge and also regained his lost father. These debates of

Aṣṭāvakra with the king and Vandin are described in the Vanaparva of *Mahābhārata* (chaps. 133-34).

One of the most crucial debates in *Mahābhārata* occurs when Viśvāmitra, facing death out of starvation, stole dog's meat from the house of an untouchable (*cāṇḍāla*), just to keep himself alive in the days of famine. Caught red-handed in this act, he is questioned about the propriety of his action, which is so unbecoming of him, by the *cāṇḍāla*, who appears to be more concerned about the loss of *dharma* which this theft would cause for the noble sage. The whole episode presents a feast of arguments and counter-arguments in the prolonged debate between the sage and the untouchable. It examines a man's action in utter crisis with an analysis of his choice between his own death and a harmless sin. *Cāṇḍāla* starts preaching the sage on the importance of saving the *dharma*. "This act of yours would not be called a sin had it been to save some other person" — he says. Viśvāmitra retorts by saying that his own body is his friend, and allowing this friend to die out of hunger would cause a bigger loss of *dharma* to him than the sinful act of stealth.[75]

Nirukta as a Documentation of Debates

Yāska, who authored the first authentic text (*Nirukta*) on etymology and hermeneutics on Vedic texts around 700 BCE, has been referred as a legatee of an argumentative tradition earlier. He refers to a number of debates on issues related to interpretation of the Vedas in *Nirukta*. There have been two opposite schools with regard to reading any meaning in the *mantras* of Veda. Kautsa as cited by Yāska opined that there is no meaning in *mantras*: *anarthakā vai mantrāḥ*.[76] The justification for this theory lies in the belief that *mantras* are for application in rituals, their application is defined by the Brāhmaṇa

---

[75] *Mahābhārata*, Śāntiparva, 141 (Gita Press edn).

[76] अथापीदमन्तरेण मन्त्रेष्वर्थो न विद्यतेऽर्थमप्रतियतो नात्यन्तं स्वरसंस्कारोद्देशस्तदिदं विद्यास्थानं व्याकरणस्य कार्त्स्न्यं रुन्यं स्वार्थसाधकं यदि मन्त्रार्थप्रत्ययायानर्थकं भवतीति कौत्सोऽनर्थका हि मन्त्रास्तदेतेनोपेक्षितव्यं नियतवाचोयुक्तयो नियतानुपूर्व्यां भवन्त्यथापि ब्राह्मणेन रूपसम्पन्ना विधीयन्ते। — *Nirukta* I.15, pt. I, p. 87

texts. They have a fixed order of words and syllables (*niyatānupūrvī*) and a defined method for recitation or chanting which cannot be violated; and learning them for derivation of a meaning is a futile exercise. Any attempt to draw sense from the *mantra*s would lead to impossible situations or contradictions. Drawing sharp difference with this view, Yāska refutes all the arguments of Kautsa one by one. He says that *mantra*s are very much meaningful and they yield the meaning through well-defined principles of etymology and grammar. A person chanting a *mantra* without knowing its meaning may commit mistakes in correct application of *svara*s, because the capability of applying the correct *svara* requires an understanding of the meaning. The words used in *mantra*s are used in the *laukika* language (Pāṇinian Sanskrit) also, if they yield meanings in the *laukika* language, how can they become meaningless when used in a *mantra*? The Brāhmaṇa texts do not describe their applications only, they also describe their meanings. *Mantra*s cannot lead to the actions being performed in a *yajña* without yielding their meaning. What Kautsa understands as impossible situations or contradictions can be resolved by taking symbolic and figurative meanings.

Kautsa's denial of a semantic status to Veda was met with a strong rebuttal not only from Yāska but from philosophers like Jaimini, Śabara and Sāyaṇa. In *Mīmāṁsāsūtra* I.1, Jaimini raises a question — does the study of Veda include only its memorization or learning it with the meanings of *mantra*s also? He then argues in favour of the second option. Pāraskara in his *Gṛhyasūtram* has defined Veda having three functions: *vidhi* (injunction), *vidheya* (application) and *tarka* (argument).

II. Tarka-kāla (The Age of Arguments)

The beginnings of the age of arguments which is spread over the whole millennium between 500 BCE to CE 1000, were marked with the emergence of the six systems of Vedic philosophy and the onslaught of various heterodox systems — Cārvāka, Ājīvaka, Jainism and Buddhism.

The essence of philosophical thought under diverse schools was put in the texts comprising the Sūtras. The word heterodox is an English equivalent of the term *nāstika* and has been used in a wider sense not only to denote śramaṇa and Jaina traditions alone, but also all *nāstika* (non-orthodox, not subscribing to the final authority of the Veda or Śruti) systems.

The school of Cārvāka is perhaps the oldest of all philosophical systems. It was cultivated in non-Vedic traditions, although the ideas of Cārvāka philosophy are reflected in the Vedic Saṁhitās and the Upaniṣads. In *Mahābhārata*, a brāhmaṇa named Cārvāka, said to be a friend of Duryodhana, confronts Yudhiṣṭhira with disturbing questions, and is eventually killed by other brāhmaṇas. Subsequently, Śrīkṛṣṇa explains the genesis of Cārvāka and his philosophy through a story. Cārvāka accordingly was a *rākṣasa*, who attained brāhmaṇahood by performing rigorous penance.[77]

The course of the development of the Cārvāka philosophy incorporates several stages during the course of its prolonged development. It was ritualistic during the stage of its early formulation, then had affiliations with tantric cults, and gradually embraced epistemological considerations. Some of the hymns of *Ṛgveda* record the earliest versions of the propositions by the Cārvākas. There are copious references to non-believers and transgressors.[78] The view that *sat* (being) came out of *asat* (non-being) — is repeatedly cited in Vedic and Upaniṣadic texts and taken up for a debate. It can be taken as the first assertion by the Cārvākas. The seer of *Ṛgveda* X.72 is Laukya Bṛhaspati. The word *laukya* would mean the son of Loka. On the basis of this, Athawale[79] believes that Loka, father of Bṛhaspati, was the originator of the Lokāyata philosophy. Bṛhaspati is said to be the founder of

---

77 *Mahābhārata*, Śāntiparva IXL (Gita Press edn).

78 *Ṛgveda* III.3.9, IV.23.7, V.2.3, V.42.9, etc.

79 S. Athawale, 1997, *Cārvāka: Itihāsa āṇi Tattavajñāna* (1997), Preface, p. 14.

this philosophy. *Lokāyatasūtra*, supposed to have been authored by him, is no more extant. Patañjali informs in his *Mahābhāṣya* (VII.3.8) that a philosopher named Bhāguri had authored *vārttikas* (a form of commentary) on Bṛhaspati's *Lokāyatasūtra*. Athawale has referred to Bharadvāja, son of Bṛhaspati, who also upheld the Lokāyata philosophy.[80] Bharadvāja has given a detailed exposition of Bhūtavāda (materialism) as described at length in *Mahābhārata*.[81] Cārvāka, the demon appearing after the Mahābhārata war and rudely questioning Yudhiṣṭhira, is identified as Cārvāka the philosopher.[82]

That Lokāyata continued to be a dominating force is evidenced by its presentation in several literary works: *Samrāiccakahā* of Haribhadra, a narrative in Prākṛt; *Triṣaṣṭiśalākāpuruṣacarita* of Hemacandra or *Yaśastilakacampūḥ* of Somadeva.

Brahmasūtra of Bādarāyaṇa, *Mīmāṁsāsūtra* of Jaimini, *Sāṁkhyasūtra* of Kapila, *Yogasūtra* of Patañjali, *Nyāyasūtra* of Gautama and *Vaiśeṣikasūtra* of Kaṇāda were composed in the BCE era. These herald the beginning of six systems of orthodox philosophy — all of them accepting the Veda as authority. Of these, Vedānta alone is pure idealist, Sāṁkhya and Yoga are realists but have leanings towards idealism; remaining systems of the orthodox philosophy are all realists.

Of these, the Sāṁkhya system is one of the oldest and has remained a potential challenge in the debate for all other systems except the Yoga. Kapila, its proponent, was of the earliest of non-conformists. He stood against the rituals. *Baudhāyana* II.vi.30 says that before Kapila there were three *āśramas* — *brahmacarya*, *gṛhastha* and *vānaprastha*. Kapila introduced the fourth — the *saṁnyāsa*. The order of Kapila was accepted by Āsuri of *asura* descent.

80 S. Athawale, 1997, op. cit., p. 18.

81 Śāntiparva, chaps. 186, 188, 190.

82 *Sanskrit Worterbuch* (Perterburgh Dictionary), pt. II, p. 997.

The Mīmāṁsā system had its beginnings in theoretical/ interpretative discussions and speculations. Mīmāṁsā has also been termed as Vicāraśāstra (the discourse in thinking) in the chapter on Mīmāṁsā in *Sarvadarśanasaṁgraha*. The process of analysing was also termed as *mīmāṁsā*. *Taittirīya Brāhmaṇa* III.5.7 says : *mīmāṁsante brahmavādinaḥ* (the philosophers speculate). The means of arriving at truth is Mīmāṁsā. The Upaniṣads therefore describe the philosophers conducting the Mīmāṁsā with regard to the questions about what is self, what is *Brahman*?[83]

The Vaiśeṣika system was not basically concerned with physics, rather than metaphysics and devoted itself to the study of nature. The Ārambhavāda (atomic theory) as envisaged in this system viewed the universe as formed by the conjunctions of atoms — the subtlest form of matter.

Rājaśekhara, a well-known poet, dramatist and rhetorician of tenth century CE, enumerates six philosophical systems as Ānvīkṣikī, all of them being argumentative. Out of these, Buddhism, Jainism and Cārvāka system form the prima facie view, and Sāṁkhya, Nyāya and Vaiśeṣika belong to the *uttara-pakṣa* (the theory to be accepted). These six systems utilize the techniques of debate — *vāda, jalpa* and *vitaṇḍā*.[84]

There are grounds for agreement between the orthodox and heterodox schools, especially between Śāṅkara-Vedānta and Buddhist schools of Śūnyavāda and Vijñānavāda who regard the knowledge acquired through *pramāṇas* as not absolutely real. They assign to it a level of practical reality — *vyāvahārika sattā* or *saṁvṛti-satya*. On the other hand, Nyāya-Vaiśeṣika, Mīmāṁsā and Mādhva Vedāntin regard knowledge gained through *pramāṇas* as

---

83 महाश्रोत्रिया: समेत्य मीमांसां चक्रुः — को नाम आत्मा, किं ब्रह्मन्? — *Chāndogya Upaniṣad* V.Xi.1

84 द्विधा चान्वीक्षिकी - पूर्वोत्तरपक्षाभ्याम्। अर्हद्भदन्तदर्शने लोकायतं च पूर्वः पक्षः। साङ्ख्यं न्यायवैशेषिकौ चोत्तरः। त इमे षट् तर्काः। तत्र च तिस्रः कथाः भवन्ति - वादो जल्पो वितण्डा च। — *Kāvyamīmāṁsā*, chap. II, pp. 24-25

absolutely real. There is no place for *māyā* (illusion) in the world-view of Nyāya-Vaiśeṣika and Mādhva Vedānta. To the Naiyāyika the whole world is formed of real entities, which become objects of *pramā* (knowledge) that cannot be contradicted. The existence of these entities is defined by *jāti* or *sāmānya.*

Even though the six systems — Vedānta, Mīmāṁsā, Nyāya, Vaiśeṣika, Sāṁkhya and Yoga — are said to be the Vedic *darśanas*, there are fundamental differences and issues for debate amongst them. One very crucial question is with regard to the validity of the means of knowledge (*pramāṇa*). Both the Nyāya and Vaiśeṣika systems uphold the principle of *parataḥ pramāṇa*, i.e. the validity of a *pramāṇa* is to be ascertained by a source other than the *pramāṇa* itself. Jaimini on the other hand, postulated *svataḥ prāmāṇya* — the theory of holding that a *pramāṇa* does not require its validation from an external source, it is valid by itself. These two opposite views create a situation of a neck-to-neck fight between the Nyāya and Mīmāṁsā systems. To the Vaiśeṣika and Naiyāyika, even the authority of the scriptures is not to be considered as something independent and irreducible, it has to be established through inference. To the Mīmāṁsaka, the Veda is eternal — not created by any conscious being — divine or human, and does not require validation.

The Sūtra texts are structured as quintessential of several prolonged discourses and discussions in search of certain specific queries. The word *jijñāsā* (inquiry) occurring in the very first aphorism of *Brahmasūtra* and *Mīmāṁsāsūtra* is suggestive of inherent questions and discussions. Jaimini used another term *parīṣṭi* (investigation) for a critical examination of diverse views on any issue.[85] In its prescriptive and descriptive forms, the Mīmāṁsā system appears to be least concerned with issues for debate. But even as a Sūtra text, it searches for the solutions of certain fundamental questions, whether *vidhi*, *arthavāda*, *mantra*

---

[85] *Mīmāṁsāsūtram* I.I.2.

and *nāmadheya* are *pramāṇas* or not in the first chapter of the *Mīmāṁsāsūtra*.

The Continuance of Ānvīkṣikī

Even though the proponents of the Nyāya system treated their philosophy at par or identical with Ānvīkṣikī, the Ājīvakas and Cārvākas continued to practise Ānvīkṣikī in their own way. Sañjaya Kātyāyana, Purāṇakaśyapa, Makkaliputta Gosāla (Maṅkhaliputra Gośāla), Ajitakeśakambalin, Kakuda Kaccāyana belonged to this tradition of philosophy. They argued against ritualism, theories of *karma* and denied the moral consequences of all actions. Maṅkhali Gośāla (died about 493 BCE) was a contemporary of Mahāvīra. He came from the lowest strata of society. His father was a beggar. Bhadrā, his mother, gave birth to him in a cow's pan; hence he was called Gośālaka or Gośāla. He embraced maverick asceticism. He spent a few years of his life in association with Mahāvīra and quit him to found the Ājīvaka sect. The Ājīvakas propounded the thesis of 84,000 *yonis* (births circles) to explain the evolutionary process. This process also imbibes an unalterable destiny for the human beings, as there is no escape from it. Sagar Mal Jain finds him identical with the Sage Maṅki, as described in *Mahābhārata*. Maṅki is also said to have propounded the philosophy of Niyativāda.[86]

Amongst the Upaniṣadic seers there were some who propagated materialism. Uddālaka argued that mind, life and speech have their genesis in the intake of food, water and heat respectively. A man's comprehension, retention and memory depend upon the way he feeds himself.[87]

Buddha's Dialectical Method of Discourse

Buddha developed a unique method of resolving contradictions. It seems that he was often criticized for accepting opposite stand-points. He himself is reported to have remarked that he has

---

[86] *Isibhāsiyāin*, pp. 102-03.

[87] *Chāndogya Upaniṣad* IV.5.3.

propounded the doctrines which are *ekāṁśikas* (one-sided) and also the doctrines which are *anekāṁśikas* (many-sided). Matilal (1981: 6) says that "the word *anekāṁśika* was probably another name for *anekānta* and Buddha's method of *anekāṁśika* could be taken to be a precursor of the Jaina Anekānta doctrine".

In *Majjhimanikāya* (*sutta* 99) Buddha proclaims that he is not an Ekāntavādin, he is a Vibhajyavādin. Through Vibhajyavāda, Buddha presented his own analytical method. Vibhajyavāda consisted of division, classification, qualified negations or qualified affirmation. The analysis is to be made by way of questioning each part of a theory to be discussed, with the acceptance or rejection of each one on fair grounds. Vasubandhu defines a Vibhajyavādin in the following terms:

> Those who say that everything exists — past, present and future — are Sarvāstivādins. But there are Vibhajyavādins who say that only certain things exist, viz. — the present *karma* as well as the past *karma* which have fructified — they exist. The future *karma* which have not fructified do not exist.[88]

By his analytical method, Buddha classified all the philosophical questions into four categories — *ekāṁśa-vyākaraṇīya* (answerable in affirmative or negative terms), *vibhajyavādena-vyākaraṇīya* (answerable by division and analysis), *pratipraśnena-vyākaraṇīya* (answerable by putting counter-questions) and *sthāpanīya* (to be answered by silence or to be set aside). This was in accordance with his philosophy of avoiding extremes — the *madhyamā pratipad* (the middle path). There can be two aspects emerging out of any theory and they may form two extremes. Avoidance of these two extremes is *madhyamā pratipad*. Buddha followed the middle path by rejecting the two extremes. In the theory of Anekānta also, middle path is accepted albeit with acceptance of the two extremes as well. Matilal (1981: 18) explains Buddha's way as "exclusive middle" and the Anekānta theory as "inclusive middle".

---

[88] *Abhidharmakośabhāṣya*, chap. V, p. 805.

The way Buddha applied the technique of Vibhajyavāda in his discourse led to the development of Anekāntavāda. He not only presented an alternate world-view, he also encouraged arguments and discussions. Before his enlightenment he had met a number of philosophers and thinkers of his times. His quest for enlightenment has been termed *ariyapariyesana* (The Noble Quest) in Pāli canons. During his restless wandering and search for knowledge, he met Ālāra Kālāma and Uddaka Rāmaputta.[89] Sañjaya Kātyāyana, Purāṇakaśyapa, Makkali Gosāla and Ajitakeśakambalin — these were Buddha's contemporaries. Kakuda Kaccāyana was a hump-backed philosopher, belonging to the Ājīvaka sect in fifth century BCE. These philosophers have been raising questions on prevailing norms. It is perhaps to condemn them that the interpolation in Vālmīki's *Rāmāyaṇa* comprising Jābāli's conversation with Rāma was added. Buddha rejected their views. He is reported to have described, Makkali Gosāla, an exponent of Ājīvaka sect, as "a burden on earth" a person responsible for leading people astray.[90] He also launched a crusade against the hypocrisy of the priestly class. Pratap Chandra (1977) says:

> There is little doubt that Buddha treated the priestly class with a contempt and rejected their claims of supremacy with disdain. They are always treated as ideal gossipers with no worthwhile contribution to make to general religious debate.

Rather than launching a movement for protest, Buddha kept open all the doors for debate and discussion. It was because of the dialogic nature of his discourses, the correspondences between Vedic philosophies and Buddhism were accepted and Buddha was accepted as one of the ten incarnations of Viṣṇu. Buddha also did not launch a rebellion against the prevalent religions. A rebel

---

[89] G.C. Pande, 1957, *Studies in the Origin of Buddhism*, p. 377.

[90] Quoted by Pratapchandra in "Study of Ideological Discord in Ancient India: Search for a Suitable Model" in *Dissent, Protest and Reform in Indian Civilization*, p. 95.

would not consider an established viewpoint he is refuting at par with his own views. In all fairness, Buddha limited all his debates to a fair criticism without being hostile or destructive, never to cause any violence.

Buddha and his followers developed a specific method of indulging in *kathā* (discussion). It has been termed as *paṭipucchā kathā* (*pratipṛcchā kathā* — delivering a discourse by the way of asking questions). In *Nandakavāda Sutta* of *Majjhimanikāya*, Nandaka exemplifies this method of *kathā*. In the same way, *Anumānasutta* and *Upālisutta* in the same scripture present the concept of inference and *vāda* in the sense of a controversy. The debating skills of the monks like Vāseṭṭha and Bhāradvāja are described in the Piṭakas or Buddhist scriptures. Buddha's debate with Saccaka is also described.[91] The genre of *dhammakathā* (discussion of *dhamma*) was cultivated and practised with the advent of Buddha. The basic tenets of the theory of *kathā* were also evolved with Buddha's discourse on *dhamma*. *Kathāvatthu* in *Abhidhamma Piṭaka* which composed around 255 BCE mentions *anuyoga* (inquiry), *udāharaṇa* (illustration), *paṭiññā* (proposition), *upanayana* (application of reason), *niggama* (conclusion) and *niggaha* (capture or defeat) as various techniques of *kathā*.[92]

Mahāvīra and the Tradition of Debate

The practice of Vibhajyavāda in later śramaṇic traditions culminated into the theory of *anekānta*. Avoidance of *ekānta* (one-sidedness) is Anekānta. Matilal (1981: 1) explains the philosophy of Anekānta as "the theory of non-one-sidedness" or "the theory of many-sidedness of reality". Because of its acceptance of many-folded nature of reality, Anekānta had the capability of traversing on different *nayas* (standpoints) offering justification of each. Each standpoint has its conditionality and if stated without any conditionality, it remains unjustified. Accepting any doctrine or system unconditionally would mean exclusion of all rival

---

91 Solomon, 1976, *Indian Dialectics*, vol. I, pp. 30-31.

92 Ibid., p. 34.

doctrines and systems. Anekānta requires an understanding of the truth behind diverse standpoints and also the conditions of these standpoints, overruling every prejudice.

Accepting the view of Dalsukhabhai Malvania that the practice of Vibhajyavāda in later śramaṇic traditions culminated into the theory of Anekānta, Matilal (1981: 4) further suggests that the moral doctrine of *ahiṁsā* (non-violence) was "partly responsible for the development of the Anekānta attitude in Jaina philosophy".

Matilal (1981: 25) rightly described the methodology of Anekāntavāda as taking its flights on two wings — Nayavāda (the doctrine of standpoints) and the Saptabhaṅgī (the doctrine of sevenfold predications). The later is also named as Syādvāda and is also taken as synonymous to Anekānta, because the prefix *syād* in it signifies manifold nature of any category.

In fact, the philosophy of Saptabhaṅgīnaya developed from the *trairāśika* as propounded by Ājīvaka Gosāla. Gosāla said that everything has triple character — existence, non-existence and both. Matilal (1981: 49) finds this doctrine of triple character of every entity as more akin in spirit and logically closer to the later Jaina doctrine of sevenfold formula as well the Anekānta.

Haribhadra in his *Anekāntavijayapatākā* (pp. 13-26) explains the theory of Anekānta as Saṁhāravāda (the theory of integration), Sarva-vastu-śabala-vāda (the theory of manifoldness of every real entity), Ākulavāda (theory of accepting opposites) and Saṅkīravāda (the theory of intermixture).

With this kind of openness, Mahāvīra's tradition of *vāda* distinguished between *naya* and *durnaya. Naya* is accepting one standpoint with full awareness of other standpoints in relation to it, and *durnaya* is accepting one standpoint by excluding others. The correct method of *vāda* therefore would be to explore the *naya* and expose *durnaya* (Matilal 1981: 30).

Solomon has referred to vigorous debates between the followers of Mahāvīra with Buddha or his disciples which are recorded in

Jaina Āgamas like *Rājapraśnīya* or *Bhagavatīsūtra*. A team of *vādins* (debaters) accompanied Mahāvīra. The Jaina Āgamas also describe types of *vādas*, as well as their qualities and defects.[93]

Arthaśāstra as a Text of Debates

Kauṭilya's *Arthaśāstra*, a comprehensive text on governance, management, polity and economics, was written most probably during the reign of Candragupta Maurya in fourth century BCE. Throughout his discourse, Kauṭilya refers to the views of earlier authorities on Dharmaśāstra (law, ethics) and Arthaśāstra, and records his agreements or disagreements with them. They are — the Mānavas (the followers of the school of Manu), Bārhaspatyas (the followers of the schools of Bṛhaspati), Auśanasas (the followers of the school of Uśanas or Śukra), Bhāradvājas (followers of the schools of Bharadvāja), Viśākhila, Pārāśaras (disciples of Parāśara), Piśuna (identified as Sage Nārada), Kauṇapadanta, Vātavyādhi, Bāhudantīputra and Āmbhīyāḥ (followers of the schools of Āmbhi?).

Because of the profuse references to diverse views and their critique, *Arthaśāstra* has become a text in debate. The following passage can be cited as an elucidation of the method and diction of Kauṭilya:

> *Ānvīkṣikī* (logic), *trayī* (the three Vedas), *vārtā* (agriculture, animal husbandry and trade) and *daṇḍanīti* (governance) —these are the *vidyās* (branches of learning).
>
> The Mānavas (the followers of the school of Manu) accept *trayī*, *vārtā* and *daṇḍanīti* as three *vidyās* (they omit *ānvīkṣikī*, saying that) *ānvīkṣikī* is a special branch of *trayī* itself. Bārhaspatyas (the followers of the schools of Bṛhaspati) accept only two *vidyās* — *vārtā* and *daṇḍanīti*, being atheists, for them *trayī* is just for concealment for a pragmatic man. The Auśanasas (followers of the school of Uśanas) hold *daṇḍanīti* alone as the *vidyā*, because it encompasses the beginnings of all *vidyās*. Kauṭilya opines that *vidyās* are four, because by all the four, one attains *dharma* and

[93] Solomon, 1976, op. cit., vol. I, pp. 42-43.

artha and a *vidyā* is that which leads to *dharma* and *artha*.[94]

After this Kauṭilya proceeds to explain in detail how these four *vidyā*s lead to the accomplishment of *dharma* and *artha*.

The discussion on *tantra-yukti*s (devices for a discourse) in *Arthaśāstra* presents a complete structural design for the analysis of a *vāda* text. The thirty-two *tantra-yukti*s enumerated by Kauṭilya are — *adhikaraṇa* (chapter), *vidhāna* (table of contents), *yoga* (scheme of sentences), *padārtha* (explanation of words), *hetvartha* (indicating the reasons), *uddeśa* (listing of contents), *nirdeśa* (elaboration of contents), *upadeśa* (advice), *apadeśa* (reference to other views), *atideśa* (incorporation of one theme in the other), *pradeśa* (separating the topics to be discussed subsequently), *upamāna* (explaining through similitude), *arthāpatti* (implication), *saṁśaya* (doubt), *prasaṅga* (application of one context to the other), *viparyaya* (vice versa, contrariety), *vākyaśeṣa* (incomplete sentence to be explained through inherent meaning), *anumata* (acceptance of the views of others), *vyākhyāna* (heightened speech), *nirvacana* (etymological explanation), *nidarśana* (illustration), *apavarga* (ending), *svasaṁjñā* (explaining a word through another one), *pūrva-pakṣa* (the prima facie view), *siddhānta-pakṣa* (the principle),

---

94 आन्वीक्षिकी त्रयी वार्ता दण्डनीतिश्चेति विद्याः। त्रयी वार्ता दण्डनीतिश्चेति मानवाः, त्रयीविशेषो ह्यान्वीक्षिकीति। वार्ता दण्डनीतिश्चेति बार्हस्पत्याः, संवरणमात्रं हि त्रयी लोकयात्राविद इति। दण्डनीतिरेका विद्येत्यौशनसाः, तस्यां हि सर्वविद्यारम्भाः प्रतिबद्धा इति। चतस्र एव विद्या इति कौटिल्यः। ताभिर्धर्माधर्मौ विद्यात्, तद् विद्यानां विद्यात्वम्। — *Arthaśāstra* I.2.1
That Kauṭilya is presenting real traditions of multifarious views is attested by Rājaśekhara's discussion on *vidyā*s. He also cites several views with regard to the knowledge systems.

वार्ता कामसूत्रं शिल्पशास्त्रं दण्डनीतिरिति पूर्वैः सहाष्टादश विद्यास्थानानि - इत्यपरे। आन्वीक्षिकी त्रयी वार्ता दण्डनीतिश्चेति विद्याः। दण्डनीतिरेवैका इत्यौशनसाः। धर्मभयाद्धि कृत्स्नो लोकः स्वेषु स्वेषु कर्मस्ववतिष्ठते। वार्ता दण्डनीतिर्द्वे विद्ये इति बार्हस्पत्याः। वृत्तिर्विनयग्रहणं च स्थितिर्लोकयात्रायाः। त्रयी वार्ता दण्डनीतयस्तिस्रो विद्या इति मानवाः। त्रयी हि वार्तादण्डनीत्योरुपदेष्ट्री। आन्वीक्षिकीत्रयीवार्तादण्डनीतयश्चतस्रो विद्या इति कौटिल्यः। आन्वीक्षिक्या हि विवेचिता त्रयी वार्तादण्डनीत्योः प्रभवति। पञ्चमी साहित्यविद्येति यायावरीयः।
— *Kāvyamīmāṁsā*, chap. II, pp. 24-25

ekānta (exclusive view), *anāgatāvekṣaṇa* (summing up the issues to be taken up later), *atikrāntāvekṣaṇa* (resume), *niyoga* (demarcation), *vikalpa* (option), *samuccaya* (simultaneity) and *ūha* (investigation).[95]

In fact, Kauṭilya has employed all these thirty-two *tantra-yuktis* to make his voluminous compendium a subtle text in *vāda*. At the very outset of *Arthaśāstra*, he has used the first four of the above *tantra-yuktis* by the way of giving a complete outline of the whole text. On each and every topic, he takes into account all the *pūrva-pakṣas* (the prima facie views), then the *uttara-pakṣa* (rejoinder) together with *ekānta*. Along with these, he discusses the facts, gives copious references and illustrations, agreements and disagreements, contrarieties, resume, summing up, etc. References to previous portions and the alternatives are provided, and implications are specified.

Other Knowledge Texts

Mahābhāṣya of Patañjali reflects the maturity and growth of *vāda* traditions. It also uses several technical terms related to the theory of *vāda*, viz. — *anaikāntika* (inconclusive), *itaretaraśraya* and *anyonyasaṁśaya* (mutual dependence), *atiprasaṅga* (over-application), *lāghava* (parsimony), *ubhayataḥ pāśā rajjuḥ* (dilemma), etc.[96]

Kāmasūtra of Vātsyāyana (around second century BCE) is also structured on these very lines; it cites several views on any issue and then presents a resolution.

Buddhist Councils, Debates and Split

Buddha could instill the essence of *vāda* tradition in the dialogues and discussions he engaged in with his followers. After his final departure, his followers continued his legacy. This necessitated *vādas*. Differences with regard to interpretations of *buddha-vacanas* surfaced. This led to calling a number of *saṅgītis* (councils). These

---

[95] *Arthaśāstra*, pt. III, pp. 241-47.

[96] Solomon, 1976, op. cit., vol. I, p. 29.

councils provided platforms for debates and they also caused split in the *saṁgha*.

Raising doubts and questioning must have been a practice in the order founded by Buddha. The repercussions of this practice are reflected in *Kathāvatthu*, a text which has already been referred here. Sometimes such doubts and questions could also cause a split in the order. One Mahādeva, as referred in *Kathāvatthu,* had questioned the very authenticity of the *arhat*, alleging that the *arhat* might be sexually tempted, might have a residue of ignorance, might have doubts himself, or might depend upon others for his own enlightenment.[97]

Buddha had a premonition of this situation and had forewarned his disciples of the possibilities of split. The split cannot be caused by reasons external. Monk Nāgasena in *Milindapañho* rightly said:

> The householders do not break the order, nor a nun, nor a newly initiated nun under probation, nor a novice (*sāmanera*). It is the ordained monk, belonging to the same communion, to the same parish, living within the same boundary, who can break the order.[98]

In response to a question by Upāli in *Cullavagga* of *Vinayapiṭaka* (chap. VII) he enumerates eighteen possible causes for the split of the *saṁgha*. There can be a split if the followers of the *saṁgha* start explaining non-*dhamma* as *dhamma*, non-obedience as obedience, attributing things to *tathāgata* which he did not say, attributing practices to him which he did not practise, attributing tenets to him which he did not propound, explaining no offence as offence, slight offence as serious offence, a curable offence as incurable, a bad offence as a good offence; as well as the vice versa of these take

[97] Ujjawal Kumar, 2014, "Grounds of Saṁghabheda: Division or Split in the Saṁgha", *Pāli-Prakṛt-Anuśīlanam*, I(2): 64.

[98] न गिही संघं भिन्दति, न भिक्खुणी, न सिक्खमाना, न सामनेरो, न सामणेरी संघं भिन्दति, भिक्खु पकतत्तो समानसंवासको समानसमीमायां छितो संघं भिन्दतीति। – *Milindapañho*, p. 108

the number up to eighteen. These causes are enlisted in the chapter on the split of *saṁgha* (*saṁghabhedasutta*) of *Aṅguttaranikāya* (5.93) in a more compact way, reducing the number to ten.

Saṁghabheda (split in the organization) as a category is repeatedly discussed in Buddhist canons. Forming a separate circle for any practice to be done collectively in the *saṁgha* causes *cakrabheda,* and *cakrabheda* leads to *saṁghabheda.* The canons differentiate between the division amongst the monks by forming separate circles within the order and the split. The former is called *saṁgharāji,* and the latter is already described as *saṁghabheda*. The *saṁghabheda* will be supposed to have occurred if the total number of the monks raising a dispute exceeds nine. The canons also describe the situations of *cakrabheda* which were already occurring in the *saṁgha.* The causes of split rested either on doctrinal differences or adoption of different practices.[99]

Buddha is reported to have propagated *nairātmya* (the theory of no soul), but even amongst his followers there were reputed philosophers like Sthavira Vatsa who believed in the existence of soul. He was a contemporary of Kālāśoka (395-67 BCE). The followers of Sthavira Vatsa had formed their own school and were known as the Vatsīputrīyas or Sammatīyas during the rule of Nanda, the grandson of Kālāśoka. There are records to prove that this school continued to exist during the third-fourth centuries and became influential during the reign of the King Harṣa (CE 606-47). Harṣa's sister, Rājyaśrī was a Sāmmatīya.

After Buddha, a number of councils were held to systematize his ideas and precepts. These councils fall in two categories — the canonical and the non-canonical. The sole purpose of the former had been to compile and systematize the *buddha-vacanas*. The first council was held in the year of Buddha's death itself in 483 BCE. King Bimbisāra sponsored it by donating a site. Five hundred monks were selected to participate in the proceedings. Upāli, one of the

[99] Ujjawal Kumar, op. cit., pp. 61-62.

direct disciples of Buddha, recited the Vinaya texts comprised of the disciplinary rules for monks, and Ānanda recounted Buddha's discourses which were then called as a *Suttapiṭaka*.

One hundred years after Buddha's *mahāparinirvāṇa* (final departure), the second council was held at Vaiśālī. Seven hundred monks are said to have attended this council to debate on the issues related to indiscipline in the *saṁgha*. A concord was re-established. A non-canonical council after 137 years of Buddha's *mahāparinirvāṇa* was held in Pāṭaliputra, when King Mahāpadma Nanda was requested to mediate in a dispute between rival groups of monks. This council initiated Buddhism as a sectarian movement. The first division in Buddhist *saṁgha* occurred in this council. The monks of Vaiśālī vehemently disagreed with regard to the status of the *sthavira*s (elders), and alienating from the conservative *sthavira*s (the elders); they formed a liberal group of their own. This group was known as the *mahāsaṁgha* (great community) and its members were called the *mahāsāṁghika*s.

The third canonical council was convened by King Aśoka around 250 BCE in Pāṭaliputra. Moggaliputta Tissa alias Upagupta supervised over its proceedings. Around one thousand monks are reported to have joined this council. Lively debates between the orthodox Theravādins and orthodox/heterodox sects concerning various doctrinal points were held in this council. These debates have been recorded in *Kathāvatthu* (points of debate) a Pāli text, which forms the fifth book of *Abhidhammapiṭaka* under the Theravāda tradition.

One of the earliest councils related to Theravāda was organized in 25 BCE when King Vattagmaṇī's rule was restored at the Mahāvihāra of Anurādhapuram, the capital city of Sri Lanka, to resolve religious unrest in Buddhist community. The compilation of Tripiṭakas — the Buddhist scriptures as per the Theravāda tradition — was initiated in this council.

Another important council was organized by Kaniṣka in the country of Gāndhāra around CE 100 at the instance of Pārśva, a

Sarvāstivādin monk. Vasumitra, one of the foremost philosophers of Buddhism, presided over it. The council was attended by 499 monks and Aśvaghoṣa, a great Sanskrit poet and scholar of Buddhism, actively participated in it. It is also said that under the guidance of Vasumitra commentaries in Sanskrit on all the three Piṭakas — *Suttra, Vinaya* and *Abhidhamma* — were prepared in this council. Composition of a commentary *Mahāvibhāṣā* on *Jñānaprasthāna* of *Abhidhamma* was taken up in this council. *Mahāvibhāṣā* was later on accepted as a standard text on *Abhidhamma. Abhidharmakośa* of Vasubadhu is one of the most important texts in Buddhist literature. It is based on *Mahāvibhāṣā.*

Kuṇḍalakeśī: The Lady Debater

There is no doubt that Buddha and his followers initiated debates that have sustained the intellectual discourses for more than a millennium in India. Bhadrā, as described in *Therīgāthā,* first accepted the Nirgrantha order. She was called Kuṇḍalakeśī when her curly locks grew up again. She learned the texts from the Nirgrantha monks and became adept in debating. She had debates with the great scholars and preachers of her times. She would visit villages and cities and at the gate or entrance of the city or village she would place a rose apple tree on the heap of sand with the declaration that who so ever tramples this bough of the rose apple tree will have to enter into a debate with her; she would wait for a challenger for one week and depart to other place to resume her victorious journey. When she reached Śrāvastī, Sāriputra had a debate with her. First Kuṇḍalakeśī chose to ask him the questions. When the stock of her questions was exhausted and Śāriputra had answered them all, it was the latter's turn to confront her with questions. He asked only one question to her — What is that which is one? And she fell silent.

Milindapañho

Milindapañho is a meta text of debate in Pāli compiled around second century BCE. It forms the dialogues and debates between Milinda

(Greek ruler Minander) and Buddhist monk Nāgasena. Milinda is said to be well versed in the practice of *vitaṇḍā* (destructive debate) and it was difficult to conquer him in arguments.[100]

He first asked monk Nāgasena — "Bhante Nāgasena! will you enter into *saddhi* (debate) with me?" Nāgasena said — "If you want to have Paṇḍitavāda with me, I will talk to you, but if you want to have Rājavāda with me I will not talk to you." Asked about the difference between Paṇḍitavāda and Rājavāda, Nāgasena says:

> The *paṇḍitas* argue with each other, one of them would refute what the other has said, but he will not be punished for this refutation. This is Paṇḍitavāda. But if one enters into a debate with the king and refutes what the king has said, he will be punished. This is Rājavāda. I can have a Paṇḍitavāda with you and not the Rājavāda.

Being assured by King Milinda or Minander that he intends to enter simply into a Paṇḍitavāda with the monk,[101] the latter enters into a discussion with the king, which leads to one of the most fascinating, intense and profound debates in the world history of *vāda* as recorded in *Milindapañho.*

Milinda is inquisitive; he goads the monk with piercing queries, but also allows and facilitates the discussion with persistent request for illustrations. Nāgasena obliges him by using profuse illustrations to corroborate his theses.

It is in the fourth chapter titled as Meṇḍakapañho that Milinda assumes a challenging tone, and confronts the monk with sharp questions. The word *meṇḍaka* stands for the horns of rams ready to fight. Milinda finally praises the debating skills of Nāgasena and agrees that Nāgasena has crushed the theories of the rivals (*paravādas*).[102]

---

100 वितंडवादी, दुरासदो दुप्पसहो पुथुतित्थकरानं अग्गमक्खायति। — *Milindapañho,* p. 6

101 *Milindapañho*, p. 35.

102 Ibid., p. 150.

Nāgasena rules out the migration of soul from one body to other and also establishes the theory of rebirth. He explains it with the example of lamp enlightened by another lamp.[103]

Sometimes the debates turned into secret talks, not to be made public. For this both the debaters had to be highly proficient in their own branch of learning. Earlier this had happened in the debates of scholars with Yājñavalkya. During the course of prolonged discussions between Monk Nāgasena and King Milinda, both the discussants felt the needs to move to a secluded place. Milinda prepared for such a debate after observing eight vows for seven days,[104] and then sought a meeting with the monk in a completely secluded place where they might not be disturbed.

Aśvaghoṣa: His Debates with Buddhists and Non-Buddhists

The life and history of Aśvaghoṣa, a great poet and Buddhist philosopher, provide a glorious exemplification of the *vāda* tradition. He wrote *Vajrasūcī* in refutation to the caste system. This text is being discussed in Chap. 5 of the present work. According to the biographical details about him as recorded in Chinese sources, Aśvaghoṣa was born in a brāhmaṇa family and was very proud of his scholarship. Kumārajīva has given a life sketch of Aśvaghoṣa. Accordingly, Pārśva, a monk who commanded scholarship with spiritual powers, reached a monastery in central Asia. To his surprise, he learnt that the monks and novices in the monastery do not strike the bell as a part of the ritual. Upon asking the reason for this departure from the norm, he was informed that a heretic recluse has forewarned the members of the monastery not to strike the bell, as striking it would mean a challenge to him for a debate. Since the members in the monastery are afraid of entering into a debate with the awesome recluse, they have since long stopped ringing the bell. Hearing this, Pārśva asked the monks to strike the bell. This being done, the recluse appeared and asked Pārśva

[103] *Milindapañho*, p. 90.

[104] Ibid., pp. 114-15.

whether he intends to enter into a debate with him. A debate between Pārśva and the recluse was ensued on the condition that the loser will become the disciple of the winner. Pārśva used his spiritual powers to silence the opponent. The opponent became his disciple and received ordination under him. He continued to display his skills in debate for propagation of Buddhist order and he was named Aśvaghoṣa because of his resounding voice.[105]

Debates within Buddhist Schools

In the first millennium CE, various philosophical schools grew under the Hīnayāna and Mahāyāna Buddhism and *bhāṣyas* on the Sūtra texts were composed. This was the age of interpretation and reasoning. These Buddhist schools also initiated intense philosophical debates with non-Buddhist rivals on problems of universals, philosophies of logic, language and other issues. Nāgārjuna rejected the concept of *svabhāva* and emphasized the idea of *madhyamā pratipad* (the middle path). He also established the invariable relationship of the philosophy of Śūnyavāda with Buddha's concept of *pratītyasamutpāda* (interdependent origination). *Nirvāṇa* and *saṁsāra* to him are the forms of one and the same reality.

The difference between the Sautrāntika (Representationalism) and Vaibhāṣika (Direct Realism) lies in their view of cognition of external phenomena. The Vaibhāṣikas hold that all external things are known through perception. The Sautrāntikas say that they are known only through *anumāna* (inference). The Vaibhāṣika developed as a branch of Sarvāstivādin School under the Hīnayāna.

Śūnyavāda and Vijñānavāda attempt a liberal interpretation of *buddha-vacanas* and they are more inclined towards metaphysical thinking. These two fall under the Mahāyāna (the great vehicle) and the other two, i.e. the Sautrāntika and Vaibhāṣika fall under the Hīnayāna (the little vehicle).

---

105 Li Rong XI, Taisho XI, vol. 50, no. 2046 cited in Ramesh Bharadwaj, 2007, *Vajrasūcī of Aśvaghaṣa and the Concept of Varṇa-Jāti Through the Ages*, pp. 148-53.

But there were divergences of opinions and differences of views even amongst the followers of Śūnyavāda as well as those of Vijñānavāda. The different interpretations of Buddhapālita (CE 470–540) and Bhāvaviveka, also known as Bhavya (CE 490–570) created a split in the Mādhyamika system or Śūnyavāda. Buddhapālita stuck to the dialectical demolition of all theories. Bhavya, however, postulated that *śūnya* or *niḥsvabhāva* can be understood in a positive way.

Debates between Buddhist Logicians and Naiyāyikas

The history of intellectual debate between the orthodox schools of Indian philosophy on one hand and the schools of Buddhist philosophy on the other is a unique phenomenon as far as world philosophy is concerened. It presents one of the finest examples of intellectual refinement through *vāda*. As both the sides sharpened their weapons for attacking their adversaries, they enriched and sharpened their own systems of thought and tools of analysis. Nāgārjuna was the forerunner of one of the most prolonged traditions of scholastic debate. He vehemently criticized Gautama's logic in his *Vigrahavyāvartanī* and *Vaidalyasūtra*. While acknowledging the greatness of Nāgārjuna as a philosopher, it must also be accepted that he was able to take the argumentative traditions to the peaks through the steps of logic as envisaged by Gautama in his *Nyāyasūtra*.

Nāgārjuna flourished between CE 150–250. The essence of his Mādhyamikaśāstra lies in shunning all standpoints:

> When one accepts any standpoint, one is captured by the cunning poisonous serpent of the impurities. Those, having their mind cleansed of every standpoint, are not captured.[106]

His *Mūlamādhyamikakārikā* of twenty-seven chapters and approximately 450 verses is the greatest sourcebook for Mādhyamikaśāstra. *Dvādaśadvāraśāstra* and *Vigrahavyāvartanī*

---

[106] *Yuktiṣaṣṭikārikā* 51.

are his other works. *Vigrahavyāvartanī* heralded an era of debate between the Buddhist philosophers and Naiyāyikas, which became one of the most enduring, most fruitful and long-living intellectual fights. Nāgārjuna was also the first philosopher to have used the method of *vitaṇḍā* (cavil) through which he could dismantle his opponents on the basis of their own arguments.

Nāgārjuna provided a firm footing to the intellectual discourse leading to a prolonged series of *vāda* between the Buddhist logicians and the orthodox Naiyāyikas. He became a legendary name subsequently. In *Laṅkāvatārasūtra*, the Buddha is made to issue the following prophesy:

> In Vedāli, in the southern part, a *bhikṣu*, most illustrious and distinguished [will be born], his name is Nāgāhvaya (Nāgārjuna), he will be the destroyer of the one-sided views based on being and non-being.
>
> He will declare my vehicle, the unsurpassed Mahāyāna, to the world; attaining the stage of joy he will go to the land of bliss.[107]

In fact, Nāgārjuna came to be deified as second Buddha.

Nāgārjuna challenged the followers of the rival schools of orthodox philosophies and initiated debate with them. He discarded all labels and ideologues — absolutism, monism, radical pluralism, nihilism, negativism, relativism or any form of dialectics. He appears of be elusive but his philosophy is solely based on the middle path "which can be termed the ontological inclusiveness, excellence, purity and supreme state of being".[108] He restrained himself from adopting any counter-thesis, "because that would entail yet another position".[109] His philosophy is defined as the philosophy of no-position. He himself declares that "he has no

---

[107] *Laṅkvatārasūtra*, Sagāthakam, vv. 165-66, quoted in *Mūlamādhyamika-kārikā*, ed. Kenneth K. Inada.

[108] *Mūlamādhyamikakārikā*, ed. Kenneth K. Inada, p. 22.

[109] Ibid., p. 24.

views to offer and therefore he must be absolved from all errors".[110] Nāgārjuna asserted that common intellect is unmindful of the four relational conditions: *hetu-pratyaya* (causal component), *ālambana-pratyaya* (objective component), *samānāntara-pratyaya* (sequential component) and *ādhipateya-pratyaya* (dominant component).[111] Any reality or experience therefore can only be categorized in negative terms, viz. non- extinction, non-origination, non-destruction, non-eternal, non-identity, non-differentiation, non-coming into being and non-being. In fact, by *śūnyatā*, Nāgārjuna gave a potential tool for reasoning and refuting the opponents view:

> When a refutation is based on *śūnyatā*, and an opponent refuses, he is not able to counter everything since counter-refutation will be the same nature as the contention (*sādhya*). When an exposition is based on *śūnyatā*, and an opponent censures, he is not able to censure everything since the censorship will be the same (nature) as contention.[112]

Gautama, the author of *Nyāyasūtras,* is said to have criticized Nāgārjuna in some places, but these portions appear to be interpolations.[113] Vātsyāyana, the author of *Nyāyabhāṣya,* certainly gives a refutation to Nāgārjuna's *Mādhyamikakārikā* in his discussion on *Nyāyasūtra* V.1.39-40 (without naming him) for his (Nāgārjuna's) acceptance of only three categories (*pratijñā, hetu* and *dṛṣṭānta*) out of the group of five as propounded by Gautama. The Buddhist

---

110 *Mūlamādhyamikakārikā*, ed. Kenneth K. Inada, p. 25.

111 चत्वारः प्रत्यया हेतुश्चालम्बनमनन्तरम् ।
तथैवाधिपतेयं च प्रत्ययो नास्ति पञ्चमः।। — *Mūlamādhyamikakārikā* I.2, p. 39

112 विग्रहे यः परीहारं कृते शून्यतया वदेत् ।
सर्वं तस्यापरिहृतं समं साध्येन जायते।
व्याख्याने य उपालम्भं कृते शून्यतया वदेत्।
सर्वं तस्यानुपालम्भं समं साध्येन जायते। — Ibid. IV.8-9, p. 56

113 *Nyāyasūtras* IV.1.39-40 appear to be referring to Nāgārjuna's *Mādhyamikakārikā* 15th and also *Nyāyasūtras* IV.2.31-32 to *Mādhyamikakārikā* 7th.

institutions and Buddhism were confronted with forceful challenges of a reinvigorated Brāhmanism.

Āryadeva flourished around CE 200. He is also referred as Kāṇadeva for being blind with one eye. He was one of the most renowned direct disciples of Nāgārjuna. Candrakīrti who commented on Āryadeva's *Catuḥśataka* informs that he was the son of a king and was born in Siṁhala. Having renounced the world as a crown prince, he came to south India and studied Mādhyamikaśāstra with Nāgārjuna to become one of its foremost champions. He is said to have moved to Nālandā from Śrīparvata to defeat Mātṛceṭa in debate.

Asaṅga and Vasubandhu are also referred to as brothers, the former being the elder. They probably belonged to Puruṣapura (modern Peshavar) and flourished around CE 320–400.

Debates within Orthodox Systems of Philosophy

The doctrine of cumulative pursuit of *karma* and *jñāna* continued till Śaṅkara vehemently discarded it. He was criticized by his contemporaries and his immediate followers like Bhāskara also for this. They even called him a non-conformist and the charge heterodoxy was levelled against him.

This era is also marked with serious debates and the employment of tactics of *jalpa*, *chala*, *jāti*, *nigrahasthāna* and *vitaṇḍā*. The term *vāda* came in vogue in this era and *brahmodyas* were replaced by *vādas* (in the sense of friendly as well as hostile debates). With growth of diverse philosophical schools, the debates assume a tone of confrontation and challenge, and are carried through written texts and public platforms with ferocity.

Philosophical systems referred to as *matas* or *siddhāntas* and later on as *darśanas* developed under two schools — the realist and idealist. A more rational grouping of various *darśanas* has been attempted by Mādhavācārya, who authored a Saṁgraha text on these *darśanas* — *Sarvadarśanasaṁgraha*. Accordingly, *darśanas* are divided into two groups — the *nāstikas* and *āstikas*. The former are of two types — Ādhyakṣikas (those who uphold perception as the only means of knowledge) and Tārkikas (rationalists). The *āstika* philosophers are also of two kinds — the Saguṇātmavādins and the Nirguṇātmavādins. The Saguṇātmavādins are of two type — Tārkikas (rationalists) and Śrautas (those who hold the authority of Śruti or scriptures alone). The Tārkikas are again of two types: Spaṣṭatārkikas (direct rationalists) and Pracchannatārkikas (indirect rationalists).

The proponent and the respondent (*vādin* and *prativādin*) stood before each with daggers drawn, abuses we are hurled and piquant satires we are used. And this was the era when India's intellectual genius reached its zenith reverberating with its fertile thinking and presenting sumptuous feasts in intellection. Philosophy became a celebration of intellectual skills. Both intra-sectarian and inter-sectarian debates were fought by Bādarāyaṇa, Vātsyāyana, Nāgārjuna, Diṅnāga, Kumārila, Prabhākara, Dharmakīrti, Śaṅkarācārya and Udayana. Buddhist philosophers like Nāgārjuna, Diṅnāga and Dharmakīrti exemplified the theory and practice of debate not only through their writings, they also participated in debates on public platforms. *Vāda* was a means of propagation of Buddha's message for them.

Diṅnāga was a debater par excellence. He remained conspicuous by his presence in the debates held at Nālandā University. There are references to some of the debates in which he proved the brilliance of his intellect. In one such debate, Sudurjaya, a brāhmaṇa scholar, received debacle at his hands.[114]

The diversity of sects and their tolerant symbiosis were brought out by Bāṇa (seventh century CE) in his description of the hermitage of Divākaramitra. Harṣa sees here,

> devotees dead to all passion, Jaina monks in white robes, mendicants in white dress, followers of Kṛṣṇa, religious students,

[114] T. Stcherbatsky, 1962, op. cit., p. 40.

> ascetics who had plucked off their hairs, followers of Kapila, Jainas, Lokāyatikas, followers of Kaṇāda, followers of Upaniṣads, theists, students of Dharmaśāstras, students of Purāṇas, experts of Vedic rituals, grammarians, followers of Pāñcarātra system of Āgama, all diligently following their own tenets, pondering, registering objections, raising doubts, resolving the objections and doubts, giving etymologies, disputing, studying, and explaining . . . .[115]

Vātsyāyana had refuted the propositions of Nāgārjuna. Diṅnāga (CE 450–520) gave befitting rebuttal to him. Udyotakara subsequently refuted Diṅnāga, and then Dharmakīrti suitably replied to his critique of Diṅnāga. It was Vācaspati Miśra who further carried the fight against the Buddhist philosophers like Dharmakīrti. Kumārila had attacked the very foundation of Nāgārjuna's philosophy and questioned the validity of grading the truth — *saṁvṛti-satya* (the relative) and *paramārtha-satya* (the ultimate). But to Mādhyamika all phenomena remain indeterminate and indefinable.

Bhāvaviveka (CE 490–570), also known as Bhavya and also as a commentator of Nāgārjuna's *Mūlamādhyamikakārikā,* founded Svātantrika school under Mādhyamika Buddhism. He opposed Buddhapālita (CE 470–540), the founder of Prāsaṅgika school of Mādhyamika philosophy. He differed with Buddhapālita with reference to the concept of *paramārtha* (the ultimate) and *saṁvṛti* (the relative).

Śāntarakṣita (CE 680–740) was one of the most brilliant philosophers of Buddhist thought. In collaboration with his disciple Kamalaśīla (CE 700–750), he criticized Bhāvaviveka and repositioned it under Yogācāra-Mādhyamika system. In his *Tattvasaṁgraha,* Śāntarakṣita presented a critique of Sāṁkhya theories of *Prakṛti* and *Puruṣa* and examined the concepts of *Ātman* and God in Nyāya-Vaiśeṣika systems, Syādvāda and Cārvāka systems. Kamalaśīla wrote a *pañjikā* on *Tattvasaṁgraha.*

---

[115] *Harṣacaritam*, chap. VII.

The deliberations of Bhāvaviveka, Śāntarakṣita, Kamalaśīla and other followers of Nāgārjuna show the sharp differences and debates even within the Mādhyamikas.

Amongst the Jaina philosophers who entered into debate both with the Naiyāyikas and the Buddhist logicians mention may be made of Nīlakeśī, whose debates are described in the Tamil *kāvya* of the same name. Myth and imagination are interspersed in the whole texture of this text. By the time the text was created around fourth-fifth century CE, Nīlakeśī had become a mythical name. The debates described in *Neelakesi* are fictitious, but they bring out the perspectives with which Jainism encountered the other systems. Different sections in the text are named on the schools of thought or the masters belonging to these schools who are conquered by Nīlakeśī in debates, viz.:

daruma curaic carukkam
kuṇḍalakeśivāda carukkam
arulkkacandravāda carukkam
moggalavāda carukkam
biddhavāda carukkam
ācīvakavāda carukkam
saṁkhyavāda carukkam
vedavāda carukkam
bhūtavāda carukkam.

The debates are said to have been held at Ujjain, Padmapura, Kapilapura, Attināpura (Hastināpura) and Kākkalandī or Kāveripoompattinam.[116]

Nīlakeśī is said to have debated with Bhadrā Kuṇḍalakeśī (referred above) at Campillī in the country of Pāñcāla; with Buddhist philosopher Arkacandra at Ujjayinī and Mokkala at Padmapura. After defeating these three, she went to Kapilapura and challenged Buddha himself and defeated him in the debate! In the same way Sāṁkhya-teacher Parāśara was routed at Hastināpura and

[116] C.S. Sundaram, 1999, *Contribution of Tamilnadu to Sanskrit*, p. 103.

Vaiśeṣika-teacher Lokajit at his hermitage. Nīlakeśī then met Vedic scholar Bhūtika in the town Kākanti and having defeated him finally she vanquished the teacher of Bhūtavāda (materialism), named Piśācaka in the royal court of King Madanajit.

The issues taken up in the debates offer strong refutation from the Jaina point of view to various philosophical concepts in all the rival systems, but as Nīlakeśī is supposed to win all the debates, and the rival has to be silenced, the counter-positions from the opponents have not been properly stated.

Haribhadra (6th century CE) enriched the Indian tradition of philosophical debates by his enormous contributions. He is one of the very few philosophers who always engaged in a constructive debate. Haribhadra exhibited extraordinary sensitivity to understand the point of view of his opponent. Even though he was a devout follower of Mahāvīra, he wrote a commentary on *Nyāyapraveśakasūtram* of Diṇnāga, in which he very faithfully elaborated upon the aphorisms of Diṅnāga. The propitiatory verse in the beginning of his commentary (*praṇipatya jineśvaram* . . .) is supposed to be a salutation for Mahāvīra and Buddha both. Haribhadra declared his commitment for remaining unbiased in his *Lokatattvanirṇaya*:

> I do not have any prejudice for Mahāvīra, nor do I foster any grudge for Kapila and others. (I believe in the principle that) whosoever speaks logically, must be respected.[117]

It is said that Haribhadra had authored as many as 1,444 works, as he was asked to compose that many works by his *guru*, as an atonement for having finished 1,444 Buddhists (in debate?).

Notable amongst his philosophical works are: *Ṣaḍdarśana-samuccaya* and *Śāstravārtāsamuccaya, Anekāntajayapatākā* (Victory Flag of Perspectivism) and *Lokatattvanirṇaya.* In the last work he

---

[117] पक्षपातो न मे वीरे न द्वेषः कपिलादिषु।
युक्तिमद्वचनं यस्य तस्य कार्यः परिग्रहः। — *Lokatattvanirṇaya* I.38, quoted in the Preface of *Nyāyapraveśakasūtram*, p. 46

refuted the concepts of *Īśvara* (God) and *Ātman* and considered the world as essential. With his faith in the theory of Anekānta, he criticized the opponent's view, but also tried to see it with another perspective and to unveil its validity. This way of looking at another's view embraces both agreements and disagreements. Also, in his attempt to justify the view of his rival, Haribhadra gave it a twist, which might not at all be acceptable to the opponent. He was guided by the philosophy that ideologies aim at one and the same target, i.e. *mokṣa*, therefore the points of disagreement between them might be rectified. For the refutation of *nairātmya* (theory of non-soul) he even cited the authority of Veda: *svayaṁ jyotiḥ sadā eva ātmā tathā vede api paṭhyate.*[118]

Besides well-established schools of philosophies, several ideologues and schools of thought like Daivavāda (fatalism), Svabhāvavāda (naturalism), Kālavāda (pessimism) and Puruṣakāravāda (activism) had existed. Vātsyāyana in his *Kāmasūtra* and Yājñavalkya in his *Smṛti* had criticized some of these. Haribhadra also presented refutation of Daivavāda (fatalism), Svabhāvavāda (naturalism), Kālavāda (pessimism) and Puruṣakāravāda or Karmavāda (activism) in his *Śāstrārthavārtāsamuccaya.* He did not completely overrule these theories, he simply said that none of them was sufficient to explain the theory of causality singularly. *Kāla, svabhāva, niyati* and *karma* all collectively become the cause for world.[119]

During sixth-seventh centuries, the Pallava and Pāṇḍya courts in south India had become vibrant centres of debates between diverse sects. Sundara Pāṇḍya, a philosopher of Advaita Vedānta who flourished before Śaṅkarācārya in Tamil Nadu, was also known as Pāṇḍyarāja Kubjavardhana and Kūna Pāṇḍya. He is said to have converted from Jainism to embrace Śaivism after discussions with Jñānasambandhar. He is worshipped amongst the sixty-three Nāyanārs (devotees of Śiva). Akalaṅka, one of the most brilliant

---

[118] *Śāstrārthavārtāsamuccaya* I.87.

[119] Ibid. II.191.

logicians, was contemporary of the Rāṣṭrakūṭa king Śubhatuṅga or Kṛṣṇa I (eighth century CE). He is said to have defeated the Buddhists in the debates held in Pallava court, so that they were forced to migrate to Laṅkā.

Debates between Buddhists and Naiyāyikas

In his *Pramāṇasamuccaya*, Diṅnāga had presented a refutation of *Nyāyasūtra* of Gautama together with the *bhāṣya* on it by Vātsyāyana. Udyotakara came in support of the traditional Nyāya system and in his *Nyāyavārttika*, he gave a strong rebuttal to Diṅnāga. Dharmakīrti took up the position of Diṅnāga to give a rejoinder to Udyotakara in this work.

It is Diṅnāga who posed a real challenge to these systems. His illustrious predecessor, Nāgārjuna was an arguer par excellence. The philosophers of the rival schools, however, could possibly ignore Nāgārjuna, it was not possible to ignore Diṅnāga or to avoid a tacit or a spoken confrontation with him. Diṅnāga also set the rules of the game. The challenges posited by Diṅnāga also led them to reconsider the scheme of their categorizations and postulations as well. Diṅnāga also criticized Bhartṛhari's philosophy of Śabdabrahmavāda in his *Traikālyaparīkṣā*.

Dharmakīrti came in the line of disciples of Diṅnāga. His *Pramāṇavārtika* occupies a pivotal position in the debate between the Gautamīyas and Buddhist logicians. With rare brilliance and insight, he exhibited so subtle an understanding of Diṅnāga's texts that his teacher is reported to have conceded his superior understanding. It was at the instance of Īśvarasena, his *guru*, that Dharmakīrti started writing commentaries on Diṅnāga's works.

Haribhadrasūrin calls Dharmakīrti as "Vādimukhya" (the chief debater). From other accounts about the life and deeds of Dharmakīrti, we learn that he was given the titles like *vādivṛṣabha* (a bull amongst the debaters), *vādipuṅgava* (best of the debaters), etc.[120]

---

[120] *Nyāyapraveśakasūtram*, Preface, p. 27.

In the mythological accounts of the life and deeds of Dharmakīrti, the Tibetan traditions record that he combated with the two great apostles of orthodox philosophies (Kumārila and Śaṅkara) on the public platforms and emerged victorious. This is historically impossible. Such stories must have been fabricated out of a wishful thinking and also out of appreciation for Dharmakīrti's talents in logic — suggesting that had Dharmakīrti been alive when Kumārila and Śaṅkara dominated the scene, he might have humbled them by his arguments.

Stories of Dharmakīrti's contemptuous behaviour and sneering nature became current owing to his remaining undaunted and unwavering on philosophical positions. He did not hesitate to criticize his teacher Īśvarasena and to express his disagreement even with great Diṅnāga whom he emulates. Similarly, he attacked the views of his senior contemporaries like Udyotakara, Bhartṛhari and Kumārila also, who were much respected philosophers of their times.

In fact, the history of intellectual debate between the orthodox schools of Indian philosophy on one hand and the schools of Buddhist philosophy on the other is unique in world philosophy. It presents one of the finest examples of intellectual refinement through *vāda*. As both the sides sharpened their weapons for attacking their adversaries, they enriched their own systems of thought and tools of analysis.

The fierceness of these debates led to an intensive study of rival schools. As a result, Kumārila and Śaṅkara displayed an extraordinary knowledge of Buddhist philosophy. Mādhava in his *Śaṅkaradigvijaya* informs that Kumārila accepted initiation in Buddhism in order to study the texts of Buddhist philosophy. He was found out on the occasion when tears started rolling from his eyes hearing the eulogy of *tathāgata* on his demolition of Vedic system.[121] Pt. Baldeva Upadhyaya believes that this teacher was

[121] तदा तदीयं शरणं प्रपन्नः सिद्धान्तमश्रौषमनुद्धतात्मा।
अदूदुषद् वैदिकमेवमार्गं तथागतो जातु कुशाग्रबुद्धिः॥

→

the famous Ācārya Dharmapāla.[122] Dharmapāla taught at Nālandā during CE 530-61.[123]

D.N. Shastri says:

> The story of protracted conflict between the realist school and the Diṅnāga school in which the Nyāya-Vaiśeṣika is the chief combatant on the orthodox side is one of the most fascinating chapters of Indian philosophy. The conflict lasted some six hundred years from fifth century CE to the eleventh.[124]

Vādas after Dharmakīrti

Arcaṭa wrote a commentary on *Hetubindu* of Dharmakīrti, presenting an exhaustive analysis of the text along with references to the proponents and opponents. Pt. Sukhalal Singhavi has compared him with Vācaspati Miśra. He gave a rejoinder to Kumārila's objections on Dharmakīrti's treatment of the *pramāṇas.* Kumārila had said that there would be *regressus ad infinitum* (*ānantyadoṣa*) the way Dharmakīrti has enumerated the theory of inference (*anumāna*). According to the Buddhists, when fire is inferred due to the presence of smoke, the smoke is the inferential mark (*liṅga*) for fire which is *sādhya.* The orthodox Naiyāyika would find the smoke cognized through direct perception — it is an object visible through eyes therefore there is contact between this object and the sense-organ (*indriyārthasannikarṣa*). But in Buddhist epistemology, the object smoke is not cognized through perception, it is only the *sāmānya lakṣaṇa* of the smoke that is inferred. But for having the inference of this smoke, some other mark of inference (*liṅga*) will be required and for that other mark of inference again one more

---

← तदापतद् मे सहसाश्रुबिन्दुः तदा विदुः पार्श्वनिवासिनोऽन्ये।
तदा प्रभृत्येव विवेश शङ्का मय्याप्तभावं परिहृत्य तेषाम्।
— *Śaṅkaradigvijaya* VII.94-95

122 Śrī Śaṅkarācārya (1963), Baldeva Upadhyaya, p. 73.

123 For details, see Dharmakīrti 2014: 27-28.

124 D.N. Shastri, 1976, p. 15.

inference mark will be needed — this chain will continue in an unending way.

Arcaṭa gave a rebuttal to this objection by Kumārila, because Buddhists do not hold that all generalized reality (*sāmānya lakṣaṇa*) is cognized through inference only. But then this argument of Arcaṭa has gone against the dictum of Dharmakīrti himself, and thus misunderstood the theory of Diṅnāga and Dharmakīrti. D.N. Shastri rightly points out that followers of Buddhist philosophy like Arcaṭa as well as the adherents of orthodox Nyāya philosophy misunderstood Dharmakīrti. The idea of inference in Diṅnāga and Dharmakīrti is different from its counterpart in orthodox Nyāya.

Besides, the commentary on *Hetubindu*, Arcaṭa had written at least two more works — *Kṣṇabhaṅgasiddhiḥ* and *Pramāṇadvitvasiddhiḥ.*

Durveka Miśra, who flourished between the last quarter of the tenth and the first half of the eleventh century CE, wrote a sub-commentary on Arcaṭa's commentary on *Hetubindu.* The appellation *miśra* added after his name indicates that he must have been a brāhmaṇa and belonged to Mithilā. (Perhaps from a poor family as the very name Durveka is suggestive of.) He became a disciple of Jitāri, the head of Vikramaśilā University.[125] He had written five more works as referred in the sub-commentary — *Dharmottarapradīpa, Svayūthyavicāra, Viśeṣākhyāna, Kṣṇabhaṅgasiddhiḥ* and *Catuḥśatī.*

Ratnakīrti was one of the brilliant disciples of Dharmakīrti. In continuation to Dharmakīrti's *Santānāntarasiddhi,* he wrote *Santānāntaradūsaṇa* (Refutation of Other Mind-streams) in which he further developed and refined the themes of substantiation of other mind-streams. He did not refute the tenets of *Santānāntarasiddhi,* but further developed the topic from an empirical one, that is, where there are manifold minds cognized by one's experience of others' mental processes attributed through the perceived actions of other sentient beings to an absolutist view, there is only "one mind-

[125] Jitāri, a student of Dīpāṅkarajñānaśrī, had migrated to Tibet afterwards. (*Hetubinduṭīka*, Preface of Pt. Sukhalal Singhavi, p. 12.)

stream" (*ekacitta*). Ratnakīrti's argument is that the valid cognition (*pramāṇa*) of another's mind-stream is an inference (*anumāna*) and not a direct perception (*pratyakṣa*). Moreover, Ratnakīrti introduced the two truths doctrine as key to the nature of the discussion as inference is trafficking with illusory universals (*sāmānya*), the proof of the mind-streams of others, whilst empirically valid in relative truth (*saṁvṛti-satya*), does not hold ultimate metaphysical certainty in absolute truth (*paramārtha-satya*).

Both the proponents and the opponents of Buddhist philosophy extensively used Arcaṭa's commentary for support and refutation of Dharmakīrti's postulations. Amongst the orthodox Naiyāyikas, Śālikanātha, the author of *Prakaraṇapañcikā*, Jayanta Bhaṭṭa and Vyomaśiva refer to Arcaṭa. Udayana, one of the most outstanding philosophers in the tradition of the orthodox Nyāya and Vācaspati Miśra — known as a towering figure for his overall mastery of systems of philosophy known by that time — seem to have consulted Arcaṭa for sharpening their weapons against Buddhist philosophers like Dharmakīrti.

Amongst Dharmakīrti's opponents, Vyomaśiva, Akalaṅka, Haribhadra and Jayanta came a little later after him, and all of them criticized him.

Vācaspati Miśra, one of the most celebrated philosophers of India, entered into a debate with Dharmakīrti in his *Tātparyapariśuddhi*. He was followed by several other authors like Vyomaśiva in his text on Vaiśeṣika philosophy, Śālikanātha in his text on Mīmāṁsā and Akalaṅka, a Jaina philosopher. Dharmakīrti, who had lamented for having been left alone in his pursuits of philosophy, was actually supported by a host of his followers. Jñānaśrīmitra, Śāntarakṣita, Ratnakīrti and others sharply criticized Vācaspati Miśra for his attack on Dharmakīrti and presented a threadbare analysis of his arguments to demolish the prima facie views of Vācaspati Miśra. Finally it was Udayana, one of the greatest philosophers who entered into this scholastic debate and provided a sound defence for the Gautamīya Nyāya. Even though Udayana was countered by his critics from the Buddhist schools, the vigorous exercise which Dharmakīrti had initiated in one of the most enduring philosophical debates almost came to an end with Udayana.

The opponents of Dharmakīrti on the other hand attacked the logistics of inference as envisaged by him. Amidst the works by the orthodox Naiyāyikas, *Nyāyavārttikatātparyaṭīkā, Nyāyavārttikatātpary aṭīkāpariśuddhi, Nyāyamañjarī* and *Nyāyabhūṣaṇa* vehemently criticize him. The first two accept Dharmakīrti as an original thinker, the other two however find his theses as the derivative of *Nyāyasūtra* of Gautama. A staunch critic of Dharmakīrti, Jayanta Bhaṭṭa, specifically said that Dharmakīrti was indebted to Akṣapāda Gautama.

The adherents of the orthodox schools had extra-logical considerations in their attempts to demolish the logical structures proposed by Dharmakīrti, as his theory of *anumāna* stood against the authenticity of the Veda. Bhāsarvajña, Vyomaśiva and Śrīdhara are some other most brilliant stars on the terra firma of philosophy that dominated the debate between Buddhists and followers of Gautamīya Nyāya.

Return of Cārvāka

Jayarāśi Bhaṭṭa, the author of *Tattvopaplavasiṁha,* flourished between CE 770–830. He was a staunch follower of a very hard-core school of Cārvāka system. But his harsh criticism of the epistemologies of all systems establishes him as a nihilist and non-believer. A votary of scepticism, Jayarāśi did not postulate any viewpoint and declared that he had excelled even Bṛhaspati, the first proponent of Cārvāka school. *Tattvopaplavasiṁha* is a great exercise in *vitaṇḍā* (cavil). He refuted all epistemological categories of Nyāya, called the views of Kumārila Bhaṭṭa as *bālavalgitam* (child's quibbling).[126] He not only refuted the theses of Buddhist philosophers, he also refuted their refutation of the Naiyāyikas on *jāti* (universal).[127] He had refuted

---

[126] *Tattvopaplavasiṁha*, p. 115.

[127] Ibid., pp. 188-210.

the concept of *pramāṇa* as propounded in the philosophies of Nyāya, Mīmāṁsā, Sāṁkhya, Buddhism, Vyākaraṇa and Purāṇa. In his treatment of Mīmāṁsā, he quoted the definitions of *pramāṇa* given by Kumārila and for Buddhism he cited Dharmakīrti's definition only. But he gave prominence to the refutation of Nyāya system and cited the definitions of all the four *pramāṇas* from *Nyāyasūtra* for their rejection. He seemed referring to *Vākyapadīyam* of Bhartṛhari for the denouncement of the philosophy of grammar.

Vijñānavāda to him was *mugdha-vilasita* (fancy of fools).[128] The Naiyāyikas were described by him as animals (p. 14), fools or childish (pp. 29, 32). Since even *pratyakṣa* (perception) is invalid, there is no scope for holding the other *pramāṇas* like *anumāna,* etc. The theory of Anekānta is also negated. All the concepts of *mokṣa* (liberation) are in same way demolished. On the other hand, he cited Bṛhaspati with respect adding the appellation *Bhagavān* before his name.[129]

Jayarāśi had adopted a specific methodology for demotion of any system of thought resting on discursive analysis. He would present a number of alternatives for any category and then taking each one by one would show the impossibility of each one. He cited Dharmakīrti's definition of perception (*pratyakṣam kalpanāpauḍhaṁ* – *Nyāyabindu* I.4) and then gave twelve alternatives for *kalpanā* and refuted them all.[130]

Jayarāśi proclaimed himself as a follower of Bṛhaspati, but he even demolished the very first aphorism of his mentor, which says that there are only four elements – the earth, the waters, the fire and the wind. Offering justification for this overruling, Jayarāśi said that Bṛhaspati actually did not propose the existence of these four elements; he was just referring to the popular belief.[131] With a gusto,

---

[128] *Tattvopaplavasiṁha*, Veliyanad, 2013, p. 210.

[129] Ibid., p. 183.

[130] Ibid., p. 32.

[131] *Tattvopaplavasiṁha,* ed. Pt. Sukhalalji Singhavi, Varanasi, 1987, p. 1.

Jayarāśi prided in himself claiming that the varieties of thoughts occurring to him that eradicate the arrogance of the hypocrites, were unforeseen even by Bṛhaspati, the teacher of the gods.[132]

Like Nāgārjuna and Śrīharṣa, the author of *Khaṇḍanakhaṇḍakhādya* (see Chap. 1), Jayarāśi shunned all positions, but unlike these two he was neither a Śūnyavādin nor a Vedāntin. He had presented his magnum opus as an exercise in *vikalpas* (alternatives).[133] The purpose of composing a text in *vitaṇḍā* like this for him might have been to repeal the hypocrisies that got attached to every dogma and also to show the way to win a debate.

Jayarāśi became a model for the practitioners of *vāda*. A number of Jaina monks utilized his method for debating with rival systems.[134] Vidyānanda, a Jaina philosopher who flourished between CE 810-75, had not only cited *Tattvopaplavasiṁha* by name in his *Aṣṭasahasrī*, but also produced excerpts from Jayarāśi's text with a view to refute him.

Debates on Philosophy of Language

Even though, Bhartṛhari with his *Vākyapadīyam* provided a sound footing to Vyākaraṇa as a philosophical system, an intense debate continued for a few centuries pertaining to the acceptability of Vyākaraṇa as a philosophy. Somānanda, the author of *Śivadṛṣṭi*, strongly rejected the idea of Vyākaraṇa as a philosophical system. Vyākaraṇa should occupy itself with accuracy of language and not with pursuit of *vijñāna*.[135] The main arguments of the opponents of the view of Vyākaraṇa as *darśana* were:

---

132 ये याता नहि गोचरं सुरगुरोर्बुद्धैर्विकल्पा दृढाः।
प्राप्यन्ते ननु तेऽपि यत्र विमले पाखण्डदर्पच्छिदि। — *Tattvopaplavasiṁha*, p. 125

133 पाखण्डखण्डनाभिज्ञा ज्ञानोदधिविवर्धिताः।
जयराशेर्जयन्तीह विकल्पा वादिजिष्णवः।। — Ibid.

134 Preface to *Tattvopaplavasiṁha* by Muni Sukhalal Singhavi, p. 13.

135 वैयाकरणतां त्यक्त्वा विज्ञानान्वेषणेन किम् ।
भवतामप्रस्तुतेन न केवलमिहोदितम् ।।

1. Vyākaraṇa is meant to teach correct usages, it is not expected to indulge in philosophizing.
2. Vyākaraṇa does not have any epistemology and ontology.
3. A mere study of language cannot lead to *mokṣa* which is the purpose of *darśana.*

Before Patañjali and Bhartṛhari, Jaimini in his *Mīmāṁsādarśana* had already provided a firm footing to the philosophy of language. Jaimini had discussed the debatable question whether the word is eternal or ephemeral, and various systems of philosophy as well as the Vyākaraṇa are sharply divided on the question of nature of speech.

Śaṅkara's Conquests

In the biographies of Śaṅkarācārya, the debates occurring between him and the representatives of rival schools of philosophy are called *vādas*. His journey for *vāda*, also known as his *digvijaya* in later literary tradition, is said to cover almost each and every part of the whole country. Descriptions of his debates with some of his contemporaries — Maṇḍana Miśra, Umveka, Padmapāda, etc. — are available.

There are very interesting accounts as to how Śaṅkarācārya inquired and located the house of Maṇḍana Miśra. His meeting with Maṇḍana Miśra is described by Govindanātha in his *Śaṅkarācāryacaritam*; with Viśvarūpa by Rājacūḍāmaṇi Dīkṣita in his *Śaṅkarābhyudayam*; and his debate with Maṇḍana's wife by Anantānanda Giri in his *Śaṅkaravijayam*; by Codvila in his *Śaṅkaravijayavilāsaḥ;* and by Tirumala Dīkṣita in his *Śaṅkarābhyudayaḥ.*[136]

Mādhava, the author of *Śaṅkaradigvijaya* also known as *Mādhavīyaśaṅkaradigvijaya*, mentions Śaṅkarācārya entering into debates with poets and philosophers like Bāṇa, Daṇḍin, Mayūra, Abhinavagupta, Śrīharṣa, the author of *Khaṇḍanakhaṇḍakhādya*,

[136] G.C. Pande, 1998, *Life and Thought of Śaṅkarācārya*, p. 33.

Bhaṭṭa Bhāskara and Udayanācārya — none of them was actually a contemporary to Śaṅkara.

In *Śaṅkaradigvijaya*, Śaṅkara challenges Maṇḍana Miśra with the following words: "Let there be *vādakathā* (debate) between us. Let the pains taken by us in the scriptures fructify".[137] Maṇḍana also replies: "No doubt, I will enter into *vāda* with you".[138]

The methodology that was adopted during the course of a *vāda* is also indicated in *Śaṅkaradigvijaya*. The two wings in the *vāda* (*pakṣa* and *vipakṣa*) are to be represented by the *vādin* and the *prativādin*. Then each of the two should declare his *pratijñā* (thesis) and the *pramāṇas* (means of knowledge) desired to be adopted by him, they should also decide the terms of reference — the binding condition, etc.[139] In case of the debate between Śaṅkarācārya and Maṇḍana Miśra, the former agreed that if he is routed in the debate he will give up his saffron cloth and will embrace *gṛhasthāśrama* (life of a householder); whereas Maṇḍana Miśra declared that in case of his defeat, he will give up *gṛhasthāśrama*. However the law that a *gṛhastha* cannot be ordained for the *saṁnyāsa* without the permission of his wife was not to be overruled.

Śaṅkarācārya agreed to the nomination of the very wife of his opponent, Bhāratī Miśra, as the only jury (*sadasya*).[140] The *vāda* between the two combatants continued for several days. Bhāratī Miśra eventually conceded that her husband has been defeated, but not completely. As per law, she is the half of her husband, and without defeating her, Śaṅkarācārya cannot be declared as the

---

[137] भवतु सम्प्रति वादकथाऽऽवयोः फलतु पुष्कलशास्त्रपरिश्रमः।
— *Śaṅkaradigvijayam* VIII.42

[138] वादं करिष्यामि न सन्दिहेऽत्र — Ibid. VIII.46

[139] वादे हि वादिप्रतिवादिनौ द्वौ विपक्षपक्षग्रहणं विधत्तः।
का नौ प्रतिज्ञा वदतोश्च तस्यां किं मानमिष्टं वद कः स्वभावः।।
— Ibid. VIII.47

[140] विधाय भार्यां विदुषीं सदस्यां विधीयतां वादकथा सुधीन्द्र। — Ibid. VIII.47

winner.[141] In some accounts Śaṅkara is reported to have expressed his reluctance to enter into the debate with a woman. However, when Bhāratī Miśra reminded him of the discussion between Gārgī and Yājñavalkya, he accepted her challenge.

Mostly the *vāda*s lasted for several days and continued from the morning till evening with a break in noon.[142] *Madhyastha* and *sadasya* two words have been used for jury.

In some of the biographies of Śaṅkarācārya, Kumārila asks Śaṅkara to go for a debate with Maṇḍana Miśra.[143] According to *Padmapādacaritam* of Durgāprasāda Yatin, the *vāda* between Śaṅkara and Umveka was held in a temple in the presence of Umveka's wife. Śaṅkara defeated Umveka thrice in the debate. The reason for holding the debate for a second and third time was the overruling by the wife of Umveka. When her husband was defeated for the third time, she placed a stick and a jug (*daṇḍa* and *kamaṇḍalu*) before her husband and said: "O *vipra*! now you are really defeated, do whatever you wish now!" — and went to her home.[144]

Śaṅkarācārya's dialectic method involved arguing through the textual authority. He also construed the texts to support his own thesis. For example *Bṛhadāraṇyaka Upaniṣad* VI.17 describes a ritual to be performed for begetting a daughter who must be a *paṇḍitā*, obviously meaning a scholar. Śaṅkara in his *Bhāṣya* on this passage says that *paṇḍitā* here cannot mean "learned" because Vedic study is denied to women; hence the work can mean only a lady skilled in household management.

Biographies of Śaṅkarācārya also describe some other debates he held with the philosophers who became his disciples after being

---

[141] अपि तु त्वयाऽद्य न समग्रजितः प्रथिताग्रणीर्मम पतिर्यदहम् ।
वपुरर्धमस्य न जिता मतिमन्नपि मां विजित्य कुरु शिष्यमिमम्। — Ibid. IX.56

[142] भविष्यते वादकथा ऽपरेद्युर्माध्याह्निकं सम्प्रति कर्म कुर्याम्। — *Śaṅkaradigvijayam* VIII.49

[143] *Padmapādacaritam* IV.1-16.

[144] C.S. Sundaram, 1999, *Contribution of Tamilnadu to Sanskrit*, p. 80.

routed in the debates. Amongst them, Padmapāda, the author of *Pañcapādikā* came from Tamil Nadu; whereas Sureśvara was associated with Kāñcī. Sarvajñātman another disciple of Śaṅkara had conquered Jainas in debates.[145]

Udayana

Udayana, one of the most brilliant stars in the firmament of philosophy, was born in the second half of the tenth century CE in a village near Darbhanga in Bihar. The period of his activity extends to the first half of the eleventh century. One of the greatest Naiyāyikas, he acquired legendary fame for countering Buddhism through scholastic debates and through his writings. In *Bhaktimāhātmya,* he is eulogized as an incarnation of Viṣṇu, who delighted the scholars by his *Kiraṇāvalī* (cluster of rays, the title of one of his works).[146] As per textual evidence, *Kiraṇāvalī* the text referred by *Bhaktimāhātmya* with a pun was composed in CE 984. Śrīdhara, a well-known author of *Nyāyakandalī,* another eminent Naiyāyika, who lived in Bengal, was his contemporary and both Udayana and Śrīdhara seem to criticize each other in *Kiraṇāvalī* and *Nyāyakandalī,* respectively. He has cited a verse of Buddhist philosopher Jñānaśrī and has also refuted his views.

His *Nyāyakusumāñjali* is a brilliant dissertation in defence of the existence of God. For this treatise, Udayana came to regarded as a saviour in the theistic tradition. In fact, credit goes to him for having convincingly established theism in the system of Nyāya-Vaiśeṣika. His *Ātmatattaviveka* is also known as *Bauddhādhikāra* and better by *Bauddhadhikkāra* (Condemnation of the Buddhists).

Udayana established the existence of the self (*ātman*) as an

---

[145] भगवानपि तत्रैव मिथिलायां जनार्दनः।
श्रीमदुदयनाचार्यरूपेणावततार ह।
बौद्धसिद्धान्तमुग्धान्तःसुखाय हितकारिणीम् ।
व्यातेने विदुषां प्रीत्यै विमलां किरणावलीम् । — quoted by Ācārya Viśveśvara in the Preface of his *Nyāyakusumāñjali.*

[146] Ibid., p. 1.

object of internal perception. There has to be cognizer for every cognition. The Vijñānavādin refuses to accept this distinction and maintains that the cognizer and the cognition are one and the same. Udayana traps the Vijñānavādin on the basis of latter's acceptance of two types of parallel streams of cognitions — *ālaya-vijñāna* (self cognition) and *pravṛtti-vijñāna* (object cognition). The former works as a storehouse to generate the object cognitions. Udayana questioned the very logistics of this genesis.

Several stories of his public debates with contemporary philosophers are known in the tradition. He is said to have defeated Hīra, a *paṇḍit* in the court of King Vijayacandra of Kānyakubja. To have his revenge, Hīra devoted himself to training his son, Śrīharṣa. Śrīharṣa became one of the intellectual giants of his time and a celebrated poet also, but his rival had already passed away by the time he was prepared to challenge. Śrīharṣa had to contend by refuting Udayana's theories of Nyāya in his *Khaṇḍanakhaṇḍakhādya.* Caṇḍū Paṇḍita, a commentator of Śrīharṣa's *Naiṣadhīyacarita,* says: "Śrīharṣa refuted the works of Udayana, who had defeated his father, in the text entitled *Khaṇḍanakhaṇḍakhādya*".

There is a whole section devoted to *Udayanamāhātmya* (glory of Udayana) in *Bhaviṣya Purāṇa Pariśiṣṭa* (chap. XXX) describing Udayana's debate with some Bauddhācārya. The king of Mithila announced that if the *paṇḍit*s of his court are defeated by the Bauddhācārya then he will accept ordination under him, and if the *paṇḍit*s defeat him, then he will remain a slave to them. Udayana alone accepted the challenge. The debate between him and the Buddhist scholar continued for several days. Then the Bauddhācārya created some magic (*māyā*). Ultimately, both agreed that they will give a taste by falling from a tall palmyra tree, and whosoever remains alive will be the winner. Udayana escaped after falling from the heights of the tree and his enemy died. But then he had to incur the sin of causing the death of a religious figure and when he visited Jagannātha Temple at Purī, the doors of the temple closed at his face. Undaunted, Udayana recited a stanza addressed to Lord Jagannātha, which said:

You are despising me
Intoxicated by your prowess
But when the Buddhists come
Your very existence depends on me.

The story goes that the doors of the temple were flung open at this and Lord Jagannātha appeared before the priests of the temple in a dream to tell them that Udayana, having proved his existence through logic, is His form.

Such was the glory attained by Udayana that Cāritravardhana, a commentator on *Meghadūta* of Kālidāsa, understood a reference to King Udayana in the poem as reference to Udayanācārya and explained that the famous Naiyāyika was a resident of Ujjayinī, and the tales about him were told by the elderly people even in the villages there.

In his *Ātmatattvaviveka* Udayana counters for oppositional stands — Kṣaṇabhaṅgavāda (theory of momentariness), Guṇaguṇibhedabhaṅgavāda — theory of non-difference between the quality and qualifier and *anupalambha* (non-perception).

Udayana ultimately created a synthesis of Nyāya and Vaiśeṣika systems to form a complete unity. His *Nyāyapariśiṣṭa* also known as *Pariśiṣṭa, Bodhasiddhi* or *Prabodhasiddhi* can be regarded as a commentary on *Nyāyasūtras* of Gautama, whereas *Kiraṇāvalī* by him is the only available commentary on *Padārthadharmasaṁgraha* of Praśastapāda which is a basic text of the Vaiśeṣika system. Udayana also wrote another work on Vaiśeṣika philosophy, i.e. *Lakṣaṇāvalī*.

Next to Udayana, Gaṅgeśa stands as one of the most outstanding logicians. He "scrupulously analyses and rejects the opponent's views and makes *Īśvarānumāna* a perfected syllogism".[147]

---

[147] K.N. Neelkantha's Prefatory Note in John S.J. Vattanky, *Gaṅgeśa's Philosophy of God*, p. ix.

III. Vistāra-kāla (The Age of Diversification)

Udayana was perhaps the last great philosopher to have cast an everlasting impact on the philosophical traditions through *vādas*. Like his illustrious predecessors, he engaged in public debates as well as debates through writings. With the overpowering and authoritative status that the Navya-Nyāya as developed by Gaṅgeśa attained, and the chief combatant — the Buddhist philosopher — having gone out of the scene, the glorious age of *vāda* seems to be over now. There are various reasons for this decline. "Both realism and the power of abstraction may be seen at their extreme in Navya-Nyāya method of universalizing."[148] The onslaught of Vaiṣṇavism that swept over almost the whole peninsula replaced public debates as well as debates through new texts by the religious faith and devotional fervour. The spirit to fight mellowed down with the onslaught of Bhakti movement. On the other hand, interfaith dialogues and syncretic approaches to philosophical and religious issues were encouraged. The debates between diverse schools of Vedānta — Advaita, Dvaita, Dvaitādvaita, Śuddhādvaita, etc. — continued generation after generation.

Revived by Madhva, Rāmānuja, Vallabhācārya (1479–1531), Caitanya (1485–1533), Tukārāma (1609-49) and other saints, the Bhakti movement had a dominating effect even in the area of philosophical reasoning. Sadānanda who flourished in Kashmir in the seventeenth century made an attempt to synthesize *bhakti* and *yoga* in his *Svarūpaprakāśa*, a text of Advaita Vedānta. He also introduces the concept of Para-Vāsudeva from Vaiṣṇava Pāñcarātra system[149] and discusses the concept of *sākṣī* (witness) different from the individual soul (*jīva*) and elaborates upon it by giving the illustration of the lamp in a theatre. Just as the lamp in the theatre illuminates the patron, the audiences and the performer

---

148 Daniel H.H. Ingalls, 1988, *Materials for the Study of Navya-Nyāya Logic*, Introduction, p. 1.

149 *Svarūpaprakāśa*, Preface by G.C. Tripathi, pp. x-xi.

simultaneously remain illuminated in itself without all these also, *sākṣī* illuminates the ego, the intellect and the objects and remains self-luminous. In the light of this illumination, *buddhi* (intellect) dances like a performer.[150] After Śrīharṣa, Citsukhācārya wrote *Citsukhī* in the same vein.

Amongst the Jaina works, *Hetuviḍambanopāya*[151] is a manual on the science of debate. Devasūrin (CE 1186–1269) was a brilliant logician amongst the Jaina philosophers. He severely criticized Udayana and Jayanta of Kashmir.

Vādirāja, so named because of his debating skills, flourished in eleventh century CE under the rule of Cāḷukya king Jagadekamalla Jayasiṁha (CE 1018-42). In his *Nyāyaviniścayavivaraṇa,* Vādirāja has refuted several rival doctrines. He brilliantly defends Syādvāda against the vehement criticism of Śaṅkarācārya, he also argues against Kumārila, Praśastapāda, Īśvarakṛṣṇa and Maṇḍana Miśra.

Scholastic debates were fiercely conducted for the propagation of religious order. Jñānasambandhar, a Naynār and a Śaiva saint, is said to have defeated the Jainas in a public debate and converted Pāṇḍya rulers of Mathurā.[152]

At the juncture of the third and fourth phases stands Al-Biruni, with his extraordinary hermeneutic awareness and masterly command over the textual material in Greek, Arabic and Sanskrit. He evaluated the knowledge systems of both the Greeks and Hindus from a perspective developed through the Islamic monotheism and failed to understand the pluralistic outlook in Indo-Greek cultures. He complains of the lack of scientific perfection in them.

> I can only compare their mathematical and astronomical literature, as far as I know it, to a mixture of pearl shells and sour dates, or of pearls and dung, or of costly crystals and common

---

150 *Svarūpaprakāśa*, p. 26.

151 Preface to *Tattvopaplavasiṁha* by Muni Sukhalal Singhavi, p. 20.

152 G.C. Pande, 1998, op. cit., p. 61.

> pebbles. Both kinds of things are equal in their eye since they cannot raise themselves to the methods of a strictly scientific deduction.[153]

He searches affinities in the methods of calculations between Indian astronomers and *alfazari*.[154] He was aware of the debates on various issues amongst the intellectuals in India. He refers to differences of opinions on the question whether the people of lower castes can attain *mokṣa*.[155] He draws comparisons the concepts, cultures and traditions. In fact, he displayed the techniques of *vāda* in a novel way when he criticized Brahmagupta and made an assessment of Varāhamihira. Al-Biruni finds an inner contradiction in Brahmagupta for accepting the myth of Rāhu and Ketu on one hand and also discussing the scientific reason for the eclipse on the other.[156] There are many other issues on which he differs with Brahmagupta.[157] He cites Varāhamihira; criticizing him on the claim of giving respects to the *yavanas* and *mlecchas* if they are knowledgeable. But from this passage of Varāhamihira alone you see what a self-lauding man he is, whilst he gives himself airs as doing justice to others.[158] Only Al-Biruni could have unleashed such a scathing attack on a stalwart like Varāhamihira:

> . . . . you mostly find that even the so-called scientific theorems of the Hindus are in the state of utter confusion, devoid of any logical order, and in the last instance always mixed up with the silly notions of the crowd, e.g. immense numbers, enormous

153 *Al-Beruni's India*, ed. Edward C. Sachan, 2005, vol. I, p. 25.

154 Ibid., p. 315.

155 Ibid., vol. I, p. 104; Al-Biruni wrongly attributes the Sāṁkhya theory of twenty-five elements to Vyāsa here, but rightly cites Kṛṣṇa's statement from *Gītā* that even women and śūdras can attain salvation.

156 Ibid., vol. II, pp. 110-11.

157 Ibid., vol. I, pp. 267-68.

158 Ibid., vol. I, pp. 267-68, p. 23.

> spaces of time, and all kinds of religious dogmas, which the vulgar belief does not admit of being called into question.[159]

He severely criticizes Balabhadra, a commentator on Brahmagupta's text,[160] and also questions some of the propositions of Āryabhaṭṭa, the junior.[161]

Al-Beruni entered into *vāda* with Indian intellectual discourses by viewing them in relation to the Greek thought. His way of doing *vāda* lied in finding out the contours of *saṁvāda*.

> He seems to have thought that the philosophers both in ancient Greece and India, whom he most carefully and repeatedly distinguishes from the ignorant, image-loving crowd, held in reality the very same ideas, the same as seem to be his own, i.e. those of a pure monotheism, that in fact, originally all alike pure and virtuous, worshipping one sole Almighty God, but that the dark passions of the crowd in the course of time had given rise to the difference of religion, of philosophical and political persuasions and of idolatry.[162]

In his own way, Al-Beruni was anticipating Dara Shikoh by the way of seeing

> Hindu scholars as "enjoying the help of God" which to a Muslim means as much as inspired by God, guided by divine inspiration.[163]

He was viewing India in the context of Iranian and Greek cultures[164] and at the same time was preparing a manual for his fellow countrymen to train them to be able to enter into a conversation with India.

---

[159] *Al-Beruni's India*, op. cit., vol. I, p. 25.

[160] Ibid., p. 144.

[161] Ibid., p. 246.

[162] Ibid., Preface by Edward C. Sachan, p. xviii.

[163] Ibid., p. xviii.

[164] Ibid., p. 24.

With the withdrawal of the Buddhists from the scene, the intensity and profoundness of debate were gone. *Vāda* was also shifted to vernaculars. Sectarian debates are sustained through generations. There are interfaith dialogues between the *paṇḍits* and sufis.

Some of the most spectacular debates that became the parts of Itihāsa (collective memory of nation) can be studied from various sources documenting them. The debates between Madhva and Trivikrama Paṇḍita, etc. are examples of such debates.

There are interesting accounts of the debates between Jaina *ācāryas* and the Buddhists in Prabhācandrasūri's *Prabhāvakacarita* (thirteenth century CE).[165] *Jalpakalpalatā* gives an account of the historical event of the fierce debate between Māṇikya Sūri and a Naiyāyika from Varanasi, named Śaṅkara. The author, Ratnamaṇḍana, was a disciple of Nandīratna. Māṇikya Sūri, the respondent in the debate, was a disciple of Devasūrin. Deva Sūri was a renowned ascetic and a contemporary of Hemacandra. He had defeated Kumudacandra, a Digambara ascetic, in a famous debate held in the court of the King Siddharāj. Kumudacandra himself is described as a ferocious debater, and is said to have defeated as many as eighty-four adversaries. The masterly skills of Deva Sūri in debate have been described in *Mudritakumudacandra*, a play (see Chap. 7) as well as in some other medieval works.[166] His disciples Ratnaprabha, Māṇikyamuni and Mahendrasiṁha were also adept in debates.

During the visit of Deva Sūri to Anahilapattana, Śaṅkara challenged him for a *kāvyagoṣṭhī* or a *vāda*. On behalf of his *guru*, Māṇikyamuni took up the challenge. The subject of *vāda* between Māṇikyamuni and Śaṅkara was God as the creator of the world.

---

[165] Solomon, 1976, op. cit., vol. I, pp. 852-59.

[166] The editor of *Jalpakalpalatā* quotes the following verses, perhaps from a text *Gurvāvalī*, in the eulogy of Deva Sūri — श्रीदेवसूरिरपरश्च जगत्प्रसिद्धो वादीश्वरोऽस्तगुणचन्द्रमदोऽपि बाल्ये। येनार्दितश्चतुरशीतिसुवादिवेलालब्धील्लसज्ज्यरम-मदकेलिशाली वादाहवे कुमुदचन्द्रदिगम्बरेन्द्रः श्रीसिद्धभूमिपतिसंसदि पत्तनेऽस्मिन्।

Śaṅkara started with the simple reasoning that every effect has an intelligent agent, and then proceeded to prove how this invariable concomitance, formed by God as the agent and the world as effect, is free from all sorts of fallacies. Māṇikyamuni gave reasons why God cannot be accepted as the creator of the world. The proposition that God has created this world cannot be proved by *pratyakṣa* (perception) and the inference upheld by his opponent does have fallacies.

Challenges to Śaṅkara's Advaitavāda

In the period between twelfth to eighteenth centuries, some of the renowned philosophers who created history by entering into diversified debates were Rāmānuja, Madhva and Madhusūdana Sarasvati. Rāmānuja derived his concept of soul from Śaṅkara and to an extent his philosophy of Viśiṣṭādvaita corroborated Śaṅkara's postulations. The fundamental difference between Śaṅkara and Rāmānuja lies in their world-views. To Śaṅkara, the world is a *vivarta* (an appearance) while Rāmānuja regards it an evolution. According to Rāmānuja, the soul and the matter are different from *Brahman* in relation to the matter as being an object of enjoyment, and they are identical with Him as constituents of His body. The world of our perception is His *kāryāvasthā* (effected state). He exists in causal state when the world stands dissolved. All *jīva*s (souls) exist in him in subtle state and they just become manifest when He exercises His Will and creates them.

Madhva, on the other hand, posited a potent challenge for the Advaitin with his uncompromising logic to prove the difference between God and the world. His basic argument is — if there is only one *Brahman* and nothing else, who then is making this statement that there is only *Brahman* and nothing else? He questions the ontological status of "nothing which is negated in God".[167]

With their virulent of attacks and uncompromising adherence to dualism, Madhva and his followers, Vyāsatīrtha and Jayatīrtha, emerged as strongest critics of Śaṅkara's monism. The debate

[167] K. Satchidananda Murty, 2007, *Evolution of Indian Philosophy*, p. 219.

continued till twentieth century. Madhva's works are also known as vāda granthas. His philosophy became the most powerful rival of Advaita Vedānta and stimulated a tooth and nail fight between very opposite juxtapositions — Advaita vs. Dvaita, idealism vs. realism, identity vs. difference, etc.

Veṅkaṭanātha also known as Vedāntadeśika (CE 1278–1369) stands next to Rāmānuja as a votary of Viśiṣṭādvaita. He was born at Tuppal near Kāñcī. He travelled far and wide including northern India to hold discussions on philosophical issues.

Veṅkaṭādhvarin in his *Viśvaguṇādarśacampūḥ* (see Chap. 6) describes Vedāntadeśika as a great debater who could explain most difficult propositions in the debates and repeal the intoxication of the opponents.[168] Veṅkaṭādhvarin devotes as many as twelve verses to Vedāntadeśika (CE 1289–1300) with some very succinct prose passages. Unable to tolerate the praise showered on Vedāntadeśika, Kṛśānu, the reviler, asks his opponent Kṛśāśva in *Viśvaguṇādarśacampūḥ* — how can the words of a poet tender like the *campaka* flowers decorating the head of Goddess Sarasvatī be able to break the hearts of opponents in debates hard like stones?[169] Viśvāvasu, the protagonist, replies that the speech of the master of Vedānta is as tender as flowers and pleases the noble, but it is able to break the hearts of the enemies (the opponents in debate) like the tender foot of child Kṛṣṇa, the touch of which delighted Nandin and it could become as hard as a diamond in killing the demon Śakaṭāsura.[170]

---

168 भेदाभिदा विषयवादापतद्दुरुपपादार्थसाधकमदो-
त्सादावहाद्भुतमखादापगास्यादविनोदाभिजातभणितिः।
पादारविन्दनतखेदापहारचतुरोदारमाधवगुणा-
स्वादाभितुष्ट इह मोदाय वो भवतु वेदान्तदेशिकमणिः।।
— *Viśvaguṇādarśacampūḥ*, p. 226, v. 290

169 कथं नाम द्रुहिणगृहिणीचिकुरनिकुरम्बचुम्बिचम्पककुसुमसुकुमारतराः कविकथककण्ठीरवगुरोरपि गिरो दुस्तरप्रस्तरनिष्ठुरबंहिष्ठसासूयहृदयनिर्भेदाय जायन्ते? — Ibid., p. 232, prose 117

170 वेदान्तार्यगिरः प्रसूनमृदवो मोदं दधीनाः सतां
प्रौढग्रावकठोरकाण्यपि परं भिन्दन्ति हृन्दि द्विषाम्।

→

Vedāntadeśika wrote in Sanskrit, Tamil and Maṇipravāḷam (a mixture of Tamil amd Prākṛt) also. His *Śatadūṣaṇī* is a treatise in refutation of the Advaita system, which started a chain of critiques (*dūṣaṇa* texts). Vedāntadeśika's *Vāditrayakhaṇḍana* is also a work of similar nature. He became a legendary figure even in his lifetime and several stories are current about his extraordinary scholarship and eloquence. It is said that he was blessed by the Lord Hayagrīva for always being a champion in the *vādāhavas* (battles of debates)[171] and was supposed to be an incarnation of the bell given to his parents by Lord Veṅkaṭeśa Himself.[172] Many of his contemporaries like Varadarāja, his own son, and Yatirāja had composed a *Dhyānalokas* (verses for meditation) in his worship.[173] Rāmānuja, the propounder of Viśiṣṭādvaita, was his maternal uncle and *guru*.

Veṅkaṭanātha was challenged by Diṇḍimakavi Sārvabhauma, who sent him in verse describing himself as a lion having reached *pakkaṇa* — the habitat of outcasts, and like Garuḍa being forced to roam in the assembly of water-snakes.[174] Veṅkaṭanātha sent him

← नन्द्याद्यार्यजनाभिनन्दितमृदुस्पर्शोऽपि पादो हरे-
दुर्भेदे शकटासुरे तु शतकोट्याकारमागान्न किम्? — *Viśvaguṇādarśacampūḥ* , pp. 232-33, v. 299

171 *Saṅkalpasūryodaya*, Upodghāta, p. 62.

172 The editor of *Saṅkalpasūryodaya* has given a detailed account of the legend narrating Veṅkaṭanātha as an incarnation. He has also enlisted as many as forty-one Sanskrit texts on the life and deeds of Vedāntadeśika. — *Saṅkalpasūryodaya*, pt. I, Upodghāta, p. 57

173 श्रीमान् वेङ्कनाथार्यः कवितार्किककेसरी।
वेदान्ताचार्यवर्यो सन्निधत्तां सदा हृदि।। — Ibid., pp. 69, 71

174 छित्वा सर्वाण्यरण्यान्यतिविषमलतागुल्मदुर्गाणि सद्यः
प्राप्तं मां पक्कणान्तं बत भषकततिर्बुक्कणैर्द्विक्करोति।
लज्जन्ते हन्तुमेनां मदकरटिघटाकुम्भपीठीविपाक-
क्रीडाधौरेयधारा मम खलु कराः किं करोमि क्व यामि।।
प्राज्ञानामेव राज्ञां सदसि न सहते जल्पमल्पेतरेषां
क्षुद्रेष्वाक्षेपमुद्रां न खलु गणयते डिण्डिमः सार्वभौमः
भाङ्कुर्वद्भेककुक्षिम्भरिषु भयकरभ्रान्तभोगीन्द्रसुभ्रू-

→

two verses as a befitting rejoinder[175] which wrecked the ego of Diṇḍimakavi. After listening to the readings of Veṅkaṭanātha's epic *Yādavābhyudaya*, he became an ardent admirer of Veṅkaṭanātha and composed fine stanzas in his eulogy.[176]

Veṅkaṭanātha was a very amicable person. In a quarter of night he is said to have composed one thousand verses of the poem *Pādukāsahasram*. Unable to tolerate the overwhelming applause showered on him for this extraordinary feat, Varavara, poet, also started composing a poem of one thousand verses but his inspiration lasted only for a few verses and he was put to shame. Veṅkaṭanātha consoled him by dedicating a stanza. The stanza said:

> The she-pig produces hundred cubs instantly; a she-elephant after a long time gives birth to only one cub, but he becomes dear to kings.[177]

At the initiative of Vidyāraṇya, Harihara I (CE 1336-56), the king of Vijayanagara, sent a letter to him requesting him to grace the

---

← भ्रूणभ्रंशी किम्भःफणिषु पतगराट् सम्भ्रमी बम्भ्रमीति।।
— quoted in *Saṅkalpasūryodaya*, op. cit., p. 65

175 स्पर्धन्तां सहजं नु कुञ्जरतया दिक्कुञ्जरैः कुञ्जरा
ग्राम्या वा वनवासिन मदजलप्रस्विन्नगण्डस्थलाः।
हा कालस्य विपर्ययं शृणु सखे प्राचीनपालीमला-
स्वादस्निग्धकपोलभित्तिरधमः कोलोऽपि संस्पर्धते।।
बाह्यैर्वर्णाडम्बरैर्मा भ्रमन्तु च्छित्वा गर्भाभ्यन्तरं शोधयन्तु।
निर्णेतारो नीरसत्वेन को वा डिण्डीराणां डिण्डिमानां च भेदः।। — Ibid., p. 66

176 घोटीघाटीकठोरस्फुटविकटकथाटोपवाचाटकोटी-
कोटीराघाटपेटीपुटघटितमणीसङ्घसङ्घट्टिताङ्घ्रिः।
खर्वीकुर्वन् स गर्वं जयति पवितते: सर्वतन्त्रस्वतन्त्रो
वेदान्ताचार्यवर्यो विघटितजडधीसङ्कटो वेङ्कटेशः।
वेदे सञ्जातखेदे मुनिवरवचने प्राप्तनित्यावमाने
सङ्कीर्णे सर्ववर्णे सति तदनुगुणे निष्प्रमाणे पुराणे।
मायावादे समोदे कविकलुषवशाच्छून्यवादे विवादे
धर्मत्राणाय योऽभूत् स जयति भगवान् विष्णुघण्टावतारः।। — Ibid.

177 सूते शूकरयुवतिः सुतशतमत्यन्तदुर्भगं झटिति।
करिणी चिराय सूते सकलमहीपाललालितं कलभम्।। — Ibid., p. 67

royal court of Vijayanagara. Sarvajña Siṁhabhūpāla (CE 1330-80), considered himself his disciple and approached him for enlightenment on the issues of *dharma*. Veṅkaṭanātha composed *Tattvasandeśa*, a text in Tamil and *Subhāṣitanīvī*, an anthology of verses in Sanskrit and sent him. He was constantly harassed by persons who were unable to tolerate the heights he had scaled.

Veṅkaṭanātha had authored 115 works; of these sixty were in Sanskrit, the rest are bilingual — mixing Sanskrit and Tamil in Maṇipravāḷa style; or purely in Tamil.

Śatadūṣaṇī (declamation of one hundred tenets) examines the various theories of Advaitavāda from the viewpoint of Rāmānuja's philosophy. Out of one hundred sections called *vādas*, only sixty-six are presently available. *Vāditrayakhaṇḍana* is also a text refuting three *ācāryas* — Śaṅkara, Bhāskara and Yādava. Other works by Vedāntadeśika are — commentary on *Īśāvāsyopaniṣat*, *Tātparyacandrikā* (a commentary on *Gītābhāṣya* of Rāmānuja) and *Tattvamuktākalāpaḥ* (on Viśiṣṭādvaita philosophy in 500 verses). The last work has been cited by Mādhava in his *Sarvadarśanasaṁgraha*. *Adhikaraṇa* is a compendium of *Śrībhāṣya* on *Brahmasūtra* in 562 verses. This work was composed after *Śatadūṣaṇī*. *Saccharitrarakṣā* propounds the tenets of Viṣṇavism in three *adhikāras* citing profusely from Vedic Saṁhitās and Smṛtis. *Nikṣeparakṣā*, *Pāñcarātrarakṣā* and *Rahasyarakṣā* are his sectarian works. In *Nyāyapariśuddhi*, Veṅkaṭanātha establishes the authenticity of *Nyāyasūtras* of Gautama according to Vedas. Many of his works, viz. *Adhikaraṇadarpaṇa*, *Nigamaparimala* and *Vedārthasaṁgrahavyākhyāna*, etc. have been lost. He also authored *Seśvaramīmāṁsā*, *Mīmāṁsāpādukā*, *Tātparyacandrikā*, *Gītārthasaṁgraharakṣā*, *Nyāyaysiddhāñjana*, *Tattvaṭīkā*. *Cakārasamartham* is a *maṇḍana* text, written as a rejoinder to Vidyāraṇya's criticism of the use of *ca* at a place in his *Śatadūṣaṇī*. *Nyāsaviṁśatiḥ* explains the concept of *nyāsa* or *prapatti*. *Damiḍopaniṣattātparyaratnāvalī* is a commentary in 130 verses on the Tamil *Divyaprabandha* of Śaṭhakopasūri. *Damiḍopaniṣattātsāraḥ* is a work of similar nature. His works in Maṇipravāḷa style are *Amṛtarañjanīrahasya, Amṛtavādinīrahasya, Paramatabhaṅga, Hastinīmāhātmya, Paramapadasopāna, Rahasyatrayasāra,* etc. Of these eighteen texts are known as *Laghurahasyas* explaining the core of his faith. Again eighteen texts are known as Drāviḍagāthās or Deśikaprabandhas. *Nigamaparimala* is not available. In *Paramatabhaṅga* he presents critiques of Lokāyata, Buddhism, Śaṅkara's Advaita, Bhāskara and Yādava, Vyākaraṇa, Vaiśeṣika, Nyāya, Kaumārila, Prabhākara, Sāṁkhya, Yoga, Pāśupata, etc. Many other works in Sanskrit and Tamil are ascribed to him.[178] *Acyuasa-a-am* (*Avyutaśatakam*) is in Prākṛt, presenting a confluence of *bhakti* and *śṛṅgāra*. Apart from these, Veṅkaṭanātha composed twenty-four *strotrakāvyas*.

Stories of his having defended the Draviḍa Āmnāya (scriptures in Tamil) when their authenticity was questioned by the followers of other faiths on the occasion of a Brahmotsava are also current.[179] At Raṅgapaṭṭana or Śrīraṅgam, when Sudarśanasūrya was challenged by some rivals to have debate with them, otherwise stop the daily worship of God Raṅganātha according to Pāñcarātra system, the former entrusted Vedāntadeśika to enter into a debate with them and when Vedāntadeśika emerged victorious in the debate he was given the title of Vedāntācārya by the God himself.[180] His detractors did not leave him even when he had moved to Ahīndranagaram and was delivering discourses for the King Devanātha there. At the behest of the king he debated with the adversaries again and after defeating them was honoured with the title of Kavitārkikacakravartī (sovereign of poets and philosophers) by the king. His followers documented these debates and compiled an anthology of them entitled *Paramatabhaṅga*.

Madhva builds up a world-view through difference at five levels. God and soul differ from each other, God differs from the matter

---

178 C.S. Sundaram, 1999, *Contribution of Tamilnadu to Sanskrit*, p. 102.

179 *Saṅkalpasūryodaya*, Upodghāta, p. 63.

180 Ibid.

and matter differs from the soul. One soul differs from another, and there is difference from one matter to another. This difference is a reality. The world is also a reality. Bondage is also real and it is really destroyed by the grace of God and not through knowledge alone. This concept gave a pivotal position to *bhakti* (devotion to God) in Mādhva Vedānta, and enabled it to attract the masses. There is some affinity with Sāṁkhya, as *Prakṛti* is accepted as the material cause of the world. Madhva's Dvaita therefore became a chief combatant for the post-Śaṅkara Advaitins as Sāṁkhya was for Śaṅkara.

Many of the works on philosophy, that were composed basically for challenging opponent schools, formed the base for a series of debates. *Tarkatāṇḍava* of Vyāsatīrtha,[181] the fourth pontiff in Mādhva tradition, presents the interesting compendium of debates. There are works detailing debates between Śaivites and Vaiṣṇavites or between other sects. Campakeśācārya (fifteenth century) was an adherent of Viśiṣṭādvaita system. In his works like *Vedāntakaṇṭakoddhāra* and *Vādārtharatnamālā* he has taken up issues with the followers of other systems. He had written a prose-poem and a *prabandha* on *Rāmāyaṇa* theme, which are referred in his *Vādārtharatnamālā.* Tātadeśika or Tātārya (CE 1526-67) authored *Pañcamatabhañjana,* criticizing the Śaivites and upholding the tenets of Vaiṣṇavism.

The tradition of debate between *Nyāyāmṛta* and *Advaitasiddhi* is spread to a span of 500 years and continued in the form of texts constantly composed from both the sides. Nṛsiṁhāśrama, one of the most celebrated philosophers in Advaita tradition of Vedānta, gave a rebuttal to *Nyāyāmṛtam.*

Vādirāja

Vādirāja was born in the village of Huvunakere, near Kumbhāsi in the Kundūpur Taluka of the present South Kanara district of Karnataka. He was son of Rāmācārya and Gaurī. Madhvācārya

[181] Published in four volumes from Vanivilasa Press.

established eight *maṭhas* in Udupi, the pontiffs of these *maṭhas* were ordained by rotation. Amongst these, the Kumbhāsi Maṭha was headed by Viṣṇutīrtha, Madhva's younger brother. Vādirāja became the twentieth pontiff of this *maṭha*, and it later was named after him as Śrīvādirāja Maṭha. Vādirāja is said to have lived till the age of 120 years and then he entered the Vṛndāvana a sacred tomb, which he had got constructed through his royal disciple and disappeared. In consideration to his debating skills and soundness of arguments, he was honoured with the title of *Prāsaṅgikābharaṇa* (Ornament of Polemics) in the court of the King Veṅkaṭadevarāya of Vijayanagara. It is believed that he helped the kings of Vijayanagara Kṛṣṇadevarāya (CE 1509-29) and Acyutadevarāya (CE 1529-42) in their dire circumstances by the way of taking them to the cave of Vālin and discovering the hidden treasure there for them.[182]

He was adept in the use of *vākovākya alaṁkāra* which reflects *vāda*. Amongst his works *Yuktimallikā* is one of the great philosophical classics in the field of Dvaita Vedānta. It consists of 5,379 verses as an extensive commentary on *Brahmasūtra*. Vādirāja's brother presided over as the sixteenth pontiff of the Bhaṇḍārakere Maṭha and had written a commentary on *Yuktimallikā*.

Nyāyaratnāvalī by Vādirāja is a refutation of Śaṅkara's Advaita Vedānta in 901 verses and five chapters:

> He tries to flabbergast his opponent by judicious mixture of theology and metaphysics using homely analogies and persuasive rhetoric.[183]

Śrutitattvaprakāśikā vindicates Dvaita philosophy by interpreting Upaniṣadic sentences *neha nānāsti, aham brahmāsmi, ekam eva advitīyam, tattvamasi* and *kevalo nirguṇaś ca* in 507 verses. *Saṁskṛtasūtrārtha* presents the essence of Dvaita philosophy in condensed aphorisms. *Adhikaraṇanāmāvalī* documents the sections

---

[182] D.N. Shanbhag, 1996, *Vādirāja, the Dvaita Poet: Great but Ignored*, pp. 14-19.

[183] Ibid., pp. 14-19, 28.

of *Brahmasūtra*. His *Pāṣaṇḍimatakhaṇḍana* and *Kalpalatā* are also polemic works in refutation to *Pramāṇanirṇaya* of Vādirāja Sūri, a Jaina philosopher. *Kalpalatā* especially disapproves Syādvāda and Saptabhaṅgīnaya. *Upanyāsaratnamālā* is supposed to have contained ten discourses on philosophy out of which only three are available. In *Bhūgolanirṇaya*, Vādirāja describes the Indian geography on the basis of *Bhāgavata Purāṇa*. In his *Vivaraṇārṇava* he refutes the *Pañcapādikā* of Prakāśātma Yati. Besides these, Vādirāja had written a work on omens, and several other works on rituals, *mudrās*, etc. He also authored commentaries on *Mahābhārata* and Puruṣa-Sūkta of *Ṛgveda*, along with glosses on the *bhāṣya* of Madhva on *Talvakāropaniṣad, Kaṭhopaniṣad, Taittirīya Upaniṣad* and also on the commentaries of Jayatīrtha — *Nyāyasudhā* and *Tattvaprakāśikā*.

Madhusūdana Sarasvatī made a threadbare analysis of the Mādhva system as propounded in *Nyāyāmṛtam* and demolished its arguments against Śāṅkara-Vedānta in his *Advaitasiddhi*. He was born in a village under Faridpur (Bengal). He learnt Nyāya at Navadvīpa from Harirāma Tarkavāgīśa. Gadādhara Bhaṭṭācārya was his classmate at Navadvīpa. With his all-round scholarship he entered into debates with his contemporaries and challenged his predecessors through his writings. Baldeva Upadhyaya (1994: 42) refers to an incident of his having created a sensation during his visit to Navadvīpa. Gadādhara had to bow down before him after persistent discussions. The following verse cited by Sures Chandra Banerji (2004: 16) sums up the awesome effect created by Madhusūdana by his debates:

> *navadvīpe samāyāte madhusūdanavākpaṭau* ।
> *cakampe tarkavāgīśāḥ kātaro 'bhūd gadādharaḥ* ॥
>
> At the arrival of Madhusūdana, skilled in oratory, in Navadvīpa, the masters in arguments trembled and Gadādhara was stunned with fear.

Rāmārya in his *Nyāyāmṛtataraṅgiṇī* gave a reply to his criticism of Madhva. It is said that he became a disciple in disguise to learn

Vedānta from Madhusūdana himself to be able to give a suitable rebuttal to Madhusūdana's critique of Madhva. Madhusūdana makes a sarcastic and derogatory reference to one *kumati* (conceited person), who is jittering in a meaningless way and presenting pseudo-refutations, and need not be given a notice.[184] Baldeva Upadhyaya (1994: 43) conjectures that the person hinted upon here is Rāmārya.

Tulasīdāsa, who authored one of the most popular devotional epic *Rāmacaritamānasa* in Awadhī, was being criticized and tortured by the *paṇḍits* of Kāśī for having disgraced Rāma by the way writing poetry in the language of common people. It was the interference of Madhusūdana that led the whole controversy to rest and give Tulasīdāsa an honourable place amongst the devotees of Rāma.

Appayya Dīkṣita, a well-known philosopher and rhetorician, flourished in the sixteenth century. He is known for his very severe criticism of Mādhva system in his *Madhvatantramukhamardana*. (Smacking the Face of the Mādhva System) and *Madhvamatavidhvaṁsana* (Demolishing the Views of Madhva). Appayya's criticisms were answered by his contemporary Mādhva scholar Vijayīndra in his work *Madhvādhvakaṇṭakoddhāra* (Removing Thorns from the Path of Madhva). Vijayīndra is also said to have vehemently criticized Appayya Dīkṣita in his *Appayyakapolacapeṭikā* (Slap on the Cheek of Appayya). Vijayīndra's *Bhedavidyāvilāsa* (Beauty of the Doctrine of Difference), is a critique of Nṛsiṁhāśrama's *Bhedadhikkāra* (Denunciation of the Doctrine of Difference). The anti-Appayya trend continued in the Mādhva tradition with works like Nārāyaṇācārya's *Advaitakālānala* (Deadly Fire for Advaita) and Satyanātha Yati's *Abhinavagadā* (New Mace [to Crush Advaita]). The five chapters of *Abhinavagadā* are titled as *yuddhas* (battles)

---

[184] इह कुमतिरतत्त्वे तत्त्ववादी वराकः
प्रलपति यदकाण्डे खण्डनाभामुच्चैः।
प्रतिवचनममुष्मै तस्य को वक्तु विद्वान्
नहि रुतमनुकरोति ग्रामसिंहस्य सिंहः।।
— Cited by Baldeva Upadhyaya (1994: 43)

with an obvious allusion to the *gadā-yuddha* between Bhīma and Suyodhana.[185]

Bhaṭṭoji Dīkṣita was Appayya's disciple. He continued the intellectual wrestling with the rival school of Madhva in his *Tattvakaustubha*. He dared to attack even his teacher Śeṣakṛṣṇa, as the latter belonged to the Mādhva school of philosophy in his *Prauḍhamanoramā*. Paṇḍitarāja Jagannātha was also a disciple of Śeṣakṛṣṇa and he wrote *Prauḍhamanoramākucamardinī* (Crushing the Breasts of Prauḍhamanoramā) as an answer to Bhaṭṭoji's work. Jagannātha had challenged a *mullāh* of Jaipur and won him in debate. His fame as a scholar extraordinary reached the court of Shahjahan who called him to his court and honoured him. Dara Shikoh came in contact with him and some other *paṇḍits* and Hindu saints of his times. French doctor and intellectual François Bernier stayed in the Mogul court for twelve years and initially worked as a physician to Dara, and then became an interpreter of recent development of science and philosophy in Europe to Daneshmund Khan, secretary of State for Foreign Affairs in Delhi court.

Madhav M. Deshpande has discussed conflicting accounts of a philosophical debate that occurred in Ikkeri during the early seventeenth-century (before CE 1629) at the court of Nāyaka king Veṅkaṭappā between the Advaitin court scholar Raṅgoji Bhaṭṭa (younger brother of the well-known grammarian Bhaṭṭoji Dīkṣita) and his opponent, a *Dvaitin* scholar named Vidyādhīśa.

Vidyādhīśa was the sixteenth pontiff of the Uttarādi Maṭha of the Mādhva tradition from 1619 to 1631. Even at the age of sixteen he was known for his mastery over various Śāstras and had started participating in scholarly debates. After his ordination in the *maṭha*, he started travelling to various parts of the country and entering

---

[185] Madhav M. Deshpande, 2011, "Will the Winner Please Stand Up: Conflicting Narratives of a Seventeenth -Century Philosophical Debate from Karnataka", in *Knowing India: Colonial and Modern Constructions of the Past — Essays in honour of T.R. Trautmann*, ed. Cynthia Talbot, pp. 366-67.

into debates with the proponents of rival sects. It was in the course of these travels that he visited Ikkeri, where the most "debatable debate" happened.

There are varying accounts of the debate from both the sides. *Mādhvasiddhāntabhañjanī* by Raṅgoji Bhaṭṭa most probably contained an account of this debate from the Advaitin's side, but this work is unfortunately lost. Kauṇḍa Bhaṭṭa in his *Bṛhadvyākaraṇabhūṣaṇa* pays tributes to his father, Raṅgoji Bhaṭṭa, with the claim that he (Raṅgoji) had defeated the Dvaitin Vidyādhīśa. On the other hand, in *Raṅgojibhaṭṭadhikkāra* which is available in manuscript, the most intense and fierce debate of these times between Raṅgoji Bhaṭṭa and Vidyādhīśa, both in the words of Vidyādhīśa himself, as well as in the words of his followers and opponents is described.

An account of this debate from the Dvaitin's side is also available in *Śrīvidyādhīśavijaya* of Janārdana Sūri. According to Janārdana, the debate between Raṅgoji Bhaṭṭa and Vidyādhīśa lasted for three months. Janārdana describes Raṅgoji as a demon (*danuja*) born in the garb of a brāhmaṇa, barking like a dog at his opponent.

In fact, the question as to who won this debate in itself became one of the issues of a series of hot debates. The narratives given from both the sides are full of abuses for the opposite camp. After giving an account of a number of tracts and narratives describing this debate from both the sides, Deshpande says:

> The debate probably ended in a stalemate of sorts, with each party claiming victory, and finding fault with the claims seen in written documents like the *jayapatras*. With the charge that the written documents were falsified, probably both sides were free to make statements that were contrary to what one might have found in the written documents, as the probative value of such documents was already discounted by the imputation of falsification. Thus, any possibility of verification is rejected out of hand, as all sources of information are tainted in some way, except one's own perception of what happened as seen in Vidyādhīśa's own words, and the perception of the followers about what must have

> happened. For the followers it is inconceivable that their hero could have been defeated at a debate. Positives from the received information are accentuated, and the negatives are discounted with disbelief.[186]

Short tracts like *Raṅgojibhaṭṭadhikkāra* (Condemnation of Raṅgoji Bhaṭṭa) and *Bhaṭṭojikuṭṭanam* continued to be written in series. The opposition to the line of Dīkṣitas by the way of composing Khaṇḍana-granthas (texts in refutation) has continued till the twentieth century. Vyākaraṇa Setumādhavācārya wrote a voluminous critique of the *Tattvakaustubha* of Bhaṭṭoji under the title *Tattvakaustubhakuliśa* (1957).[187]

The debates not only were constantly carried on between some religious sects, between rival families of scholars as well. Paṇḍitarāja Jagannātha was opposed to the Dīkṣita family. If Bhaṭṭoji Dīkṣita wrote *Manoramā*, a commentary of Pāṇinian system of grammar, Paṇḍitarāja Jagannātha came out with its strong rejoinder in his treatise under the provocative title *Manoramākucamardanī*.

Creating Bridge through Vāda

Then there are efforts at synthesis and evolving through dialogues. The Arabs invaded Iran and the Islamic order came to be established there around CE 651. There was exodus of the followers of Zoroastrianism. Some of them settled in Gujarat in tenth century CE. In their enthusiasm to propagate Zoroastrianism in the country that sheltered them and to enter into dialogue with the people of other faiths, the scholars amongst them started translating *Avesta* and other texts from Pahalavī into Sanskrit. Naryosang, who was a Persian priest and son of Dhavala, translated *Avesta* into Sanskrit. Naryosang was a resident of modern Gujarat in the first half of fourteenth century.[188] He also transcribed many texts from Pahalavī

---

186 Deshpande, 2011, op. cit., pp. 377-78.

187 Ibid.

188 This information is based on *Iranshah* by M. Patel, pages accessed through google.

script to Avestan script. Of these translations, *Skanda-Gumanig-vizar*, a Pahalavī text of ninth century by Mardan Farrukh is noteworthy. It argues in favour of the religion of the Pārsīs, presenting refutation of other faiths, especially, Islam.[189]

By this time Sufism had started making inroads in Indian milieu. It was the beginning of a great dialogue between diverse Asian traditions, which had been prefaced in the writings of poets like Jalāl ad-Dīn Muhammad Rumi. The commentaries, poems, songs and sayings of saints like Caitanya (1486–1533), Jñāneśvara, Ekanātha (1533-99), Nāmadeva, Tukārāma, Kabīr, Mīrābāī, Dādū (1544–1608) and Nānak (1469–1539) paved the way for this dialogue. The idea of *sahaja* as elaborated upon by saints even ridiculed the discarding of *viṣayabhoga* (enjoyment of worldly things). The Sahajīyās regarded love and natural life as the core of the religion. Sarahapā is said to have been the founder of this school. He was born in eastern India at a place called Sarolī in the city of Rājī. He used to listen to the discourses by Amita and developed interest in Buddhist philosophy. Afterwards he deviated from Buddhism. Bringing in empiricism in his philosophy of pure bliss, he said:

> *tanutaracittāṅkurakaḥ viṣayarasair yadi na sicyate śuddhaiḥ* ।
> *gaganavyāpī phaladaḥ kalpatarutvaṁ katham labheta* ।।
>
> — *Caryāgītikośa*

> The subtle sprout of mind should be irrigated with the waters of pure worldly pleasure, otherwise it will not grow as a great tree of *kalpavṛkṣa*.

Under the philosophical moorings of Śaivism, Tantra made a unique journey in the world of mysticism and spiritual pursuit. Geographically, Tantra had two major centres — one in Kashmir and the other in Karnataka. A revolutionary mystic like Lal-Dêd was

---

189 At the very outset of his translations, Naryosang says — इदं स्कन्दगुमानीगुजारनाम पुस्तकं मया नैर्योसंघेन धवलसुतेन पहलवीभाषाया: संस्कृतभाषायां अवतारितं विषमपारसीकाक्षरेभ्यश्च अविस्ताक्षरैर्लिखितम्। (version provided by Balram Shukla).

born in Kashmir to spell out the essence of the Kashmir Śaivism as seen and experienced by her. Basaveśvara represents the Śaivite philosophy in Karnataka developed under the Liṅgāyata sect.

In fact, the philosophy of Tantra gave a vision of transforming this world and the lower levels of consciousness into higher level. Basaveśvara says:

> The body and the lower senses of labour and actions being transcended, the senses are now one with the *liṅga*, the higher self. I have together with *manas* (a sense-organ) and awareness served the *jaṅgama*, that working energy and the *manas* are now one with the Jaṅgamaliṅga — the moving higher self.[190]

Vakh of Lal-Dêd and *Vacanas* of medieval saints like Basaveśvara presented a new vision of religion and life. Through the inculcation of the element of devotion, the hard and atrocious practices of Tantra melted into compassion. The philosophical sophistries gave place to practical wisdom and search for freedom. Instead of intellectual discourse, *vacanas* revealed real experiences of a liberated soul. The female voices, silenced and lying dormant in the course of the male dominated history of more than two millennia also resounded with a revived gusto. Āṇḍāla, Akkā Mahādevī, Lal-Dêd, Habbā Khātūn, Mīrā and many other female mystic saints created their literary oeuvre with spontaneous verbalization of experiences on the path of enlightenment. The mystic experiences in their sayings are expressed through rare images in subtle phrases. Their feminine discourse had *śakti* (power) and insight to unravel the truth and address the human beings and the God created by them for the inconsistencies and inner contradictions.

Satsaṅga provided a platform for the meeting of the *siddha* with the *sādhaka*s and creating bridges across diverse strata of the society. It served as a link between the seeker and the common people. The *bhajanas, vacanas, vakh* assigned a performative character to *satsaṅga.*

---

[190] Sushma Kannan, 2014, *Indian Literature*, Sep.-Oct., p. 11.

If Muhammad Azam Dedamari and Dawood Mishqati are enamoured of the Lal-Dêd's message of *vakh*, Rupa Bhavani (1620–1720), a great Kashmiri woman mystic poet in her *Rahasyopadeśa,* acknowledges Lal-Dêd as her *guru.* On her poetry also she relives the spirit of Lal-Dêd. The correspondences and dialogues of Lal-Dêd with contemporaries like Sheikh Baba Nasr-ud-Dīn and philosophic successors like Sheikh Nur-ud-Dīn (Nund Rishi) exemplify the wide horizons and vision which seek to demolish the barriers and compartmentalizations created through religious sects and dogmas. Her mystic interactions with these saints and mystics are mentioned in the Old Persian sources titled *Nūranāmā* and *Ṛṣināmā.*

The onslaught of Bhakti movement created new platforms for dialogues across cultures, sects and societies. Hindus were visiting the shrines occupied by *pīrs*, *fakīrs*, *darveśas*; the Muslims were being immersed in the streams of love for Kṛṣṇa and Rādhā. The ripples of the Bhakti movement incepted by Caitanya (CE 1486–1533) swept the country far and wide, many Muslims accepted his cult. Shekh Mohammad of Shrigonde was a *bhakti* poet from Ahmednagar; his *guru*, Chand Boddhale was also the mentor of Janārdana. This Janārdana was the *guru* of Ekanātha.[191]

Even though the interaction with Arabs was going on in the first millennium CE, and *Yavanadarśana* (Islamic philosophy) has been listed as one of the disciplines to be studied by Śukra in his *Śukranīti*, the arrival and intrusion of Turks in the socio-political order gave a jolt to the existing systems and thought processes. There were conversions and also resistance to conversions. Many Hindus, even kings, chose to embrace Islam at their own choice also, to escape the oppression and inequalities of the caste system and hierarchies. Describing the situation after the annexation of Bengal by Sultan Muhammad Tughlak (succession CE 1325), Sures

---

[191] Elleanor Zelliot (tr.), 1982, "A Medieval Encounter between Hindu and Muslim: Eknath's Drama-poem 'Hindu-Turk-Saṁvāda'', ed. E.W. Clothy, p. 67.

Chandra Banerji says:

> Jitmal or Jaymal, popularly known as Yadusena, embraced Islam, but after some time, reverted to his ancestral religion. This fickle-minded man again embraced Islam and after the death of his father, occupied the throne under the name of Jalāluddīn.[192]

It was in this background that Ekanātha (1533-99) wrote a unique *bhāruḍ* (drama-poem) titled *Hindu-Turk-Saṁvāda.* The saint-poet appears as an interlocutor between the two debaters — the Turk and the Hindu, and his address at the very outset sets the tone for this poem:

> *The goal is one, the ways of worship are different,*
> *Listen to the dialogue between these two,*
> *The Turk calls the Hindu* kāfir,
> *The Hindu answers — "I will be polluted, get away!"*
> *A quarrel broke out between the two*
> *A great controversy began.*[193]

Both the debaters — the Turk and the Hindu — make allegations and counter-allegation of the religious and sectarian practices of each other. But their disagreements eventually culminate into an agreement — that there are fundamental unities and each tradition must be respected in its distinctiveness.

> *Hindu:* *The brāhmaṇa says O yes Swāmi*
> *As a matter of fact you and I are one,*
> *This controversy grew over caste and* dharma
> *When we go to God, there are no such things,*
>
> *Turk:* *this is the truth,*
> *For God there is no caste,*
> *There is not separation between the devotee and the God*
> *Even though the prophet has said — the God is hidden.*[194]

---

[192] Sures Chandra Banerji, 2004, *Sanskrit Culture of Bengal*, p. 7.

[193] Elleanor Zelliot, 1982, op. cit., p. 64.

[194] Ibid., p. 76.

Ekanātha's other *bhāruḍs* include dialogue between a brāhmaṇa and a *mahār*, between a brāhmaṇa and a dog, or words spoken my fortune tellers, untouchables, snake-charmers, prostitutes, etc.[195]

Dabistān-e-mazahib, a Persian text by unknown author, presents debates and dialogues between various faiths; it was written in seventeenth century under the patronage of Akbar. The text also gives a glimpse of debates and discussions held in the court of Akbar (1542–1605). The authorship of this work has remained a subject of much controversy. It is divided in twelve chapters named as *tālīms*. Each *tālīm* is again divided into several *naẓar*s (views). The first *tālīm* takes into account the faiths and beliefs of Parsis and Iranis, especially of Zoroastrianism, in fifteen *naẓar*s. It is also possible that the author of this work was a follower of the Parsi religion. He describes the tenets of this religion, its prophets and saints and major texts, including several sects and communities within it. The second *tālīm* is concerned with Hinduism. It is comprised of twelve *naẓars*. The author introduces the basic principles of Hindu religions and also compares it with Zoroastrianism. In the second *naẓar* of this *tālīm* he describes the theories of creation according to Purāṇas. He also provides details of the geography and *avatāra*s (incarnations) according to *Bhāgavata Purāṇa*. He supports idol worship because of its symbolism. The third *naẓar* deals with the Smārta view. It describes sixteen *saṁskāra*s, the Vedas and the Smārta *karmas*. Vedānta is dealt within the fourth *naẓar*. The author not only describes major texts and philosophers, he also enumerates many interesting stories as *dṛṣṭānta*s (illustrations). The fifth and sixth *naẓar*s deal with Sāṁkhya and Yoga systems and the seventh and eighth with the Vaiṣṇavas and Śāktas, respectively. The Cārvākas are taken up in the ninth. The sect of *tyāgī*s is described in the tenth *naẓar*. The eleventh presents the Buddhist philosophy and the twelfth one takes notice of diverse faiths and philosophies.

The third *tālīm* describes a Karāvatī sect, the fourth ones deals with Judaism. The author has referred to the original texts and

---

[195] Elleanor Zelliot, 1982, op. cit., p. 65.

has even translated the first chapter of *Tauret*. In the fifth *tālīm* on Christianity, the author has presented the life and acts of Christ as well as the beliefs and practices of the Christians. The sixth *tālīm* introduces Islam. The differences between the Sunnīs and the Śiyās are enumerated and the twelve sects under Śiyā are described. The seventh *tālīm* is on the Sādiks. It describes the tenets of the Ismāilīs and those who believe Ali as the God. The ninth *tālīm* is related to the tenets of Vāhidiyā and Vāyajīd. The tenth *tālīm* on *Dīn-e-Ilāhī*, propagated by Akbar, forms the core of this work. Akbar is described as Ḳhalīftullāh or the representative or the Prophet. It is comprised of four *naẓar*s, in which the author describes the birth of the Prophet, the debates organized and presided over by him, his divine attributes and finally his message. The eleventh *tālīm* discusses diverse faiths. The last *tālīm* is concerned with Sufism.

The tenth *tālīm* also furnishes the first-hand account of the debates held in the court of Emperor Akbar. In the first debate brings out a very bitter fight between the Sunnīs and Śiyās. The author says that he has presented this debate at the instance of the adherents of both these orders and he only intends to examine the truth of each. The Śiyā scholar argued that the Sunnīs are non-religious because they do not consider the Prophet Mohammad infallible, and they treat him like a ordinary human being. The follower of Zudaism interferes here to support the Śiyā. But then the Śiyā also enters into an argument with him and establishes that the present scripture of the Zudaism is but an interpolation. He also narrates the tragic episode of Mohammad not being given material for writing to enable him to frame his will and declare his daughter and the son-in-law as his inheritors and illegal seize of the land belonging to Fātimā, his daughter by Abu Bakr. Sunnī gives a rejoinder here by pointing out that the prophets do not declare a will. Śiyā then accuses the Sunnī of character assassination of the Nabī by the way of making him dance to please his wife Ayesha. He describes various illegal acts of the previous *khalifā*s and the glory of Ali. The Śiyā and the Sunnī appear to be daggers drawn at each other and the Emperor Akbar orders for their being taken out. Next the debate of a Christian scholar with a Muslim is described. The former says that no Prophet named Mohammad is described in his scriptures, and cites the Christ having said that many untruthful persons will come after me claiming the prophethood, but they should not be believed in. On the contrary, the followers of Islam already regard Christ as a Prophet. Replying these allegations the Muslim alleges that the Christian texts have been tampered with. Upon which the Christian asks him whether he is in possession of the untampered texts, eliciting a negative answer from the later. Why don't you respect the Christ just as we respect Musa? — he then asks the Muslim. The Muslim starts describing the miracles performed by Mohammad. The Christian retorts by saying that if such miracles happened, they should have been referred in the history books of all faiths. The followers of some other faiths then are called for to give an attestation to the miracle of the Mohammad, which they promptly deny. The debate between a Zew and a Christian is then taken up. The Zew asked his opponent whether there occurs any reference to Christ in Touret. The Christian in his reply pointed out that it is the text of his opponent that describes the birth of Christ from a maiden. The Zew said — Mariam is not described in our text as a virgin, she was already married to Yousuf. The Christian retored — this is true, but he had not even touched Mariam". The Zew then shouted — how can you prove that? The Christain fell silent. In the next episode a wise person confronts with the representatives of various faiths — Hinduism, Islam, Christianity, Judaism, etc. taken all together. The wise man challenged the validity of the prophethood of the prophets of all these faiths citing the following grounds — a prophet must always speak logical things, he should be civilized and not an oppressor. Musa killed his own foster mother by drowning her in the river, it is not correct to say that the river did not make a way for her. Christ had allowed killing of the animals and Musa was involved in looting. In this way the wise man found fault with all the prophets and decried them. Replying to him, the followers of various faiths started recounting the miracles performed by the respective prophets. The wise man pointed out the inner contradictions in their narratives and found fault with Hindu *avatāras* of Rāma, Kṛṣṇa, etc. also. In the end the text describes the new faith being proposed by Akbar.

Padmanābha Miśra wrote *Kaṇādarahasyam*, an exposition of *Vaiśeṣikasūtras* of Kaṇāda in vs 1640 (CE 1583). He discussed the prima facie views of other systems and refuted them according to the theories of the Vaiśeṣika system.[196]

Dara Shikoh was born in 1625 after the Emperor Shah-e-Jahan offered a *mannat* at the shrine of Khwaja Moinuddin Chishti at Ajmer and remained deeply steeped in the discourses of *pīrs* and *faqīrs* belonging to Sufism. He was trained in Islamic lore by Latif Sultanpuri, Miran Shekh, Ajhamad Dehalvi and others. The discourses of Sufi saint Miyan Mir Dehalvi and Bābā Lāldās Bairāgī, a Kabīrpanthī *sādhu*, made great impact on his mind. He was mercilessly butchered in 1659.

The Reconciliation

At the age of 42, five years before his untimely demise, Dara Shikoh had completed *Samudrasaṅgama* — translation of his Persian work *Mazm-ul-Baharain* into Sanskrit. *Sirr-e-Akbar*, comprises his translations of fifty-two Upaniṣads into Persian. In *Samudrasaṅgama* he envisaged the bridges across two powerful streams of ideologies and created a synthesis of Sufi traditions of Islam and Upaniṣadic philosophy. "I have called this text as *Samudrasaṅgama* because it is a confluence of two seas of knowledge" he says in the beginning (*jnānyor dvayar api matasamudrayor iha saṅgama iti ca asya nāma ca asthāpayaṁ — Samudrasaṅgama* I.2). There are twenty sections in *Samudrasaṅgama* covering comparative studies between Vedāntic

196 Walkhaede Bhupendra has made a study of this unpublished work in "Padmanābhaviracitakaṇādarahasyamiti Pāṇḍulipeḥ Samīkṣaṇaṁ", Abstracts of 16th World Sanskrit Conference, Bangkok, p. 480.

concepts and Islamic view with regard to the five elements, sense-organs (*indriyas*), meditation, qualities of God, concept of soul and its relations with God, concept of creation, concept of light (*nūra*), realization of God, names of God and other terms related to Him, the concept of *siddhas*, concepts of time and space, earth and its localities as described in both the traditions, other worlds, the cosmos, concept of *pralaya* (dissolution) and the concept of *mokṣa*. After juxtaposing the theories on these categories in Vedic and Islamic thoughts and analysing them in contrast to each other, Dara opines that only terms and definitions differ, the fundamentals do not. He sees *ekavākyatā* (unity) and says that those who find difference between these two are devoid of wisdom (*bhedavādinastu kuṇṭhitamatayaḥ*). The sufis to Dara are Aikātmyavādins (advocates of unity between the two traditions).

There are differences on the border lines which Dara minutely notes. For example in Islamic philosophy there are five types of inner organs whereas the Vedic view upholds four types of *antaḥkaraṇas*.

In fact, *Samudrasaṅgama* is a condensation of ideas Dara had developed after prolonged discussions with *maulavīs*, *pīrs*, *faqīrs*, scholars like Paṇḍitarāja Jagannātha, saints like Bābā Lāldās Bairāgī and others. He calls the philosophy thus developed by him as Satyaikātmatāvāda (true monism). He refers to the scholars of Hinduism as *paripūrṇa vaidikas*. There are records of seven dialogues between him and the saint Bābā Lāldās whom he has described as *caitanyasvarūpa-jñānamūrti* in his *Samudrasaṅgama*. These dialogues with Bābā Lāldās were recorded by Ray Jadhav Das and Chandrabhan Brahman, who was a scholar of Persian and Sanskrit. He helped in rendering these texts into Persian. Translation of fifty-two Upaniṣads in his *Sirr-e-Akbar* was aimed at building the bridges between diverse philosophical traditions and creating an understanding of the Asian spirit and philosophy. At the same time, he must have had a political angle as the heir apparent — he wanted to translate his vision of Asian culture as well, by the way of inculcating his ideas in the socio-political system.

Dara sees certain obvious equations between Vedānta and Islam. The five elements *ākāśa, vāyu, tejas, jala* and *pṛthvī* are named as *unsūre ālam, vāda, ātaśa, āba* and *ṣoka* in Islamic philosophy and in the same way they are supposed to be the material causes of the universe. By creating hermeneutics, Dara further develops the concept of *ākāśa*, which is of three types — *bhūtākāśa*, *cidākāśa* and *cittākāśa*. The former envelops all material, the second envelops the cosmos and the third one is the Ultimate Reality. In the same way Dara locates affinities to finding out the similarities in terms for sense-organs and the subjects of the sense-organs (*tanmātras*). He based his critique on *Bṛhadāraṇyaka Upaniṣad*, *Yogavāsiṣṭha* and *Vedāntaratna-mañjūṣā*. The presiding deities of the three *guṇas* (*sattva, rajas* and *tamas*) are Brahmā, Viṣṇu and Śiva and they are equated with Jibariāla, Mikaila and Īsarāphīla in Islamic concepts. The concepts of *jīvātman* and *paramātman* have their counterparts in Islamic traditions as *rūhajūjaī* and *rūhakulī. Rūha-e-Azam* is the Supreme God. He produces Sanskrit translation of Koran IV.35 to support the contention that Almighty God can be seen. In the same way the idea of *mukti* (salvation) also gets new dimensions through hermeneutics.[197]

Mazm-ul-Baharain, the Persian original of *Samudrasaṅgama,* made an everlasting impact on world thought. Within 100 years of its composition, it was translated into Arabic.

Dara Shikoh was not alone in visualizing the harmony and meeting grounds between diverse faiths. Parallel to verbal duals or clashes in debates there were stalwarts seeking resolution of differences and envisaging a unifying approach. A series of Cāturmatasāmarasya works (on the harmony between four tenets) continued with this approach. Appayya Dīkṣita authored *Nayamañjarī, Nayamayūkhamālā, Nayamaṇimālā* and *Nayamuktāvalī*.

---

[197] For further details see my paper (Tripathi 2008) "Life and Philosophy of Dara Shikoh" in *Glory of Sanskrit Tradition*, vol. I, pp. 71-76.

These four texts by him taken together are called *Adhikaraṇasāra*. Madhusūdana Sarasvatī also worked with a holistic perspective. The tradition of Sāmarasya-texts has continued till the recent times in the works of Polaga Rama Shastri and Lakshmipuram Shrinivasacharya.

Mahānirvāṇatantra, a text marking the beginnings of modern Indian philosophy, was created at the end of this phase between 1775–1875, by unknown author/authors, most probably in Bengal. It is different from *Nirvāṇatantra* and could be a revised version of a Buddhist text recast in Vedāntic garb.[198] Sures Chandra Banerji suggests that the entire text is a fabrication by Hariharānandanātha, preceptor of Raja Rammohun Roy (1772–1833), as it reflects the reformist views and the first edition of the text was brought out by Ādi Brahma Samāj, which was founded by Roy.[199]

Deviating from the earlier Tantras and tāntric cults, *Mahānirvāṇatantra* specifies the method of *brahma-dīkṣā* as the best form of initiation. The following topics have been dealt it in the fourteen *ullāsa*s (chapters) — liberation, meditation, Supreme *Brahman*, meditating upon the *parā-prakṛti*, rescuing the *mantra*s and purifying the *tattvas*, etc., *śrīcakra* and *homacakra,* the *kavaca*s (protecting spells) and the concept of *kula, varṇāśramācāradharma* (duties of different castes), *kuśaṇḍikā* (the pedestral for *havana*) and ten secraments, *śrāddha* and *abhiṣeka* rites, *prāyaścitta* (expiation rites), *vyavahāra* (legal matters), *vāstu* and *grahayāga*, establishment of *śivaliṅga* and four kinds of *avadhūta*s (ascetics). It makes a unique synthesis of Vedic ritualism with tantric Śaivism and prescribes two types of *sandhyās* — *vaidikī* and *tāntrikī*; differing on the type of *upāsanā.* It also preserves the chanting of *brahma-mantra*, and *gāyatrī-japa.*[200]

In fact, this Tantra seeks to envisage a new social order by

---

[198] S.C. Banerji, 2004, op. cit., p. 89.

[199] Ibid.

[200] *Mahānirvāṇatantra* VIII.76-77.

synthesizing Vedāntic and Śaivite world-views, the Upaniṣadic philosophy and reformist social thoughts, the Tantra and Smṛti, the Śākta monotheism and the cult of Durgā, Mahāvidyā and Lakṣmī. It also advocates a balanced and precautionary use of five *makāras* — *madya* (wine), *māṁsa* (meat), *matsya* (fish), *mudrā* (parched cereals) and *maithuna* (sexual union — normally with one's wife) for the members of the *cakra* (circle), warning against their misuse.[201] The initiation in Tantra leads to the annihilation of caste, but caste system is to be accepted before the initiation. *Mahānirvāṇatantra* even introduces a fifth caste — the *sāmānya* — or the common class formed by the mixture of all castes and both śūdras and the members of the fifth *sāmānya* caste to perform the rites prescribed in the Āgamas to.[202] In this way, it leads to a demolition of the caste system itself. It also authorizes all the five *varṇas* to get initiation as *avadhūtas*.[203] There are ideas providing the glimpses of the dawn of a new age — admonition against any brutality against one's wife[204] and recommendation on women education, etc.[205] *Dāna* (charity), according to *Mahānirvāṇatantra,* is the best practice leading to all kinds of *siddhis* in the age of Kali, but only the poor person engaged in good deeds is eligible to be the beneficiary of charity.[206]

Mahānirvāṇatantra is a law book for modern men, culling out essentials from various Smṛtis, Tantra texts and even

---

[201] विवाहो भैरवीचक्रे तत्त्वचक्रेऽपि पार्वति।
सर्वथा साधकेन्द्रेण कर्तव्यः शैववर्त्मना।।
बिना परिणयं वीरः शक्तिसेवां समाचरन्
परस्त्रीगामिनां पापं प्रापनुयान्नात्र संशयः।। — *Mahānirvāṇatantra* VIII.177-78

[202] Ibid. VIII.80.

[203] Ibid. VIII.224.

[204] न भार्यां ताडयेत् क्वापि मातृवत् पालयेत् सदा।
न त्यजेत् घोरकष्टेऽपि यदि साध्वी पतिव्रता।। — Ibid. VIII.39

[205] S.C. Banerji, *Sanskrit Culture of Bengal*, pp. 89-93.

[206] कलौ दानं महेशानि सर्वसिद्धिकरं भवेत्।
तत्पात्रं केवलं ज्ञेयो दरिद्रः सत्क्रियान्वितः।। — Ibid. VIII.95

Śrīmadbhagavadgītā. Rabindranath Tagore had been studying *Mahānirvāṇatantra* and he has cited some of its verses in his writings.[207]

With the arrival of the East India Company and the beginning of the Oriental studies, debates assume political overtones. This is being taken up here in Chap. 6.

[207] *Mahānirvāṇatantra*, p. 402.

3

Vādaśāstra
The Theories of Debate, Dialogues and Discussions

THE profundity of the debates in the areas of philosophy, *dharma* (ethics and law) and Āyurveda, etc. led to the theoretical discussion on *vāda*, and a conceptual universe of Vādaśāstra was thus created. A theoretical framework on the art of debates had been evolved in the Vedic period. Besides documenting some of the most profound debates in their times, the Vedic texts also present a few technical terms and key concepts related to this discipline. The terms like *yukti, tarka, smṛti, pratyakṣa,* and *aitihya* are used in the Brāhmaṇas, Āraṇyakas and Upaniṣads.[1]

Theory of Vāda in Mahābhārata

Mahābhārata presents the first authentic exposition on the theory of debate through the discourse of Sulabhā which has been referred in the previous chapter. This discourse can be termed as "a conversation about how to converse well".[2] Sulabhā enumerates eighteen blemishes of speech which corrupt the wisdom. Of these, nine belong to the structure and stylistics of the discourse and nine to intent of the interlocutor. They are as under:

The flaws of expression:

- *Gurvarthasaṁyuktam* (verboseness),
- *Parāñmukhasukham* (not easy to understand),

---

[1] Solomon, 1976, *Indian Dialectics*, vol. I, p. 24.

[2] Chakrabarti and Bandhyopadhyaya (eds.), 2014, *Mahābhārata Now*, p. 246.

- *Anṛtam* (false),
- *Trivargeṇa viruddham* (flouting the human ends — *dharma*, *artha* and *kāma*)
- *Asaṁsakṛtam* (uncultured/ungrammatical)
- *Nyūnam* (laconic),
- *Kaṣṭam* (full of strained phrases),
- *Vikramābhihataṁ* (full of words reflecting arrogance),
- *Śeṣam* (incomplete), and
- *Niṣkāraṇaṁ* (unreasonable)

Nine flaws of intent pertain to making a statement out of *kāma* (lust), *krodha* (rage), *bhaya* (fear), *lobha* (greed), *dainya* (self-pity), *anāryatva* (disgrace), *hrī* (bashfulness), *anukrośa* (pity) and *māna* (ego).[3]

These are the virtues which the speech imbibes when free from these blemishes:

- *Anapetārthatā* (wholeness),
- *Abhinnārthatā* (coherence),
- *Nyāyārthatā* (judiciousness),
- *Anyūnādhikya* (conciseness),
- *Ślakṣaṇatā* (grace), and
- *Asandigdhatā* (being free from doubt),

A sentence not corrupted by the blemishes as above is replenished by eighteen qualities.

During the course of a discussions in the assembly of intellectuals, the statements made by the interlocutors should reflect the five qualities — *saukṣmya* (minuteness), *sāṁkhya* (enumeration of qualities and blemishes), *krama* (order), *nirṇaya* (conclusion) and *prayojana* (purpose, motif). The arrangement of the contents in a statement justifying the sequence of their occurrence

---

[3] कामात् क्रोधात् भयाल्लोभात् दैन्याच्चानार्यकात् तथा।
ह्रीतोऽनुक्रोशतो मानान्न वक्ष्यामि कथञ्चन।।

is *krama* (order). *Nirṇaya* (conclusion) relates to the goals of human life. The inclination to control the confluence of sorrows caused by desire and jealousy is *prayojana* (motif).

A sentence should not become cumbersome with too much load of contents. It should be easy to understand, should be true and should not stand against the three aims of life (*dharma, artha* and *kāma*). It should be refined, complete, unhurting, and non-violating any order. It should have proper reasoning and no statement should occur aimlessly.

A discourse is illuminated when the speaker, listener and statement come together in unison. The communication does not develop if the speaker disregards the listener and simply promotes his self interest. On the other hand, if he gives up his own issues and simply promotes the issues of the other, then also his discourse is subjected to doubts and the statement becomes defective. A true speaker therefore takes into account the view of the listener and also puts up his own propositions in a balanced way.[4]

---

[4] नवभिर्नवभिश्चैव दोषैर्वाग्बुद्धिदूषणैः।
अपेतमुपपन्नार्थमष्टादशगुणान्वितम् ।
सौक्ष्म्यं साङ्ख्यक्रमौ चोभौ निर्णयः सप्रयोजनः।।
पञ्चैतान्यर्थजातानि वाक्यमित्युच्यते नृप।।
एषामेकैकशोऽर्थानां सौक्ष्यमादीनां सलक्षणम्
शृणु संसार्यमाणानां पदार्थपदवाक्यतः।।
दोषाणां च गुणानां च प्रमाणं प्रविभागतः।
कञ्चिचदर्थमभिप्रेत्य सा सङ्ख्येत्युपधार्यताम्।
इदं पूर्वमिदं पश्चाद् वक्तव्यं यद् विवक्षितम्।
क्रमयोगं तमप्याहुर्वाक्यं वाक्यविदो जनाः।।
धर्मार्थकाममोक्षेषु प्रतिज्ञाय विशेषतः।
इदं तदिति वाक्यान्ते प्रोच्यते स विनिर्णयः।।
इच्छाद्वेषभवैर्दुःखैः प्रकर्षो यत्र जायते।
तत्र सा नृपते वृत्तिस्तत् प्रयोजनमुच्यते।।
तान्येतानि यथोक्तानि सौक्ष्म्यादीनि जनाधिप।
एकार्थसमवेतानि वाक्यं मम निशामय।।
अपेतार्थमभिन्नार्थमव्यावृत्तं न चाधिकम्।
नाश्लक्ष्णं न च सन्दिग्धं वक्ष्यामि परं ततः।।

→

Sulabhā's enumeration of the qualities and blemishes of the speech can be compared to Marcus Tullius Cicero's delineation of the qualities of conversation.[5]

Categorizations related to *vāda* find a mention at a number of places in *Mahābhārata*. The terms like *tarka, jalpa, vitaṇḍā,*

← न गुर्वर्थसंयुक्तं पराङ्मुखसुखं न च।
नानृतं न त्रिवर्गेण विरुद्धं नाप्यसंस्कृतम्।
न न्यूनं कष्टशब्दं वा विक्रमाभिहितं न च।
न शेषमनुकल्पेन निष्कारणमहेतुकम्।
कामात् क्रोधात् भयाल्लोभात् दैन्याच्चानार्यकात् तथा।
ह्रीतोऽनुक्रोशतो मानान्न वक्ष्यामि कथञ्चन।।
वक्ता श्रोता च वाक्यं च यदा त्वविकलं नृप।
सममेति विवक्षायां तदा सोऽर्थः प्रकाशते।।
वक्तव्ये तु यदा वक्ता श्रोतारमवमन्य वै।
स्वार्थमाह परार्थं तत् तदा वाक्यं न रोहति।।
अथ यः स्वार्थमुत्सृत्य परार्थं प्राह मानवः।
विशङ्का जाते तस्मिन् वाक्यं तदपि दोषवत्।
यैस्तु वक्ता द्वयोरर्थमविरुद्धं प्रभाषते।
श्रोतुश्चैवात्मनश्चैव स वक्ता नेतरो नृप।

5 Conversation then, in which the Socratics are the best models, should have these qualities – It should be easy and not in the least dogmatic; it should have spice of wit. And the one who engages in conversation should not debar others from participating in it, as if he is entering upon a private monopoly, but, as in other things so in a general conversation he should think it not unfair for each to have his turn. He should observe, first and foremost, what the subject of conversation is. If it is grave, he should treat it with seriousness, if humorous, with wit. And above all, he should be on watch that his conversation shall not betray some defect in his character. This is most likely to occur, when people in jest or in earnest take delight in making malicious and slanderous statements about the absent, on purpose to injure their reputations. (Cicero, *De Ificiis, XXXVII* (Cicero 1913: 134) quoted by Arindam Chakrabarti (2014) in "Just Words: An Ethics of Conversation in Mahābhārata", in Chakrabarti and Bandhyopadhyaya (eds.) *Mahābhārata Now*, p. 244.)

nirṇaya and pramāṇa, nyāya, anumāna, have been used in this epic in the contexts of argumentation.[6] The concept of *pañcāvayava-vākya* (five-member syllogism) had been developed long before Gautama wrote his *Nyāyasūtra*, as there is a reference to it in *Mahābhārata*.[7]

Vāda and Nyāyadarśana

Even though the tradition of intellectual discourses, debates and discussions was assiduously pursued for more than a millennium, it was the Nyāya philosophy that made it a part of an epistemology within the system. *Nyāyasūtra* of Gautama (sixth-fifth century BCE) discusses the theory of debate in detail. Out of the sixteen *padārthas* (categories) that are supposed to be essential for the discipline of Nyāya, the following fourteen *padārthas* are directly related to debate — *saṁśaya* (doubt), *prayojana* (purpose/motive), *dṛṣṭānta* (illustration/example), *siddhānta* (theory/tenet), *tarka* (argument), *avayava* (members of a syllogism/parts of sentence presenting the thesis), *nirṇaya* (conclusion), *vāda* (conversation), *jalpa* (debate, wrangling), *vitaṇḍā* (cavil), *hetvābhāsa* (fallacy), *chala* (trick/quibbling), *jāti* (legitimate objection/rejoinder) and *nigrahasthāna* (points of capture/checkmates/clinchers); and the remaining two — *pramāṇa* and *prameya* — are indirectly linked with debate.

There are four *pramāṇas* — *pratyakṣa* (perception), *anumāna* (inference), *upamāna* (analogue) and *śabda* (scripture).

The knowledge arising out of sense contact with an object, and which is determinate, unnamable and non-erratic, is *pratyakṣa* (perception). Inference is knowledge preceded by perception and is of three kinds — *pūrvavat* (a priori), *śeṣavat* (a posteriori) and *sāmānyatodṛṣṭa* (commonly seen). A discourse from an authentic source is *śabda* (scriptural authority). Knowledge of an object

---

[6] *Mahābhārata* XIII.90.45, II.33.4, VII.61.13.

[7] See Chap. 1.

through similarity is *upamāna* (analogue).[8]

Of these, *anumāna* (inference) is crucial for sustaining any conversation or debate. It has three cases in relation to *hetu* (reason/cause) — *pakṣa, sapakṣa* and *vipakṣa. Pakṣa* is the thesis case, *sapakṣa* is the observed case in which *hetu* is essentially present, and *vipakṣa* another observed case in which *hetu* is essentially absent. Inference is employed in two ways — for the understanding of one's own self and for the understanding of the other one (a disciple or an opponent in debate). The former is called *svārthānumāna* and the latter *parārthānumāna. Pañcāvayava-vākya* is required for *parārthānumāna.* The five *avayavas,* comprised in five statements, are *pratijñā* (thesis), *hetu* (reason), *dṛṣṭānta* or *udāharaṇa* (illustration), *upanaya* (application) and *nigamana* (conclusion).

The statement of *sādhya* (probandum) is *pratijñā.* The cause or probans for proving the probandum by similarity or dissimilarity is *hetu. Udāharaṇa* is *dṛṣṭānta* having similarity with the probandum. Application of the illustration is *upanaya.* Reaffirming the statement of probandum on the basis of justification from *hetu* and *upanaya* is *nigamana.*[9]

In the well-known instance "there is fire on the mountain, because smoke is arising out of it", the *pañcāvayava-vākya* will be formulated in the following manner:

- There is fire on the mountain — *pratijñā.*
- Because there is smoke arising from its top — *hetu.*
- Wherever there is smoke, there is fire, just as we see it in the kitchen — *dṛṣṭānta.*

---

[8] इन्द्रियार्थसन्निकर्षोत्पन्नं ज्ञानमव्यपदेश्यमव्यभिचारि व्यवसायात्मकं प्रत्यक्षम् तत्पूर्वकं त्रिविधमनुमानं पूर्ववच्छेषवत्सामान्यतोदृष्टं च। प्रसिद्धसाधर्म्यात् साध्यसाधनमुपमानम्। आप्तोपदेशः शब्दः। — *Nyāyasūtra* I.1.4-7

[9] साध्यनिर्देशः प्रतिज्ञा। उदाहरणसाधर्म्यात् साध्याधनं हेतुः। तथा वैधर्म्यात् साध्यसाधनसाधर्म्यात् तद्धर्मभावी दृष्टान्त उदाहरणाम्। तद्विपर्ययाद् विपरीतम् उदाहरणापेक्षस्तथेत्युपसंहारो न तथेति वा साध्यस्य उपनयः। हेत्वपदेशात् प्रतिज्ञायाः पुनर्वचनं निगमनम् । — Ibid. I.1.33-39

- So is on the mountain — *upanaya.*
- Therefore the fire burning on this mountain — *nigamana.*

The enunciation of any *anumāna* is not complete without the five *avayavas*, and in the very first aphorism of his *Nyāyasūtra*, Gautama says that the forms of debate are initiated through the five *avayavas* and the system of thought in Nyāya rests on debates.

Mahāvidyā syllogisms comprising of other members were first formulated by Kulārka Paṇḍita in eleventh century. They were refuted by Vādīndra in his *Mahāvidyāviḍambana* and the system sank into oblivion.[10]

Vyāpti (invariable concomitance) is the rule of unfailing relationship between the cause and its effect. A statement specifying the invariable relation between the proban and the probandum is also called *vyāpti.* Wherever there is smoke, fire is there — this is *vyāpti.* There are two *vyāptis* — *anvaya* and *vyatireka*, the positive concomitance and the negative concomitance.

Saṁśaya (doubt) is an irresolute judgement about the precise character of an object arising from recognition of common properties in many objects, or properties uncommon to any from the conflicting testimony or irregularity of perception and non-perception.[11]

Prayojana is the aim for which the discourse is initiated.[12]

Dṛṣṭānta (illustration) is the statement comprising an example on which both an ordinary person and an expert would have the similarity in understanding.[13] It is used in the five member syllogism as stated above.

---

[10] Solomon, 1976, op. cit., vol. I, 306-37.

[11] समानधर्मोपपत्तेर्विप्रतिपत्तेरुपलब्ध्यनुपलब्ध्यव्यवस्थातश्च विशेषापेक्षो विमर्शः संशयः
— *Nyāyasūtra* I.1.23

[12] यमर्थमधिकृत्य प्रवर्तते तत् प्रयोजनम्। — Ibid. I.1.24

[13] लौकिकपरीक्षकाणां यस्मिन्नर्थे बुद्धिसाम्यं स दृष्टान्तः। — Ibid. I.1.24

Siddhānta (theory) is a position resting on the authority of a certain treatise, a section of a treatise or implication.[14] It is of four types — *sarvatantra siddhānta* (the theory followed by all systems), *pratitantra siddhānta* (theory in the system followed by the proponent not followed by the opponent), *adhikaraṇa siddhānta* (theory in the system followed in a treatise required for the validation of other sections) and *abhyupagama siddhānta* (the theory to be validated).

Tarka (argument/reasoning) is the confutation carried out on ascertaining the real character of an unknown entity by showing the absurdity of all other characters.[15] Incorrect application of *tarka* leads to *tarkābhāsa* (fallacious reasoning). Udayana has propounded five types of blemishes of *tarka* — *ātmāśraya* (self-dependence), *anyonyāśraya* (mutual dependence), *cakraka* (vicious circle), *anavasthā* (infinite regress) and *aniṣṭaprasaṅga* (*reductio ad absurdum*).

Arriving at a decision after hearing both the sides — *pakṣa* and *pratipakṣa* — is *nirṇaya.*[16]

Kathā (conversation) is a generic term for all kinds of debates, discourses and dialogues. *Vāda* (discussion), *jalpa* (debate) and *vitaṇḍā* (cavil) — these are the three forms of *kathā* according to *Nyāyasūtra*. *Jalpa* (debate) is a defence or attack with the aim of winning over the opponent. *Chala* (quibble), *jāti* (objection) and *nigrahasthānas* (clinchers) are essentially employed in it.[17] Mere attack on the opposite side is *vitaṇḍā* (cavil). The proponent in *vitaṇḍā* makes refutations of other systems without ascertaining

---

14 तन्त्राधिकरणाभ्युपगमसंस्थितिः सिद्धान्तः। सर्वतन्त्रप्रतितन्त्राधिकरणाभ्युपग संस्थित्यर्थान्तर-भावात् सर्वतन्त्राविरुद्धस्तन्त्रेऽधिकृतोऽर्थः सर्वतन्त्रसिद्धान्तः। समानतन्त्रसिद्धः परतन्त्रा-सिद्धः प्रतितन्त्रसिद्धान्तः। यत्सिद्धावन्यप्रकरणसिद्धिः स अधिकरणसिद्धान्तः। अपरीक्षिताभ्युपगमात्तद्विशेषपरीक्षणम् अभ्युपगमसिद्धान्तः। — *Nyāyasūtra* I.1.26-31

15 अविज्ञाततत्त्वेऽर्थे कारणोपपत्तितस्तत्त्वज्ञानार्थमूहस्तर्कः। — Ibid. I.1.40

16 विमृश्य पक्षप्रतिपक्षाभ्यामर्थावधारणं निर्णयः। — Ibid. I.1.41

17 यथोक्तोपपन्नश्छलजातिनिग्रहस्थानसाधनोपालम्भो जल्पः। — Ibid. I.2.2

his own position.[18] *Jalpa* is thus a tricky debate whereas *vitaṇḍā* is destructive debate involving scholastic exercise with arguments from one side only. The practitioner of *vitaṇḍā* does not argue for establishing his own theory, but demolishes all the other theories, so that his theory alone remains vindicated. Texts written exclusively in the genre of *vitaṇḍā* have been discussed earlier (see Chap. 2). There are two categories of *vitaṇḍā*. The higher category of *vitaṇḍā* serves its *siddhānta-pakṣa* through refutation of all rival systems. The second category is comprised in the misuse of *vitaṇḍā* just for scholastic exercise. Those who practise this basic form of *vitaṇḍā* are called the *durvaitaṇḍika*s by Śrīharṣa.[19]

Vāda is a pervasive concept. It is defined by Gautama as the conversation between the master and the disciples or between peers involving discussions of friendly nature. Both the sides of a theory are discussed in *vāda* employing five-member syllogism.[20] In his presentation of *Nyāyadarśana*, Haribhadra (sixth century CE) in his *Ṣaḍdarśanasaṁgraha*[21] defines *vāda* in the following way: The means for the practice of discourse between the master and the disciple with taking up positions and counter-positions is *vāda* (discussion).[22]

The gamut of *vāda, jalpa* and *vitaṇḍā* is named as *kathā*. The author of *Tārkikarakṣā* defines *kathā* in the following manner: Expansion of sentences by various speakers deliberating upon a particular topic is *kathā*. It has six and according to some, four

---

18 स्वप्रतिपक्षस्थापनाहीनो वितण्डा। – *Nyāyasūtra* I.2.3

19 *Khaṇḍanakhaṇḍakhādya*, chap. I, p. 12.

20 प्रमाणतर्कसाधनोपालम्भस्सिद्धान्ताविरुद्धः पञ्चावयवोपपन्नः पक्षप्रतिपक्षपरिग्रहो वादः।
— *Nyāyasūtra* I.2.1

21 Doxography is a nineteenth century term made famous by Hermann Diels. The text of doxography presents the views of different philosophers or systems in different chapters.

22 आचार्यशिष्ययोः पक्षप्रतिपक्षपरिग्रहात्।
यः कथाभ्यासहेतुः स्यादसौ वाद उदाहृतः।। – *Ṣaḍdarśanasaṁgraha* II.29

divisions.[23]

In *Milindapañho*, King Milinda asks Monk Nāgasena — "let there be *kathāsallāpa* (discussion and dialogue) between us".

Śaṅkara Miśra in his *Vādivinoda* takes up the following alternate theses with regard to *kathā* and refutes them one by one:

1. Sanātana's theory of a different kind of *vitaṇḍā*, consisting of *tattvabubhutsuvāda*, i.e. exposition of the own theory alone by the proponent and its vilification only by the respondent.
2. The proposition of the author of *Ratnākara*, holding a fourth category of *kathā* in the form of the exploration of the theory of the proponent only.
3. The theory of *kathā* as a unified single form of debate without any categorizations.

Śaṅkara Miśra also discusses the concept and verities of *vipratipatti* (disagreement) in *kathā*.[24]

There are seven regulations of *kathā* as defined in *Tārkikarakṣā*. They are:

- *Nirūpyanirūpakaniyama* — regulations for using signifiers and signs.
- *Kathāviśeṣavyavasthā* — arrangements for special types of debates.
- *Vādiprativādiniyama* — rules for the opponent (*vādī*) and respondent (*prativādī*).
- *Sadasi anuvidheyasamvaraṇa* — codes of conduct for the juries defining scopes for their interference and maintaining restraint by both the head of assembly (*sabhā*) and the juries.

---

23 विचार्यविषयो नानावक्तृ को वाक्यविस्तरः।
कथा, तस्याः षडङ्गानि प्राहुश्चत्वारि केचन।। — *Tārkikarakṣā*, *kārikā* 76, p. 206, quoted by Rajeshwar Shastri Dravid in *Śāstrārthavicārapaddhatiḥ*, *Prakhyā*, vol. III, p. 100

24 *Vādivinoda*, pp. 4-9.

- *Nigrahasthānasāmastya* — deciding the clinchers.
- *Asāmastyodbhāvanapratijñāna* — ascertaining the extent to which the clinchers have been completely/incompletely pointed out.
- *Kathāparyavasānasaṁvittiḥ* — regulating the debate for winding up.

On the other hand, some of the theorists have accepted four divisions. They are — two types of *vādiprativādiniyama* (rules for the opponent and respondent) and two types of *sadasi anuvidheyasamvaraṇa* (codes of conduct for the juries).

Kathaka is a person participating in a *kathā*.

Rajeshwar Shastri says that when a *kathā* is being conducted in the form of a debate, both the participants should be of equal stature in erudition, otherwise the very purpose of *kathā* — dissemination of knowledge in a particular field — will be lost, and due to inequality of the debators, the juries may take a decision without the debate.

The orthodox tradition of Nyāya philosophy regards *vāda* as something sacred. As a *vāda* was supposed invariably to culminate in an understanding of *tattva* (reality), only the teacher and his disciple as well as those engaged in the pursuit of knowledge are entitled to participate in a *vāda*. Organizing an assembly for a *vāda* was supposed to yield merit equal to performance of a *yajña*. The understanding of *tattva* (reality) is said to be of three types — (i) that which imparts the knowledge of the unknown, (ii) that which substantiates the knowledge of the known, and (iii) that which eradicates the doubts.[25]

Gautama has defined five *hetvābhāsas* (fallacies) — *savyabhicāra, viruddha* (contrary), *prakaraṇasama, sādhyasama* and *atītakāla*. The

[25] तत्त्वावसायफलत्वादस्यां वीतरागाणामेव शिष्याचार्यसब्रह्मचारिणामधिकारः। न च विजिगीषूणामित्युक्तं - वीतरागकथेति। . . . अज्ञातज्ञापनम्, ज्ञातस्य स्थिरीकरणम्, संशयनिवर्तनम् इति त्रिविधस्तत्त्वनिर्णयः। — *Śāstrārthavicārapaddhati, Prakhya,* vol. III, p. 101

first occurs when the probans leads to other probandums also. The probans leading to the opposite probandum is *viruddha*. Making probans identical with the probandum is *prakaraṇasama*. Unproved probans is *sādhyasama*. Mistimed statement on the probans is *atītakāla* or *kālātīta*.[26] Other authors in the field of Nyāya have redefined these *hetvābhāsas* as *asiddha* (unproven), *viruddha* (contrary), *anaikāntika* (inconclusive), *satpratipakṣa* (counter-balanced) and *kālātyayāpadiṣṭa* or *bādhita* (contradicted).

Assumption of alternate meaning in the proposition of an opponent is *chala* (cheating). It is of three types — *vāk-chala*, *sāmānya-chala* and *upacāra-chala*. On the basis of the ambiguous use by a speaker, the opponent misconstrues his statement — this is *vāk-chala*. Imagining an impossible situation from a statement describing a possibility is *sāmānya-chala*. *Upacāra-chala* consists of deriving the metaphorical meaning.

An attack or denial of a proposition on the basis of similarity or dissimilarity is *jāti*,[27] so named because it is generated or born instantly. As per *bhāṣya* of Vātsyāyana, *jāti* involves objections on *hetu* (cause). When *hetu* is intended to prove a proposition through the similarity of the example cited, *jāti* proceeds to counter it by producing an example based on dissimilarity and vice versa. Udyotakara however disagrees with the definitions of Gautama and Vātsyāyana with regard to restricting *jāti* to opposing a hypothesis on the basis of similarity or dissimilarity of the example alone. It is like positioning a *wazīr* against a *wazīr* in the game of chess. *Jāti* thus forms a counter-argument exhibiting the futility of the arguments already presented, right argument against the right one and a futile argument against the equally futile one, showing flaws in opponent's argument. Gautama has described twenty-four *jātis* based on:

- Homogeneity (*sādṛṣyasama*)

---

[26] *Nyāyasūtra* I.2.5-9.

[27] Ibid. I.2.18.

- Heterogeneity (*vaidharmyasama*)
- Addition (*utkarṣasama*)
- Deficiency (*apakarṣasama*)
- Uncertainty (*varṇyasama*)
- Certainty (*avarṇyasama*)
- Alternative (*vikalpasama*)
- Probandum (*sādhyasama*)
- Co-presence (*prāptisama*)
- Mutual absence (*aprāptisama*)
- Infinite regress (*prasaṅgasama*)
- Counter-instance (*pratidṛṣṭāntasama*)
- Non-production (*anutpattisama*)
- Doubt (*saṁśayasama*)
- Issue under reference (*prakaraṇasama*)
- Cause (*hetusama*)
- Implication (*arthāpattisama*)
- Non-difference (*aviśeṣasama*)
- Proof (*upapattisama*)
- Apprehension (*upalabdhisama*)
- Non-apprehension (*anupalabdhisama*)
- Evanescence (*anityasama*)
- Eternity (*nityasama*)
- Effect (*kāryasama*).[28]

The knowledge of *jātis* makes a debater to expose the futility of the arguments made by his opponent.

When a refutation of the hypothesis of *vādī* is equally defective, then this yields *ṣaṭpakṣī* (six options). Of the six ways employed in this *ṣaṭpakṣī*, *vādī* and *prativādī* both get three chances each to prove the infallibility of their position. *Vādī* makes a statement, the opponent gives futile rejoinder and the proponent is unable to point out the flaw in this rejoinder. According to Udayana, the debate can be put to an end by the jury here itself, so that there

[28] *Nyāyasūtra* V.1.1.

are only three ways. But the respondent is allowed again to point out that the proponent has not been able to point out his flaw, failing which the proponent again will get one more chance, and then the opponent will be asked to give his view. This makes six presentations all in all. Of these, the first, third and fifth belong to *vādī*, and the second, fourth and sixth belong to *prativādī*.[29]

The concept of *nigrahasthāna* (clincher) is very crucial in the theory and practice of debate. It occurs when one of the debaters gets himself trapped due to his own deficiency.[30] Śrīharṣa in his *Khaṇḍanakhaṇḍakhādya* has used the term *pratidvandīgraha* for the situation when a *vādī* overlooking the defect in his own thesis, starts displaying the same defect in the discourse of his opponent.[31]

In *Gautamīya Nyāya* the following twenty-two *nigrahasthānas* are accepted:

(a) *nigrahasthānas* based on defect in the statement or probans (5):
  - *pratijñāhāni* (loss of thesis)
  - *pratijñāntara* (change of thesis)
  - *pratijñāvirodha* (contradicting one's own thesis)
  - *pratijñāsaṁnyāsa* (abandonment of thesis)
  - *hetvantara* (shifting the reason)

(b) *nigrahasthānas* based on defective syntax and semantics (4):
  - *arthāntara* (digression)
  - *nirarthaka* (gibberish)
  - *avijñātārtha* (incomprehensible speech)
  - *apārthaka* (nonsensical)

(c) *nigrahasthānas* based on wrong formulation of thesis (3):

---

[29] *Nyāyasūtra* V.1.39-43.

[30] Ibid. I.2.10-19.

[31] *Khaṇḍanakhaṇḍakhādya*, *vṛtti* on I.5, p. 37.

- *aprāptakāla* (reversal of order of five-member syllogism)
- *nyūna* (omission of one or more steps)
- *adhika* (addition of steps not required)

(d) *nigrahasthāna* based on repetition (1):
- *punarukta* (repetition)

(e) *nigrahasthānas* arising out of inconsistency (4):
- *anuvāda* (reiterating)
- *arthapunarukta* (repetition of contents)
- *ananubhāṣaṇa* (silence)
- *ajñāta* (lack of intelligence)

(f) *nigrahasthānas* with acceptance of one's own defective proposition (3):
- *apratibhā* (incapability to respond)
- *vikṣepa* (dispension, making excuses)
- *matānujñā* (allowance to the view of the opponent by saying that this defect lies in your statement also)

(g) *nigrahasthānas* based on inner contradiction (2):
- *paryanuyojyopekṣaṇa* (neglecting the one's own defeat or objections raised on it)
- *niranuyojyānuyoga* (inadvertent proclamation of the defeat of the opponent by the disputant himself).

Caraka on the Theory of Vāda

The discussions on the theory of *vāda* and cultivation of the methodology related to it was not confined to Nyāya system of philosophy alone, nor was it the prerogative of philosophers only. Theory and practice of *vāda* were taken up by authors in the field of other disciplines like Āyurveda, Arthaśāstra and Dharmaśāstra also. Each text defines it own parameters of the theoretical discussion.

The extensive treatment of the concept of *vāda* and its techniques by Caraka in his *Caraka Saṁhitā* has led a modern scholar of philosophy like S.N. Dasgupta to suggest that in Indian philosophy "dialectic emerged from discussions of Āyurveda physicians". E.A. Solomon rightly disagrees with this view. To quote her:

> We may not so far as to give all the credit to the Āyurveda-physicians, but we can certainly say that we have evidence that the school of Yājñika-Mīmāṁsakas and the medical school through their discussions and disputes contributed considerably to the field of logic and dialectic.[32]

According to Caraka, the whole discourse in his text is delivered through four sections/segments: *tantra* (text), *sthāna* (section), *adhyāya* (chapters) and *praśna* (queries and their answers) by the *pravaktṛ*s (spokesmen/proponents) of this *śāstra*. The themes are to be explained in brief and in detail through the five stages of *pratijñā, hetu, udāharaṇa, upanaya* and *nigamana*, so that the discussion is made comprehensible for all the three types of disciples — brilliant, average and dull.[33] Caraka has also given the model of questions and answers that can proceed between a *guru* and his *śiṣya* of this *śāstra*.[34] He has used the term *sambhāṣā* (conversation) instead of *kathā* (discussion). Themes for discussions or questions between two *vaidya*s have also been defined by Caraka. They comprise of a group of eight categories — *tantra* (treatise or the text), *tantrārtha* (contents of the text), *sthāna* (sections in the text), *sthānārtha* (contents of the sections), *adhyāya* (chapters), *adhyāyārtha* (contents of the chapters), *praśna* (topics) and *praśnārtha* (contents of the topics).[35]

---

[32] Solomon, 1976, op. cit., vol. I, p. 12.

[33] तत्रायुर्वेदविदस्तन्त्रस्थानाध्यायप्रश्नानां पृथक्त्वेन वाक्यार्थशोऽर्थावयवशश्च प्रवक्तारो मन्तव्याः। तत्राह - कथं तन्त्रादीनि वाक्यशो वाक्यार्थशोऽर्थावयवशश्चोक्तानि भवन्तीति। अत्रोच्यते - तन्त्रमार्षं कार्त्स्न्येन यथाम्नायमुच्यमानं वाक्यशो भवत्युक्तम्। बुद्ध्या सम्यगनुप्रविश्यार्थतत्त्वं वाग्भिर्व्याससमासप्रतिज्ञाहेतूदाहरणोपनयनिगमनयुक्ताभिस्त्रिविधशिष्यबुद्धिगम्याभिरुच्यमानं वाक्यार्थशो भवत्युक्तम्। तन्त्रनियतानामर्थदुर्गाणां पुनर्विभावनैरुक्तमर्थावयवशो भवत्युक्तम्। — *Caraka Saṁhitā*, Sūtrasthāna, 30.16-19

[34] Ibid. 30.20.

[35] Ibid. Sūtrasthāna, 30.30.

Through the theory of *vāda,* Caraka has reformulated the epistemology for Āyurveda. He has also developed a theory of *vāda* as applicable to his discipline and calls it *bhiṣagvāda* (debates between the physicians).[36] He also gives a clear directive to his fellow physicians — all the discussions or dialogues that they carry with their colleagues should pertain to Āyurveda only and not to other disciplines.[37] Here, *pratyakṣa* (perception) is not cited as the first valid means of knowledge, it is *āptopadeśa* which is the first *pramāṇa.*[38] The concept of *āpta* also differs. *Āpta*s to Caraka are the knowledgeable ones who have perfect memory of the *śāstra* and can give a discourse on it in an unambiguous way without any partiality and prejudice.[39]

Debates between the practitioners of Āyurveda were assiduously cultivated and were regarded as essential for a healthy growth of the discipline itself. Caraka regards the employment of debating techniques to defeat the designs of the pseudo-*vaidyas*. He equates such *vaidya*s to wolves terrorizing poor folks who are like weak animals. The knowledgeable *vaidya* should assert himself as an *āpta* (authority on the subject) so that he appears as a wolf for dispelling the appearances of the ignorant one. A *vaidya* knowing nothing but boasting of his expertise should be confronted with eight questions pertaining to the fundamentals of the discipline. In the course of the debate his adversary who is feigning to be a great *vaidya* then is exposed like a *babhru* or *nakula* (mongoose) covered by his woollen hair. The knowledgeable *vaidya* should carry on a hostile debate to such a fake practitioner. A *vaidya* should face the challenge in the debate and should not tolerate pedantry and misconstrued notions.

---

[36] *Caraka Saṁhitā*, Vimānasthāna, IV.27.

[37] वादस्तु खलु भिषजां प्रवर्तमानो प्रवर्तेतायुर्वेद एव, नान्यत्र।

— Ibid. VIII.66

[38] त्रिविधं खलु रोगविशेषविज्ञानं भवति। तद्यथा — आप्तोपदेशः, प्रत्यक्षम्, अनुमानं चेति।

— Ibid. IV.3

[39] Ibid. IV.4.

A debate is necessary for revelation of true knowledge in the field of Āyurveda. A true *vaidya* would carry *sadvāda* (fair debate) and would put an end to *Asadvāda* (unfair debate). Through the real debate, the *āpta* (authentic expert) is recognized. *Ānāptas* (non-authorities) start boasting of their knowledge and become rude out of hypocrisy. They are actually *dūṣakas* (revilers) of the *śāstra.* One should avoid them and approach the real *vaidyas* to arrive at true knowledge of the *śāstra.*[40]

After describing the pedagogy and methods of teaching Āyurveda in chap. IV (VIII in some other editions) of Vimānasthāna in his text, Caraka discusses the theory of debate in detail. The debate between physicians encourages the pursuit of knowledge and its advancement provides expertise, improves the art of oratory, illuminates fame, provides opportunity to remove doubts with reference to what was listened earlier by listening to it again with the removal of the doubts; it inculcates decisiveness and introduces new ideas hitherto unknown. Sometimes the teacher reveals the secrets of his discipline before a disciple with whom he may be pleased, but he also reveals these secrets in the course of a discussion with an opponent out of the desire of winning the debate. Therefore the experts recommend that a physician should enter into debates only with those physicians who are adept in their field.

---

[40] पृच्छातन्त्राद् यथाम्नायं विधिना प्रश्न उच्यते। प्रश्नार्थो युक्तिमांस्तस्य तन्त्रेणैवार्थनिश्चयः।। निरुक्तं तन्त्रणात् तन्त्रं स्थानमर्थप्रतिष्ठया। अधिकृत्यार्थमध्यायनामसंज्ञाप्रतिष्ठिता।। इति सर्वं यथाप्रश्नमष्टकं सम्प्रकाशितम्। कार्त्स्न्येन चोक्तस्तन्त्रस्य सङ्ग्रहः सुविनिश्चितः।। पशुः पशूनां दौर्बल्यात् कश्चिन्मध्ये वृकायते। स सत्यं वृत्तमासाद्य प्रकृतिं भजते पशुः।। तद्वदज्ञोऽज्ञमध्यस्थः कश्चिन्मौखर्यसाधनः। स्थापयत्याप्तमात्मानमाप्तं त्वासाद्य भिद्यते।। बभ्रुर्गूढ इवोर्णाभिरबुद्धिरबहुश्रुतः। किं वै वक्ष्यति सञ्जल्पे कुण्डभेदी जडो यथा।। सद्वृत्तैर्न विगृह्णीयाद् भिषगल्पश्रुतैरपि। हन्यात् प्रश्नाष्टकेनादावितरांस्त्वाप्तमानिनः।। दम्भिनो मुखराः ह्यज्ञाः प्रभूताबद्धभाषिणः। प्रायः प्रायेण सुमुखाः सन्तो युक्ताल्पभाषिणः। तत्त्वज्ञानप्रकाशार्थमहङ्कारमनाश्रितः। स्वल्पाधाराज्ञमुखरान् मर्षयेन्न विवादिनः।।
परो भूतेष्वनुक्रोशस्तत्त्वज्ञाने परा दया। येषां तेषामसद्वादनिग्रहे निरता मतिः।। असत्पक्षाक्षणि-त्वार्तिदम्भपारुष्यसाधनाः। भवन्त्यनाप्ताः स्वे तन्त्रे प्रायः परविकत्थकाः। तान् कालपाशसदृशान् वर्जयेच्छास्त्रदूषकान्। प्रशमज्ञानविज्ञानपूर्णाः सेव्या भिषक्तमाः।। — *Caraka Saṁhitā*, Sūtrasthāna, 30.69-83

The debate is of two types from the point of view of purpose — *sandhāya saṁbhāṣā* (friendly debate) and *vigrāhya saṁbhāṣā* (hostile debate). The former is conducted with a spirit of coordination. The latter is aggressive and involves disputes. Caraka has also used the term *anuloma sambhāṣā* for the friendly debate.[41]

The friendly debate is held with a learned and knowledgeable *vaidya* who is able to express himself well and is prompt in responding; is not irritable and jealous; is ready to be convinced and able to convince others; can take pains in carrying out the discussion and is endearing in speech. In the course of a discussion being carried out with such a *vaidya*, one should talk to him without reservations, should ask him questions without hesitation and upon his raising any query, should tell him in an elaborate manner. He should not be detracted by the fear of defeat in the debate, should not rejoice at winning a debate, should not boast before others, should not be obsessed with his own stand, should not explain things which are unknown, should be perfectly convincing with humility and maintain restraint. This is the way *anuloma sambhāṣā*s (friendly discussions are conducted).

On the other hand, one should enter into a hostile debate with a fake physician, considering himself superior to his adversary. Before proceeding to make rejoinders, he should examine the difference between his speech and the speech of the opponent, difference between himself and the other one, and also the qualities of the juries. Proper examination gives an understanding when one should initiate the discussion and when he should wind it up.

---

41 सम्भाषाविधिमत ऊर्ध्वं व्याख्यास्यामः - भिषक् भिषजा सह सम्भाषेत। तद्विद्यसम्भाषा हि ज्ञानाभियोगसंहर्षकरी भवति, वैशारद्यमपि चाभिनिवर्तयति, वचनशक्तिमपि चाधत्ते, यशश्चाभिदीपयति, पूर्वश्रुते च सन्देहवतः पुनः पुनः श्रवणाच्छ्रुतसंशयमपकर्षति, श्रुते चासन्देहवतो भूयो भूयोऽध्यवसायमभिनिवर्तयति, अश्रुतमपि कञ्चिदर्थं श्रोत्रविषयमापादयति, यच्चाचाचार्यः शिष्याय शुश्रूषवे प्रसन्नः क्रमेणोपदिशति गुह्याभिमतमर्थजातं तत् परस्परेण सह जल्पन् पिण्डेन विजिगीषुराह संहर्षात् - तस्मात् तद्विद्यसम्भाषामभिप्रशंसन्ति कुशलाः। द्विधा तु खलु तद्विद्यसम्भाषा भवति - सन्धायसम्भाषा विगृह्यसम्भाषा च। — *Caraka Saṁhitā*, Vimānasthāna, IV.15-16 in Priyavrata Sharma's edn VIII.

Hence the experts recommend proper examination. When making such an examination, one should also examine the merits and demerits of the speaker in a proper way, viz. — his knowledge, understanding, retention, brilliance and eloquence — these are the merits. The demerits are — irritability, lack of skill, cowardice, lack of retention and unawareness. One should compare the advantages and disadvantages in respect of these merits and demerits.[42]

In accordance with these merits or demerits, the opponent may be of three types — superior, inferior or equal.[43]

The assembly of experts or juries is of two types — learned or ignorant. From other point of view, it is of three types — friendly, neutral and prejudiced. Before a prejudiced assembly, even if it is a congregation of learned and knowledgeable ones, one should not carry discussion. But if the assembly consists of friendly or neutral persons, one should carry on discussion with his opponent whether he is ignorant or knowledgeable one. In discussions with such an opponent, a *vaidya* is advised to use long incomprehensible sentences loaded with aphorisms, to ridicule the opponent again and again with movements of hands before the gathering and

---

[42] तत्र ज्ञानविज्ञानवचनप्रतिवचनशक्तिसम्पन्नेनाकोपनेनानुपस्कृतविद्येनानसूयकेनानुनेयेनानुनय-कोविदेन क्लेशक्षमेण प्रियसम्भाषणेन च सह सन्धयसम्भाषा विधीयते। तथाविधेन सह कथयन् विस्रब्धः कथयेत्, पृच्छेदपि च विस्रब्धः, पृच्छते चास्मै विस्रब्धाय विशदमर्थं ब्रूयात्, न च निग्रहभयादुद्विजेत, निगृह्य चैनं न हृष्येत, न च परेषु विकत्थेत, न च मोहादेकान्तग्राही स्यात्, न चाविदितमर्थमनुवर्णयेत्, सम्यक् चानुनयेनानुनयेत्, तत्र चावहितः स्यात् इत्यनुलोमसम्भाषा विधिः।

अत ऊर्ध्वमितरेण सह विग्रहसम्भाषायां जल्पेच्छ्रेयसा योगमात्मनः पश्यन्। प्रागेव च जल्पाज्जल्पान्तरं परावरान्तरं परिषद्विशेषांश्च सम्यक् परीक्षेत। सम्यक् परीक्षा हि बुद्धिमतां कार्यप्रवृत्तिनिवृत्तिकालौ शंसति, तस्मात् परीक्षामभिप्रशंसन्ति कुशलाः। परीक्षमाणस्तु खलु परावरान्तरमिमान् जल्पकगुणाञ् श्रेयस्करान् दोषवतश्च परीक्षेत सम्यक्, तद्यथा - श्रुतं विज्ञानं धारणं, प्रतिभानं वचनशक्तिरिति, एतान् गुणान् श्रेयस्करानाहुः, इमान् पुनर्दोषवतः, तद्यथा - कोपनत्वमवैशारद्यं भीरुत्वमधारणत्वमनवहितत्वमिति। एतान् गुणान् गुरुलाघवतः परस्य चैवात्मनस्तुल्येत्। — *Caraka Saṁhitā*, Vimānasthāna, IV.17-18

[43] तत्र त्रिविधः परः सम्पद्यते - प्रवरः, प्रत्यवरः, समो वा, गुणविनिक्षेपतः, न त्वेव कार्त्स्न्येन। — Ibid. IV.19

not allow him to speak and while using difficult words and seeing the opponent at the loss of words, he should say why are you not speaking now? Or should tell him, in an assertive way, that your propositions do not stand. He should tease him by saying:

> You should learn for one more year, it seems that you have not learned under an able *guru*. The opponent even when defeated for once only, should be taken as defeated and should not be entertained again. Some say that this very method can be applied for discussions with a superior one, but Caraka recommends that confrontation with a superior *vaidya* is not desirable.[44]

A hostile debate with a person who is inferior in knowledge or with the one who may be a peer can be conducted before a friendly assembly. If the assembly consists of neutral persons, who are attentive, prompt in listening, and equipped with knowledge, comprehension and retention; are able to respond through speech and give a rejoinder; one should carefully weigh the merits as well as the strong and weak points of the opponent. If he finds the opponent superior, he should avoid debate without apparently exhibiting the discontinuance. But where he finds the opponent inferior, he should overpower him there (on the weak points). And these are the means to subdue the inferior opponents quickly — he should overpower the opponent having no knowledge of the text by long citations

---

[44] परिषत्तु खलु द्विविधा - ज्ञानवती, मूढ़परिषच्च। सैव द्विविधा सती त्रिविधा पुनरनेन कारणविभागेन-सुहृत्परिषत्, उदासीनपरिषत्, प्रतिनिविष्टपरिषच्चेति। तत्र प्रतिनिविष्टायां परिषदि ज्ञानविज्ञानवचनप्रतिवचनशक्तिसम्पन्नायां मूढ़ायां वा न कथञ्चित् केनचित् सह जल्पो विधीयते, मूढायां तु सुहृत्परिषद्युदासीनायां वा ज्ञानविज्ञानवचनप्रतिवचनशक्तीनित-रेणाप्यदीप्तयशसा महाजनविद्विष्टेनापि सह जल्पो विधीयते। तद्विधेन च सह कथयता आविद्धदीर्घसूत्रसङ्कुलैर्वाक्यदण्डकैः कथयितव्यम्, अतिहृष्टं मुहुर्मुहुरुपहसता परं निरूपयता पर्षदमाकारैर्ब्रुवतश्चास्य वाक्यावकाशो न देयः, कष्टशब्दं च ब्रुवता वक्तव्यो नोच्यते, अथवा पुनर्हीना ते प्रतिज्ञा इति। पुनश्चाहूयमानः प्रतिवक्तव्यः - परिसंवत्सरो भवान् शिक्षस्व तावत्, न त्वया गुरुरुपासितो नूनं, अथवा पर्याप्तमेतावत्ते, सकृदपि न परिक्षेपकं निहतं निहतमाहुरिति नास्य योगः कर्तव्यः कथञ्चित्। अप्येवं श्रेयसा सह विगृह्य वक्तव्यमित्याहुरेके, नत्वेवं ज्यायसा सह विग्रहं प्रशंसन्ति कुशलाः। — *Caraka Saṁhitā*, Vimānasthāna, IV.20

from the text; the opponent weak in comprehension by producing long and difficult sentences; the opponent weak in retention of the sentences by cluster of sentences making complicated structure; the unintelligent opponent by speaking a sentence with more than one meanings; the opponent lacking in power of speech by intercepting when he has uttered half of the sentence; the unskilled opponent by putting him in an embarrassing situation; the irritant opponent by teasing; if the opponent is a coward then by terrorizing him; if he is not attentive, then by controlling him. Thus by these means one should subdue an inferior opponent quickly.[45]

In a hostile debate, one should always stick to logic. A position once adopted should not be relinquished. One should keep the fact in mind that the hostile debate sometimes creates enmity in some persons. If a person really gets angry in the hostile debate, he can cross limits in action and speech. The experts do not recommend real quarrel in the assembly of noble persons.[46]

Prior to the start of the debate, one can do some planning. If the assembly of judges is friendly, he should get such a topic selected in which he is well-versed, or that which may be difficult for his opponent. Or the opponent can be assigned the uneasy side of the

---

45 प्रत्यवरेण तु सह समानाभिमतेन वा विगृह्य जल्पता सुहृत्परिषदि कथयितव्यम्, अथवाऽप्युदासीनपरिषद्यवधानश्रवणज्ञानविज्ञानोपधारणवचनप्रतिवचनशक्तिसम्पन्नायां कथयता चावहितेन परस्य साद्गुण्यदोषबलमवेक्षितव्यम्, समवेक्ष्य च यत्रैनं श्रेष्ठं मन्येत नास्य तत्र जल्पं योजयेदनाविष्कृतमयोगं कुर्वन्, यत्र त्वेनमवरं मन्येत, तत्रैवेनमाशु निगृह्णीयात्। अत्र खल्विमे प्रत्यवराणामाशु निग्रहे भवन्त्युपायाः, तद्यथा – श्रुतहीनं महता सूत्रपाठेनाभिभवेत्, विज्ञानहीनं पुनः कष्टशब्देन वाक्येन, वाक्यधारणहीनमाविद्धदीर्घसूत्रसङ्कुलैर्वाक्यदण्डकैः प्रतिभाहीनं पुनर्वचनेनैकविधेनानैकार्थवाचिना, वचनहीनशक्तिमर्धोक्तस्य वाक्यस्याक्षेपेण, अविशारदमपत्रपेण, कोपनमायासनेन, भीरुं वित्रासनेन, अनवहितं नियमेनेति। एवमेतैरुपायैः परमभिभवेच्छ्रीघ्रम्। — *Caraka Saṁhitā*, Vimānasthāna, IV.21

46 तत्र श्लौकौ –
विगृह्य कथयेद्युक्त्या युक्तं च न निवारयेत्।
विगृह्य भाषा तीव्रं हि केषाञ्चिद् द्रोहमावहेत्।।
नाकार्यमस्ति क्रुद्धस्य नावाच्यमस्ति विद्यते।
कुशला नाभिनन्दन्ति कलहं समितौ सताम्।। — Ibid. IV.22-23

theme of the debate. After making these arrangements, he should say these are learned experts, it is improper for us to say anything in their presence, the assembly of learned juries itself will decide the norms and guidelines as they deem fit and desire to decide. Having said this he should sit quiet.

The norms for winning or losing a debate can be like this — the debaters will use such and such terms, they will not use such and such terms, and either of them speaking in such and such way will be declared defeated and so on.[47]

After this Caraka produces a long list of technical terms with which the participants in a debate should be well-acquainted.[48] Out of the forty categories cited by him, the following are in addition to the ones defined by Gautama: *drava, guṇa, karma, sāmānya, viśeṣa, samavāya, sthāpanā, pratiṣṭhāpanā, uttara, aitihya, aupamya, jijñāsā, vyavasāya, arthaprāpti, sambhava, anuyojya, ananuyojya, anuyoga, pratyanuyoga, vākyadoṣa* and *vākyapraśaṁsā*. *Siddhānta* is included in sixteen *padārthas* (universal categories) of *Nyāyadarśana*. Some of his terms like *atītakāla, upalambha, parihāra, pratijñāhāni, abhyanujñā, hetvantara* and *arthāntara* cited here by Caraka are included in the *nigrahasthānas* and whereas some others may fall under the *hetvābhāsas* (fallacies). He has used the term *ahetu* for fallacious

---

[47] प्रागेव तावदिदं कर्तुं यतेत – सन्धाय पर्षदाऽयमनभूतमात्मनः प्रकरणमादेशयितव्यम्, यद्वा परस्य भृशदुर्गं स्यात्, पक्षमथवा परस्य भृशं विमुखमानयेत्, परिषदि चोपसंहितायां शक्यमस्माभिर्वक्तुम्, एषैव ते परिषद् यथेष्टं यथायोगं यथाभिप्रायं वादं वादमर्यादां वा स्थापयिष्यतीत्युक्त्वा तूष्णीमासीत।

तत्रेदं वादमर्यादालक्षणं भवति – इदं वाच्यम्, इदमवाच्यम्, एवं पराजितो भवतीति।

— *Caraka Saṁhitā*, Vimānasthāna, IV.25-26

[48] इमानि तु खलु पदानि भिषग्वादमार्गज्ञानार्थमधिगम्यानि भवन्ति, तद्यथा – वादः, द्रव्यं, गुणाः, कर्म, सामान्यं, विशेषः, समवायः, प्रतिज्ञा, स्थापना, प्रतिष्ठापना, हेतुः, दृष्टान्तः, उपनयः, निगमनम्, उत्तरम्, सिद्धान्तः, शब्दः, प्रत्यक्षम्, अनुमानम्, ऐतिह्यम्, औपम्यम्, संशयः, प्रयोजनम्, सव्यभिचारं, जिज्ञासा, व्यवसायः, अर्थप्राप्तिः, सम्भवः, अनुयोज्यम्, अननुयोज्यम्, अनुयोगः, प्रत्यनुयोगः, वाक्यदोषः, वाक्यप्रशंसा, छलम्, अहेतु, अतीतकालम्, उपालम्भः, परिहारः, प्रतिज्ञाहानिः, अभ्यनुज्ञा, हेत्वन्तरम्, अर्थान्तरम्, निग्रहस्थानमिति।
— Ibid. IV.27

reason and has defined here three types of *ahetus*: *prakaraṇasama*, *saṁśayasama* and *varṇyasama*.

Six out of this whole gamut — *dravya, guṇa, karma, sāmānya, viśeṣa* and *samavāya* — relate to universal categories of Vaiśeṣika philosophy and Caraka has described them at the very outset of his text (in Sūtrasthāna) in the context of the cosmogony.[49]

He follows Vaiśeṣika closely here, but differs with Gautama to a considerable extent. It is Caraka who actually understands the term *vāda* in the sense of a formal or proper debate, where one party differs with the other and each adopts a position as per their system of thought or discipline. Instead of grouping *jalpa* and *vitaṇḍā* as types of *kathā* (discussion) Caraka defines these two as types of *vāda*.[50]

Caraka has added two more categories — *sthāpanā* and *pratiṣṭhāpanā* — after *pratijñā* (proposition). The statement of probandum is *pratijñā*. *Sthāpanā* involves the other four categories of the five-member syllogism for substantiating the *pratijñā*. *Pratiṣṭhāpanā* is the counter-proposition reversing the proposition of the opponent. Caraka has reformulated the concept of *hetu* (probans). That which leads to the attainment of the probandum is *hetu*, and it is a resultant of four *pramāṇas* — *pratyakṣa*, *anumāna*, *aitihya* and *upamāna*.[51] There is slight difference in his concept of

---

49 द्रव्यगुणकर्मसामान्यविशेषसमवायाः स्वलक्षणैः श्लोकस्थाने पूर्वमुक्ताः। — *Caraka Saṁhitā*, Vimānasthāna, IV.29

50 तत्र वादो नाम स यत्र परेण शास्त्रपूर्वकं विगृह्य कथयति। स च द्विविधाः सङ्ग्रहेण – जल्पः, वितण्डा च। तत्र पक्षाश्रितयोर्वचनं जल्पः, जल्पविपर्ययो वितण्डा। यथा एकस्य पक्षः पुनर्भवोऽस्तीति, नास्तीत्यपरस्य। तौ च स्वस्वपक्षहेतुभिः स्वस्वपक्षं स्थापयतः, परपक्षमुद्भावयतः एष जल्पः। जल्पविपर्ययो वितण्डा। वितण्डा नाम परपक्षे दोषवचनमात्रमेव।। — Ibid. IV.28

51 अथ प्रतिज्ञा – प्रतिज्ञा नाम साध्यवचनम् यथा – नित्यः पुरुष इति। अथ स्थापना। स्थापना नाम तस्या एव प्रतिज्ञाया हेतुदृष्टान्तोपनयनिगमनैः स्थापना। — Ibid. IV.30-31
अथ प्रतिष्ठापना। प्रतिष्ठापना नाम या तस्या एव परप्रतिज्ञाया विपरीर्थतास्थापना। यथा अनित्यः पुरुष इति अथ हेतुः। हेतुर्नामोपलब्धिकारणम्, तत् प्रत्यक्षम्, अनुमानम्, ऐतिह्यम्, →

dṛṣṭānta, *upanaya* and *nigamana* also. A *dṛṣṭānta* should be intelligible to fools and scholars alike, and *upanaya* as well as *nigamana* are to be seen in the context of *sthāpanā* and *pratiṣṭhāpanā*.[52] *Uttara* is a rejoinder. If the proponent explains *hetu* on the basis of similarities, the opponent would explain the same on the basis of dissimilarities. For example, if a patient is suffering from *śītavyādhi* (flu), the proponent would say that the causes of this disease are contact with chill air in winter. The opponent would reply — the same causes, i.e. the contact with chill air, etc. would function as favourable when one is suffering from heat.[53] In Gautama's system, this category is incorporated in the treatment on *jāti*.

Caraka's concepts of *siddhānta, aupamya, saṁśaya* and *prayojana* are very much in affinity with their counterparts in Nyāya,[54] while his *savyabhicāra* is treated as a *hetvābhāsa* in Nyāya. His treatment of *śabda*, *pratyakṣa* and *anumāna* also follows the Nyāya system.[55] He defines *aitihya* as *āptopadeśa* (advice from ancient reliable source).[56] This is treated as a category separate from *śabda-pramāṇa*, because *śabda-pramāṇa* to Caraka lies in the statements of reliable

---

← औपम्यमिति, एभिर्हेतुभिर्यदुपलभ्यते तत् तत्त्वम्।। — *Caraka Saṁhitā*, Vimānasthāna, IV.33

52 अथ दृष्टान्तः। दृष्टान्तो नाम यत्र मूर्खविदुषां बुद्धिसाम्यं यो वर्ण्यं वर्णयति। उपनयो निगमनं चोक्तं स्थापनाप्रतिष्ठापनाव्याख्यायाम्। — Ibid. IV.35

53 अथोत्तरम्। उत्तरं नाम साधर्म्योपदिष्टे हेतौ वैधर्म्यवचनं, वैधर्म्योपदिष्टे वा हेतौ साधर्म्यवचनम्। यथा - हेतुसधर्माणो विकाराः, शीतकस्य हि व्याधेर्हेतुभिः साधर्म्यं हिमशिशिरवातसंस्पर्शाः इति ब्रवुतः परो ब्रूयात् - हेतुविधर्माणो विकाराः यथा शरीरावयवानां दाहौष्ण्यकोथप्रपचने हेतुवैधर्म्यं हिमशिशिरवातसंस्पर्शा इति। एतत् सविपर्ययमुत्तरम् ।
द्रव्यगुणकर्मसामान्यविशेषसमवायाः स्वलक्षणैः श्लोकस्थाने पूर्वमुक्ताः।
— Ibid. IV.29, 36

54 अथ सिद्धान्तः। सिद्धान्तो नाम यः परीक्षकैर्बहुविधं परीक्ष्य हेतुभिः साधयित्वा स्थाप्यते निर्णयः। स चतुर्विधः सर्वतन्त्रसिद्धान्तः, प्रतितन्त्रसिद्धान्तः, अधिकरणसिद्धान्तः, अभ्युपगमसिद्धान्तश्चेति। . . . अभ्युपगमसिद्धान्तो नाम स यमर्थमसिद्धमपरीक्षितमनुपदिष्टम-हेतुकं वा वादकालेऽभ्युपगच्छन्ति भिषजः। — Ibid. IV.37

55 Ibid. IV.38-40.

56 अथैतिह्यम् - ऐतिह्यं नाम आप्तोपदेशो वेदादिः। — Ibid. IV.41

physicians. *Jijñāsā* is a typical category in Caraka's discourse. It is like diagnosis. The advice given after examining a patient is *jijñāsā.*[57] *Vyavasāya* is decision.[58] *Arthaprāpti* (implication) is like the *arthāpatti* in Māmāṁsā, *sambhava* (origination), *anuyojya* (questionable statement), *ananuyojya* (unquestionable statement), *anuyoga* (question) and *pratyanuyoga* (counter-question) are other categories, according to Caraka, to be utilized in debate.[59]

He has discussed five *vākya-doṣas* (blemishes of a sentence) — *nyūna* (laconic), *adhika* (having excess of words, etc.), *anarthaka* (senseless), *apārthaka* (misleading) and *viruddha* (contradictory). The reversal of these yields five *vākyaprasaṁśās* — *anyūna, anadhika, arthavat, anapārthaka* and *aviruddddha.* Caraka perhaps is indebted to Sulabhā's categorizations of good and bad conversations as discussed in *Mahābhārata.*

Chala has been defined by Caraka as mere verbosity full of deceit and pseudo-meanings. Examples are given from Āyurvedic debates. He defines two types of *chala* only – *vāk-chala* and *sāmānya-chala*, and omits *upacāra-chala.*[60] The categories like *atītakāla* are repeated here and they are taken up as *nigrahasthānas* also. Caraka has used the term *ahetu* for *hetvābhāsa. Ahetu* is of three types — *prakaraṇasama, saṁśayasama* and *varṇyasama. Upālambha* is remonstration. *Parihāra* is retribution of the defect. *Pratijñāhāni* and *abhyanujñā* are also defined as *nigrahasthas* in *Nyāyasūtra. Hetvantara* is referred to a defective cause instead of the cause in the context. *Arthāntara* is digression.

Caraka defines *nigrahasthāna* as the occasion of defeat. He cites the following *nigrahasthānas* — *triḥ abhihitasya aparijñānam*

---

57 जिज्ञासा नाम परीक्षा यथा भेषजपरीक्षोत्तरकालमुपदेक्ष्यते। — *Caraka Saṁhitā*, Vimānasthāna, IV.46

58 व्यवसायो नाम निश्चयः। — Ibid. IV.47

59 Ibid. IV.48-52.

60 अथ छलम्। छलं नाम परिशठमर्थाभासमनर्थकं वाग्वस्तुमात्रमेव। तद्विविधम् - वाक्छलम्, सामान्यच्छलं च। — Ibid. IV.56

(inability to understand even when a proposition is repeated thrice), *ananuyojyānuyogaḥ* (asking a question not to be asked), *anuyojyasya ananuyogaḥ* (not asking a question that ought to have been asked), *pratijñāhaniḥ* (loss of statement), *abhyanujñā, kālātītavacana, ahetu, nyūna, adhika, vyartha, punarukta, viruddha, hetvantara* and *arthāntara.*[61]

In the terminology of Dharmakīrti, *sandhāya saṁbhāṣā* (friendly debate) and *vigrāhya saṁbhāṣā* (hostile debate) are known as *tattvabubhutsuvāda* (debate with the desire to seek the truth) and *vijigīṣuvāda* (debate with the desire for winning).

Asaṅga on the Types of Vāda

Next to Gautama and Caraka, Asaṅga (around fourth century CE) discussed the concepts and categories of debate in a most elaborate way in his *Yogācārabhūmi* and *Abhidharmasamuccaya.* He used the term *hetuvidyā* for logic and defined it as "perception at hand by reason of careful consideration".[62]

---

[61] अथाहेतुः। अहेतुर्नाम प्रकरणसमः, संशयसमः, वर्ण्यसमश्चेति। अथातीतकालम् अतीतकालं नाम यत् पूर्वं वाच्यं तत् पश्चादुच्यते, तत् कालातीतत्वादग्राह्य भवति। पूर्वं वा निग्रहप्राप्तमनिगृह्य परिगृह्य पक्षान्तरितं पश्चान्निगृहीते तत् तस्यातीतकालत्वान्निगृहवचनमसमर्थं भवतीति। अथोपालम्भः। उपालम्भो नाम हेतोर्दोषवचनम्, यथा पूर्वमहेतवो हेत्वाभासा व्याख्याताः। अथ परिहारः। परिहारो नाम तस्यैव दोषवचनस्य परिहरणम्।
अर्थान्तरम् - अर्थान्तरं नामैकस्मिन् वक्तव्येऽपरं यदाह। यथा ज्वरलक्षणे वाच्ये प्रमेहलक्षणमाह। अथ निग्रहस्थानम् निग्रहस्थानं नाम पराजयप्राप्तिः। त्रिरभिहितस्य अपरिज्ञानम्, अननुयोज्यस्यानुयोगोऽनुयोज्यस्याननुयोगः, प्रतिज्ञाहानिः, अभ्यनुज्ञा, कालातीतवचतनम्, अहेतुः, न्यूनम्, अधिकम्, व्यर्थम्, अनर्थकम्, पुररुक्तम्, विरुद्धम्, हेत्वन्तरम्, अर्थान्तरं च निग्रहस्थानम्। वादस्तु खलु भिषजां प्रवर्तमानो प्रवर्तेतायुर्वेद एव नान्यत्र। अत्र हि वाक्यप्रतिवाक्यविस्तराः केवलाश्चोपपत्तयः सर्वाधिकरणेषु। ताः सर्वाः समवेक्ष्यावेक्ष्य च सर्वं वाक्यं ब्रूयात्, नाप्रकृतशास्त्रमपरीक्षितमसाधकमाकुलमव्यापकं वा। सर्वं च हेतुमद् ब्रूयात्। हेतुमन्तो ह्यकलुषाः सर्व एव वादविग्रहाश्चिकित्सिते कारणभूताः, प्रशस्तबुद्धिवर्धकत्वात्, सर्वारम्भसिद्धिं ह्यवहत्यानुपहता बुद्धिः।। — *Caraka Saṁhitā*, Vimānasthāna, IV.58-67

[62] A. Wayman, 1958, "The Rules of Debate according to Asaṅga", *Journal of American Oriental Society*, 78: 31.

Asaṅga defined six kinds of *vāda* — (i) *vāda* (utterance in general), (ii) *pravāda* (worldly declarations), (iii) *vivāda* (quarrels), (iv) *apavāda* (rebukes), (v) *anuvāda* (consistency of remarks), and (vi) *avavāda* (precepts, guidelines).[63]

On the basis of *pratijñā* (thesis) *vāda* is of two kinds — *svabhāva* (*vāda* of intrinsic nature) and *viśeṣa* (*vāda* of particular nature). On the basis of *hetu* it is of eight kinds — (i) *pratijñā* (upholding the thesis), (ii) *hetu* (giving the reason), (iii) *udāharaṇa* (example), (iv) *sārūpya* (similarity of example), (v) *vairūpya* (dissimilarity of example), (vi) *pratyakṣa* (right perception), (vii) *anumāna* (inference), and (viii) *āptāgama* (concluding with reference to the authorities).

All in all, this makes ten kinds of *vāda*. Asaṅga has expanded *pañcāvayava-vākya* (five-member syllogism) as defined in *Nyāyasūtra* to make these ten types. But he has further elaborated upon the varieties based on similarity and dissimilarity of the examples. There are five varieties based on *sādṛśya* (similarity) — *liṅgasādṛśya, svabhāvasādṛśya, karmasādṛśya, dharmasādṛśya* and *hetuphalasādṛśya*. Asaṅga has extensively dealt with the varieties of *pratyakṣa* (perception) which do not generally come in practical use. His treatment of *vādālaṁkāra* (adequacies of debate) is noteworthy. He describes five types of *vādālaṁkāras*: *svaparasamayajñāna* (the debaters have knowledge of their own and other's systems), (ii) *vākkaraṇasampannatā* (they are equipped with the accomplishment in oratory), (iii) *vaiśāradya* (they are skilful), (iv) *sthairya* (they are firm), and (v) *dākṣiṇya* (they are generous). Under *vākkaraṇasampannatā*, Asaṅga enumerates five *guṇas* (qualities) and nine *ākārās* (gestures). The five *guṇas* are *agramyatā* (being non-rustic), *laghutā* (being at ease), *tejasvitā* (brilliance), *sambaddhatā* (coherence) and *svārthatā* (meaningfulness). The nine gestures are *anākula* (remaining undisturbed), *asaṁrabdha* (not exhibiting violence), *gamaka* (communicability), *mita* (being precise), *arthayukta* (being cogent), *kālana* (maintaining time),

[63] Wayman, 1958, op. cit., p. 32.

sthira (sticking to the point), *dīpta* (illumination of speech, clarity) and *prabaddha* (continuity). The concept of surrender by one of the debaters (*kathātyaya*) is very significant in Asaṅga, in the Nyāya traditions it has not been taken into account independently. Asaṅga takes a detailed note of it in his treatment of *vādinigraha* (capturing a disputant). If none of the debaters is unable to continue the discussion then it is *kathāsāda*. If there are defects in the debate, they are treated as *vāg-doṣas*. Asaṅga elaborates upon thirteen kinds of surrenders through declaration (*vāg-vijñapti*) — by the way of saying that mine was not good, yours was good, mine was not well-considered, yours was well considered, mine was not cogent, yours was, etc. The blemishes are *ākulavacana* (confused language), *samrambha* (violence), *agamakatva* (incomprehensibility), *amita* (digressions), *akālana* (mistimed), *asthira* (inconsistent), *adīpta* (obscure) and *aprabaddha-vacana* (staggering). A disputant should proceed for debate only after careful consideration of merits and demerits of the assembly and of skills. Knowledge, confidence and ingenuity are the three desired attributes for any debater.[64]

Debate on the Debate: Buddhist Critique of the Naiyāyika

The concept of triple probans prevailed since the time of Gautama. Afterwards, the orthodox Naiyāyikas adopted the idea of sixfold probans adding additional three categories. This model of the probans was rejected by the Buddhists. Dharmakīrti has given considerable space to the refutation of the concept of six types of probans. As a result of his criticism, the later Naiyāyikas readjusted the concept of sixfold probans and accepted five categories of *hetu*.[65]

---

[64] Wayman, 1958, op. cit., pp. 33-37.

[65] Jayanta Bhaṭṭa, Bhāsarvajña and Vācaspati Miśra accepted the following five categorical elements of *hetu* — *pakṣadharmatva* (presence of *hetu* in the thesis case), *sapakṣadharmatva* (its presence in the similar case), *vipakṣavyāvṛtti* (its absence in the dissimilar case), *abādhitaviṣayatva* (validity) and *asatpratipakṣatva* (absence of counter-probans). They deleted the sixth category — *jñātatva* (being known).

The orthodox Naiyāyikas gave the concept of *pañcāvayava-vākya* — the sentence stating the five steps of inference, as elaborated earlier. Both Diṅnāga and Dharmakīrti rejected the concept of *pañcāvayava-vākya*. They emphatically stated that without using the five-member syllogism a *vādī* can prove *sādhya* and all the argument should invariably lead to it and not to any other attribute. For drawing an inference, *pakṣa* and *dṛṣṭānta* these two premises only are sufficient and they make *vyāpti* (invariable concomitance). *Pratijñā* (statement of proposition) and *nigamana* (conclusion) are redundant.[66] Having rejected the structure of *pañcāvayava-vākya,* he also demolishes the sequential order of the five categories there, proposing to abolish the restriction that the probans should be stated first and the instance in the last. He finds any such sequence absurd, because argument can be employed both ways and the aim of causing authentic cognition should be realized, rather than maintenance of an order in the statement of categories.[67] He also holds the use of two *vyāptis* (*anvaya* and *vyatireka* — the positive concomitance and the negative concomitance) as redundant, because one of them naturally implies the other.[68]

The idea that the invariable concomitance can be understood without reliance on examples was elaborated first by the Jainas. It was taken over by Buddhists and became known as Antarvyāptivāda (theory of intrinsic implication of invariable concomitance). Dharmakīrti argues in support of Antarvyāptivāda. He redevelops it through his idea of *sāmarthya,* i.e. the invariable concomitance in itself is capable of leading to the conclusion and out of two types of *vyāptis* one is capable of leading to the other.

The concept of *āpta* (reliable person) has been a contentious issue between the orthodox Naiyāyikas and the Buddhists. Even the

---

66 *Pramāṇavārtika* II.3-4.

67 Ibid. II.5.

68 Ibid. II.6.

system of grammar so scientifically and meticulously cultivated under Pāṇinian tradition relied on *āptas* or *śiṣṭas*. Patañjali states that the usage of *śiṣṭa* (learned) should be accepted as the standard norm. He identifies *śiṣṭas* as "those brāhmaṇas who live in Āryāvarta (the home of *āryas*), whose daily intake of food is the grain only in one little earthen pot, who are not greedy, do not seize upon a cause and are well versed in all the Śāstras (knowledge systems)".

Buddhist logicians like Diṅnāga and Dharmakīrti do not agree with the theory of *parārthānumāna* as postulated by Gautama and his followers. *Parārthānumāna* was also named as *sādhana* by Diṅnāga. *Pakṣa* (thesis), *hetu* (cause or signifying analogy) and *dṛṣṭānta* (instance) — these are the three constituents of *parārthānumāna* according to Diṅnāga. The unsound nature of these three makes three fallacies, called *sādhanābhāsas* by Diṅnāga — *pakṣābhāsa, hetvābhāsa* and *dṛṣṭāntābhāsa.*

Diṅnāga believed that *parārthānumāna* will not be possible if any one of the three elements, i.e. *pakṣa, hetu* and *dṛṣṭānta,* is defective. In the same way he also holds that all of three elements — *pakṣa, sapakṣa* and *vipakṣa* — also form the essential requisites for the inference. Dharmakīrti in his *Nyāyabindu* agrees with Diṅnāga and criticizes the orthodox Naiyāyikas.[69]

The Buddhist logicians differ from orthodox Naiyāyikas as *vāda* to them is not a means for winning the arguments, it is meant to help the opponent in seeing the truth. The conceptual framework for the theory of debate was further substantiated in the discussions on *anumāna* (inference).

Again there is a basic difference between Gautamīya Nyāya and

---

[69] त्रिरूपलिङ्गाख्यानं परार्थानुमानमित्युक्तम्। तत्र त्रयाणामेकस्यापि रूपस्यानुक्तौ साधनाभास उक्तावप्यसिद्धौ सन्देहे वा प्रतिपाद्यप्रतिपादकयोरेकस्य रूपस्य धर्मिसम्बन्धस्यासिद्धौ सन्देहे चासिद्धौ हेत्वाभासः। यथा - अनित्यः शब्द इति साध्ये चाक्षुषत्वमुभयासिद्धम्। चेतनास्तरव इति साध्ये सर्वत्वगपहरणे मरणं प्रतिवाद्यसिद्धं विज्ञानेन्द्रियायुर्निरोधलक्षणस्य मरणस्याभ्युपगमात् तस्य च तरुष्वसम्भवात्। अचेतना सुखादय इति साध्य उत्पत्तिमत्त्वमनित्यत्वं वा सांख्यस्य स्वयंवादिनोऽसिद्धम्। — *Nyāyabindu*, pp. 87-90

Buddhist philosophers with regard to the concept of *nigrahasthāna*. In the former *nigrahasthāna* is defined as a *parājayavastu* (a point of defeat), whereas Dharmakīrti views *nigrahasthāna* as a *parājayādhikaraṇa* (forfeiture of the right to continue debate).

Dharmakīrti has divided *nigrahasthānas* into two categories — *asādhanāṅga-vacana* (non-statement of a constituent proof) and *adoṣodbhāvana* (failure to point out the fault of the opponent). The former belongs to *vādī* (disputant) and the latter to *prativādī* (opponent or defendant). In the former, the digression by the opponent leads to disruption in the debate. Dharmakīrti advises the juries that if the opponent starts employing this malpractice, the debate should be adjourned. *Asādhanāṅga-vacana* would become an occasion of defeat of the disputant only when the opponent points it out, otherwise none of them can be held victorious or defeated just on the basis of the use of *asādhanāṅga-vacana* by the disputant. Dharmakīrti prescribes a gap between the occurrence of *nigrahasthāna* and actual declaration of defeat and in this way has avoided a paradoxical situation which occurs in the framework of Gautamīya Nyāya, viz. if the disputant commits the fault of using a *hetvābhāsa* and the opponent at the same time is guilty of *paryanuyojyopekṣaṇa* — by the way of not pointing out this fault of the disputant, then both of them are to be declared defeated! But this kind of peculiar situation has an occurrence in Dharmakīrti's concept of *adoṣodbhāvana* as well. The inability to point out the defect in presenting *sādhana* (proof) of the disputant is naturally an occasion of defeat of the opponent. This is the first *nigrahasthāna* for the opponent called *adoṣodbhāvana*. But what happens if the disputant points out or fails to point out his opponent's inability to point out his (disputant's) defect? Dharmakīrti says that in either case neither the disputant nor the opponent loses a point, and the debate should be taken up again.

Dharmakīrti rejects *chala* (cheating) and *jātis* as parts of *vāda*, as well as the whole framework of *nigrahasthāna* proposed by Gautama.

Like the parliaments, judicial courts have also functioned as platforms for very lively debates on social, moral and ethical issues. These courts also initiated new techniques and methodologies for discussions and debates. Smṛti texts furnish in depth analysis of these techniques. *Bṛhaspatismṛti* (1.17) lays down four steps of the judicial process involving debate — *pūrva-pakṣa* (petitioners view), (ii) *uttara* (reply by the respondent), (iii) *kriyāpāda* (specifying the action to be taken), and (iv) *nirṇaya* (judgment). Reply under no. (ii) is divided by *Śukrasmṛti* into four categories — *satya* (factual), *mithyā* (false), *pratyavaskandana* and *pūrvavyavahāravidhi*. The first is also named as *pratipatti*. It is the acceptance of the points raised by the petitioner. The second is negation of the points raised by the petitioner. *Pratyavaskandana* is partial acceptance with a view to denounce the case as presented by the petitioner. This is done by adding rejoinders. The fourth involves citations of previous arguments and victory acquired by the respondent in the same or similar cases.

Kauṭilya specifies the arrangements to be made for proper recording of *vāda* or *vyavahāra* (case) brought up in *dharma-sthāna* (court of law). The questions and objections of *vādī* and *prativādī* should be written in proper order.[70]

Kātyāyana (16-40), Bṛhaspati (2.8-9) and Śukra also describe certain defects in the language. Śukra defines these defects as under:

- *anyārthaṁ* (carrying a different meaning)
- *arthahīnaṁ* (without meaning)
- *pramāṇāgamavarjitaṁ* (without proper evidence)
- *hīnāṁ* (laconic)
- *adhikaṁ* (excessive)
- *bhraṣṭaṃ* (corrupt).

Codes for Conducting the Debate

Prāśnika and *sadasya* these two terms have been used for a jury. Diṅnāga says that *prāśnika* (jury) is not supposed to know the

[70] *Arthaśāstra* III.1, vol. II, p. 5.

conclusions being derived by the disputants when a debate is started.[71] Commenting on him, Haribhadra explains — it is not that *prāśnikas* are ignorant, but they do not know the way to support either of the debaters.[72] In his commentary on *Nyāyapraveśakasūtram*, Haribhadra defines *prāśnikas* as "unbiased like a balance which can equally weigh both the debaters, having knowledge of their systems and the systems of others, born in a good family, tolerant, and devoted to debates".[73]

Minimum three juries should be nominated with the consent of both *vādī* and *prativādī*. They should always be in odd numbers.[74] The advantage of having juries in odd numbers lies in felicitating a decision by majority, as odd numbers will eliminate any possibility of a tie.

The concept of jury has cast an impact even on the textual debates. Śaṅkara in his *bhāṣya* on *Praśna Upaniṣad* (VI.2) introduces an imaginary *madhyastha* (impartial arguer) who accepts both the sides.

Holding a debate is treated at par with organizing a *yajña* ritual.[75] The similarity of the structural designs between *yajña* and *vāda* is maintained to a large extent, so that the performers involved in the performance of a *yajña* are called *sadasyas*, the juries deciding the debate in favour of the two disputants are also called *sadasyas*. The *sadasyas*, seven, five or three in number, should be free from prejudices against or any biases in favour of any of the debaters.

---

71 पक्षहेतुदृष्टान्तवचनैर्हि प्राश्निकानामप्रतीतोऽर्थः प्रतिपाद्यते। — *Nyāyapraveśa* l.iv, p. 1

72 ये यथोक्ताः प्राश्निकाः कथं तेषां कश्चिदप्रतीतोऽर्थ इति। उच्यते - न तत्परिज्ञानमङ्गीकृत्य अप्रतीतः। किन्तु वादिप्रतिवादिपक्षपरिग्रहसमर्थनासहस्तदन्तर्गत इत्यतोऽप्रतीतोऽर्थः प्रतिपाद्यते। — *Nyāyapraveśavṛtti of Haribhadra,* on *Nyāyapraveśa*, p. 14

73 स्वसमयपरसमयज्ञाः कुलजाः पक्षद्वयस्थिताः क्षमिणः।
वादपथेष्वभियुक्तास्तुलासमाः प्राश्निकाः प्रोक्ताः।। — Ibid., p. 16

74 *Śāstrārthavicārapaddhatiḥ*, Prakhya, vol. III, p. 99.

75 रागद्वेषविनिर्मुक्ताः सप्त पञ्च त्रयोऽपि वा।
यत्रोपविष्टाः विप्राः स्युः सा यज्ञसदृशी सभा।। — quoted, ibid.

They are also called *vipras* (scholars).

Mallinātha, in his commentary titled *Niṣkaṇṭaka*, says that the juries should submit a written declaration at the end of *kathā*, that they have taken the decision in all fairness.

The head of this assembly is called *sabhāpati*. A *sabhāpati* should be elected with the consent of both the debaters as well as the *sadayas*. He is supposed to declare the result of the debate after the juries have given their verdict.

It seems that the arrangements with regard to *sadasyas* differed with the nature of *kathā* (type of discourse) to be held. The assembly for a *vāda* (discussion) does not require any jury; *vāda* being a dialogue between the teacher and the taught or conversation between persons of like-mindedness. But if by any chance *sadasyas* arrive on the scene, they can be co-opted as juries with the mutual consent of the discussants. This is done with a view to overrule the charge of *kathābhāsa* (a fake discussion). But such infiltrators will not be allowed to decide the terms of reference or *prameya* (topics) for the debate. In *jalpa* (debate) and *vitaṇḍā* (cavil) the situation is different. There the *sadasyas* regulate the terms of reference.

Before the start of *kathā*, both the discussants should agree on their premises. The jury sees to it that none of them has violated these norms. Śrīharṣa says:

> Both the parties in the debate should be made to enter into an agreement before the start of the *kathā* (debate) that the debater who will observe the limits of the rules will win and the one who transgresses these limits will be the loser.[76]

Kauṭilya in his *Arthaśāstra* describes the assemblies in which discussions on political, social or moral issues are held. He issues

---

76 तस्माद् यादृग् व्यवहारनियमः कृतस्तेन मर्यादाऽनेन नोल्लङ्घिता - इति यद् वादिवाग्व्यवहारे मध्यस्थावगमः, स विजयते, यस्य तु वचसि नैवं तस्यावगमस्तस्य पराजयः, यत्र वाग्युक्त-निग्रहसत्त्वावगमः, स निगृहीतः, तदितरस्तु न तथा इत्यादिनियं एव कथारम्भाय ग्राह्यः। —*Khaṇḍanakhaṇḍakhādya*, chap. I, p. 23

guidelines for the royal officer specifying the codes of conduct and maintaining decorum in such assemblies. He should enter the assembly after being permitted by the officer-in-command, should neither sit far away nor very near to his senior officer, should not sit on a seat higher than his senior; should avoid interruption, vulgarity, citations not attested by perception, propositions which are unbelievable or false; should not speak loudly; should not laugh without an occasion, should not break wind or spit. He should also avoid talking with the members, contradicting the view emerging out of consensus, should dress decently.[77]

[77] *Arthaśāstra*, vol. II, pp. 209-10.

4

Vāda in Darśana
Philosophical Debates

Tussle between Action, Knowledge and Devotion

ONE of the recurring themes for debate is the conflict between *karma* (action) and *jñāna* (knowledge). The Indian mind has been occupied with the two opposite ways of *pravṛtti* (empiricism) and *nivṛtti* (renunciation). *Mahābhārata* repeatedly discusses such conflicting views and their resolution (see Chap. 2).

Even within the fold of Advaitins, Śaṅkara is countered by the theorists who hold the Jñānakarmasamuccayavāda (theory of synthesis between knowledge and action). Śaṅkara at least concedes to it as a possibility in his *bhāṣya* on *Kaṭhopaniṣad* (1.17). But then he firmly refutes the synthesis between action and knowledge as his final verdict in his *bhāṣya* on *Taittirīya Upaniṣad* (I.11.4). On the very first aphorism of *Brahmasūtra*, Śaṅkarācārya in his *bhāṣya* raises the question of the non-essentiality of *dharma-jijñāsā* (inquiry in *dharma*) and asserts that it is not a prerequisite for pursuing inquiry into the Ultimate Reality or *Brahman*. *Brahma-jijñāsā* can be acquired even before the acquisition of *dharma*; and that nothing remains to be done after the acquisition of the true knowledge of *Brahman* is the beauty of the Advaita system.[1]

The two divergent views — Kevalajñānavāda and Jñānakarmasamuccayavāda — are linked to the diverse visions of human life. The Kevalajñānavāda upheld by Śaṅkarācārya

---

[1] अलङ्कारो ह्यमस्माकं यद् ब्रह्मावगतौ सत्यां सर्वकर्तव्यताहानिः कृतकृत्यता चेति।
— *Brahmasūtra, Śāṅkarabhāṣya*, p. 19

would lead to the lifestyle of *aikāśramya* (absolute asceticism). Jñānakarmasamuccayavāda on the other hand would support *caturāśramya* or *āśramasamuccaya* (theory of a synthesis of all the four *āśramas*).

Śaṅkara had to dispute with the authors of Dharmaśāstras like Manu who gave the highest status to *gṛhasthāśrama*. Bhāruci, who supported the Jñānakarmasamuccayavāda, flourished two or three centuries before Śaṅkara. G.C. Pande sees an internalization of the conflict between the Brāhmanical and Śramanic traditions in the opposite views of Bhāruci and Śaṅkarācārya.[2] On the other hand, *Gītā* presents a resolution of conflict between *karma*, *jñāna* and *bhakti* before these philosophers.

Śaṅkara again stands against Manu, as the latter allows an honourable space for *kāma* (desire). Desire leads to motivation, and this motivation subsequently will lead to the inclination for performing religious duties. Bhāruci agrees with Manu in giving the highest status to *gṛhasthāśrama*. He permits the option between *aikāśramya* and *caturāśramya* or *āśramasamuccaya*.

The Jñānakarmasamuccayavāda also presupposes the combination for intellectual and practical methods like *upāsanā* and meditation for liberation. Śaṅkara does not find them absolutely desirable.

On the relationship between *karma* and *jñāna* Maṇḍana also holds a position strikingly different from Śaṅkara and Sureśvara.[3] Maṇḍana cites at least seven theories in this connection. Of these, he favours a peculiar variety of *jñānakarmasamuccaya*; whereas Śaṅkara and Sureśvara do not regard performance of ritual as compatible with the knowledge of *Brahman*.

Revisionism

Sāṁkhya stands as a *pradhānamalla* (main combatant) before the

---

[2] G.C. Pande, 1998, *Life and Thought of Śaṅkarācārya*, pp. 233-35.

[3] Ibid., p. 285.

Vedāntin of monist system and the Buddhists as well. In sixteenth century, Vijñānabhikṣu reformulates the whole system of Sāṁkhya and brings it closer to Upaniṣadic thought. *Puruṣa,* according to him, is the sovereign of the whole world (*akhileśvara*) and the agent (*kartā*) of this world.[4] He refers to Seśvara Sāṁkhya.[5] The terminology of *Brahman, ātman* and *ānātman* — which was earlier alien to classical Sāṁkhya, is introduced, the Upaniṣads are cited, and Prakṛti is treated as synonymous to *avidyā, ajā śakti* and *māyā.*[6] Still, Vijñānabhikṣu does not make any compromise with Vedānta and remains unwaveringly offensive for his old rival. He interprets the concept of *dṛṣyatva* (the quality of being seen) in a way very much different from that of Advaitites or even Dvaitavādins. The Vedāntin establishes *ātman* as the seer and the world as to be seen. Vijñānabhikṣu, on the basis of the Upaniṣadic aphorisms, makes even *ātman* as liable to be seen.[7]

Debates between Idealism and Materialism

Cārvāka "may possibly be characterized as primitive proto-materialism".[8] It is the oldest philosophical school in India. It has been a challenge to rest of all philosophical systems emerged during the past three millennia. The philosophy of materialism is discussed in the Upaniṣads. *Bṛhadāraṇyaka Upaniṣad* (IV.12) says:

> The consciousness is generated out of matter and dissolves in the matter, there is no life after death.

---

[4] पुमानेव जगत्कर्ता जगद्भर्ताऽखिलेश्वरः।
स्वाम्यर्थे भृत्यवद् यस्माज्जडवर्गः प्रवर्तते।।
— *Sāṁkhyasāra* of Vijñānabhikṣu, Uttarabhāga V.13, p. 33

[5] Ibid. V.24, p. 34.

[6] प्रकृतिशक्तिरजा प्रधानमव्यक्तं तमो मायाऽविद्येत्यादयः प्रकृतेः पर्यायाः।
— Ibid., Pūrvabhāga, chap. III, p. 9

[7] यत्तु आधुनिका वेदान्तिब्रुवा दृश्यत्वेनैव प्रकृत्यादीनां दृष्ट्रत्वेन च प्रकृत्याद्यखिलजडेभ्य आत्मविवेकं मन्यन्ते . . ., तन्न; आत्मा वा अरे द्रष्टव्यः इत्यादिश्रुतिभिरात्मनोऽपि दृश्यत्वात्, साक्षाद् दृश्यत्वविवक्षया च प्रकृत्यादेरसङ्ग्रहात् करणद्वारेणैव तद्दर्शनात्। — Ibid., p. 7

[8] *Lokāyata*, Introduction, p. xvii.

The Āgama texts of Jaina tradition refer to the Cārvākas as Bhūtavādins or Bhūtacaitanyavādins.[9]

The Cārvāka system is refuted by all other systems and regarded to be one of the toughest rivals.[10] Of all the Indian philosophical systems, this seems to be the most misunderstood and misrepresented one also. Cārvākas are supposed to be licentious and indulging in vandalism.

In fact, Cārvāka is not a single and unified philosophical school. Various groups of Cārvākas have been flourishing in different periods of the history of Indian philosophy for the past two/three millennia. The materialist is one of them. Kṛṣṇa Miśra in his play *Prabodhacandrodaya* presents the materialist Cārvāka's view in a precise way. Accordingly, perception is the only valid means of knowledge; there are four elements — earth, fire, air and water; and consciousness is indivisible with the body. There was another group of Cārvākas that accepted inference also as the second means of knowledge or *pramāṇa*. Sāṁkhya and Vaiśeṣika were also categorized as Cārvākas. The Ājīvaka sect formed one of the strongest of Cārvāka groups (see Chap. 2).

The Cārvākas were known for their debating skills and for centuries had been challenging the other systems which had developed very subtle and intricate categorizations and conceptual frameworks and sufficient textual material. This is very much evidenced by Jayarāśi's text on the deconstruction of all philosophies (see Chap. 2). The Cārvākas excelled in disputation and deconstruction of prevalent theories and norms. The methodology developed by them for disputing with others came to be defined as *vitaṇḍā*. Buddhaghoṣa described Lokāyata as Vitaṇḍāvādaśāstra.

Bṛhaspati is said to be the first preceptor of this philosophy.[11]

---

[9] *Tattavopaplavasiṁha*, Preface by Muni Sukhalalji Singhavi, p. 22.

[10] दुरुच्छेदं हि चार्वाकस्य चेष्टितम्। — *Sarvadarśanasaṁgraha*, chap. I, p. 3.

[11] Kṛṣṇa Miśra's *Prabodhacandrodaya* is being discussed in Chap. 6. The antagonist in this play is the follower of Cārvāka philosophy. →

He is said to have composed the *sūtras* (aphorisms). Some of them are quoted in later works. Max Müller calls Bṛhaspati "a perplexing character".[12] One Bṛhaspati was a Vedic seer. Several hymns in *Ṛgveda* are attributed to him.[13] Bṛhaspati is also a Vedic deity.[14]

In Purāṇic mythology Bṛhaspati is known to be the *guru* of the gods. The identity of Bṛhaspati — the author of *Bārhaspatyasūtra* — and the mythological Bṛhaspati has been mingled in later texts. *Maitrāyaṇī Upaniṣad* says that Bṛhaspati, the *devaguru*, became Śukrācārya and faked a philosophy of materialism to trap the *asuras* (demons) and ensure their defeat.[15] Even Haribhadra, a Jaina philosopher, confirms the story of Bṛhaspati's disguise as Cārvāka.

Jayarāśi, the author of *Tattvopaplavasiṁha*, is a devout Cārvāka, but his voluminous work is only concerned with deconstructing all the systems of philosophy rather then establishing the Cārvāka system.

Cārvāka philosophy developed in three stages. The Cārvākas were initially known as debaters, who undauntedly questioned all prevailing norms. They were nihilists. Subsequently, some

---

← Appreciating the Cārvāka, he says: सर्वथा लोकायतमेव शास्त्रम्, यत्र प्रत्यक्षमेव प्रमाणम्, पृथिव्यप्तेजोवायवस्तत्त्वानि अर्थकामौ पुरुषार्थौ, भूतान्येव चेतयन्ते। नास्ति परलोकः, मृत्युरेवापवर्गः। तदेतदस्मदभिप्रायानुबन्धिना वाचस्पतिना प्रणीय चार्वाकाय समर्पितम्। तेन च शिष्योपशिष्यद्वारेणास्मिंल्लोके बहुलीकृतं तन्त्रम्। — *Prabodhacandrodaya*, Act II, pp. 70-71

12 Max Müller, 1919, *Six Systems of Indian Philosophy*.

13 *Ṛgveda* X.71-72.

14 Ibid. VIII.96.15.

15 बृहस्पतिर्वै शुक्रो भूत्वा इन्द्रस्याभयायासुरेभ्यः क्षयायेमां विद्यामसृजत् तया शिवमशिवमित्यादिसदशिवं शिवमिति वेदादिशास्त्रहिंसकधर्माभिध्यानस्त्विति वदन्ति। — *Maitrāyaṇi Upaniṣad* VII.9. It is said that Bṛhaspati struck Gāyatrī and smashed her head into pieces. Gāyatrī being immortal, every bit of her brain remained alive. Again in *Mahābhārata*, Bṛhaspati is described as a sceptic and has a long discussion with Manu who finally prevails upon him to accept the Vedic order.

of them thought of formulating a system of philosophy, which can be termed as Svabhāvavāda (naturalism). This came in the second stage. At the third stage of the development some sort of epistemology and cosmology came to be introduced. It was at this stage that the philosophers like Ajitakeśakambalin, Purāṇakaśyapa and Kambalāśvatara were associated with the system of Lokāyata. Philosophers like Purandara accepted inference also as a valid means of knowledge. In fact, the Cārvāka came to be understood as an umbrella term incorporating various groups of philosophers who opposed all orthodox philosophies and systems that created dogmas and sects. Lokāyatikas (materialists), Svabhāvavādins (naturalists) and Ucchedavādins (nihilists) — these three major schools under the Cārvākas are taken up for refutation by other philosophies. *Rāmāyaṇa* of Vālmīki is one of the earliest text that mentions the Lokāyatikas (see Chap. 2) who employed the wisdom from Ānvīkṣikī (logic, probably including Sāṁkhya and Yoga also as per the definition given by Kauṭilya — [see Chap. 2]) for misuse. Kumārila Bhaṭṭa has used the word *cārvākamata* in the sense of atheism in general.[16]

In seventh-eighth centuries, the philosophy of Cārvāka was reborn in the form of the Sahajīyā sect. The Sahajīyās regarded love and natural life as the core of the religion. Sarahapā is said to have been the founder of this school. He was born in eastern India at a place called Sarolī in the city of Rājī. He used to listen to the discourses by Amita and developed interest in Buddhist philosophy. There are stories about his having taken wine and the brāhmaṇas in the locality going to the king with a complaint and plea for his banishment. Sarahapā proved his innocence by coming out unscathed in the tests of fire, water, etc. Then onwards he came to be worshipped. Bringing in empiricism in his philosophy

---

16 प्रायेणेव हि मीमांसा लोके लोकायतीकृता। तामास्तिकपथे कर्तुमयं यत्नः कृतो मया।। *Ślokavārttika,* Pratijñāsūtra, X. *Nyāyaratnākara* says — नित्यकर्मणां फलं नास्तीति बह्पसिद्धान्तपरिग्रहेण मीमांसा भर्तृमित्रदिभिर्लोके लोकायतीकृता। — quoted in *Cārvākaṣaṣṭi*, Gagandeo Giri, fn. 1, p. 43

of pure bliss, he said:

> The sprout of mind should be irrigated with the waters of pure bliss revived from the worldly pleasure, otherwise it will not grow as a great tree of *kalpavṛkṣa*.[17]

This is a critique of all systems which are based on *aparigraha* (non-possession) and *saṁnyāsa* (renunciation).

The Sahajīyās stood against renunciation and deliberately renouncing worldly pleasures. It is the *rāga* (attachment to the objects of the world) that binds and it is the *rāga* that liberates — says the author of *Hevajratantra*.[18]

Bengali poet Caṇḍīdāsa was a follower of Sahajīyā school. In his *Dohākośa* Sarahapā refuted all the systems of the orthodox philosophy like Vedānta and Sāṁkhya, and also various systems under Jaina and Buddhist philosophy.

Chiranjib Bhattacharya in his *Vidvanmodataraṅgiṇī* recorded all the views belonging to the schools of non-believers. In twentieth century Dakshina Ranjan Shastri wrote a treatise *Cārvākaṣaṣṭi*.[19]

The texts belonging to the orthodox systems of Indian

---

[17] तनुतरचित्ताङ्कुरको विषयरसैर्यदि न सिच्यते शुद्धैः।
गगनव्यापी फलदः कल्पतरुत्वं कथं लभते।। — *Caryāgītikośa*

[18] रागेण बध्यते लोको रागेणैव विमुच्यते। — *Hevrajratantra* II.2.51

[19] Dakshina Ranjan Shastri served as professor of Sanskrit at the Sanskrit College of Calcutta which was one of the premier institution for traditional education of Sanskrit. He also taught at Krishnanagar Sanskrit College in Nadia. His father Pt. Candrakishore had earned the title of Vidyāvācaspati and was also known as a poet. He dedicated the Bangla edition of his *Cārvākadarśana* published in *Kolkata-purogāmī* in 1959 to his elder brother and teacher Pt. Durga Prasad, and the Sanskrit treatise *Cārvākaṣaṣṭi* to his father Pt. Candrakishore. It is interesting to note that he describes his father as a man devoted to *dharma*, a *vajra* (lethal weapon) for the lofty mountain of the *nāstika mata*. Pt. Anand Jha was another traditional Sanskrit scholar who wrote a work called *Cārvākadarśana*.

philosophy cite[20] and criticize Cārvāka, but Cārvāka philosophy as such was not included in the curricula in the *gurukulas* or *āśramas*. The Buddhists took Cārvākas more seriously. Max Müller has referred to a *Ambaṭṭhasutta* where Lokāyata is mentioned as a subject for the study of a brāhmaṇa.

Critique of Cārvāka Philosophies

Cārvākas are criticized in *Arthaśāstra, Tattvaṭīkā, Kāmasūtra, Rāmāyaṇa, Mahābhārata*[21] and Purāṇas like *Viṣṇu*[22] and *Padma.*[23] *Ṣaḍdarśanasamuccaya* and *Śāstrārthavārtāsamuccaya* of Haribhadra, *Tattavasaṁgraha* and *Prabodhacandrodaya,* and several Buddhist works like *Samantaphalasutta* and *Payasisuttanta.* Philosophers like Āryadeva, Śāntarakṣita, Śaṅkarācārya, Jayanta Bhaṭṭa, Kamalaśīla, Vācaspati Miśra, Bhāskarācārya and Varadarāja, present critiques of Cārvāka philosophy. The Cārvāka is referred in several works as a *pūrva-pakṣa* (prima facie view), viz. the *Śāṅkarabhāṣya* of *Brahmasūtra,*[24] *Tattvasaṁgrahapañjikā* of Kamalaśīla, *Vivaraṇaprameyasaṁgraha, Nyāyamañjarī*, chap. I of *Sarvasiddhāntasaṁgraha, Khaṇḍanakhaṇḍakhādya* and *Naiṣadhacarita* of Śrīharṣa, etc.

The Lokāyata view is also described as something unethical leading to sin.[25] Jayanta Bhaṭṭa calls Cārvākas as doers of undoable things (*vikarmastha*) or transgressors, hypocrites (*vaidalavratikas*) and logicians (*haitukas*).

---

[20] The following aphorisms of Brahaspati are cited by Bhāskarācārya in his *bhāṣya* on *Brahmasūtra* III.3.53 – पृथिव्यप्तेजोवायुरिति तत्त्वानि (1), तत् समुदाये शरीरेन्द्रियविषयसंज्ञा (2), तेभ्यश्चैतन्यम् (3), किण्वादिभ्यो मदशक्तिवत् (4)।

[21] *Mahābhārata,* Śāntiparva, chaps. 38-39.

[22] *Viṣṇu Purāṇa* III.17-18, 82, 85.

[23] *Padma Purāṇa,* Sṛṣṭikhaṇḍa, V.13.318-40.

[24] *Brahmasūtra, Śāṅkarabhāṣya* II.3.5.

[25] लोकायतमतं प्राज्ञैर्ज्ञेयं पापौघकारणम्।
इत्थं तत्त्वविलोमं यत् तन्न ज्ञानविवर्धनम्। — *Śāstrārthavārtāsamuccaya* I.110

The ground on which the Cārvākas are vehemently criticized by all other schools of philosophy lies in their view of body as soul or matter as the cause for consciousness. Haribhadra finding *avyāpti* (narrow extension) in this view, says that if body be taken as the material cause of soul or consciousness, then all matters should be imbued with consciousness.[26] Cārvāka may say that consciousness is generated in particular type of matters and not in all matters. Haribhadra retorts by saying that it amounts to the acceptance of a soul in a particular substance or body.[27] Udayana gives the following reasons for the unacceptability of the theory of identifying body as soul — Just as the objects seen by someone cannot be remembered by some other person, body as soul cannot remember as it is constantly changing, it is not the same body after some time. The Buddhists explain remembrance on the basis of *vāsanāsaṁkrama* (transit of traces); the Cārvāka does not accept the theory of momentariness, so he cannot explain the remembrance on that basis.[28]

Treating body as the soul and philosophy of pleasure are similar to Epicureanism. Epicurus (4th century BCE) also accepted only four elements — earth, air, fire and water — and rejected space.

Debates on the Nature of Reality

The four schools of Buddhist philosophies have been mentioned in Chap. 2. The Sautrāntika (Representationism) and the Vaibhāṣika (Direct Realism) are the earliest. The other two schools, the Śūnyavāda and the Vijñānavāda attempt a liberal interpretation of the *buddha-vacanas* and they are more inclined towards metaphysical thinking. These two fall under the Mahāyāna (great vehicle), whereas the Sautrāntika and the Vaibhāṣika fall under the Hīnayāna (little vehicle).

---

[26] *Śāstrārthavārtāsamuccaya* I.31-34.

[27] Ibid. I.39.

[28] *Nyāyakusumāñjali* I.15.

The difference between the Sautrāntika and the Vaibhāṣika lies in their view of cognition of external phenomena. The Vaibhāṣikas hold that all external things are known through perception. The Sautrāntikas argue that external things are known only through *anumāna* (inference). The Vaibhāṣika developed as a branch of Sarvāstivādin school under the Hīnayāna. They upheld the simultaneous existence of the past, present and future, the Sautrāntikas differed with them. The Sarvāstivādins also propounded the atomic theory of creation. Accordingly, the *paramāṇu* (atom) is the basic unit of the matter. It is imperceptible. A combination of seven *paramāṇus* makes an *aṇu* and an *aṇu* is perceptible. This theory of *paramāṇu* is criticized by the other Buddhists — the Vijñānavādins on one hand and the Nyāya-Vaiśeṣika system on the other. The proponents of *paramāṇu*-theory as per the tenets of Nyāya-Vaiśeṣika systems hold that *paramāṇus* can exclude each other as they possess magnitude and actuality.[29] Both of these — the Sarvāsivādins and the theorists of Nyāya-Vaiśeṣika — are contested by the Vijñānavādins who ask whether an atom is united with another atom partially or wholly, showing impossibility of both alternatives. An atom being indivisible cannot unite with another.

Udayana utilizes the same logic to refute Vijñānavādin's theory that the external reality is a manifestation of consciousness only. He asks whether the cognition is related to its contents partially or wholly. Since consciousness and cognition have no parts, partial relation is impossible. Vijñānavādin would challenge Naiyāyikas for the theory of difference between the *avayavin* (whole) and the *avayavas* (parts).

Regarding the aggregates (*skandhas*), bases (*āyatanas*) and elements, the Vaibhāṣikas believe that the word *skandha* means *rāśi*. It is an aggregate of the following:

- Past, present and future,

---

[29] K. Vishweshvari Amma, 1985, *Udayana and His Philosophy*, p. 36.

- the external and the internal,
- the gross or the subtle depending upon its status as resistant (*sapragraha*) or non-resistant (*apratigraha*),
- the inferior or the superior, and also depending upon whether it is sullied (*kliṣṭa*) or unsullied (*akliṣṭa*) with vices (*kleśa*s), and
- the far or the near — depending upon whether it is past, present or future.

These attributes belong to either the four aggregates, with the difference that gross consciousness is that of the five material sense-organs, whereas subtle consciousness is mind consciousness; or consciousness is gross or subtle, depending upon whether it belongs to the lower or higher stage.

The Sautrāntikas reject the last three attributes; they stipulate that the third category — the gross form aggregate — is one which is perceived by the five material senses-organs, all other forms being subtle, and the fourth category — inferiority or superiority — depends on the form aggregate's quality of being either pleasant or unpleasant; the last category — distance or proximity — depend on its being either in an invisible or visible place.[30]

In Buddhism, an individual existence is regarded as an aggregate, a stream of transient factors.[31] In its earlier phase, the doctrine of momentariness was essentially a doctrine of the transience of psychic states without any permanent substratum. It did not mean in early phase the unqualified denial of all substances.[32] There were debates within Buddhist sects on the concept of momentariness, as recorded in *Abhidharmakośa*. Finally, the momentariness came to be accepted at the level of experience.

Nāgārjuna rejected the concept of *svabhāva* and emphasized the

---

[30] Zahiruddin Ahmed, 2007, *Introduction to Buddhist Philosophy in India and Tibet*, p. 30.

[31] G.C. Pande, 1998, op. cit., p. 256.

[32] Ibid.

idea of *madhyamā pratipad* (the middle path). He also established the invariable relationship of the philosophy of Śūnyavāda with Buddha's concept of *pratītyasamutpāda* (interdependent origination). *Nirvāṇa* and *saṁsāra* to him are the forms of one and the same reality.

The essence of Mādhyamikaśāstra lies in shunning all standpoints.

> When one accepts any standpoint, one is captured by the cunning poisonous serpent of the impurities. Those, whose mind has shunned any standpoint, are not captured.[33]

The idealism in both the Mādhyamika and the Advaita Vedānta ultimately hinges upon some kind of mysticism, indirectly or directly subsisting on the Upaniṣadic philosophy. This becomes a basis for the accusations of indebtedness by the followers of each of these two systems, and this also remains a hidden ground for their affinity and their differences.

The externalists attack the theory of momentariness. Haribhadra, who is otherwise keen to agree with his opponents in his *Śāstrārthavārtāsamuccaya,* has devoted largest space to the refutation of this theory. He revisits the theory by adding that instead of a substance being dissolved and reborn every moment, it is proper to say that the substance stays, only the *dharma*s as born every moment. Also, everything can be said to be momentary to motivate people for renunciation of the mundane world.[34] In this way, Haribhadra sends an ontological issue to the domain of ethics. He gives a rebuttal to the Śūnyavādin arguing that if everything is void, then the arguments given for this voidness are also void. The acceptance of Vijñānavāda would put an end to the possibility of liberation, because there is nothing beyond *vijñāna* according to it.

Haribhadra also revises the Advaitin's position that at the

---

[33] *Yuktiṣaṣṭikārikā* 51.

[34] *Śāstrārthavārtāsamuccaya* VI.464-66.

pārmārthika level everything is *Brahman*. This can be said to inculcate the view of equanimity in a subsidiary sense and not in the primary sense.

Śaṅkara refutes Vijñānavādin, Sāṁkhya and Vaiśeṣika together on one ground — they are not based on the knowledge of *Brahman* as revealed from the Śruti.[35] In fact, he corners the Sāṁkhya, Nyāya, Vaiśeṣika, Vijñānavādin and Cārvāka for their realist, dualist and materialistic views. At the very outset of his *bhāṣya* on *Brahmasūtra*, he gives a resume of various prima-facie views and takes together all of them.[36] The Vaiśeṣika's concept of *ātman* appears equally absurd to him as he would regard the *ātman* as *acetana* (inanimate) and *dravya* (substance).[37] Neither view of *vijñāna* is acceptable as it is momentary.[38]

Sāṁkhya becomes the chief combatant for Śaṅkara because it cites the Śruti (scriptures) and also takes recourse to arguments to support it. For Śaṅkara it is appropriating the scriptures for the categories which are validated by other *pramāṇas* (means of knowledge).[39]

Arguing against the Naiyāyika for his dependence on arguments, Śaṅkara cites the maxim of the Upaniṣad — *naiṣā tarkeṇa matir āpaneyā* (the wisdom cannot be acquired through arguments).[40] He differs with Gauḍapāda on the latter's concept

[35] *Śāṅkarabhāṣya* on *Kena Upaniṣad* 2.3.

[36] देहमात्रं चैतन्यविशिष्टमात्मेति प्राकृता जना लौकायतिकाश्च प्रतिपन्नाः। इन्द्रियाण्येव चेतनान्यात्मेत्यपरे। मन इत्यन्ये। विज्ञानमात्रं क्षणिकमित्येके। शून्यमित्यपरे। अस्ति देहादिव्यतिरिक्तः संसारी कर्ता भोक्तेत्यपरे। भोक्तैव केवलं न कर्तेत्येके। अस्ति तद्व्यतिरिक्तः सर्वज्ञः सर्वशक्तिरिति केचित्। आत्मा स भोक्तुरित्यपरे। एवं बहवो विप्रतिपन्नाः युक्ति-वाक्यतदाभाससमाश्रयाः सन्तः। — *Brahmasūtra*, *Śāṅkarabhāṣya*, p. 6

[37] *Śāṅkarabhāṣya* on *Kena Upaniṣad* 2.4.

[38] Ibid.

[39] सांख्यादयस्तु परिनिष्ठितं वस्तु प्रमाणान्तरगम्यमेवेति मन्यमानाः प्रधानादीनि कारणान्त-राण्यनुमिमानास्तत्परतयैव वेदान्तवाक्यानि योजयन्ति। — *Śāṅkarabhāṣya*, p. 26

[40] *Kaṭha Upaniṣad* II.9.

of the physical world as dream. Applying five-member syllogism of inference he shows the inconsistancy in Gauḍapāda's view. He uses the same argument to rebut the Vijñānavādin. The experience of physical world is different from the experience in the state of a dream. The dream is obliterated when a man is awakened; the empirical reality is not cancelled after self-realization.

The followers of Rāmānuja refute the Advaitins on the score of their concept of *ajñāna*. How can the idea of the ignorance that has neither a subject nor an object be accepted? — they ask.[41] There is no evidence of a cosmic illusion and the Anirvacanīyatāvāda (indescribability of cognition). They maintain the difference between *jīva* (individual soul) and *Paramātman* (Absolute Being) but also treat *jīvātman* at par with *Paramātman*. The world to them is of two types — sentient and non-sentient. The non-sentient is of three kinds — *bhogya* (object), *bhogopakaraṇa* (instrument) and *bhogāyatana* (site of fruition). Rāmānuja Darśana also differs from Śāṅkara-Vedānta by the way of holding *karman* as necessary.

I have already referred to the long history of scathing debates between the Advaitins and the Mādhvas (see Chap. 2). The Advaita Vedānta views world as *mithyā* (false) which is *anirvacanīya* (indescribable), and is not the locus of being-not-being (*sadasattva-anadhikaraṇarūpaṁ*). Here *sadasattva-anadhikaraṇarūpaṁ* signifies absolute absence of being and absolute absence of non-being. It is here that the Mādhvas apply their most pricking clinchers for goading the Advaitins by bringing out the impossibilities of the concept of absolute absence of being and absolute absence of non-being.

The *anirvacanīyatākhyāti* (indescribability of cognition) of the Advaitin has been vehemently opposed by the Mādhva philosophers Vyāsatīrtha and Jayatīrtha. Madhusūdana Sarasvatī not only defends Advaitin's position, and but also raises fundamental objections on the view of reality in the Mādhva system. Vyāsatīrtha

---

[41] *Sarvadarśanasaṁgraha*, p. 131.

defines reality as that which is not the counter-positive of absolute negation. The question is how the perception of this negative entity is possible. Replying to Madhusūdana, Rāmārya in his *Taraṅgiṇī* says that it is not possible to perceive a negation, but it is possible to perceive an entity that has been negated. This rejoinder is further reviewed by the author of *Laghucandrikā*.

The Naiyāyika also questions the position of the Advaitin with reference to the status of world. He says that the negation of something, which is *alīka* (false) in itself, is not possible. The world therefore cannot be regarded as the locus of absolute negation, of non-being-as-characterized by being (*sattva-viśiṣṭa sattvābhāva*).[42] The law of contradiction is also violated — the world cannot be taken as the locus of absolute absence of *sattva* (being) and *asattva* (non-being) simultaneously.

It was Madhusūdana Sarasvatī who could counter Vyāsatīrtha's terrible triade of arguments against Śaṅkara's concept of Reality. Vyāsatīrtha had shown fallacies including *ativyāpti* (wide extension) and *avyāpti* (narrow extension) in Śaṅkara's concepts of *ajñāna* and the world as *vivarta* (illusory negation). According to him *ajñāna* cannot be the material cause of something that is illusory. A *bhāva* cannot create *abhāva*. Madhusūdana pointed out that Vyāsatīrtha misunderstood the concepts of *bhāva* and *abhāva* here. *Bhāva* to Śaṅkara is difference from negation and not the state of being. Again to Vyāsatīrtha's objection that *ajñāna* having a different *jāti* (generality) that the so-called effect of it — the world — cannot really function as the cause, Madhusūdana gave a rebuttal by pointing out that complete similarity between the cause and effect is not feasible, there has to be some difference between them. With his subtle reasoning Madhusūdana could save the Advaitin's stand, i.e. that *avidyā* can be adjusted as the material cause of illusory negation.[43]

---

42 *Advaitasiddhiḥ*, tr. and ed. Karuna Bhattacharya, p. 10.

43 K. Narain, 1986, *Critique of Mādhva Refutation of Śaṅkara School of Vedānta*, pp. 166-67.

The Advaitin does not describe *sattva* (being) as the negation of *asattva* (not being). Therefore there is no contradiction. *Sattva* is the quality of not being cancelled (*abādhitatva*) and *asattva* is the character of not being present in any locus.

Brahman is *sadrūpa* (being itself) only and neither *sat* or *asat.*

The concepts of *pratītyasamutpāda* (dependent origination) and *kṣaṇabhaṅga* (momentariness) stand in a sharp contrast to the absolutism of Vedānta on one hand and the idea of synthetic principles of *dravya* (substance) and *jāti* (universal) in Nyāya-Vaiśeṣika systems on the other. There is no place for a permanent and abiding substance in Buddhist world-view, where only reality is *svalakṣaṇa* (point instant). The Buddhists deny the status of reality to *jāti* (universal or generality) of Nyāya, for them any universal is a *vikalpa* (logical construct) only, comprised in the exclusion of a common counter-correlate. "A universal is in its very essence the exclusion of the other", says Dharmakīrti in *Pramāṇavārtika* (*sāmānyaṁ anyavyāvṛttilakṣaṇaṃ* — III.30). Kumārila had attacked the very foundation of Nāgārjuna's philosophy and questioned the validity of grading the truth — *saṁvṛti satya* and *paramārtha-satya.* But to the Mādhyamika all phenomena remain indeterminate and indefinable.

The Nyāya-Vaiśeṣika school advocated realism in the sense that it maintained difference between *dharma* (attribute, substrata) and *dharmin* (substance). Because of this, it came to be sharply divided not only with idealists like the adherents of the Mādhyamika and Yogācāra schools of Buddhist philosophy, but with Pūrva-Mīmāṁsā and Vedānta as well. Vedānta holds *dharmin* alone as real and all its *upādhis* (attributes) as *vivartas* (unreal effects). Contrary to this, the Diṅnāga–Dharmakīrti school regards only *dharmas* in the form of discrete moments — as real, *dharmin* — the substance is just a mental construct and unreal.

The categories mentioned by Gautama in his *Nyāyasūtra* and by Kaṇāda in his *Vaiśeṣikasūtra* form the idea of reality in both these schools. They are not ideal constructs. Vaiśeṣika's conceptual framework for reality is comprised of six categories – *dravya* (substance), *guṇa* (quality), *karma* (action), *sāmānya* (generality), *viśeṣa* (particularity) and *samavāya* (inherence). Later philosophers, i.e. Śivāditya, Śrīdhara, Udayana, etc. accepted the seventh additional category – *abhāva* (non-existence) – also. Śivāditya Miśra wrote a treatise – *Saptapadārthī* – on seven categories, where he firmly stood for accepting negation as the seventh category. The perception of reality undergoes a change with the introduction of *abhāva* as the seventh category, and the reality assumes a pluralistic dimension. Naiyāyika's concept of Reality is comprised in the gamut of sixteen categories mentioned earlier (see Chap. 1).

A shift in the concept of categories occurs in Raghunātha Śiromaṇi (CE 1500). In his *Padārthatattavanirūpaṇa*, he reduced the number by denying *abhāva* as a category. He was criticized by Veṇidatta in his *Padārthamaṇḍana* who accepts only four positive categories.[44]

It was Vātsyāyana who suggested that *abhāva* (non-existence) can become a *prameya* and can be used as a way to comprehend reality in his *bhāṣya* on *Nyāyasūtra* II.2.8. From a pile of marked and unmarked clothes, if somebody is asked to bring the clothes that are unmarked, the absence of mark becomes the means to locate the clothes asked for. In Navya-Nyāya, the category of *abhāva* assumed special significance, it was utilized to define the reality by positing the category of *pratiyogin* (couter-positive) which is invariably conspicuous by its absence. Kumārila stands on the opposite pole from Advaitavādin by viewing non-existence as a reality. But Prabhākara opposed Śabarasvāmin and Kumārila on one hand and the Nyāya-Vaiśeṣika on the other by denying *abhāva* an entity and a *pramāṇa* means of knowledge. For Buddhist also, non-existence is not a reality, it is an inferential judgement.

The Prabhākara school of Mīmāṁsā holds *sādṛśya* (similarity),

---

[44] Dhirendra Sharma, 1974, *The Negative Dialectics*, p. 230.

saṁkhyā (number) and *śakti* (potency) also as categories. Udayana and other Naiyāyikas had to combat with them for the rejection of these.

The Ārambhavāda as proposed in the Nyāya-Vaiśeṣika system, visualizes the world as created out of the *paramāṇus* (atoms) serving as basic building blocks. Their concept of reality lies in its pluralistic view and diversity. In fact, there are two different theories of causation of the world — Ārabhyārambhakavāda (transitive causation) and Ārambhavāda (intransitive causation). Udyotakara, Vācaspati Miśra and Udayana stand for the transitive causation and sharply criticize the former theory.

The Pariṇāmavāda of the Sāṁkhya stands in sharp contrast to both the theories — Ārabhyārambhakavāda (transitive causation) and Ārambhavāda (intransitive causation) and also to the Vivartavāda of the Advaita Vedāntin. It views the physical world as a transformation of one single, unitary and all-pervasive substance, named as *prakṛti* (primordial matter). The universe is evolved out of this *prakṛti*. The Naiyāyikas like Udayana criticize the Sāṁkhya, questioning the possibility of diversity evolving out of singularity. They also point out the inner contradiction of *prakṛti* being *acetana* (insentient) but having the power of creation.

The idea of multiplicity evolving out of unity is taken up in Vedānta also but with a different view of reality. The Bhāskara school of Vedānta, known as the school of Tridaṇḍins, advocates Brahmapariṇāmavāda, viz. the theory of the *Brahman* transforming itself into the multifarious world. He being the material cause, the phenomena are His real *vikāras* (modifications). *Brahman* in fact is an undifferentiated unitary mass of pure consciousness.

On the concept of *paramāṇus* (atoms), the Vaiśeṣika is cornered by orthodox schools as well the Buddhist schools. The Vaiśeṣikas propound that the *paramāṇus* function as the basic building blocks for creating this world and their coalesceance creates larger and larger forms. Āryadeva and Śāntarakṣita argue that the no *yoga* (integration) between *paramāṇus* can create the universe. The *yoga* of *paramāṇus* can be of two types — complete and partial. If there is complete integration (*sarvātmanā yoga*) between two *paramāṇus*, it would not lead to any increase in the volume or quality nor would it create a larger form. If it is a partial integration, it would be multifarious, and hence will be impermanent.

Sāṁkhya is attacked from all corners for its concept of *puruṣa* and *prakṛti* and the world as *pariṇāma* (transformation). Haribhadra objects this postulation by saying that if *puruṣa* is *vibhu* and *nitya* (changeless and eternal), then there is no point in putting him in the stages of bondage and liberation. And if *prakṛti* is inanimate and eternal, then also it cannot transform itself to create the world. He then goes on to revise the Sāṁkhya concept of *prakṛti*, suggesting that it may be viewed as *karma-prakṛti*, which in Jaina ontology, is just a part of *pudgala-jagat*. In this way he does not find any problem in accepting the Prakṛtivāda of Sāṁkhya.[45]

The Kṣaṇabhaṅgavāda (theory of momentariness) in the Diṅnāga–Dharmakīrti school presents the nominalist view of outer reality where the universe is in a constant flux. It proposes that every point-instant (*kṣaṇa*) stays just for a moment and vanishes to be replaced immediately by the other one, and this point-instant is reality. Reality for Diṅnāga and Dharmakīrti lies in constant movement or change, it is always becoming and not being.

There is no place for *jāti* (generality) in this system; the *svalakṣaṇa* (unique particular) is only reality. Whatever that is supposed to be *sāmānya lakṣaṇa* (universal) is unreal; it can be described linguistically, but then any such description ought to be fictional. The *svalakṣaṇa* functions as a reality from moment to moment. It is the *paramārthasat* (ultimate reality) and is *sarvato vyāvṛtta* (distinguished from everything else).

Dharmakīrti employs a series of arguments in refutation of generality (*sāmānya* or *jāti*). These arguments fall into three

---

45 *Śāstrārthavārtāsamuccaya* III.232-37.

categories — intuitive, metaphysical and logistic. Acceptance of the generality is beset with the "one-many" problem, i.e. generality is said to be present in one object and at the same time in many as well, and then it is *vyabhicāra* (defect of variance). The universal would share the multiple natures of the various particulars, that too would be at variance, therefore to Dharmakīrti it is a pseudo-entity. Describing *jāti* as a fiction, he says:

> It neither comes from somewhere nor it was there already, nor is it subsequently produced; nor does it have any parts. [And even when in other places] it does not leave the previous locus. Oh! It's just one disaster after another![46]

Any substance to be real must occupy just one location in time (*kāla*) and space (*deśa*) and have only a singular nature (*svabhāva*). It cannot be present in several distinct objects over different times and places, and possess the many natures of the various particulars. The proponents of *jāti* or *sāmānya* envisage manifold placements of one and single *jāti* once and always. The concept of *tiryag lakṣaṇa* (horizontal placements) as well as *ūrdhvatā lakṣaṇa* (vertical placements) for the universals is not admissible in a universe that functions as per the theory of *kṣaṇabhaṅga* or *kṣaṇikatva* (momentariness).

In fact, Dharmakīrti utilizes the concept of inference to disapprove the idea of *jāti* (universal) as proposed by the orthodox Naiyāyikas on one hand, and to support the concept of *kṣaṇikatva* (momentariness) on the other. He devotes a major portion of his *Hetubindu* to prove the invariable concomitance *yat sat tat kṣaṇikam* (whatever that exists, is momentary) and also to the theory of *pratītyasamutpāda* (dependent origination). An effect is produced by a cause and subsequently functions as the cause for another effect, this chain of causality subsists in a series of *samartha kāraṇas* (capable causes).[47]

---

[46] *Pramāṇavārtika* I.152.

[47] *Hetubindu* II.15.

Jāti — the technical term for generality used by the Naiyāyika — also denotes caste and hierarchy in day-to-day language. Dharmakīrti and his followers like Śākyabuddhi and Karṇakagomin attribute a link between *jāti* as generality and *jāti* as a caste hierarchy. The metaphysical categories in orthodox systems of philosophy were seen as foundations for social organizations and hierarchy under Brāhmanism, and any attempt at the disapproval of these provided impetus to the Buddhists for demolishing the organizational hierarchy of their opponents.

Debates on Scriptural Authority

The debates on the specific doctrinal questions as discussed above become more intense as they move to the question of scriptural authority. Even on the nature of the authority of the Veda the so-called Vedic *darśana*s differ one from the other. Kumārila regards Sāṁkhya, Yoga, Pāñcarātra and Pāśupata as *avaidika* (non-Vedic) *darśanas*.[48] Bhīmācārya in his *Nyāyakośa* classifies Sāṁkhya and Advaita Vedānta amongst the *nāstika-darśana*s. Mīmāṁsā would hold the *svataḥ prāmāṇya* — the theory that the knowledge acquired through the *pramāṇa*s is valid in itself; whereas the Nyāya upholds the theory of *parataḥ prāmāṇya* (the theory that the knowledge acquired through the *pramāṇa*s needs to be validated from an outside agency). This implies that the knowledge acquired even from Śruti or Veda is not valid by itself and it needs to be validated by other means of knowledge.

Dharmakīrti proceeds to a detailed attack on the authority of the Vedas, the brāhmaṇas that expound them, the Brāhmanical ideas about the efficacy of *mantra*s, and the system of caste in his *Pramāṇavārtika.*

The Mīmāṁsaka school established Vedas as eternal, *apauruṣeya* (not created by humans) and hence authoritative being free from any fault or error liable to occur as a result of human influence.

---

[48] *Tantravārtika* I.3.4.

Against this, the Buddhists argued that if scriptures were *apauruṣeya*, they would be incomprehensible being devoid of *vivakṣā* (speakers' intention).

Tagged with the question of scriptural authority is the question of validity of the words coming from a reliable person termed as *āpta* by the ancient Indian philosophers. Those who believe in the authority of the Śruti do not uphold, the authority of the reliable persons. With some reservations, Al-Beruni even prefers spoken or written word over the testimony of the *pratyakṣa pramāṇa* (perception). Caraka had given more importance to the authority of *āpta* (see Chap. 3). Al-Biruni clubs both the written and spoken words under his concept of hearsay and his speculations about the validity of "hearsay" are noteworthy:

> No one will deny that in questions of historic authenticity, hearsay does not equal eye-witness, for in the latter the eye of the observer apprehends the substance of that which is observed, both in the time when and in the place where it exists, whilst hearsay has its peculiar drawbacks. But for these, it would even be preferable to eyewitness; for the subject of eyewitness can only be actual momentary existence, whilst hearsay comprehends alike the present, the past and the future, so as to apply in a certain sense both to that which is and to that which is not (i.e. which either has ceased to exist or has not yet come into existence). Written tradition is one of the species of hearsay — we might almost say — the most preferable.[49]

Debates on the Theory of Knowledge

Vyāpti is a universal relation to be known only through *anumāna*. This proposition of Dharmakīrti poses a problem. If we hold *vyāpti* to be known through *anumāna* and again, *anumāna* to be known through *vyāpti* this leads to *anavasthā* (infinite regress) — forming an unending chain of *vyāptis* and *anumānas*. The Naiyāyikas of Gautamīya tradition had an easy solution for avoid this trap — they

[49] *Al-Beruni's India*, p. 3.

held *vyāpti* as dependent on perception. In Dharmakīrti's conceptual framework, this is impossible, because of his insistence on the presence of probans in all the similar cases (*sapakṣas*) and one cannot observe all the *sapakṣas* in a given life. To Dharmakīrti, an inference should result in both positive and negative concomitances (*anvaya* and *vyatireka vyāptis*). The Naiyāyika does not consider it essential. Dharmakīrti asks the Naiyāyika if there is any *kevalānvayī hetu* — the cause that goes only with the positive concomitance. The Naiyāyikas succeeded in breaking the Dharmakīrtian framework of inferential knowledge by devising an instance of *kevalānvayī hetu-adṛṣṭa;* which is perceived by God. In forming the *vyatireka vyāpti* of this concomitance, it is not possible to cite an instance, therefore here the *hetu* (*adṛṣṭa*) does not have a *vipakṣa*.

Dharmakīrti begs to differ from his *paramaguru* (grand-teacher) Diṅnāga in his concept of *pratyakṣa* to an extent. Diṅnāga has accepted the objects appearing in illusion or hallucination as perceived. Dharmakīrti, on the other hand, reserves the sphere of perception only for the objects of veridical perception.

The orthodox Naiyāyikas believed that *pratyakṣa* is of two types — *laukika* (this-worldly) and *alaukika* (other-worldly). Both Diṅnāga and Dharmakīrti naturally stood against the *alaukika pratyakṣa* as it does not fit in the theory of *svalakṣaṇa* — a *svalakṣaṇa* cannot be judged in terms of *laukika* (this-worldly) or *alaukika* (other-worldly).

Nyāya is opposed to the theory of *śabdānuvedha* there can be no cognition without the verbal knowledge. If *nirvikalpa jñāna* is accepted, a distinction between perception and the verbalization of perceptual state is maintained. A child has the knowledge of the deep structures of language whereas what he learns later on is its surface structure.[50]

Dharmakīrti rules out the possibility of accepting other *pramāṇas* proposed in Nyāya, Mīmāṁsā and rest of the systems.

---

[50] B.K. Matilal, 2005, *Epistemology, Logic and Grammar in Indian Philosophical Analysis*, p. 5.

He rejects *anupalabdhi* (non-apprehension) as a *pramāṇa*. The Mīmāṁsakas believe that *anupalabdhi* is a *pramāṇa* leading to the cognition of *abhāva* (absence). Any *pravṛtti* (inclination) is generated by *buddhi* (intelligence) after visualization of something that is *bhāva* (existent). A non-existent will not lead to *pravṛtti*, therefore *anupalabdhi* is not a *pramāṇa*. For Dharmakīrti *anupalabdhi* is just a type of probans. In his brilliant analysis of the apprehension of "non-apprehension" Dharmakīrti has given the concept of *ekajñānasaṁsarga* (co-cognizibility). The apprehension of *abhāva* (non-existence) in one place involves the apprehension of a co-cognizable object on the same place.[51] In difference to both Mīmāṁsakas and Naiyāyikas again, he denies *abhāva* as a separate category. Determination of an object cannot prove the non-existence of another; hence absence cannot be proved by ignorance.

Udayana proposed the reality of negation. Abhāva came to accepted as an additional ontological category in later Nyāya-Vaiśeṣika system. Out of his concern with making the theory of *anumāna* perfectly precise, Dharmakīrti dared to disapprove the postulation of Diṅnāga here also (like in the sphere of *pratyakṣa*). Diṅnāga proposed three essential categories for the validity of an *anumāna* — *pakṣa*, *sādhya* and *hetu*. But he also allowed *dṛṣṭānta* to be included for establishing an *anumāna* in a convincing way. Dharmakīrti stood against this practical consideration. *Dṛṣṭānta* not being an essential component has to be discarded from the structure of *anumāna*.

The orthodox Naiyāyikas tried to solve the problem in a different way — they opined that *vyāpti* can be grasped without establishing the causal relation, and since it is impossible to observe all the cases of *tadutpatti* in past and presence, Dharmakīrti's concept of *tadutpatti* is not acceptable to them. Similarly they also rejected Dharmakīrti's idea of *tādātmya* (common reference), as the essential condition of *vyāpti* can be fulfilled without it. They shifted

[51] *Hetubindu* IV.1.

Dharmakīrti's frame of inductive reasoning to intuitive reasoning.[52]

Ratnakīrti introduced the two-truth doctrines as key to the nature of the discussion as inference is trafficking with illusory universals (*sāmanya*), the proof of the mind-streams of others, whilst empirically valid in relative truth (*saṁvṛti-satya*), does not hold ultimate metaphysical certainty in absolute truth (*paramārtha satya*).

Debates on the Theory of Causality

The Vaiśeṣika cosmology was based on speculative physics. It stands in opposition to Vedānta and it was firmly refuted by Bādarāyaṇa in his *Brahmasūtra.* It enumerated six basic categories and a theory of causation without any place for a creator. The Vedāntin naturally viewed it as a challenge to spirituality. Bādarāyaṇa therefore attacked the very fundamental theory of atomistic cosmology postulated under the Vaiśeṣika philosophy. Vaiśeṣika was equally a challenge for the Sāṁkhya.

Dharmakīrti strongly refutes the theories of Satkāryavāda and Pariṇāmavāda advocated by the proponents of Sāṁkhya. The Sāṁkhya theory of causality (Satkāryavāda) holds that the effects live as *avyakta* (unmanifest) within the cause. Thus, the curd lies *avyakta* in the milk. All effects exist either in *vyakta* or in *avyakta* forms — there is nothing non-existing. Dharmakīrti argues that in that case, the manifestation itself will have to be termed as existent and non-existent; therefore to hold that nothing is non-existent is impossible, as it will render all negative usages (like this is without that, that is not without this, etc.) impracticable and will create a universe without existences and non-existences (which is again an impossibility).[53] With regard to the theory of *pariṇāma* (transformation), Dharmakīrti does not overrule the linguistic usages like "the milk has been transformed into curd" — but he

---

52 P.P. Gokhale, 1992, *Inference and Fallacies Discussed in Ancient Indian Logic,* p. 125.

53 अनन्वयव्यतिरेकं विश्वं स्यात्, भेदाभावात्। — *Vādanyāya*, p. 26

would like this transformation to be understood in the light of the Buddhist theory of causality — as a series (*santāna*) of cause and effect, rather than its Sāṁkhyaite implication of the unity of the cause and the effect. The Sāṁkhya theorist holds that the substance remains the same, only there is a cessation of some of its property and generation of some different property in it. Dharmakīrti points out the inner contradiction of the Sāṁkhya here, how can the substance remain the same if some of its properties perish and some other properties within it are generated? The Sāṁkhyaite will have to answer the question whether the properties are the same as substance or different from the substance. Both the situations are impossible as per the Sāṁkhya tenets, because if the properties are one and same with the substance, then the change of properties will involve the change of the substance also, and if the properties are different from the substance, then the theory of *pariṇāma* will be vindicated, as the substance will not undergo through the transformation, only its properties will be transformed. If the Sāṁkhyaite says that we will hold the transformation of the substance also, then he will have to accept the transformation of consciousness as well. For Dharmakīrti, there is no relation except the relation of the cause and the effect; he will not accept the *dharma-dharmī* relationship.

Mīmāṁsā postulates the theory of *śakti* (power) in the cause which leads to the genesis of the effect. Udayana and other Naiyāyikas refute their arguments. To them, the cause itself is an aggregate of causal power and the absence of counteracting agents.

Debates on the Absolute and God as Creator

Īśvaravāda (theory of the existence of God) is one of the most contentious issues that has always provoked vigorous fights not only between the non-believers and the believers, but amongst the theistic schools as well. The proponents of Nyāya-Vaiśeṣika schools claimed that unknown can be known with the apparatus of facts that are known. They developed such apparatus through the process of logic based on *anumāna* (inference). The followers of Advaita Vedānta vehemently opposed any move to make the Supreme Being a subject of inference.

The whole discourse on *Īśvarasiddhi* in the tradition of Nyāya is based on the edifice of the following three aphorisms in Gautama's *Nyāyasūtra*:

> *īśvaraḥ kāraṇaṁ, puruṣakarmaphalyadarśanāt* ।
> *na puruṣakarmābhāve phalāniṣpatteḥ* ।
> *tatkaritatvād ahetuḥ* । — IV.1.19-21

> God is the cause (of the world), because actions of men (by themselves) do not yield fruits. (The opponent says): This is not so, because there is no fruit without the action by men. It is improper to say so, because, God makes men to take actions.

Following Vātsyāyana's *bhāṣya* on these aphorisms, Ganganath Jha in his commentary entitled *Khadyota* suggests that these three aphorisms refute certain other systems and approve some systems. The first aphorism (IV.1.19) refutes the prima-facie view of Vedānta which accepts God as the *upādāna kāraṇa* (inherent cause) of world. The third aphorism (IV.1.21) again disapproves the Vedāntic view that God is the *nimitta kāraṇa* (efficient cause) of the world. Accordingly Vātsyāyana's view of Iśvara establishes Him as the observer and regulator of this world, and not as the creator. He does not transform himself in the form of this world. If we accept the theory of *pariṇāma* (transformation), the question would arise as to whether God transforms Himself partly or fully to create this world. There will objections both ways. If he transforms Himself parly then he would not remain *akhaṇḍa* (whole). If he transforms Himself fully then He will not remain eternal.

Even though the Naiyāyika combated with Sāṁkhya, Mīmāṁsā and Vedānta on the issue of Īśvaravāda, it is the Buddhist with whom he had to fight tooth and nail in this field. The Naiyāyikas and the Buddhist philosophers displayed remarkable ingenuity of reasoning here. John Vattanky says:

> From the discussions of these arguments and counter- arguments, we can easily see, if we are objective and unprejudiced, that these philosophers manifest an admirable spirit of rigorous thinking and often scale the very heights of human thought. The Buddhist attacks shorn of their ancient form and technical vocabulary have not since been surpassed by any system of human thought that denies the existence of God. And it could be said without exaggeration that the Nyāya arguments in their spirit and intent have gone as far as human spirit has ever gone in search of an answer to these objections and problems. They have established the existence of God with arguments as exact and as sure as it has been so far possible for human thinking. And this should evoke the appreciation and admiration of any objective historian of ideas.[54]

Vasubandhu was first to attack the idea of God as propounded by Gautama and his *bhāṣyakāra* Vātsyāyana. He gave the following arguments:

1. If there is a single cause for all the things, then all the things should originate at one time.
2. If God be accepted as the creator, he must have a purpose for creating this world. If the purpose is His satisfaction, then his very status as God becomes doubtful, as He is not satisfied with Himself. If the purpose is to keep others satisfied, then this world should not have been full of mysery.
3. Acceptance of God as the cause of all results in negation of other causes producing different effects.

Even though these assertions by Vasubandhu were directed against Vātsyāyana's exposition of *Nyāyasūtra*, they were taken up for refutation by Sāṁkhya and Mīmāṁsā systems.[55]

Udyotakara attempted to resolve the dilemma of commentators on the three aphorism of *Nyāyasūtra* (IV.1.19-21) as cited above by

---

[54] John S.J. Vattanky, 2011, *Gaṅgeśa's Philosophy of God*, pp. 147-48.

[55] Ibid., p. 16.

establishing God as the *nimitta kāraṇa* of the world. The crux of his reasoning lies in the necessity of accepting God as activator of atoms, without being activated, the atoms cannot combine to produce things.

Dharmakīrti devotes a sizeable portion in the first chapter of his *Pramāṇavārtika* on refuting the concept of the Absolute. The logic that there is always a creator for a cause would lead to fallacies. If there is a pot, then its creator is a *kumbhakāra*. This would make the *kumbhakāra* a creator of *valmīka* (anthill) also. In this way all the *hetus* cited for proving the existence of God are fallacious. The logic proving one substance as the causality of an effect can be employed to prove the non-causality of the same substance for the same effect.[56] Further acceptance of an eternal God as the cause of the world leads to fallacy, because it is not possible to formulate an invariable concomitance, rendering the inference invalid. When it is said that God is the cause of the world, one will have to accept that God was not the cause of this world when it was not created, and He becomes the cause of the world at the time of creation. This implies a change in the nature of God again rendering Naiyāyika's position untenable.

Vācaspati Miśra approaches the issue of Īśvaravāda with his brilliant analytical mind. He divides all phenomena into three categories comprised of: things made by human beings like pot, things known as not created by human beings, viz. atoms; and things supposed to be created by God, viz. elements like the earth. With this premise, he develops the syllogism to prove that the world is not only caused by an intelligent agent, this intelligent agent also knows the material causes of this world directly.[57] On their objection that this intelligent agent has not actually been seen by anybody, he defeats the Buddhists on their own ground, i.e. they will be denying their own idea of point-instant. Developing the

---

[56] *Pramāṇavārtika* I.23.

[57] Vattanky, 2011, op. cit., p. 51.

order of syllogisms further, Vācaspati proves that this intelligent agent is omniscient and eternal.

Udayana in his magnum opus *Nyāyakusumāñjali* created a strong argumentative defence structure for cause of God. He countered the five major theses based on different views of causality:

1. Materialist view that there is no supernatural cause of this world.
2. The Mīmāṁsā view that the other means of attaining *svarga* (heaven) rule out the necessity of a belief in God.
3. The Sāṁkhya view that there are valid means of proving that God does not exist.
4. Even if God exists, He cannot be relied upon as an object of right knowledge.
5. There are no positive arguments to prove His existence.[58]

Mīmāṁsā holds *anupalabdhi* or *abhāva* (non-existence) as a valid means of knowledge and uses it for the denial of God. Arguing against them, Udayana says — the mere non-apprehension of any entity does not prove its non-existence. It is the non-apprehension of a perceptible object that proves its non-existence. As a rebuttal to the Mīmāṁsaka, he specially gives eight proofs to prove the existence of God in chap. V of his *Nyāyakusumāñjali*. They are:

1. *Kārya*: Every effect has a cause. God is the being who conveys His intension through Veda.
2. *Āyojana*: In the beginning of the creation, the conjunction of two atoms was caused by a conscious effort.
3. *Dhṛti*: God is the preserver of this Universe.
4. *Pada*: The existence of God is proved by the use of words like Īśa or Īśvara.

---

[58] तदिह सङ्क्षेपतः पञ्चतयी विप्रतिपत्तिः। अलौकिकस्य परलोकसाधनास्याभावात्, अन्यथापि परलोकसाधनानुष्ठानसम्भवात्, तदभाववदेकप्रमाणसद्भावात्, सत्त्वेऽपि तस्याप्रमाणत्वात्, तत्साधकप्रमाणाभावाच्चेति। — *Nyāyakusumāñjali*, chap. I, p. 25

5. *Pratyaya*: Use of verbal suffixes to indicate a particular tense in the Vedas, bringing out the intentions of God.
6. *Śruti*: All the Vedas refer to God.
7. *Vākya*: The Vedas have sentences describing God or praising Him.
8. *Saṁkhyā*: Vedas refer to God in a singular number.[59]

The Cārvāka's contention that perception is the only means of knowledge is refuted by Udayana with reasons for accepting inference. Perception does not work even in the well-known example of inference, i.e. "there is fire on the mountain, because smoke is arising from its top".

Haribhadra in his *Śāstrārthavārtāsamuccaya* raises a potent objection to theism on the basis of man's choice and freedom. If a man has freedom of choice and has to decide his own course of action, God becomes unnecessary. Then trying to reconcile with theistic presumptions, he adds that the noble souls who have attained liberation may be called as gods.

Following Udayana and Śaśadhara, the author of *Nyāyasiddhāntadīpa*, Gaṅgeśa gave as many as seven formulations of *pakṣa* in the invariable concomitance to prove the existence of God and also several formulations of the prima-facie view regarding the "syllogism of" in "being-an-effect" is "having-a-cause". The universe itself being infinite cannot be taken as an individual *pakṣa*. In this way he goes on excluding everything that can be produced by human beings from the category of *pakṣa* to reach the conclusion that "what is not produced by an effort that is not produced can only by implication that which is produced by God".[60] Gaṅgeśa also takes into account the theory of conjunction of the mind and the soul (*ātmamanaḥ saṁyoga*) for production of knowledge, and argues that no such conjunction was possible in the beginning of

[59] *Nyāyakusumāñjali* V.1.

[60] Vattanky, 2011, op. cit., p. 129-30.

creation, there being no human body to make this conjunction possible. Therefore God has to be accepted here who could make the movement of mind possible. Another argument he employs in his discourse on *Īśvaravāda* is the ignorance of human beings with regard to the material cause of the universe.

Debates on the Concept of Mokṣa

The idea of emancipation or deliverance is treated in all schools of philosophy with diverse viewpoints. The Naiyāyikas hold that the state of *apavarga* (deliverance) is comprised of absolute absence of pain. The Vedāntins give the concept of *ānanda* (bliss). But *mokṣa* has distinctive nature amongst the different schools of Vedānta. In the Buddhist schools of Yogācāra and Vijñānavāda, the state of *nirvāṇa* is structured on negative dialecticism.

The Vedāntin is of the view that the Naiyāyika's proposition of *apavarga* as a state of absolute absence of pain is untenable, as the scriptures describe the soul untouched by pleasure and pain. In the state of salvation, the soul ceases to be an agent or a subject and does not have any experience or knowledge. It just becomes one with the Supreme Being — the *Brahman*.

These systems also differ with each other in respect of the process, ways and means of attaining salvation. According to Nyāya, the true knowledge of sixteen categories (see Chap. 3) leads to *niḥśreyas* (state of deliverance). The Vaiśeṣika holds that *niḥśreyas* is attained by the knowledge of similarity and dissimilarity between the six categories defined in the system. The Mīmāṁsā regards the synthesis of knowledge and action (*jñānakarmasamuccaya*) as the means for *mokṣa*. On the other hand, Vedānta enumerates step by step process of *śravaṇa* (listening), *manana* (contemplation) and *nididhyāsana* (concentration). According to Rāmānuja and Madhva, *bhakti* (devotion) leads to *mokṣa*. The Advaitin would deny any categorization and differentiation in the state of *mokṣa*. On the contrary, Madhva holds four categories of *mokṣa* as well as gradations and stages in the state of *mokṣa*. The Naiyāyikas also say that one does not attain *apavarga* simply by true knowledge of the sixteen categories. One has to undergo the process of eradication of pain and *mithyā jñāna* to reach the state of absolute painlessness. The Vaiśeṣika also holds *dharma* as a subsidiary cause for the attainment of *mokṣa* apart from the true knowledge of the categories.

In the system of Vijñanavāda, the understanding of *pratītyasamutpāda* (dependent origination) or *śūnya* leads to *nirvāṇa.*

In recent times, Dayānanda rejected the theory of identification of *jīva* and *Brahman* in the state of liberation. According to him, *ātman* (the soul) experiences *ānanda* in liberation and he is also imbued with *guṇas* like *bala* (power) and *parākrama* (valour). Badarinatha Shukla revised Naiyāyika's view of *apavarga* to make room for the experience of *ānanda* in it. Their propositions are being taken up in the last chapter here.

5

Vāda in Dharma
Socio-Political and Legal Debates

PARALLEL to the Vedic traditions which became precursors of Sanātana Dharma, the Āgamic and Śramaṇic traditions existed right from the hoary past with their own world-view and alternate lifestyles. *Ṛgveda* X.136.2 refers to *vātaraśanā munis* (sages wearing wind as girdle, i.e. the naked ascetics). *Taittirīya Āraṇyaka* also uses the appellation of *ṛṣis* (seers) as *vātaraśanās*.[1]

In Upaniṣads we find seers from all castes and classes. Bādarāyaṇa however seeks to restrict the knowledge of *Brahman* from śudras. There is a whole section in his *Brahmasūtra* — called the Apaśūdrādhikaraṇa — in defence of this restriction. Pūrva-Mīmāṁsā also upholds the ban on the śūdras for performing a Vedic ritual. On the other hand, there were some enlightened sages like Bādari, who upheld the right of the śūdras to perform rituals.

Govind Chandra Pande connects the restrictions as specified in the Apaśūdrādhikaraṇa to the desire of the priests for preserving their leadership. A reactionary outlook also emerged due to the challenge from Buddhism. "There is no doubt that liberal view of caste and religious rights was current even within the orthodoxy in this age is proved by *Mahābhārata*."[2] *Gītā* opened the doors of worship for śūdras and women. The puritans sought to counter this liberalism.

---

[1] Macdonell and Keith, 1912, *Vedic Index of Names and Subjects*, vol. II, p. 284.

[2] Pande, 1998, *Life and Thought of Śaṅkarācārya*, p. 144.

The question of nexus between *darśana* and *dharmaśāstra* arises here. Were the intellectuals soaring in the heights of philosophical spaces unmindful of the social and moral considerations? How far they considered the cultural values of the community and the social order? Navjivan Rastogi initiates a thought-provoking discussion on this question. He rightly points out that "growth of Indian philosophy had essentially been conditioned by the idea of liberation, i.e. *mokṣa*" whereas the *lokavyavahāras* – social practices and norms – were defined and regulated by the authors of Dharmaśāstras. This leads to a dichotomy between *pravṛtti* (empiricism) and *nivṛtti* (renunciation). The psycho-spiritual pursuit (*sādhanā*) looses the social context. Rastogi convincingly tries to argue for the restoration of social context by the non-orthodox systems leading to an alignment between liberation and life. He concludes that the Tantra succeeded in establishing a real nexus between the two truths – *paramārtha* and *vyavahāra.*[3]

However it is not quite correct to see an inner contradiction because of two polarities of affirmation and negation – the society-centric view and the spiritual pursuit. Within the system these contradictions were resolved by proposing alternate world-views. Realignment between *pravṛtti mārga* (empiricist way) and *nivṛtti mārga* (path of renunciation) between the society-centric view and the psycho-spiritual view was sought.

Bādarāyaṇa's postulations stand in conformity to Manu's dictates. But as Bādarāyaṇa's philosophical postulations are countered by the other philosophers like Bhāguri, *Mahābhārata* or *Gītā* within the orthodoxy; and more potentially by the onslaught of Buddhism and Jainism, counter-positions to the postulations of Manu continued to be envisaged. Unfortunately, during the regime of Warren Hastings in eighteenth century, Manu came to be regarded almost as the sole authority in respect of legal and social practices of the Hindu community. While Manu was followed

---

[3] Navjivan Rastogi, 2012, "Tantric Thought of Kashmir: A Framework of Humanistic Culture", *Sanskrit Vimarśaḥ*, new series 5.

in the larger part of the northern belt in India, there were other lawgivers for rest of the regions. Manu specifically suggests that he is standardizing the Dharmaśāstra for Āryāvarta — the land in the north of Vindhya mountain. There were other authorities in the area of Dharmaśāstra for Dakṣiṇāpatha (south), Magadha (in north-east), Gauḍa or Pāñcāla Deśas. Hundreds of *smṛtikāras* like Yājñavalkya, Parāśara, Kātyāyana, Śaṅkha and Likhita, Atri as well as the authors of *Nārada* and *Viṣṇusmṛti* provided constitutional framework for running the socio-religious and socio-political framework in diverse regions of the vast peninsula. Even though Manu ardently desired that the practices envisaged by the *agrajanmas* (brāhmaṇas) as codified by him in his law book, must be followed in the countries outside the Āryāvarta also — in the whole of the *pṛthivī* (Bhāratavarṣa), it was quite impossible that his wish would be realized. The *pṛthivī* or the vast country like India could not be governed by a single, rigid and unchanging constitution. Just as in the area of *darśana* (philosophy) so many systems and schools have been interacting and encountering with each other, and these interactions and encounters led to revisions and corrections in the systems, Dharmaśāstra offered wider and more potential field for oppositions and providing alternate systems. In all likelihood, even in the Āryāvarta, for which the codes of Manu were basically evolved, the other law books also prevailed.

The Dharmaśāstra either had to become more rigid and unitary or had to revise itself again and again in the wake of new philosophies and religious orders — Buddhists, Jainas, Tāntrikas, as well as the rise of the Bhakti movement. The revisions in the Dharmaśāstras (law books) were made in the last millennia of the BCE era, and they continued to be re-enforced or reinvigorated by fresh movements. If there was a Nigama tradition with the prevalence of *varṇāśrama*-centric and male-dominated world-view, there was the Āgama tradition. It continued in the practices of the Tantric cults, and the Bhāgavata and Vaiṣṇava schools of religious order. These cults and faiths simply overruled the hierarchies and inequalities — the differences of gender and caste, and proposed trans-varṇāśramic orders.

The lines of demarcation as well as the debates between the Vedic and non-Vedic philosophical systems — Cārvākas, Ājīvakas, Buddhists, Jainas — as well as the onslaught of philosophers like Madhva, Rāmānuja, Nimbārka and Rāmānanda within the orthodox philosophies as well as the Tantric cults need to be understood in a broad socio-cultural framework. When Dharmakīrti and other Buddhist philosophers were rejecting the whole concept of *jāti* as (generality) as a philosophical category, they were also challenging the concept of *jāti* in the sense of social hierarchy. The Tantric systems were also debating with the whole *varṇāśrama*-centric culture when they emphatically declared that after initiation in the cult, a śūdra no more remains a śūdra and a brāhmaṇa no more a brāhmaṇa. All distinctions based on caste are eliminated.[4] Abhinavagupta in this context raises a voice of protest against those who believe in the caste hierarchy. He says:

> Those, who deny liberation to women and śūdras, are possessed by the *mahāgraha* (great prejudice, great evil star), in their very limited horizon, they de-recognize the all-compassionate grace of God; their vision is marred by jealousy, concealment, and shame and they make themselves laughing stocks.[5]

These philosophies adopted a sustained strategy of debate for countering the social discordances arising out of the *varṇāśrama*-centric culture. They made strong refutations of the norms of

---

[4] गतं शूद्रस्य शूद्रत्वं विप्रस्यापि च विप्रता।
दीक्षासंस्कारसम्पन्ने जातिभेदो न विद्यते।।
— *Kulārṇava Tantra*, quoted by Navjivan Rastogi 2012

[5] केचिदाचक्षते - द्विजराजन्यप्रशंसापरमेतद्वाक्यम्, न तु, स्त्र्यादिष्वपवर्गप्राप्तितात्पर्येण इति। ते हि भगवतः सर्वानुग्राहिकां शक्तिं मितविषयतया खण्डयन्तः तथा परमेश्वरस्य परमकृपालुत्वमसहमानाः . . . . निरतिशययुक्तिप्रपञ्चसाधिताद्वैतभगवत्तत्त्वे भेदं बलादेवानयन्तो अन्यांश्चागमविरोधेन चेतयमानाः . . . परमन्तर्गर्भीकृतजात्यादिमहाग्रहाविष्टान्तःकरणाः मात्सर्यावहित्थलज्जाजिह्मीकृतावङ्मुखदृष्टय इति हास्यरसभावमात्मनि आरोपयन्ति इति।
— quoted by Navjivan Rastogi, ibid.

hierarchy. The systems they tried to evolve transgressed such norms, but ultimately achieved a reconciliation. The very term *vāma mārga* (left path) which came into prevalence for the Tantric cults denotes the adaptation of the ways and means to transgress all orthodoxy.

There are Smṛtis (law books) like the *Viṣṇusmṛti*, which reflect the alternate visions, provided by the Āgamic traditions. These Smṛti texts present as much divergence and a wide range of concrete ideas in respect of governance, polity and the social as well as the ethical norms as the philosophical systems in respect of abstract thinking.

Debates on Polity and Governance

One of the major disciplines taken up for discussions and debates was Arthaśāstra (management, polity and diplomacy). In *Rāmāyaṇa* there is a long discussion on king's duties and policies for governance initiated by Rāma during the course of his queries about the wellness when Bharata visits him in Citrakūṭa. Rāma asks Bharata:

> Is it so that you pay due regard to the preceptor Sudhanvan, who is equipped with excellent arms and is expert in Arthaśāstra?[6]

In fact, the prolonged queries here present a discussion on the subject of *prajāpālana* (nourishment of subjects by a king). The *mantraṇā* (counselling) is the base on which this polity proceeds and counselling is not be done singularly, it is always with a selected group.[7] This *mantraṇā* should properly employ *yukti*s (logic) and *tarka*s (arguments) to arrive at the *mantra*.[8] Rāma also suggests that

---

[6] इष्वस्त्रवरसम्पन्नमर्थशास्त्रविशारदम्।
सुधन्वानमुपाध्यायं कच्चित् त्वं तात मन्यसे।। – *Rāmāyaṇa* II.94.14

[7] कच्चिन्मन्त्रयसे नैकः कच्चिन्न बहुभिः सह।
कच्चित्ते मन्त्रितो मन्त्रः राष्ट्रं न परिधावति।। – Ibid. II.94.13

[8] कच्चित् तर्कैर्युक्त्या वै ये चाप्यपरिकीर्त्तिताः।
त्वया वा तव वाऽमात्यैर्बुध्यते तात मन्त्रितम्।। – Ibid. II.94.16

instead of approaching thousands of fools, a king must engage in discussions with one wise man only.[9] Further, Rāma suggests that the king should do counselling with three or four counsellors only, either together or one by one.[10]

Vajrasūcī and the Debate on the Caste System

Vajrasūcī of Aśvaghoṣa (see Chap. 2) is an essay in refutation of caste system. Aśvaghoṣa takes the following stands and refutes them one by one:

1. The *jīva* (individual soul) is brāhmaṇa,
2. a person becomes a brāhmaṇa by birth,
3. a particular human body is brāhmaṇa,
4. because of knowledge one can become a brāhmaṇa,
5. the conduct of a person makes him a brāhmaṇa,
6. the good deeds of a person make him a brāhmaṇa, and
7. the knowledge of Veda makes a person brāhmaṇa.

After giving reasons for the rejection of these views, Aśvaghoṣa presents his own thesis about what-makes one a brāhmaṇa. Accordingly, it is the spiritual attainment of a person that endows him with brāhmaṇahood. He also describes the process of observing rigorous vows and austerities, etc. that leads to this attainment. He then rejects *cāturvarṇya* — the fourfold division of society into castes — acknowledging that a man is born with only one *varṇa*.

Aśvaghoṣa cites verses from *Śukra* and *Mānava Dharmaśāstra* to support his argument. *Vajrasūcyopaniṣad* is a later text composed in Upaniṣadic style, it only repeats Aśvaghoṣa's arguments.

Laghuṭaṅka, a text written by Paṇḍit Subaji Bapu, is a rejoinder to *Vajrasūcī*. The author perhaps lived at Sehore near Bhopal and he prepared this rejoinder out of the discussions held in an assembly

---

[9] *Rāmāyaṇa* II.94.17-18.

[10] Ibid. II.94.19.

chaired by Wilkinson.[11]

Debates in Dharmaśāstras

The Smṛtis (law books) are of two types — Arthaśāstra and Dharmaśāstra. Books under the former deal with diplomacy, governance and management. Books under the second category also deal with the issues of politics and governance, etc. but they are more concerned with ethical norms, codes of conducts and rites for purification. The Smṛti texts are prescriptive in nature, but they also take up vital issues related to human destiny.

One of the questions taken up by some authors of Smṛti texts is about a person's dependence on *daiva* (fate) and *puruṣakāra* (industriousness). Yājñavalkya refers to a few divergent views here — Daivavāda (fatalism), Svabhāvavāda (naturalism), Kālavāda (pessimism) and Puruṣakāravāda (activism). In his opinion, success in life depends on *daiva* and *puruṣakāra* both. Even *daiva* is created by a man by his industriousness of the past life. Just as a chariot will not move with one wheel only, the same way without industriousness, even the fate will not materialize.[12] Which is more powerful — a man's industriousness or his fate — this question is discussed as a debatable issue by several authors and poets in Sanskrit literature.

The contradictory views in these texts on legal matters, laws of inheritance, women's rights and marriage, etc. reflect the differences of opinion and receptiveness of debates. Yājñavalkya

---

11 देशे मालव नामकेऽत्र नगरे भूपालनाम्नी शुभा तस्या अंति शिहुर नामक पुरी यस्यामजंठा-ग्रणी:विल्किन्सन्निति साहिबो विजयते तस्याश्रितानां सभामध्येऽभूल्लघुटङ्क एष विदुषां तोषाय दोषापह:। This is printed as prose in the text of *Vajrasūcyopaniṣad* produced by Ramesh Bharadwaj in his *Vajrasūcī of Aśvaghoṣa and the Concept of Varṇa-Jāti Through the Ages*. It is actually a verse in Śārdūlavikrīḍita meter and the second foot of which is to be corrected as तस्यां भाति शिहूर (सिहोर)-नामकपुरी यस्यामजण्ठाग्रणी: The text was composed in 1759 Śālivāhana year, which should CE 1837. Wilkinson's experiments in education are being discussed in the last chapter of this work.

12 *Yājñavalkyasmṛti*, Ācārādhyāya, 349-50, p. 118.

says that in case of divergence of opinions or difference in prescriptions, decision should be taken by *nyāya*. *Nyāya* here comprises of three facets — the practices of the elders who are reliable, the prevalence and the precedence. But Yājñavalkya also upholds the prominence of *dharmaśāstra* over *arthaśāstra*.[13]

Like the parliaments, judicial courts have also functioned as platforms for very lively debates on social, moral and ethical issues. Also, techniques for debates in these courts were also evolved. The Smṛti texts furnish in-depth analysis of the techniques and methodology of debates in judicial courts. The terms *vādī* and *prativādī* are used for the petitioner and the respondent. Alternately they are also called *arthī* and *pratyarthī*.[14] The model of *vāda* is taken up, *pratijñā* (statement), *sādhana* (proof, reason, probans), *pramāṇa* (evidence), *sādhya* (probandum), *vivāda* (dispute) and *siddhi* (success) — these are the terms the authors of law books have used to describe the judicial proceedings.[15]

Nārada says that for all kinds of *vyavahāras* (cases in the courts) the essence lies in *pratijñā* (statement of the disputant, the affidavit of the petitioner). If *pratijñā* is lacking, then *vādī* (disputant, petitioner) will suffer, and if it is solid, he can win the case.[16]

The gamut of these terms as well as the methodology for the conduct of judicial proceedings are based on the techniques of *vāda*. *Bṛhaspatismṛti* 1.17 lays down four steps of judicial process involving debate — (i) *pūrva-pakṣa* (the petitioner's view), (ii) *uttara-pakṣa* (reply by the respondent), (iii) *kriyāpāda* (specifying the action to be taken), and (iv) *nirṇaya* (judgement). The reply under (ii) has been divided by *Śukrasmṛti* into four categories:

---

[13] अर्थशास्त्रात्तु बलवद् धर्मशास्त्रमिति स्थितिः।
— *Yājñavalkyasmṛti*, Vyavahārādhyāya, 21, p. 145

[14] Ibid. 6, p. 130.

[15] Ibid. 7-8.

[16] सारस्तु व्यवहाराणां प्रतिज्ञा समुदाहृता।
तद्धाने हीयते वादी तरंस्तामुत्तरो भवेत्। — *Nāradasmṛti* 1.6

- *Satya* (factual) — it is also called *pratipatti*. It involves an acceptance of the points submitted by the petitioner.
- *Mithyā* (false) — is the negation of the points raised by the petitioner.
- *Pratyavaskandana* — partial acceptance with a view to denounce the case as presented by the petitioner. This is done by adding rejoinders.
- *Pūrvabhyāsavidhi* — a method involving citations of previous arguments and victory acquired by the respondent in the same or similar cases.

This structure is followed even today in submitting the counter-affidavits in the courts of law by the advocates representing the respondent.

The tactics of *chala* (cheating), *jāti* (avoiding reply) and *nigrahasthānas* (clinchers), as defined by the authors of the philosophical texts, were also practised in *dharmasabhās* (law courts). Nārada condemns the conduct of *vāk-chala* (cheating by speech).[17]

Kātyāyana (16-40), Bṛhaspati (2.8-9) and Śukra also discuss certain defects in the language or the reports prepared. Śukra defines these defects as under:

- *Anyārthaṁ* (giving a sense other than what is intended),
- *arthahīnaṁ* (nonsense),
- *pramāṇāgamavarjitaṁ* (lack of proofs),
- *hīnādhikaṁ* (having omissions and commissions), and
- *bhraṣṭaṃ* (corrupted statement).

Debates on Rights of Women

Kātyāyana prescribes death sentence for committing rape of a woman,[18] while Āpastamba differs with him and suggests that a

---

[17] सर्वेष्वपि विवादेषु वाक्छलेनापहीयते। — *Nāradasmṛti* 2.25

[18] स्त्रीषु कृतोपभोगः स्यात् प्रसह्य पुरुषो यदा
वधे तत्र प्रवर्तेत — *Kātyāyanasmṛti* 830

śūdra molesting an Āryan lady be hanged.[19] There are differences and debatable issues on punishments for adultery. Manu recommends that an adulteress should be thrown to dogs for being eaten,[20] whereas Kātyāyana is again much more human and generous here also. He directs the king to see that such a woman is freed after the declaration of her act of adultery.

It is commonly believed that the authors of Dharmaśāstras have not made any provision of divorce in marriage.[21] Dharmavir goes to the extent of alleging that the Sanskrit language does not have any word for divorce.[22] The authors of Dharmaśāstras, *Arthaśāstra* and *Kāmasūtra* do discuss the issue of separation in marriage and the term *mokṣa* has been used by them for divorce between married persons. Both man and woman are allowed to seek *mokṣa* in marriage. R.C. Majumdar rightly understands Kauṭilya when he says that "Kauṭilya permitted divorce to both husband and wife on the ground of mutual enmity".[23] Manu even recommends that a man may seek *mokṣa* from a woman who speaks harshly.[24] Kauṭilya would recommend *mokṣa* in marriage in exceptional circumstances

---

[19] वध्यः शूद्र आर्यायाम्। — *Āpastamba-Dharmasūtra* 2.10.9

[20] *Manusmṛti* 3.37.

[21] It has been seen that the Hindu marriage, being a sacrament, once performed before the nuptial fire with the sacred texts, becomes irrevocable on the completion of the ceremony of taking seven steps by the couple. There is no evidence as to the practice of divorce as such during the Vedic and post-Vedic period, . . . dissolution of marriage was not thus contemplated by the *śāstra*, for it was non-dharmic, unrighteous and sinful." — P.K. Virdi, *The Marriage*, quoted in *Dharmashastra: An Introductory Analysis*, ed. Brijkishor Swain, p. 160

[22] "सच बात यह है कि संस्कृत भाषा में तलाक के अर्थ का कोई शब्द नहीं है। यदि संस्कृत भाषा में तलाक के लिए शब्द होता, तो बुद्ध को घर छोड़कर भागना न पड़ता। . . . संस्कृत भाषा में तलाक और डाइवोर्स के अर्थ का शब्द नदारद है।"

— *Kāmasūtra kī Santāneṅ*, p. 15

[23] Swami Madhvanand, 2001, *Great Women of India*, p. 20.

[24] *Manusmṛti* IX.81.

only. Yājñavalkya, Kauṭilya and Vātsyāyana recommend remarriage for the lady who has obtained *mokṣa* from her husband. Such a lady is called *punarbhūḥ* (remarried). Such a marriage was not solemnized by Vedic rights in all cases. But then Yājñavalkya specifically prescribed that the son of a *punarbhūḥ* lady will be entitled for the property of his father. Nārada enumerates seven kinds of women who are allowed to remarry — three types of *punarbhūs* and four types of *svairiṇīs* (wanton women). The first type of *punarbhū* is a virgin, who was married but is *akṣatayoni*, i.e. never had a "penetration" with the first husband. She should be married with *saṁskāra* (Vedic rites). Second one leaves her husband for another man, but returns back to the first husband. The third one is remarried with a *savarṇa* and *sapiṇḍa* in the absence of a *devara* (husband's brother). The four *svairiṇīs* are:

1. When her husband is alive, she goes to some other man out of desire,
2. husband having died, she rejects his brother (*devara*) and chooses to live with an outsider,
3. a woman in dire circumstances sells herself for food and cloths and then accepts her buyer, and
4. a courageous lady who is given to someone in accordance with the local customs and times.[25]

Kauṭilya makes provisions for the lady choosing a second husband, when her first husband being alive or dead.[26]

These law givers prescribe divorce and remarriage in case of a lady married to an impotent person. A woman is like a field — says Nārada — "and the agricultural field cannot be handed over to a man who has no seed". Both Parāśara and Nārada make a provision for remarriage of women in five situations:

1. The husband has disappeared and his whereabouts are not

---

[25] *Nāradasmṛti* XII.45-52.

[26] *Arthaśāstra* III.2, vol. II, pp. 14-15.

known for a long time,

2. he has died,
3. he has become an ascetic,
4. he is impotent, and
5. he has committed adultery.[27]

If the husband has gone away and there is no news of him, a brāhmaṇa lady should wait for him for eight years in case she has born children from him; if she has no children then she should wait only for four years and then remarry. The time limit for the women of other castes is still lower.[28] Kauṭilya's follows Nārada in general; but he specifically instructs a lady to leave a man who has committed a sin, is convicted, is impotent, suffers from an incurable desease or is cruel.[29] He also prescribes divorce if both the husband and the wife do not like each other; but divorce is to be provided neither to the wife if she hates him for not liking her. In case both of them do not like each other, then they should be divorced. A man seeking divorce from a woman going against him may be obliged but not the woman. There is, however, no provision for a formal divorce in the marriages performed through Vedic rites.[30] But then, all law givers, cited above, make provision of going to another man in exceptional circumstances like the husband being impotent, etc. This only means that a lady having entered into a sacred bond of marriage, sanctified by Vedic rites, can leave her husband in these circumstances and start another life in a partnership. This living in partnership is in fact nothing less than marriage, as the lady gets all the benefits under the law.

---

[27] नष्टे मृते प्रव्रजिते क्लीबे च पतिते पतौ।
पञ्चस्वापत्सु नारीणां पतिरन्यो विधीयते।। — *Nāradasmṛti* XII.97

[28] *Nāradasmṛti* XII.98-100.

[29] नीचत्वं परदेशं वा प्रस्थितो राजकिल्बिषी।
प्राणाभिहन्ता पतितस्त्याज्यः क्लीबोऽपि वा पतिः।।
— *Arthaśāstra* III.2, vol. II, p. 18

[30] Ibid., p. 21.

There are sharp differences of opinion amongst the authors of Dharmaśāstras with regard to the rights of women, especially widows.[31] The views of Bṛhaspati, Kātyāyana and Parāśara are quite different from the others. Bṛhaspati would like to see that a widow lives with all the dignity of a lady. He says:

> A wife forms the half of her husband. No man can be said to have died if his wife is living.[32]

Yājñavalkya, Kātyāyana, Bṛhaspati and the author of *Viṣṇusmṛti* authorize the widow to inherit the property of her husband if he has no son.[33] If a man is not survived by his wife or sons, then the daughters would inherit his property.[34] On the other hand, there are law givers who will see that the *sapiṇḍa* relatives of the diseased person get his property. Bṛhaspati vehemently protests this practice. He goes to the extent of prescribing that the king should punish the relatives treating them as thieves, if at all they make any attempt of grabbing the property legally inherited by a widow.[35]

---

[31] In twentieth century, Jai Shankar Prasad, a prominent author in Hindi, wrote *Dhruvasvāminī* — a play in which the widow of the King Rāmagupta, after her husband is killed by his own younger brother Candragupta, marries the latter. In a very elucidative preface to this play, Prasad raised a debate on the legality of widow remarriage and cited the law books of Nārada and Parāśara. For details see "Dhruvasvāminī : Eka Ṭīkā" by me in *Naṭaraṅga 92*, April-June 2012.

[32] यस्य नोपरता भार्या देहार्धं तस्य जीवति।
जीवत्यर्धशरीरेऽर्धं कथमन्तं समाप्नुयात्।।— *Bṛhaspatismṛti* XXVI

[33] अपुत्रधनं पत्न्यभिगामी — *Viṣṇusmṛti* XVII.4, *Bṛhaspatismṛti* XXVI.93-94, *Kātyāyanasmṛti* 921

[34] पत्नी दुहितरश्चैव पितरौ भ्रातरौ तथा।
तत्सुता गोत्रजा बन्धुशिष्यसब्रह्मचारिणः।
एषामभावे पूर्वस्य धनभागुत्तरोत्तरः।
स्वर्यातस्य ह्यपुत्रस्य सर्ववर्णेष्वयं विधिः।। — *Yājñavalkyasmṛti,* Vyavahārādhyāya, 135-36, p. 238

[35] सपिण्डा बान्धवा ये तु तस्याः स्युः परिपन्थिनः।
हिंस्युर्धनानि तान् राजा चौरदण्डेन घातयेत्।। — *Bṛhaspatismṛti* XXVI.1-5

The laws of Viṣṇu, Bṛhaspati and Yājñavalkya must have made revolutionary effect on the social fabric, leading to sharp reactions from the supporters of patriarchy. *Nāradasmṛti* stoutly opposed the reformist and liberal views of the Smṛtis of Viṣṇu, Bṛhaspati and Yājñavalkya providing that the property of an issueless person will be confiscated by the state and the widow will be provided a bare maintenance.

Vijñāneśvara in CE 1100 further enlarged the scope of *strīdhana*, providing for inclusion of all property inherited by a woman in it. It is unfortunate that the Smṛtis of Prajāpati and Kātyāyana were lost, the male-dominated society did not care to preserve them, as they were fairly liberal to the other sex. Barring a few, the kings generally did not care to promulgate the laws of Viṣṇu, Yājñavalkya or Kātyāyana making the womenfolk more powerful. Kings like Kumārapāla of Gujarat were exceptions. Kumārapāla declared the right of a widow over the property of her husband in CE 1150. His court-poet praised him as more magnanimous than the illustrious kings like Raghu, Nahuṣa or Nābhāga.[36]

Manu appears to be rather insensitive in allowing liberty to women. If a woman leaves the house of her husband in a rage, she should be tied with ropes and put in the house, otherwise the husband should leave her to her father's house.[37] He levies a fine of six golden coins upon a lady going to night shows in *prekṣās* or *samājas*.[38] On the other hand, he is strictly against marrying a virgin to a man not fit for her. "It is better that a girl lives unwedded till her death, than be married to a man not suitable for her", he says. He also allows a young girl to seek a suitable match herself if the parents are unable to marry her.[39] On one hand, he deprives a married lady and

---

[36] A.S. Altekar, 1953, "Idea and Position of Indian Women in Social Life", p. 46.

[37] *Manusmṛti* IX.84.

[38] Ibid.

[39] Ibid. IX.89-90.

a daughter from inheriting the property of her husband or father, on the other he directs the brothers of a lady to provide a share of the property inherited by them to their sister; if they do not do so they are condemned.[40] But *Viṣṇusmṛti* declares in most unequivocal terms that the property of a man having died without any son will be inherited by his wife, and if he is not survived by his wife, then the property will go to his daughters.[41] Nandapaṇḍita in his commentary on *Viṣṇusmṛti* on this passage quotes Bṛhaspati's instructions to the king to punish the kin who makes an attempt to grab the property thus inherited by a widow.[42] Yājñavalkya directs that the father-in-law should provide equal part of his property for the wives of his sons if they have not inherited *strīdhana* (the money given to the bride by the parents). Even if they have been given *strīdhana*, they are to be provided with one half of the part given to the sons.[43] A widow will inherit the property equal to the share for her sons.[44]

The concept of *putrikā* — the only daughter of a man having no son is unique in this tradition. The *putrikā* is allowed to perform the last rites of her father and also to inherit his property. "Just as a son is the very soul of a man, so is the daughter" says Manu in the context of a *putrikā* — "how can any other person be allowed to take away a man's property if she is there?"[45] Most of the authors of Dharmaśāstras agree that the woman's property (*strīdhana*) will be inherited by the daughter/daughters only and not by her sons.[46]

The diversity of the opinions and concern for values of these law givers have gone a long way to sustain the Hindu society for

---

40 *Manusmṛti* IX.118.

41 अपुत्रधनं पत्न्यभिगामि। तदभावे दुहितृगामि। — *Viṣṇusmṛti* XVII.4-5

42 *Viṣṇusmṛti*, Commentary of Nandapaṇḍita, p. 288.

43 *Yājñavalkyasmṛti*, Vyavahārādhyāya, 115 (p. 221), 148 (p. 254).

44 Ibid. 123, p. 229.

45 यथैवात्मा तथा पुत्रः पुत्रेण दुहिता समा।
तस्यामात्मनि तिष्ठन्त्यां कथमन्यो धनं हरेत्।। — *Manusmṛti* IX.130

46 *Manusmṛti* IX.131.

centuries. Raja Rammohun Roy produced before Lord William Bentinck the relevant portions from the text of *Manusmṛti* describing the conduct of a widow when he was campaigning for the eradication of the practice of *satī*.[47] Swami Vivekananda and Lala Lajpat Rai also referred to these authors of Dharmaśāstras, to substantiate of their views on the rights of women.[48]

Openness for Debate

The questions whether the people belonging to lower castes (śūdras) have a right to perform Vedic rituals came to be discussed again and again. Kamalākara Bhaṭṭa, the author of *Nirṇayasindhu* (CE 1612) in his *Vivādatāṇḍava,* describes several such controversies. In his *Śūdrakamalākara*, he has discussed the rights of śūdras for performing rituals. Texts discussing the rights of śūdras for performing of rituals have been written till recent times by Sanskrit *paṇḍits* of Dharmśāstras.[49] Nāgeśa Bhaṭṭa had authored a text *Vrātyaprāyaścittavinirṇaya.* He debarred the community of kṣatriyas of his times from having the *upanayana*, because he believed that the real kṣatriyas vanished due to the massacres by Paraśurāma. The text was discussed at a *śāstra-sabhā* in Jaipur.[50]

---

[47] कामं तु क्षपयेद्देहं पुष्पमूलफलैः शुभैः।
न तु नामाऽपि गृह्णीयात् पत्यौ प्रेते परस्य तु।।
आसीतामरणात् क्षान्ता नियता ब्रह्मचारिणी।
यो धर्म एकपत्नीनां काङ्क्षन्ती तममनुत्तमम्।
अनेकानि सहस्राणि कुमारब्रह्मचारिणाम्।
दिवं गतानि विप्राणामकृत्वा कुलसन्ततिम्।।
मृते भर्तरि साध्वी स्त्री ब्रह्मचर्ये व्यवस्थिता।
स्वर्गं गच्छत्यपुत्राऽपि यथा ते ब्रह्मचारिणः।। — *Manusmṛti* V.157-60

[48] Lala Lajpat Rai, 1928, *Unhappy India*, Calcutta: Banna Publishing Co., pp. 167-68, referred in *Dharmaśāstra: A Link Between Tradition and Modernity*, ed. B.K. Swain (2003), p. 109.

[49] *Śūdrāhnikapaddhatiḥ*, ed. Jayakrishna Mishra, Puri, 2008.

[50] This statement is based on the article by Madhav M. Deshpande, 2010, "Kṣatriyas in Kali Age?: Gāgābhaṭṭa and His Opponents", *Indo-Iranian Journal*, 53: 95-120.

As long the prescriptions and codes of conduct remain open for debates and revision, the society remains free from the clutches of fundamentalism. This is brought out by the episode of Gāgā Bhaṭṭa making an allowance for the *abhiṣeka* (coronation) of Shivaji; it is an example of flexibility.

The Bhonsales were not regarded as kṣatriyas. Paṇḍit Kṛṣṇa Naraharíśeṣa, a contemporary of Akbar, had written *Śūdrācāraśiromaṇi* in support of this contention. This produced a hurdle in the coronation ceremony of Shivaji and also his enjoying the status of *Chatrapati* (lord with the royal umbrella). Local brāhmaṇas were not at all in favour of allowing a coronation ceremony with Vedic rituals. There was a bitter dispute. Paṇḍits at Kāśī were approached. Viśveśvara Paṇḍita, better known as Gāgā Bhaṭṭa (CE 1640–1700), was supposed to be the greatest authority on Dharmaśāstras amongst them. According to Paṇḍit Baldeva Upadhyaya's version, he was persuaded by Balaji who went to Kāśī for the purpose of getting the support of the *paṇḍitas*. Gāgā Bhaṭṭa not only accepted a fictitious genealogy of Shivaji establishing him a descendant of solar race, he also wrote a text *Kāyasthadharmapradīpa* in refutation of *Śūdrācāra-śiromaṇi* of Paṇḍit Kṛṣṇa Naraharíśeṣa.[51]

Baldeva Upadhyaya (1994: 38) refers to his having performed the ritual ceremony for the enthronement of Shivaji at Raigarh in 1674. He also describes Gāgā's participation in a *dharmasabhā* held at the Rājāpur village in Koṅkaṇ during 1664. The incidence is reported in *Śivadigvijaya*, a Marāṭhī chronicle.

---

[51] From the accounts given by Baldeva Upadhyaya it appears as if the huge sum of money paid by Bālājī was instrumental in changing the mindset of Gāgā Bhaṭṭa and to make give a verdict in favour of Shivaji. But as Madhav M. Deshpande informs, Gāgā Bhaṭṭa had already made his mind in favour of Shivaji ten years before the event of the coronation. He even encouraged the initiative for a proper *abhiṣekavidhi* (royal consecration ceremony) of Shivaji. — Madhav M. Deshpande, 2010, "Kṣatriyas in Kali Age?: Gāgābhaṭṭa and His Opponents", *Indo-Iranian Journal*, 53: 95-120.

In another version of the visit of Gāgā Bhaṭṭa to Maharashtra, he is reported to have met Saint Rāmdās at Paṇḍharapur with a view to hold discussions with him on philosophy. The saint called his disciple, Veṇābāī to have a sitting with the scholar par excellence with a copy of the text of his *Dāsabodha* and explain the monistic doctrine accordingly. Gāgā Bhaṭṭa is said to have satisfied by her discourse on the teachings of her master.[52]

Gāgā Bhaṭṭa composed a regulatory text, titled *Śrīśivarājyābhiṣeka-prayoga,* for the occasion of coronation. He incorporated *mantras* from *Atharvaveda*, *Aitareya Brāhmaṇa*, *Viṣṇudharmottara Purāṇa* and other tetxs in it. Yet another manual for the coronation ceremony, entitled *Śrīśivarājyābhiṣekakalpataru,* was prepared under the direction of Niścalapurī having affiliation to Tantric traditions. Madhavi Narsalaya has shown that the coronation ceremony had to be carried twice under strange circumstances.[53]

The dispute on the validity of Shivaji's coronation continued even after his death and the question of the status of Candrasenīya Kāyasthas as kṣatriyas was reopened in a massive *śāstra-sabhā* during the reign of Shahuji Bhonsale. The *sabhā* disallowed kṣatriyahood to the Candrasenīya Kāyasthas. This debate continued up to the nineteenth-twentieth centuries.[54]

---

[52] Swami Madhvanand, 2001, op. cit., p. 354.

[53] Madhavi Narsalaya, *The King with One Kingdom but Two Coronations: Analysing Śrīśivarājyābhiṣekaprayoga* and *Śrīśivarājyābhiṣekakalpataru the Two Coronation Texts for Chatrapati Śivājī Mahārāja,* abstract published in the *Book of Abstracts*, 16th World Sanskrit Conference, Bangkok, pp. 260-61.

[54] Madhav M. Deshpande, 2010, op. cit., pp. 95-120.

6

Vāda in Literary Theory and Literature

In the history of Indian intellectual discourses, *Alaṁkāraśāstra* (aesthetics and literary theory) presents some of the most fascinating and enduring debates. These debates subsist on looking at a literary discourse or a piece of art from two angles — objective and subjective.

The term *vāda* was adopted from the intellectual discourses in the realm of arts and aesthetics, especially in music and theatre. The seven musical notes (*svaras*) were classified in four categories — *vādī, saṁvādī, vivādī* and *anuvādī.*[1]

Nāṭyaśāstra as a Saṁvāda Text

Nāṭyaśāstra is one of the most voluminous texts on performing and visual arts, theatre, aesthetics, poetry and drama produced more than two thousand years ago. Bharatamuni who is said to be the author of the *Nāṭyaśāstra,* came to be regarded such a great authority on *nāṭya* (theatre) in his life, so that some other *munis* (sages) out of their curiosity and a keen desire to understand *nāṭya* approached him and asked him a number of questions about it. Bharata's replies to their questions and counter-questions in the presence of his actor-students, led to the compilation of a voluminous text — the *Nāṭyaśāstra*, which was structured in the form of a dialogue. This is the structure adopted in the Āgama texts also.

Nāṭyaśāstra starts with a debate and ends in the resolution of another debate. In the series of replies to questions and counter-

---

[1] चतुर्विधत्वमेतेषां विज्ञेयं गानयोक्तृभिः।
वादी चैवाथ संवादी विवादी चानुवाद्यपि।। — *Nāṭyaśāstra* XXVIII.22

questions, Bharata Muni narrates how *nāṭya* originated and evolved. He recounts his experiments and the failure of the debut performance under his direction. *Samudramanthana*, the play he chose to present on the occasion of the festival of Indra was disrupted by the demons who thought that the performance is a humiliation to them. Virūpākṣa, their leader started arguing and questioning the propriety of the performance. Then followed a discussion on the nature of *nāṭya* and the demons were reconciled.[2]

The debate with the demons involved physical violence, as they tried to disrupt the performance. The debate in the last chapter of *Nāṭyaśāstra* suggests that the violence of speech is much more dangerous. Bharata was aware of diverse regional theatre practices represented by the minor forms of drama which were later on termed as *uparūpakas*. In the last chapter of *Nāṭyaśāstra*, he informs that his sons, trained by him in Nāṭyaveda, later on began to perform the *śilpakas*[3] of rustic nature (*grāmyadharmaka*). The sons of Bharata, in the *śilpakas* performed by them, presented the life and deeds of the sages residing in the vicinity of Himalayas by the way of *viḍambana* (caricature) and *vyaṅgyakaraṇa* (satire). The sages being laughed at in this way, got infuriated and cursed the actors to be expelled from the divine region of the Himalayas and to become śūdras.

The first production of a play by Bharata Muni aroused a fierce debate on the character of demons portrayed there. The performance of the *uparūpaka* described at the end of dialogues and discussions by Bharata Muni also generated a heated debate. But like the first debate, this also finally resulted in reconciliation. The sages did not revoke their curse, but the disciples of Bharata who have been arguing with their mentor agreed to move from north to south to continue their activities of the *nāṭya* in a more meaningful way.[4]

---

[2] *Nāṭyaśāstra*, chap. I.

[3] *Śilpaka* is one of the *uparūpakas* (minor forms of drama).

[4] *Nāṭyaśāstra*, chap. XXXVII.

Vāda Reflected in the Conceptual Framework of Nāṭyaśāstra

In *Nāṭyaśāstra* several categories reflect *vāda* concepts. Out of the nineteen items of *pūrva-raṅga* (preliminaries to be performed before producing a play on the stage), *trigata* consists of a loose talk between *sūtradhāra* (stage manager) and his two associates involving questions, objections and sarcastic remarks on the very performance of the play to be produced. One of the two associates of the stage manager in *trigata* is necessarily the *vidūṣaka* (jester). An impromptu debate is created through *trigata* in a theatric manner by his interjections. The very concept of *pūrva-raṅga* presents the *vidūṣaka* as a character who would use his debating skills for humour.

Vāda and its categories are conspicuously employed in the theory of *vācika abhinaya* involving speech for performance. A content of a dramatic piece is structured in dialogues. The presentation of these dialogues with *abhinaya* creates theatre. The verbal content of a play in this way may have exchange of views, discussions involving repartees and rejoinders. In chap. XXII of *Nāṭyaśāstra*, Bharata has discussed twelve types of *vākyābhinaya,* some of the categories of which are imbued with skills of debate. These twelve types are: *ālāpa* (addressing), *pralāpa* (gibberish talk), *vilāpa* (lamentation), *anulāpa* (repetition), *saṁlāpa* (exchange of words, verbal dual), *apalāpa* (refutation of what has been said earlier), *sandeśa* (message), *atideśa* (agreement), *nirdeṣa* (instruction), *vyapadeśa* (concealed speech), *upadeśa* (advice) and *apadeśa* (suggestion).[5]

---

[5] काव्यवस्तुषु निर्दिष्टो द्वादशाभिनयात्मकः।
आलापश्च प्रलापश्च विलापः स्यात्तथैव च ।
अनुलापोऽथ संलापस्त्वपलापस्तथैव च।।
सन्देशाश्चातिदेशश्च निर्देशः स्यात्तथापरः।
उपदेशोऽपदेशश्च व्यपदेशश्च कीर्तितः।।
आभाषणं तु यद्वाक्यमालापो नाम स स्मृतः।
अनर्थकं वचो यत्तु प्रलापः स तु कीर्तितः।
करुणप्रभवो यस्तु विलापः स तु कीर्तितः।

→

In his treatment of thirty-six *kāvya lakṣaṇas* (characteristics of a literary discourse), Bharata Muni has incorporated some of the categories related to *vāda*. *Dṛṣṭānta* is one of the *kāvya-lakṣaṇas*. An illustration which comes in attestation to the context of *pakṣa* exemplifying the (cause *hetu*) is *dṛṣṭānta*.[6] This is an application of one of the techniques of debate as given in *Nyāyadarśana*.

In fact, the practice of *dṛṣṭānta* — exemplification of a philosophical discourse or argument by an illustration involving an episode — is very old. In Buddhism, a dārṣṭāntic sect, known for giving *dṛṣṭāntas* (illustrations) developed along with the four well-known sects (Sautrāntika, Vaibhāṣika, etc.). However, the idea of *dṛṣṭānta* as a *kāvya lakṣaṇa* in *Nāṭyaśāstra* has been directly borrowed from *Nyāyadarśana* as the use of terms *hetu* and *pakṣa* clearly suggests.

Prāpti is another *kāvya lakṣaṇa* envisaging the techniques of *vāda*. *Prāpti* incorporates the concepts of *anumāna* and *pañcāvayava vākya* from *Nyāyadarśana*. It occurs when a *bhāva* (situation) is inferred by visualizing some of the *avayavas* (components).[7] In *akṣara-saṁghāta* (confluence of letters) *chala* as defined in Nyāya philosophy is adopted. Abhinavagupta has cited dialogues from the play *Ubhayābhisārikā* to illustrate *akṣara-saṁghāta*. In the dialogue

---

← बहुशोऽभिहितं वाक्यमनुलाप इति स्मृतः।।
उक्तिप्रत्युक्तिसंयुक्तः संलाप इति कीर्तितः।
पूर्वोक्तस्यान्यथावादो ह्यपलाप इति स्मृतः।
तदिदं वचनं ब्रूहीत्येष सन्देश उच्यते।
यत्त्वयोक्तं मयोक्तं तत्सोऽतिदेश इति स्मृतः।।
स एषोऽहं ब्रवीमीति निर्देश इति कीर्तितः।
व्याजान्तरेण कथनं व्यपदेश इहोच्यते।।
इदं कुरु गृहाणेति ह्युपदेशः प्रकीर्तितः।
अन्यार्थकथनं यत्स्यात्सोऽपदेशः प्रकीर्तितः।। — *Nāṭyaśāstra* XXII.51-59

[6] सर्वलोकमनोग्राहि यस्तु पक्षार्थसाधकः।
हेतोर्निदर्शनकृतः स दृष्टान्त इति स्मृतः ।। — Ibid. XVI.142

[7] दृष्ट्वैवावयवान्कांश्चिद्भावो यत्रनुमीयते।
प्राप्तिं तामपि जानीयाल्लक्षणं नाटकाश्रयम्। — Ibid. XVI.143

between a *viṭa* (pander) and a *parivrājikā* (nun), the former tells his name as Vaiśikācala and the nun adopting *chala* (cheating), understands the meaning of his name in the sense of an adherent of the Vaiśeṣika philosophy, and quickly retorts that she has nothing to do with a person who sticks to the Vaiśeṣika philosophy. In this way the dialogue goes on presenting a fake debate.[8]

The *sandhyaṅgas* (components of junctures of plot in a drama) also incorporate elements of debate. In the third juncture named as *garbhasandhi* (embryo) the tussle reaches the peak. Some of the components of *garbhasandhi* naturally are imbued with sharp exchange of words. We can see the use of techniques of debate like *jalpa, vitaṇḍā, chala, jāti* or *nigraha-sthāna* in them. *Vyavasāya* is arriving at a decision through *pratijñā* and *hetu*. A speech in challenging tone is *dyuti*. Dialogues attributing blemishes are *paribhāṣaṇa*.[9]

Dhanañjaya in his *Daśarūpaka*, however, uses the term *jalpa* (debate) to define *paribhāṣā*.[10]

Some other *sandhyaṅgas* imbibing the tenets of *vāda* are *yukti, samādhāna, anumāna, ākṣepa, apavāda, gurukīrtana* and *nirṇaya*.

Amongst the ten major forms of drama — the *daśarūpakas* — the definitions of *prahasana* and *vīthī* as given in *Nāṭyaśāstra* include some categories of debate. In fact, *vīthī* is a theatre of debate. Unfortunately, *vithī*s exemplifying the definition in *Nāṭyaśāstra* are

---

8 द्रव्यं ते तनुरायताक्षि दयिता रूपादयस्ते गुणाः
सामान्यं तव यौवनं युवजनः संस्तोति कर्माणि ते।
त्वय्यर्थे समवायमिच्छति जनो यस्माद् विशेषोऽस्ति ते
योगस्ते तरुणैर्मनोभिलाषितैर्मोक्षोऽप्यनिष्टाज्जनात्।।
— Cited by Abhinavagupta in *Abhinavabhāratī on Nāṭyaśāstra* XVI.136, *Nāṭyaśāstra*, vol. II, Delhi, 1988, p. 257

9 व्यवसायश्च विज्ञेयः प्रतिज्ञाहेतुसंभवः।
वाक्यमाधर्षसंयुक्तं द्युतिस्तज्ज्ञैरुदाहृता।
परिवादकृतं यस्यात्तदाहुः परिभाषणम् ।। — *Nāṭyaśāstra* XIX.19

10 परिभाषा मिथो जल्पः। — *Daśarūpaka* I.52

not available. There are thirteen *vīthyaṅgas* (components of *vīthī*). Some of them are in fact built in by various forms of debate. These thirteen *vīthyaṅgas* create the structure of the prologue of a play and they also make two of the major forms of drama – *prahasana* and *vīthī*. In *prahasana*, characters like a recluse, an ascetic, a brāhmaṇa and others engage themselves in *hāsyavāda,* i.e. arguments for creating laughter. Then the play also presents *dhūrtapravivāda* (debate between the rogues).[11]

Out of the thirteen constituents of the *vīthī*, the following are imbued with some form of debate or the other — *udghātyaka, nālikā, asatpralāpa, vākkelī, prapañca, mṛdava, chala, trigata, adhibala* and *gaṇḍa.*[12]

Of these *udghātyaka* is an accidental interpretation, suggestive of the meaning of a sentence otherwise obscure. *Avaspandita* is a transferred significance, where the meaning is intrepretated otherwise. *Nālikā* is an enigmatic speech making fun of others. *Asatpralāpa* is a jittering in the form of an advice given to a fool who rejects it outright. *Vākkelī* is formed of repartees in course of a playful conversation. *Mṛdava* is advancing arguments for praise and condemnation, the intention being just opposite. It involves sarcasm. *Chala* is misrepresentation of a sentence in order to deceive another or to provoke him. *Trigata* has been discussed as one of the constituents of *prastāvanā* (prologue) of a play. *Adhibala* is strengthening an argument during the course of dialogue between two persons, each defending his own position through reasoning. *Gaṇḍa* is verbosity with anger and excitement in the form of altercation casting several aspersions.

Finally, *Nāṭyaśāstra* also opens the gateways for a *svarāja* in theatre in the treatment of an inner *vāda* which goes on inside an actor. Bharata Muni presents his own paradigm for the autonomy of his discipline and freedom of the artist. *Loka* (world), *veda* (theory)

---

[11] *Nāṭyaśāstra* XVIII.103-06.

[12] Ibid. XVIII.113-25.

and *adhyātma* (self of the artist), these three are defined by him as the *pramāṇas* (criteria) for theatre.[13] An artist has to search his own way in the context of the world around him and the framework of theories and methods that he has been tutored in.

Concepts and Categories of Vāda in Literary Theory

Alaṁkāraśāstra (literary theory) has especially adopted categories and concepts from the philosophy of *vāda*. *Vākovākya* a figure of speech defined by Bhoja comes as a direct reflection of the concept of *vāda* in poetics. As per Bhoja's definition, *vākovākya* is formed by exchange of words between two or more persons by the way of strong assertions and repartees.[14] Viśveśvara in his *Camatkāracandrikā* reproduces this definition.

There are *alaṁkāras* (figures of speech) based on the *pramāṇas* (means of knowledge). Bhoja in his *Śṛṅgāraprakāśa* has given a very profound and subtle treatment of *pramāṇālaṁkāras*. Other *alaṁkāras* based on the techniques of logic (*vāda*) are *kāvyaliṅga* (also called *hetu*), *kāraṇamālā* (series of causes), *uttara* (reply) and *asaṅgati* (incongruity).

Alaṁkāras like *Kāvyaliṅga* and *Kāraṇamālā* are based on concepts of causality in Nyāya philosophy. Whereas *alaṁkāras* like *Vakrokti* are based on the concept of *chala.* In *alaṁkāras* like *Saṁśaya* and *Bhrāntimān* a world of aesthetics is created on the edifice of their concepts of *vāda.*

Vakrokti as an *alaṁkāra* is defined as "the utterance of one person misconstrued by the other on the basis of pun or intonation".[15] *Vakrokti* in this way is an aesthetic rendering of *chala.* In Sanskrit lyric poetry, this idea of *vakrokti* led to the cultivation of a genre

---

[13] लोको वेदस्तथाध्यात्मं प्रमाणं त्रिविधं स्मृतम् ।
वेदाध्यात्मपदार्थेषु प्रायो नाट्यं प्रतिष्ठितम्। — *Nāṭyaśāstra* XXV.120

[14] उक्तिप्रत्युक्तिमद्वाक्यं वाकोवाक्यं विदुर्बुधाः।
द्वयोर्वक्त्रोस्तदिच्छन्ति बहूनामपि सङ्गमे।। — *Sarasvatīkaṇṭhābharaṇa* II.3

[15] *Kāvyaprakāśa* IX.78.

entirely resting on debate between two persons and thousands of stanzas, and even long poems were created as *vakrokti-kāvyas*. This is being taken up in a next section.

Major Debates in Literary Theory

One of the debates that continued in the history of *Alaṁkāraśāstra* (literary theory) from Bhāmaha (sixth century CE) to this date revolves around the question as to what constitutes a *kāvya* — the word or the meaning or *sāhitya* of both? Bhāmaha after spelling out the two opposite views argues in favour of *sāhitya*.

Debates have been raging in the form of agreements and disagreements as well as refutations and correspondences amongst the proponents of the six systems or theories holding one out of *rasa, dhvani, alaṁkāra, vakrokti, rīti* and *aucitya* (propriety) as the most essential element in *kāvya*. The tradition does not regard these systems as isolated schools of theory. They are related to the three aspects of literary activity — creative process, form and reception of a literary discourse involving the triangle of *kavi, kāvya* and *sahṛdaya*. The theory of *vakrokti* and *alaṁkāra* is concerned with the first, theory of *rīti* generally with the second and the theories of *rasa, dhvani* and *aucitya* with the third, i.e. receptivity.

In the realm of *rasa* discourse, Śaṅkuka and Mahima Bhaṭṭa were devout Naiyāyikas and also Ālaṁkārikas (literary critics) who understood *rasa* experience as inference. They applied the logical apparatus of inference (*anumāna*) to prove that the realization of *rasa* is *anumiti*. The Anumitivādin proves to be the most potential challenge for the Vyañjanāvāda (the theory of suggestion). Mahima Bhaṭṭa's *Vyaktiviveka* is a text in refutation to *dhvani*.

In additional to this, there are a number of texts which subsist on *vāda* for their structural design. There are texts in which *vāda* percolates in its broad sense — the whole text is conceived in a dialogic nature. *Kāvyamīmāṁsā* of Rājaśekhara (tenth century CE) may be cited as an example.

Kāvyamīmāṁsā as a Vāda Text

Rājaśekhara's views on knowledge systems and argumentative philosophies have been referred earlier (see Chap. 2). He had modelled his *Kāvyamīmāṁsā* on Kauṭilya's *Arthaśāstra*, so that the whole text is designed in the *vāda* style. He states various prima-facie views and then expounds his view. He refers to various views under the denominations such as *tad āhuḥ* (as they say), *iti ācāryāḥ* (thus speak the masters), *iti apare* (the others say this), *iti kecit* (some say so), or he will cite the names of the theorists. For example, his discourse on *vidyās* may be cited.[16]

Rājaśekhara in this lively style presents some very fascinating debates on certain fundamental issues related to poetry or belles-lettres. Amongst these debates, discussion on the relationship between poetry and the worldy phenomena is noteworthy. Rājaśekhara has referred to divergent views; some holding that the phenomena exist independent of *kāvya* or belles-lettres, while the others going to the extent of insisting that the worldly phenomena do not exist on their own, they exist as per their representation in poetry. Rājaśekhara attempts at reconciliation between these two polarities.

Another important debate elucidated by Rājśekhara pertains to the value of *kāvya*. The puritans insist on doing away with all forms of *kāvya*. Rājaśekhara has cited three statements from these opponents of *kāvya* with the respective arguments advanced by each. The detractors of *kāvya* say that no one should engage with *kāvya* because *kāvya* subsists in falsehood, sin and vulgarity.

---

[16] वार्ता कामसूत्रं शिल्पशास्त्रं दण्डनीतिरिति पूर्वैः सहाष्टादश विद्यास्थानानि – इत्यपरे। आन्वीक्षिकी त्रयी वार्ता दण्डनीतिश्चेति विद्याः। दण्डनीतिरेवैका इत्यौशनसाः। दण्डभयाद्धि कृत्स्नो लोकः स्वेषु स्वेषु कर्मस्ववतिष्ठते। वार्ता दण्डनीतिर्द्वे विद्ये इति बार्हस्पत्याः। वृत्तिर्विनयग्रहणं च स्थितिर्लोकयात्रायाः। त्रयी वार्ता दण्डनीतयस्तिस्रो विद्या इति मानवाः। त्रयी हि वार्तादण्डनीत्योरुपदेष्ट्री। आन्वीक्षिकीत्रयीवार्तादण्डनीतयश्चतस्रो विद्या इति कौटिल्यः। आन्वीक्षिक्या हि विवेचिता त्रयी वार्तादण्डनीत्योः प्रभवति। पञ्चमी साहित्यविद्येति यायावरीयः। — *Kāvyamīmāṁsā*, chap. II, pp. 24-25

Rājaśekhara enumerates these as three different prima-facie views[17] and after elaborating upon their arguments, he takes them one by one for refutation with profuse examples. This in fact is a fight against the puritans with their Platonic ideas.

Rasa Discourse: Debates and Diversities

There has been the continuity of a vigorous *bauddhika-vimarda* (intellectual wrestling) with regard to *rasa* discourse. Two factors functioned as catalysts for intensifying the debates on *rasa*. On one hand the diverse world-views that have been developing as parallels percolated in the *rasa* discourse; on the other, *rasa* discourse was also being nurtured by adopting categories and concepts from various systems of philosophy.

Jai Shankar Prasad, one of the greatest poets of twentieth century, made an interesting remark in one of his essays on art and art experience — that there are two streams of thought regarding the aesthetic experience in India — Ānandavāda and Duḥkhavāda. The former is represented by Indra and the latter by Varuṇa. The remark was made rather surreptitiously and Prasad did not cite any authentic source to support his thesis. However, we find that the theory of *rasa* as a blend of pleasure and pain (*sukhaduḥkhātmaka*) has been supported long before Abhinavagupta, who cites the Sāṁkhya view of *rasa*.[18]

Rasa was defined as the abiding or stable emotion that emerges when its determinants, ensuants and ancillaries are described or presented.[19] Bharata Muni has equated the emergence of this

---

17 असत्यार्थाभिधायित्वान्नोपदेष्टव्यम् काव्यम् इत्येके। — *Kāvyamīmāṁsā,* chap. VI, pp. 81-82
असदुपदेशकत्वात्तर्हि नोपदेष्टव्यम् काव्यम् इत्यपरे। — Ibid., p. 89
असभ्यार्थाभिधायित्वान्नोपदेष्टव्यम् काव्यम् इति च केचित्। — Ibid., p. 91

18 सांख्यदृशा सुखदुःखस्वभावो रसः। — *Abhinavabhāratī,* on chap. VI of *Nāṭyaśāstra*

19 Translated as excitants, ensuants and variants by G.N. Jha. He also translates *saṁyoga* as conjunction, *ālambana* as basic cause and *uddīpana* as inflaming cause.

emotion to creating the taste by mixing various ingradients in the cooking of a recipe. It was basically located in the characters described in a play.

Rasa is viewed as something lying at the core, and also percolating within the art form. If *kāvya* is a tree, *rasa* is the seed from which the roots of this tree sprout, and *rasa* is its flowers and fruits as well.

With this formalistic view or the view related to the structure of an art form — *rasa* was redefined with the change of the medium and form. Mātṛgupta, as quoted by Abhinavagupta and many other authors and commentators, has defined various categories of *rasa* according to the types of *abhinaya,* i.e. *vācika, nepathyaja* and *svabhāvaja. Vācika-rasa* is the aesthetic experience resulting from the dialogues of a dramatic text; *nepathyaja* or *āhārya rasa* manifests where there is a proper arrangement of external means for beautification; and *svabhāvaja rasa* manifests through the inner qualities of the characters of a play.[20]

Thus like *nāṭya rasa* (*rasa* in the structure of a theatre performance) and *kāvya rasa* (*rasa* in literary structure), there can be *nṛtya rasa* (*rasa* in dance form) and *saṅgīta rasa* (*rasa* in music) as well. *Viṣṇudharmottara Purāṇa* and Bhoja discuss *citra rasa* (*rasa* in painting) and its varieties. Accordingly, there are nine varieties of painting in accordance with these nine *rasas* — *śṛṅgāracitra, hāsyacitra,* etc.).[21] Bhoja however gives eleven types of *citra rasas*

---

[20] I have collected all the available excerpts of Mātṛgupta's *kārikās* reproduced by his successors in my *Aprāptanāṭyaśāstrīya Grantha.* The same has also been reproduced in my *Nāṭyaśāstraviśvakośa.* Regarding the three varities of *rasa* based on three types of *abhinaya,* Rāghavabhaṭṭa quotes him:

रसास्तु त्रिविधा ज्ञेया वाङ्नेपथ्यस्वभावजाः।
रसानुरूपैरालापैः श्लोकैर्वाक्यैः पदैस्तथा।
नानालङ्कारसंयुक्तैर्वाचिको रस उच्यते।।

[21] *Viṣṇudharmottara Purāṇa,* Khaṇḍa III.43.1.

by adding *preyān* and one more *rasa* in the list.[22]

To Lollaṭa, the intensification of the abiding emotion or *sthāyī bhāva* becomes *rasa* after it is originated through its *vibhāvas* (causes) and manifests through *vyabhicārīs* (auxiliaries). The actors are mistaken for the original characters through "a willing suspension of disbelief". The abiding emotions of the original characters are superimposed on these actors. This process of superimposition is combined with another process which Lollaṭa had termed *tādrūpyānusandhāna* — a searching thereafter for an identification. This search for identity leads an actor to present a semblance of the dramatis personae and the audience to perceive the intensified emotion, which is finally consummated as *rasa*. The process requires the existence of the subject and the object as two separate entities. This process presupposes a conscious effort on the part of the connoisseur for realization of *rasa*.

Śaṅkuka, criticized Lollaṭa and explained the emergence of *rasa* through the dual process of *anukṛti* and *anumiti* (inference). He anticipates the whole concepts of *sādhārṇīkaraṇa* (decontexualization, universalization) when he says that the *anukṛti* done by the actor leads the spectator to cognize this actor as the character but this cognition is different from all the four possible categories of worldly cognitions — *samyak* (real), *mithyā* (mistaken), *saṁśaya* (doubt) and *sādṛśya* (similarity). He also uses the analogy of the horse in painting (*citraturaganyāya*) to describe the trans-mundane or extraordinary nature of this process. This leads to an inference, and inferred emotion becomes *rasa*. This is made possible through the skill and training of the actor in representation, as he also has to undergo through the *anusandhāna vyāpāra*.

We thus find that the rhetoricians like Daṇḍin and Vāmana on one hand and the followers of Bharata like Lollaṭa and Śaṅkuka on the other hand upheld the formalistic and objective view of *rasa*. But then a subjective view of *rasa* was proposed with all its psychic

[22] *Samarāṅgaṇasūtradhāra*, p. 632.

ramifications. A great turning point in the development of *rasa* theory comes with Bhaṭṭanāyaka. Bhaṭṭanāyaka revolutionized the whole thinking, shifting the emphasis to the experience of *sahṛdaya* (connoisseur). To explain the psycho-somatic process of *rasa* realization, he adopted terms from four philosophical systems — Sāṁkhya, Mīmāṁsā, Vedānta and Śaivism. In earlier views of Lollaṭa and Śaṅkuka, the perceiver and the object of perception both are situated on different planes of time and space, and are interrelated only due to *anusandhāna* (search for identification) or *anumiti* (inference). In contrast to this, Bhaṭṭanāyaka found both the subject and the object uprooted from their time and space to stand on a single plane in the state of *bhoga* (bliss). Abhinavagupta, providing a subtle interpretation to his theory, calls this process of uprooting as *ubhayadeśakāla-tyāga*. Śāradātanaya in his *Bhāvaprakāśa* exhaustively explains Bhaṭṭanāyaka's theory and he also shows how the whole process can be explained through the tenets of Śaivism. Accordingly, the three elements — *rāga*, *vidyā* and *kalā* — cause an inclination in a person to the pursuits of art. Because of *rāga* the objects of poetry, even when they are contaminated with sorrow and illusion, produce *sukhābhimāna* (sense of pleasure). He suggests that the process of *bhāvakatva* or *sādhārṇīkaraṇa* tends to eradicate the intense crisis of human personality — remaining shackled with particularities. Once the mind is liberated from its limits, it attains the state of *bhoga* (bliss). The exuberance of the tranquil state of mind (*sattvodreka*) is characterized by *prakāśa* (light) and *vimarśa* (reflection). This *bhoga* involves a complex psychic process where *bhoktā* (connoisseur), *bhojya* (emotions to be relished) and *bhukti* (process) are integrated.

Bhaṭṭanāyaka also postulated Śānta Rasa as a fundamental principle. Before him, Āryarakṣita (third century CE), a Jaina author, postulated the theory of Śānta in his *Anuyogasūtra* and even before Āryarakṣita, Aśvaghoṣa had categorically stated at the end of his *Saundarānanda-mahākāvya* that he has composed this poem for ultimate peace (*vyupaśānti*) and the poem has an inherent purport of leading the listeners towards emancipation (*mokṣārtha-garbhā kṛtiḥ*). Then Udbhaṭa is perhaps the first *ācārya* in this tradition who accepts Śānta as one of the *rasas*.

This variety and multifarious nature of *rasa* embraces not only whatever that is supposed to be apparently beautiful, sweet or attractive, it equally subsists on whatever that is terrorizing, hideous or ugly, and tends to encounter the issues that disturbs us that lead to abhorrence and detestation. This is very much true in case of *Mahābhārata* or the plays like *Ūrūbhaṅga* and *Veṇīsaṁhāra*, which are based on the Mahābhārata war. The masters of *rasa* theory say that *Mahābhārata* has an ending which is completely devoid of *rasa* (*virasāvasāna*), leaving its readers in the state of *vimanaskatā* (a mind uprooted from everywhere, dismay). It is a state where we stand in aversion; repulsed by our own repulsion. But then, quite emphatically the masters also say that an ending which is completely devoid of *rasa*, leads to the fountains of real *rasa*. This leads us to the other side of *rasa* discourse, where the concept of ugly, how so ever disturbing and complicated it may be, is taken up for making an aesthetic theory. Bharata Muni therefore counts Bībhatsa (repulsive) and Raudra (terror) as fundamental *rasas* (*mūla rasas*), juxtaposing them with an equal weight with the other two — Śṛṅgāra and Vīra. Bībhatsa is said to be of two kinds — *kṣobhaja* (born out of anguish) and *udvegī* (generated by uneasiness). The former would lead to disillusionment and ultimately to liberation (*mokṣa*).[23] Unfortunately the twist and turn given to this discourse by the non-dualistic Śaivite or Vedāntic philosophers got so much propagandized when the history of our knowledge systems was being written with a colonial bias, that the line of reasoning with dualist approach to the aesthetic concepts was overlooked. In the aesthetics

---

[23] शृङ्गाराद्धि भवेद् हास्यो रौद्राच्च करुणो रसः।
वीराच्चैवाद्भुतोत्पत्तिर्बीभत्साच्च भयानकः॥ — *Nāṭyaśāstra* VI.39
शान्तो रसो रसान्तरैर्मोक्षलक्षणः पुरुषार्थः पुरुषार्थान्तरैस्तदुपसर्जनत्वेनानुगम्यमानोऽङ्गित्वेन विवक्षाविषयः। मोक्षफलत्वेन चायं परमपुरुषार्थनिष्ठत्वात् सर्वरसेभ्यः प्रधानतमः।
— Abhinava on *Dhvanyāloka*, *udyota* IV

based on absolutist philosophy, *rasa* is treated as a singular, isolated and unique experience. This is however a one-sided picture. Actually the *rasa* discourse did not run in a single stream.

Through the aesthetics of Bībhatsa Rasa, therefore, the spectator or reader undergoes the experiences of anguish, uneasiness and disgust which will finally make him liberated from the mundane and the earthly. Abhinavagupta is right in suggesting that the experience of Bībhatsa Rasa would thus lead to Śānta and to salvation.[24]

Bharata Muni was opposed to viewing *rasa* in isolation. He said that *rasa* actually emerges in *rasa-vimarda* (*rasa*s crushing and overpowering each other) or *rasavyatikara* (mixture of *rasas*) and that no *rasa* should be allowed to come alone.

Abhinavagupta gave a sound but singular philosophical base to Bhaṭṭanāyaka's views. As corollaries and rejoinders to the system that Abhinavagupta built, there are divergent views of Bhoja, Dhanika–Dhanañjaya, Mahima Bhaṭṭa, Rāmacandra–Guṇacandra and Śāradātanaya. The questions raised and the challenges posed by these return again and again in the history of *rasa* discourse running for more than two millennia, sometimes in the form of theory of *māyā rasa*; or sometimes as *navya-mata* or *para-mata*. The intellectual wrestling continues in the Sanskrit tradition till the present century.

The whole discourse assumed new dimension with the introduction of the concept of *ābhāsa* in it. It was Udbhaṭa, a predecessor of Ānandavardhana and Bhaṭṭanāyaka, who used the term for the first time. If there is impropriety in the very idea of *rasa* and *bhāva,* they become *rasābhāsa* and *bhāvābhāsa*. *Ābhāsa* is a technical term in Śaivism. The term *ābhāsa* as used in by Karṇapūra in the *vṛtti* of *Alaṁkārakastubha* also reminds of its philosophical connotation.

---

24 संसारनाट्यनायकरागप्रतिपक्षतया मोक्षसाधनहेतुत्वाच्छुद्धः। — *Abhinavabhāratī*, vol. I, Delhi edn, p. 326

It would appear that the discussions on *rasa* tend to evolve absolutist aesthetics, positing on metaphysics and holistic view through philosophical interpretations, where *rasa* is treated as a singular, isolated and unique experience. This is however a one-sided picture that presents the view of tradition of *rasa* discourse that grew in Kashmir. *Rasa* discourse would appear to be running almost in a single stream if the theorists like Bhaṭṭanāyaka and Abhinavagupta only are considered. The whole debate on *rasa* has been running in multiple streams.

Bhaṭṭanāyaka stages a comeback through Dhanika and Dhanañjaya. Parallel to the idea of *rasa* as bliss, the view of *rasa* as a mixture of pleasure and pain also recurs. Abhinavagupta refers to the *Sāṁkhya* view of *rasa* that holds *rasa* as *sukha-duḥkha-svabhāva*. This view differs from Rāmacandra's (twelfth century) theory, as it holds the very nature of *rasa* as amalgam of pleasure and pain whereas Rāmacandra would consider five *rasa*s as *sukhātmaka* (imbued with pleasure) and four as *duḥkhātmaka* (imbued with pain). It is an altogether different theory based on the Jaina view of *ahimsā* (non-violence). The proponents of Sāṁkhya system must have built up their aesthetics as well, if we consider how Īśvarakṛṣṇa in his *Sāṁkhyakārikā* used the metaphor of theatre performance to explain the process of *vivekakhyāti* (enlightenment).

Bhoja represents a very important turning point in *rasa* discourse. He establishes an equation between *rasa* and *abhimāna* (ego) and between the identification of self (*ahaṁkāra*) and *śṛṅgāra*. He does not strictly adhere to the theory of eight or nine *rasa*s as well. He suggests some new *rasa*s. The new *rasa*s proposed by Bhoja are — *udātta* with *mati* (wisdom) as its *sthāyī bhāva* and *kṣobha*.

Many other *ācārya*s added new *rasa*s to the list of eight or nine *rasa*s from this point of view. Abhinavagupta himself has referred to the theory of *laulya-rasa*, with *gardha* (greed) as its *sthāyī bhāva*. Abhinavagupta does not altogether discard *laulya-rasa*. He simply rules out the possibility of its independent existence. He says that the *sthāyī bhāva* of this so-called *laulya-rasa* can be incorporated either in *hāsa* or in *rati*. The question of this empiricist view of *rasa* recurs again in the next millennium in the treatment of some of great masters of theory — Bhānudatta, Paṇḍitarāja Jagannātha and Viśveśvara Pāṇḍe. The theory of *laulya-rasa*, which some of the predecessors of Abhinavagupta had postulated, reappears with a different name. Bhānudatta in his *Rasamañjarī* has referred to the theory of *māyā-rasa* to refute it. So does Viśveśvara Pāṇḍe in the late eighteenth century. The proponent of the theory argues that if *śānta* with *nivṛtti* (renunciation) as the dominating emotion can be accepted as *rasa*, *māyā-rasa* with *pravṛtti* (empiricism) as the dominating emotion should also be accepted.

Some of the *ācāryas* propounded the theory of twofold *rasa* — *laukika* (this-worldly) and *alaukika* (other-worldly). *Laukika rasa* is *svagata* (belonging to the character) and *alaukika rasa* is *paragata* (belonging to the connoisseur). Bhaṭṭanāyaka had stood against the theory of *svagata rasa*. But others continued to argue in favour of the other side of the *rasa* theory. They were standing on the solid ground which Bharata Muni himself had prepared. Defining *nāṭya* (theatre), Vidyānātha in his *Pratāparudrīya* says:

> *Rasa* in fact resides in the hero (or the character). But because of the delineation by a skilled actor, or by the hearing of a poem like that, the connoisseurs also experience it by perception, then Rasa can be held as *paragata* (belonging to the connoisseur) and a cause of extreme delight.

It was Paṇḍitarāja Jagannātha in seventeenth century who raised vital issues and introduced some very refreshing ideas in the discourse of *rasa* aesthetics. He not only gave a genuine Vedāntic interpretation to Abhinavagupta's Śaivite moorings, he even rejected the whole framework of absolutist aesthetics, to suggest two alternate new theories on *rasa* experience as a deliberately created and maintained illusion. He also added a fifth category in the four types of Vīra Rasa. *Dānavīra, dayāvīra, dharmavīra* and *yuddhavīra* — these are the four types of Vīra Rasa. Paṇḍitarāja Jagannātha said that there is a fifth type of Vīra Rasa, i.e. *pāṇḍityavīra*. It would find an expression in intellectual debates and intense philosophical discussions pursued with an involvement and commitment. This is in fact recasting the whole framework of *vāda* in an aesthetic framework.

Debates on the Theory of Alaṁkāra

The idea of *alaṁkāra* as extraordinary nature of art comes from the hymns of *Ṛgveda*. The *ācāryas* have termed it as *alambhāva* or *alaṁkārabhāva.* Abhinavagupta says:

> Remaining in the state of extraordinariness is *alambhāva* or *alaṁkārabhāva* (*lokottīrṇena rūpeṇa āvasthānam ityayameva asau alaṁkārabhāvaḥ*).[25]

Daṇḍin (around sixth century CE) and Vāmana (eighth century CE) accepted this broad view of *alaṁkāra* and included *rasa* as a part of *alaṁkāra*. What is *kāvya*? *Kāvya* created through *ukti* (verbal expression) but then this *ukti* is not an ordinary expression, it is *uktiviśeṣa* (an extraordinary expression). Therefore poetry is defined as *iṣṭārtha-vyavacchinnāpadāvalī* (a series of words qualified by meanings which are imbued with charm).

The poetic expression therefore has extraordinary quality which can be termed as *alaṁkāra* in a wider sense of the term. This extraordinariness in the poetic expression comes from (i) visualizing things in their real nature, (ii) describing them through extraordinary words and meanings, and (iii) expressing the emotions. Adjusting the concepts of Ḍaṇḍin in a broad framework, Bhoja therefore defined three kinds of *ukti* (verbal expression) in poetry— svabhāvokti, *vakrokti* and *rasokti*. *Rasa* also forms a part of this broad framework of the extraordinary nature of poetry, i.e. *alaṁkāra*.

The theory of *alaṁkāra* presented a holistic purview of the aesthetic structures in literature. It posited a challenge before the Dhvanivādins who used the process of *vyañjnā* to develop an idealist

---

[25] *Locana* on *Dhvanyāloka*, Varanasi edn, p. 499.

and subjective view. There have been fierce debates between these that have continued till recent times. Modern theorists in Sanskrit rhetorics treat *alaṁkāra* as the quintessence in literature. The very prefix *alam* in the term *alaṁkāra* gives its ultimate nature indicating it as the *summum bonum* in art. *Alaṁkāra* is treated as a vital and dynamic concept encompassing the process of creativity which runs on the four levels — *bhūṣaṇa* (decoration or embellishment), *vāraṇa* (negation or elimination), *paryāpti* (sufficiency) and *śakti* (capability). These levels of creativity are correlated to the surface structure, deep structure and deeper structure in an art form. The attainment of *pūrṇatā* (completeness) through this process is *alaṁkāra*. In this completeness, each and every category in an art piece would compete with the other ones in an ascending order for creating excellence, encompassing the *loka*s or the three levels of human existence, i.e. *ādhibhautika* (empirical), *ādhidaivika* (psychic) and *ādhyātmika* (spiritual). These three levels of human existence can be further correlated with the three paths in human life — *karma* (action), *bhakti* (devotion) and *jñāna* (knowledge); and their applications in literature envisage interrelationships with three functions of the word (*abhidhā, lakṣaṇā* and *vyañjanā*). *Alaṁkāra*s like *bhāvika* and *udātta* are embedded in the whole structure of a literary piece and involve a complete discourse of forms like drama or novel also.[26]

Naṭāṅkuśa: A Vāda with the Cākyārs

The theatre practices of the *cākyār*s (actors of the Sanskrit theatre — *kūṭiyāṭṭam*) are severely criticized in the fifteenth century CE by the anonymous author of *Naṭāṅkuśa* from Kerala. The author of *Naṭāṅkuśa* is a puritan and applies his vast Śāstric knowledge for the condemnation of the liberties and improvisational techniques of the *cākyār*s on the Kerala theatre. He stands for a faithful presentation of the play of an author according to the regulations

[26] I have made studies in some of the poets and authors from other languages applying the *alaṁkāra* framework in my *Nayā Sāhitya Nayā Sāhityaśāstra*, Delhi, 2012.

of *Nāṭyaśāstra*. Presenting a critique of the performance of some of the great classical plays like *Āścaryacūḍāmaṇi* of Śaktibhadra and *Pratijñāyaugandharāyaṇa* of Bhāsa by the *cākyārs*, he makes a scene by scene threadbare analysis of the transgressions and violation of the norms done by the performers. His criticism involves moral issues and the question of freedom of the performer. The following practices of the *cākyārs* are specially rejected by him:

1. Deliberate introduction of regional language (Malayalam) in addition to the dialogues in Sanskrit and Prākṛt,
2. interpretative method of performance — piecing out each and every word by the *cākyār* and enacting it, instead of cumulative and integrated performance,
3. the interference of *vidūṣaka*, his unnecessary presence on the stage continuously for hours and several days,
4. addition of dances,
5. one actor performing many roles in violation to the intention of the dramatist,
6. social criticism by the *cākyārs* — humiliation of the brahmaṇas, and
7. reconstruction of the play by the way of creating a sub text.

Naṭāṅkuśa is perhaps the most colossal exercise of generating *vāda* on an actual theatre practice — and that too of a very powerful theatre form — *kūṭiyāṭṭam* of the *cākyārs* of Kerala. No doubt the author is a great scholar, he cites *Nāṭyaśāstra* and several other texts very much authentically. The whole text is a single-handed attack; but the *pūrva-pakṣa* — the prima-facie view as the *cākyār* might have put up in his defence is also taken up extensively and then refuted point by point.

Naṭāṅkuśa is one of the most damaging, satirical and provoking texts in debate. It is a deconstruction of a very developed theatre form through a kind of bombardment of Śāstric knowledge as well as narrow ethical considerations of purity. The author is aware of the popularity of *kūṭiyāṭṭam* theatre and also of the fact that his efforts to convince the actors are going to be wasted. He says:

> The discussions of this type with the *śailūṣas* (the degraded performers) will not yield any result. They just keep the words and meaning in their own hands (to use them in whatever way they like).[27]

Vādas in Kāvya Literature

Vāda manifests in some of the hymns of *Ṛgveda*. The hymns related to dialogues of Purūravas and Urvaśī, Agastya and Lopāmudrā as well as Yama and Yamī are particularly characterized as debate on a particular issue.

Vāda traditions were captured through fascinating imageries, tales and episodes in the whole literary tradition of India. Besides the description of debates that actually occurred, the two great epics — *Rāmāyaṇa* and *Mahābhārata* — incorporate a number of debates and dialogues within the main theme of their story involving perennial questions on social, political, moral or ethical issues (see Chap. 2).

Kālidāsa's Kāvyas as Debates

Out of the seven *kāvyas* attributed to Kālidāsa (most probably first century BCE), six are imbued with inbuilt debates.

Kumārasambhava offers a refutation of Bhogavāda in the sense of Epicureanism. Śiva, the deity of piousness, cannot be obtained by physical charms; to get Him, one has to purify oneself within through *tapas* (penance). Pārvatī who was proud of her charms ultimately decries *rūpa* (beauty of the physical body) from the core of her heart (*nininda rūpaṁ hṛdayena pārvatī*) and starts vigorous penance to be united with Śiva. The later appeared before her in disguise to test her resolve and faith. This led to an altercation and argument between the two.

---

[27] *Naṭāṅkuśa* V.92.

The fifth canto of *Kumārasambhava* of Kālidāsa presents a fascinating debate between Śiva disguised as a *brahmacārī* (celibate) and Pārvatī. The former, having learnt that Pārvatī is performing extremely rigourous penance to obtain Śiva as her husband, feigns surprise and starts condemning Śiva. His arguments are — Śiva is given to inauspicious things, he wears elephant hide dripping with drops of blood, he lives in cemetery ground, he besmears himself with funeral ashes, rides on an old bull. He then concludes by saying:

> What is there in Śiva? He is ugly and uncouth because of his three eyes, the source of his birth is unknown, and his nakedness shows how rich he is! There is not a slightest trace in Śiva of whatever that is sought in a prospective bridegroom! Now two things have become deplorable by their desire to unite with that Śiva — that shining crescent of the moon and now you who are the moon light for the eyes of the world. Therefore turn your mind away from this unseemly desire. What a disparity is there between him of that type and you of auspicious qualities! Wise men do not expect the honour of a sacrificial post for a spear of cemetery!

Parvatī is extremely disturbed at such inapt remarks and she gives a very strong refutation of all the statements made by the celibate in the following words:

> You do not know Śiva in his true nature, therefore you are talking this way. Men of lesser intelligence are zealous of the extraordinary and inscrutable motives of the great. An auspicious thing is sought by one who seeks to counteract adverse circumstances, or by one who longs for prosperity. What has one, who has no desire, and is the refuse of the world, to do with the impulses that are marred by expectations? Śiva may be miser, but he is the source of all prosperity, he may be living in the cemetery, but he is the Lord of the three worlds. He appears frightful, but he is known to be auspicious. Actually no one knows Him in true nature. He is a cosmic form, one cannot comprehend his character. The funeral ashes having acquired the contact of his body attain the capacity to purify. So that, when he dances and they drop down, gods put them on their heads. Indra riding

> on his elephant, toes both the feet of him who rides on his bull and is reduced to penury.

Pārvatī concludes her arguments by saying that the celibate has talked too much, but at least one thing he said is right — that the source of birth of Śiva is unknown. How can one know the source of birth of the one who is the source of everything? She adds that she does not want to enter into any further arguments, let Śiva be what he is, her heart is completely absorbed in *bhāva* for him, such are the ways of love that the defects (of the beloved) do not matter there.

The debate between Pārvatī and the celibate in *Kumārasambhava* also reflects the controversy on Śiva's acceptability in the Vedic pantheon as a God. The initial reluctance to admit Śiva in the fold of Vedic pantheon continued in some form or the other in the later period as well when Śiva was already been given a place in the trinity of great gods along with Brahmā and Viṣṇu.

In *Raghuvaṁśa* of Kālidāsa, the discussion between Dilīpa and Kumbhodara — the lion — is as exquisite and lively from the point of view of subtle employment of categories of *vāda*. Dilīpa offers himself as the food in lieu of the cow Nandinī and Kumbhodara laughs at this proposition pointing out the irrationality of his proposal. Dilīpa countering all his arguments proves the logic of his proposal. Whatever Kumbhodara said, forms *pūrva-pakṣa*, which is perfectly answered and resolved by Dilīpa. But this debate between the King and the lion is suggestive and symbolic in many other ways. Kumbhodara (lion), as his very name suggests, represents the views of Niyativādins and Svabhāvavādins — the fatalists and the naturalists, placed against which is the philosophy of action and *dharma* which Dilīpa advocates.

In all the three plays, Kālidāsa participates in contemporary debates on philosophy through *nāndī* and *bharatavākya* — the propitiatory and concluding stanzas, by presenting a glorious, queer and subtle image of Śiva and also stating his vision of life.

The eulogy to Brahmā in canto III of *Kumārasambhava* and to Viṣṇu in the eleventh canto of *Raghuvaṁśa* brings out divergent views of Sāṁkhya, Vedānta and Śaivism with Kālidāsa's poetic fancies soaring above them and bringing out their inherent unities. All the heroines of his plays debate with men, present an alternate and feminist view. In *Mālavikāgnimitram*, supposed to be his first play, Kālidāsa initiates a debate with the traditionalists, who look down upon the contemporary creativity in comparison to the great poets of yore like Bhāsa. Kālidāsa offers a refutation to it, directly and in more subtle and suggestive way through his creativity by presenting parallel images, alternate views and critiques to Bhāsa's dramatic universe. He also agrees and disagrees with Vātsyāyana's postulations in *Kāmasūtra* and Bharata's concepts in *Nāṭyaśāstra*.[28]

Bhavabhūti's Plays as Vāda Texts

Bhavabhūti was born in a very orthodox family of traditional brāhmaṇas. He was also deeply steeped in Śāstric learning. He is rightly described as a *padavākya-pramāṇajña* (adept in Vyākaraṇa, Nyāya and Mīmāṁsā) in all the three prologues of his plays. One of the theories about Bhavabhūti that he is identical with the famous Mīmāṁsaka Umveka is yet to be testified or refuted. But then there has been a debate on the question whether a great philosopher like Bhavabhūti loses his *āptatva* (reliability) just because he has indulged in writing some piece of romantic dramas! Citsukha in his *Tattvapradīpa* holds both Bhavabhūti the poet and Umveka the Mīmāṁsaka as one and the same person and discusses the authenticity of his dramatic writings. He is of the view that Bhavabhūti is an *āpta* (authority) in philosophy; he does not become *anāpta* (non-authority) by having composed a few dramatic pieces (*nahi purā āpta eva san nāṭaka-nāṭikādiviracanamātreṇa anāpto bhavati bhavabhūtiḥ*).[29]

---

[28] For details see my lectures on *Nāṭyaśāstra* and Preface to *Kāmasūtra* edited by me.

[29] This view is reaffirmed by Jayatīrtha in his *Nyāyasudhā* – नन्वाप्तवाक्यता तावत् कपोलकल्पितेषु मालतीमाधवादिषु व्यभिचरति। न हि नाटकादिप्रबन्धं विरचयन्नपि →

Born at Padmapura in Vidarbha, Bhavabhūti migrated to the north and reached Padmāvatī (most probably modern Pavāyā near Gwalior district. in Madhya Pradesh) where his plays were performed during the *yātrā* of Kālapriyanātha.

There are debates on burning or crucial issues or philosophical dialogues in all the three plays of Bhavabhūti, viz. *Mahāvīracaritam, Mālatīmādhavam* and *Uttararāmacaritam.*

Bhavabhūti had very good relations with the repertoire which presented his plays on stage. And yet in his second play, i.e. the *Mālatīmādhavam,* Bhavabhūti expresses his anguish for being disregarded. G.K. Bhat opines that the reason for this so-called disregard lies in Bhavabhūti's neglect of his family traditions, and his indulgence in theatre. This does not sufficiently explain the outburst by Bhavabhūti. It is true that in the tradition of highly orthodox and scholarly family to which Bhavabhūti belonged, writing of poetry or play was supposed to be an inferior task of derogatory nature. However, Bhavabhūti would not expect appreciation from his family members whom he has left to seek his career as a dramatist. It is clear that he is unhappy because his first play *Mahāvīracaritam* has not been properly received. Bhavabhūti has recast the whole story of *Rāmāyaṇa* offering new interpretations to many of its characters and episodes. This redesigning of the whole story must have been somewhat startling for his audience. This in itself cannot become a reason for the disregard of which Bhavabhūti is talking in his verse — *ye nāma kecidiḥ naḥ,* etc. It is Bhavabhūti's portrayal of the character of Paraśurāma that must have caused a furor amongst a section of the society, to the extent that there was a movement to seize the copies of the text of *Mahāviracaritam* and destroy them by putting them into fire.[30]

In *Vālmīki Rāmāyaṇa* Paraśurāma is a dreadful figure, viewed

← कदाचिदुक्तलक्षणोपपन्नो नव भवति भवभूतिरिति चेन्न। — *Nyāyasudhā,* p. 273

[30] For details see my paper "Mahāvīracarita kā Paraśurāmaprasaṅga" in *Nāṭyam,* 56: 141-43.

with awe and terror. He unleashed violence and created havoc by repeated massacres of kṣatriyas. But his sacrileges as well as barbarous killings of human beings including women and children have nowhere been decried. It is Bhavabhūti who questions these acts of Paraśurāma. Unlike their counterparts in *Rāmāyaṇa*, Daśaratha, Janaka and Śatānanda in his play are not at all terrified by the onslaught of Paraśurāma; they challenge him and go to the extent of vehemently condemning his murderous acts. The prolonged debate between Paraśurāma and these persons, which covers two acts in *Mahāvīracaritam* of Bhavabhūti raises questions on the former's conduct.

The section of society that upheld Parśurāma as one of the incarnations of Viṣṇu, obviously could not tolerate this contempt of Paraśurāma. These votaries of Paraśurāma might have led a tirade against Bhavabhūti, thus causing him the anguish.

Mālatīmādhavam, a *prakaraṇa* (social drama) by Bhavabhūti is a text challenging the narrow moral and ethical norms. Mālatī, a young girl of tender age, dares to marry her lover without the permission of her parents, and quite significantly, she is guided and helped by Kāmandakī, a Buddhist nun in this venture. Bhavabhūti questions male chauvinism and the debate on harsh treatment to ladies by men is raised in the play by its female characters.

His *Uttararāmacaritam* presents one of the most sensitive and pathetic debates on Sītā's banishment by Rāma. The *pūrva-pakṣa* is formed by the contention that Sītā's modesty is under question, and Rāma should set an example by banishing her; that Rāma should forsake Sītā for duty of *lokārādhana.* In a state of introspection Rāma himself says:

> Appeasement of the people is the holy duty for the good (kings) by whatsoever means possible. That indeed was fulfilled by my father by abandoning me and his life.[31]

---

[31] सतां केनापि कार्येण लोकस्याराधनं व्रतम्।
तत् पूरितं हि तातेन मां च प्राणांश्च मुञ्चता।। — *Uttararāmacaritam* I.41

The other view is presented by Vāsantī, Janaka, Kausalyā, Anasūyā, Vasiṣṭha, Vālmīki and several others of high rank. Vāsantī was a common friend of Rāma and Sītā during the days of their sojourn in the forest. Having exiled Sītā, Rāma meets her again after more than twelve years. Extremely shaken at the news of her friend's predicament, Vāsantī asks Rāma:

You are my life, you are my second heart,
You are moon-light to my eyes and nectar to my limbs
Having pleased her the simple-hearted one
With such and other hundreds of pleasing words
Then to her . . . O peace! What to say after that![32]

When Rāma says that he had to do it as the people were intolerant, she again retorts:

O you hard-hearted one! It was your fame that was dear to you
I say, what more terrible infamy can there be than this?
What happened to the fawn-eyed one in the forest?
O lord! What do you think about that?[33]

Janaka, Kausalyā and Arundhati express their deep anguish and extol Sītā's piety in highest terms.[34] Finally Gaṅgā and Pṛthivī (Goddess Earth) appear in the play within the play and ask Sītā not to look down upon herself; it is because of her contact that their own holiness is enhanced (*āvayor api yatsaṅgāt pavitratvam prakṛṣyate* – VII.8).

---

[32] त्वं जीवितं त्वमसि मे हृदयं द्वितीयं
त्वं कौमुदी नयननयोरमृतं त्वमङ्गे।
इत्यादिभिः प्रियशतैरनुरुध्य मुग्धां
तामेव शान्तमथवा किमिहोत्तरेण। – *Uttararāmacaritam* III.27

[33] अयि कठोर यशः किल ते प्रियं
किमयशो ननु घोरमतः परम् ।
किमभवद् विपिने हरिणीदृशः
कथय नाथ कथं बत मन्यसे।। – Ibid. III.28

[34] *Uttararāmacaritam* IV.3, 11, 23-25.

Bṛhattrayī: As a Vāda Discourse

The three *mahākāvyas* of Bhāravi (around sixth century CE), Māgha (eighth century CE) and Śrīharṣa (twelfth century) are known as the Great Trinity (*Bṛhattrayī*) of Sanskrit epics. All the three are construed in inherent debate. *Vāda* is interwoven in their texture both at the surface structures and deep structures.

Kirātārjunīyam by Bhāravi begins with heated discussions between Draupadī, Bhīma, Yudhiṣṭhira and Vyāsa. After hearing how Duryodhana is prospering, Draupadī is in a furious mood and she vehemently criticizes Yudhiṣthira's passive nature. A man void of the spirit of retribution does not earn the respect of his friends nor the fear from his foes" (*amarṣaśūnyena janasya jantunā na jātahardena na vidviṣādaraḥ* — *Kirātārjunīyam* I.33), this is the view presented by her. The discussion turns on the issue of polity as Bhīma supports her. "Valour does not abide with despondency" (*nivasanti parākramāśraya na viṣādena samaṁ samṛddhayaḥ* — ibid. II.19), says Bhīma. He calls for self-respect and glory and to maintain the spirit of valience. The passionate utterance of Draupadī and Bhīma urging upon Yudhiṣṭhira to have his revenge and to immediately speed up an attack on Duryodhana form the *pūrva-pakṣa*. With all his wisdom and acquisition of polity, Yudhiṣṭhira gives a subdued and dispassionate reply to them. He patiently argues for circumspection (*vimṛśyakāritā*) and avoiding precipitation (*sahasā vidadhīta na kriyāṁ*, etc. — II.30). His views are substantiated by Vyāsa who joins them subsequently. The *siddhānta-pakṣa* is completed with Vyāsa's message. Āgama like a lamp shows the way (II.30) because when the mind follows the path the noble have trodden (*spṛhanīhaguṇair mahātmabhiś carite varmani yacchatāṁ manaḥ*) the prosperities come to men in flocks.

Bhāravi's poem is also a *vāda* for the glory of life, for a man's honour. Bhāravi has used the terms *śrī* (beauty) and *prakarṣa* (excellence) for it. The former envisaged the beauty of inner world of man, and the latter his acquisitions and proficiency in outer world. This philosophy disapproves the idea of *mokṣa* — the individual salvation. In the debate between Arjuna and Indra in canto XI of his epic, Bhāravi emphatically builds up this philosophy within the poetic form adopting *vāda* designs.

Indra appears in the disguise of an ascetic and approaches Arjuna, the ascetic. He speaks for the path of renunciation.

> The worldly objects appear charming apparently, but they give pain ultimately (XI.12). The desire is the greatest deceiver. (*śraddheyā vipralabdhāraḥ priyā vipriyakāriṇaḥ . . . kāmaḥ kaṣṭāḥ hi śatravaḥ.* —*Kirātārjunīyam* XI.35

Arjuna gives a befitting reply to Indra in his pursuits of life and he negates the whole philosophy of individual salvation.

Śiśupālavadha of Māgha similarly begins with a debate on the dilemma of Śṛī Kṛṣṇa, i.e. whether he should go to attend the Rājasūya ceremony at the invitation of Yudhiṣṭhira or should immediately launch an attack on Śiśupāla, the antagonist, who has been since long remained a threat to all who are virtuous and generous. Like Draupadī and Bhīma in *Kirātārjunīyam*, Balarāma, the elder brother of Kṛṣṇa delivers a passionate discourse in favour of vanquishing the enemy first. Māgha actually uses the word *uttara-pakṣa* (acceptable view) in a sarcastic tone for the outburst of Balarāma. Śrī Kṛṣṇa had signalled Uddhava to give his opinion, but an impatient Balarāma, seized the opportunity to speak first. Uddhava, restrained himself as if allowing the speech of Balarāma to manifest as an *uttara-pakṣa.*[35] Balarāma however appreciates the preciseness of Kṛṣṇa and elaborates upon the quality of the speech of adept persons, which can silence even the lords of speech.[36]

As a text inherently steeped in *vāda, Śiśupālavadha* presents the onslaught of Vaiṣṇavism. The abusive language which Śiśupāla used

---

[35] विवक्षितामर्थविदस्तत्क्षणप्रतिसंहृताम्।
प्रापयन् पवनव्याधेर्गिरमुत्तरपक्षताम्।। — *Śiśupālavadha* II.15

[36] विरोधिवचसो मूकान् वागीशानपि कुर्वते।
जडानप्यनुलोमार्थान् प्रवाचः कृतिनां गिरः।। — Ibid. II.25

for Kṛṣṇa, interspersed with jeering and teasing tones, forms the *pūrva-pakṣa* of the opponents of Vaiṣṇavism, whereas Kṛṣṇa, who remains silent and unmoved at the vandalism of his adversary, just gives a rebuttal by his action which culminates finally in slaying Śiśupāla.

Naiṣadhacaritam of Śrīharṣa is a masterpiece of a towering scholar and a Vedāntin of his standing and is also an example of *śāstrakāvya* where philosophy, knowledge and scholarship are combined playfully with poetry; poetry breathes in philosophy and philosophy appears in poetic garb. Canto XVII of this epic engages in a scene of intense debate. Damayantī, the beautiful princess of Vidarbha, has chosen Nala as her husband in the *svayaṁvara* and the four gods — Indra, Yama, Varuṇa and Agni — are returning after attending the event. They are confronted by the entourage of Kali on the way — the advancing multitude of dark forces is led by *kāma* (lust), *krodha* (anger), *lobha* (greed) and *moha* (delusion).[37] Moving like a storm, one of the leaders of the multitude starts delivering a discourse highlighting the heterodox systems, especially the philosophy of Cārvāka. The melodrama reaches high pitch with the four gods representing the path of *dharma* being confronted by Kali in a debate. The spirit of sin appears in the form of Kali with his accomplice Dvāpara. Infuriated by the news of Damayantī's having chosen Nala, Kali vows to take his revenge. The gods try to dissuade him and urge upon him to give up his mischievous designs. A sharp altercation and exchange of repartees follows.

The notorious Kali loiters in the city of Niṣadha utterly frustrated but awaiting his chance to devastate Nala, while King Nala performs his rituals as per routine and chants a long hymn to Viṣṇu. In the last canto (XXII) Nala entertains his beloved after duly performing the evening ablutions and the poem ends with the graphic descriptions of darkness and then bright moonlight. That Śrīharṣa wanted to design his epic as a debate between atheism

---

[37] *Naiṣadhacaritam* XVII.13-34.

and theistic schools, and projecting poetry as an assertion of his faith in Vaiṣṇavism and an argument against non-Vedic sects and schools of philosophy is evident from his discourse.

Dhuttakkhāṇa (Dhūrtākhyāna): Debates by Rogues

Haribhadrasūri, a Jaina philosopher of his own standing and a great prolific author, whose philosophical contributions have been discussed earlier (see Chaps. 1, 2 and 5), has authored a unique satirical tale — an *ākhyāna* in Prakrit, creating a masterpiece of its own kind. *Dhuttakkhāṇa* is a sheer delight in literary exercise of dispute. The whole concept of *jāti* as given by Gautama in his *Nyāyasūtra* has been utilized by Haribhadra in an imaginative way.

Dhuttakkhāṇa builds its narratives through the art of gossiping and questioning the validity of each gossip. Each of the five rogues enters into a bet to tell fantastic tales of their experiences. Each one of them describes a number of impossible situations. The narrator challenges the listeners to prove the impossible situations described by him as possible. The other members of the audience do this by citing instances from *Rāmāyaṇa*, *Mahābhārata* and the Purāṇas. If this type of things can happen there, it can happen with you also — the narrator is told. In this way, if the emergence of four classes from the body of Brahmā is possible, and the length of the huge phallus of Śiva is immeasurable for Viṣṇu and Brahmā, Mūladeva's entering into a small pot of water and an enraged elephant chasing him also entering the same pot, the chase continuing in the pot for six months and finally the elephant remaining stuck in the neck of the pot and Mūladeva coming out of it and many more such absurdities are also possible.

Dhuttakkhāṇa offers a critique of blind faith through humour, satire and application of the techniques of *vāda,* especially *jāti* as described in Chap. 3.

Āgamaḍambaraprahasana of Jayanta Bhaṭṭa

Jayanta Bhaṭṭa is well known as a Naiyāyika. His magnum opus,

Nyāyamañjarī is one of the most important treatises in logic. He hailed from a brāhmaṇa family of Gauḍadeśa. His ancestors had migrated to Kashmir in the seventh century CE. Captured and perhaps held prisoner for some time by the King Śaṅkaravarman, Jayanta as he himself informs, later on assumed the position of the minister to this very king. *Āgamaḍambara* was composed to support the royal policies of administering the religious sects and it is set in the contemporary locale of the author's times. Dharmottara, a Buddhist monk, Judge Viśvarūpa who is said to be a disciple of the Vedāntin Śaṅkara, and Vṛddhāmbhi, a scholar of *Arthaśāstra* who also represents the Cārvāka system in the play are all historical characters. Jayanta builds up a case for Brāhmanism here and the series of debates that occur ultimately culminate into a fervent pleading for the *varṇāśrama* system. The discussions that take place bear a message that all the Vedic and non-Vedic Āgamas — the Pāśupata, Śaiva, etc. — should be allowed to exist, except the Buddhists and Jainas. Saṅkarṣaṇa, the protagonist, is a *snātaka* (graduate) and a brahmaṇa. He enters into debates and discussions with various persons representing diverse faiths. He visits a Buddhist monastery in the Act I and defeats Dharmottara, the head of the monastery in debate. The philosophical discussions are not allowed to involve deeper questions and pertinent objections from the respondent's side. Saṅkarṣaṇa first attacks the theory of evanescence and finds it inconsistent as it cannot explain the consistent existence of any object being viewed by us. Then he proceeds to attack the theory of consciousness and summarily dismisses it with the question — how can consciousness become conscious of itself? Emerging victorious from the monastery in this way, the valiant hero then visits a Jaina monk, Jinarakṣita. The latter abiding to his theory of "Anekānta" refuses to enter into a debate with him, so that the victory by the hero is easily gained. The entry of a couple with indigo robes, their singing and dances are very interesting. Jayanta is referring here to some Nīlāmbara sect akin to the Sahajīyās. The hero does not favour their presence and succeeds in expelling them. Finally Vṛddhāmbhi gives a discourse on the duties of the king from the point of view of an administrator as a scholar of Daṇḍanīti. The discussion on the inference of God is initiated. The Śaiva ascetic launches a counter-attack on the Bārhaspatyas or the Cārvākas, criticizing them for holding only one means of knowledge — perception. The king arrives on the scene and in his presence Saṅkarṣaṇa delivers a speech. The play with all its graphic and colourful descriptions and interesting scenes of tussle between diverse sects does present a picture of real debates happening in Jayanta's times.

Vāda in Kāvya and Kāvya in Vāda

The intellectual scenario during the period between fifth century BCE to tenth century CE was so much dominated by debates and formulation of *vāda* techniques that many litterateurs were inspired to take up debate as a major theme in their works. Intellectual discourses and poetic vision in such writings go hand in hand.

In the realms of belles-lettres, the whole conceptual framework of *chala* (cheating) gets transformed to culminate into the subtle charms of poetic deception. *Vāda* was reformulated with an aesthetic design yielding *alaṁkāra*s like *vakrokti*. The gods and goddesses, lovers and also potent enemies were depicted displaying their debating skills to win an argument in a sportive way.

Vakrokti, a vital and pervasive concept of poetics as outlined by Bhāmaha (sixth-seventh century CE) and Kuntaka (ninth century CE), was narrowed to a small figure of speech by theorists like Mammaṭa. Interestingly, however, *vakrokti* as a figure of speech is completely based on the techniques of debate. Mammaṭa in his *Kāvyaprakāśa* defines *vakrokti* as an *alaṁkāra* where the contention of someone is misconstrued deliberately with an entirely different motive through pun on words or through intonations (*kāku*). This is defined as *chala* in Gautama's *Nyāyasūtra*. The divisions of *chala* — *vāk-chala* and *upacāra-chala* — cover both the types of *vakrokti* as defined by Mammaṭa. Literary tradition in Sanskrit abounds with beautiful examples of figurative poetry based on these categories to form *vakrokti alaṁkāra*. In the propitiatory verse of his *Mudrārākṣasa*, Viśākhadatta presents a debate between Pārvatī and Śiva through the following dialogues:

> *"Who is this blessed one seated on your head?"*
> *"It is Śashikalā (the digit of the moon)"*
> *"O, is her name Śaśikalā then?"*
> *"Yes, the digit of moon is named as Śaśikalā. You are familiar with it, how do you forget it?"*
> *"I am asking about the lady, and not the Moon!"*
> *"If you do not believe that it is moon, then let Vijayā tell you!"*
> *May the mischievousness of Lord Śiva,*
> *desirous of concealing the celestial river Ganges from Umā in this way,*
> *Protect you!*[38]

Many more such stanzas can be cited.[39] Such stanzas mostly make a creative and subtle use of the *vāda* techniques. In fact, some of the great poets like Amaruka have created moments of intense suffering and pathos in their lyrics through this kind of *vāda*.

In the *kathā* (narrative) literature, a story is quite often structured through *vāda*. This is best exemplified by *Pañcatantra*,

---

[38] धान्या केयं स्थिता शिरसि ते शशिकला किन्नु नामैतदस्या
नामैवास्यास्तदेतत्परिचितमपि ते विस्मृतं कस्य हेतोः।
नारीं पृच्छामि नेन्दुं कथयतु विजया न प्रमाणं यदीन्दु-
र्देव्या निह्नोतुमिच्छोरिति सुरसरितं शाठ्यमव्या विभोर्वः।। — *Mudrārākṣasa* I.1

[39] सन्ध्यां यत् प्रणिपत्य लोकपुरतो बद्धाञ्जलिर्याचसे
धत्से यच्च नदीं विलज्ज शिरसा तन्नाम सोढं मया।
श्रीर्याताऽमृतमन्थने यदि हरिं कस्माद्विषं भक्षितं
मा स्त्रीलम्पट मां स्पृशेति गदितो गौर्या हरः पातु वः।।
— *Subhāṣitaratnabhāṇḍāgāra*, 95, p. 7

कस्मात् त्वं पार्वति निष्ठुरासि सहजः शैलोद्भवानामयं
निःस्नेहासि कथं, न भस्मपरुषः स्नेहं बिभर्ति क्वचित्।
कोपस्ते मयि निष्फलः प्रियतमे स्थाणौ फलं किं भवे-
दित्थं निर्वचनीकृतो गिरिजया शम्भुश्चिरं पातु वः।। — *Subhāṣitaratnakośa*, p. 35

where the questions of polity and ethics are raised. The *pūrva-pakṣa* and *siddhānta-pakṣa* are presented and there is a subsidiary tale, as an illustration for them. In fact, almost every tale in *Pañcatantra* imbibes a *pañcāvayava-vākya* (the five-member syllogism). There is a statement, the reason for it is explained, a story is narrated as an illustration, then application of the same in the present context is brought out, followed by a statement of conclusion. *Śukasārikā* — a collection of tales told by a parrot to a lady wanting to visit a paramour — is another example of *vāda.*

Prabodhacandrodaya of Kṛṣṇa Miśra is known as an allegorical play. Kṛṣṇa Miśra is a devout Vedāntin, and his play is composed with a mission to impart the message of Vedānta. Of course, his achievements as a poet and dramatist are no less noteworthy. In *Prabodhacandrodaya*, Viveka, the protagonist is trying to lead the mankind to the path of renunciation whereas the antagonist, Mahāmoha is all set to lead them to delusion. As the crisis precipitates, the Vedāntic view is unfolded through dialogues and discussions. Amongst the accomplices of King Mahāmoha, Kāma and Rati are shown dallying in amorous pleasures; Lobha (greed), Dambha (arrogance), Ahaṁkāra (ego) and Cārvāka are active in misleading the people; while Viveka leads his queen Mati to the disillusionment and freedom from her bondages by making her shun the attachments. *Prabodhacandrodaya* offers a critique of society and the double standards of men. It is a play where brilliance of scholarship and knowledge combines with poetic fancy and debates are made a part of this integration.

Ahaṁkāra laughs at the pseudo-scholars:

> They have not listened to the *gurumata* (theory of Prabhākara), have not learnt Kumārila's philosophy, they do not have true knowledge of the text of Śārika (the two *pañjikā*s or sub-commentaries named *Ṛjuvimalā* and *Dīpaśikhā* on the two commentaries *Nibandhana* and *Vivaraṇa* on *Śābarabhāṣya*), what to talk of Vācaspati's text! They did not learn wise sayings of

Mahodadhi,[40] they have not seen the text of Mahāvrata.[41]

The authors of *Candrikā* and *Prakāśa* commentaries provide enlightenment on some of the *ācāryas* mentioned by Kṛṣṇa Miśra.[42]

Ahaṁkāra laughs at the Vedānta system for its inconsistencies and refers to its affinity with the Buddhist philosophies.[43]

Prabodhacandrodaya was an experiment which opened a gateway for the philosopher-poets to explore new vistas on the literary horizon with their wisdom, insight and intellect.

Saṅkalpasūryodaya of Veṅkaṭanātha in ten acts is modelled on *Prabodhacandrodaya* of Kṛṣṇa Miśra. It was composed at Śrīraṅgam, before its author flew from that place due to Mohammadan invasion.[44] Like *Prabodhacandrodaya*, the play depicts the symbolic fight between the two kings — Mahāmoha (Great Delusion) and Viveka (wisdom). Mahāmoha has followers like Vasanta (spring season), Rāga (infatuation), Kāma (love), Krodha (anger), Lobha (greed), Tṛṣṇā (thirst), Mada (intoxication), Kuhanā, Asūyā (zealousy) and Dveṣa (malice); whereas the protagonist is accompanied by his wife Sumati and is assisted by Vyavasāya (decision) as the army chief, Śraddhā (faith), Vicāraṇā (thought),

---

[40] The author of the commentary *Nibandhana*, the compendium of his wise saying is *Siddhāntarahasya.*

[41] Follower of Bhāṭṭa school, rival of Mahodadhi. Mahodadhi was a follower of Śārikanātha. He refuted Śārikanātha. Author of *Candrikā* refers to two more philosophers here Bhavadeva and Bhavanātha (II.3).

[42] नैवाश्रावि गुरोर्मतं न विदितं कौमारिलं दर्शनं
तत्त्वज्ञानमहो न शारिकगिरां वाचस्पतेः का कथा।
सूक्तं नापि महोदधेरधिगतं माहाव्रती नेक्षिता
सूक्ष्मा वस्तुविचारणा नृपशुभिः स्वस्थैः कथं स्थीयते।।
— *Prabodhacandrodaya* II.3

[43] प्रत्यक्षादिप्रमासिद्धविरुद्धार्थावबोधिनः।
वेदान्ता यदि शास्त्राणि बौद्धैः किमपराध्यते।।
— Ibid. II.4

[44] *Saṅkalpasūryodaya*, part I, Foreword by V.V. Srinivasan, p. ix.

Virakti, Viṣṇubhakti, Saṅkalpa (resolution), Buddhi (intelligence), Guru (the master) and Śiṣya (the disciple). Puruṣa (the Man) represents the Jīva (individual soul). The tussle between these two parties involves. It culminates in the emancipation of Puruṣa with the help of Viveka, Sumati, etc.

The second act of the play is specially significant as it presents a scene of debate between the disciple and the followers of rival systems, including the Advaitavādins also. The Śiṣya who symbolizes *vāda* (debate) itself, reportedly engages in verbal dual not only with the followers of non-Vedic systems, he also counters and argues against the followers of Sāṁkhya, Vaiśeṣika, Pāśupata, Pāñcarātra and Bhāṭṭa-Mīmāṁsā systems.

The play establishes Rāmānuja's philosophy through debates between his followers and their opponents. The first act is titles Svapakṣasthāpanam (establishing own view). In act II, titled Paramatabhaṅgaḥ (destroying the rival views), Mahāmoha sends the groups of Buddhists, Jainas and the followers of Bṛhaspati (Cārvāka philosophy) to debate with the supporters of Viveka. Rāmānuja himself is represented as Guru and the author of the play projects himself in the character of Śiṣya. In the third act the moves of Rāga and Dveṣa are countered by Virakti and Viṣṇubhakti and the rivals are routed. Viveka and Sumati then start working for the emancipation of Puruṣa. In the fourth act, the army of enemies, Kāma, Krodha, Vasanta, etc. corner and attack Puruṣa and try to win him over, they are forced to run away by the strategic move of Viveka. In the fifth act, these members of the rival group start blaming each other for the setback, Mahāmoha appears to boost their moral. In the sixth act, Mahāmoha is reported to have sent his spy to locate Puruṣa, whereas Viveka appears with his charioteer Tarka (argument) to search for a suitable place where Puruṣa can be engaged in spiritual practice and meditation. The seventh act presents Hṛdayamaṇḍapa (pavilion of heart) with paintings of the Universe, Vyavasāya, the army chief, shows the various profiles depicted in the paintings to Viveka and Sumati. The discussions include the process of meditating upon the form of Lord Viṣṇu. The eighth act describes the defeat of the army of Mahāmoha, and finally the ninth and tenth acts present Puruṣa attaining liberation.

Śrīyatirājavijayam or *Vedāntavilāsa* by Śrīvātsya Varadācārya (fourteenth-fifteenth century CE) is another play written in the lines of *Prabodhacandrodaya* and *Saṅkalpasūryodaya*. The author hailed from Kāñcī. He was the son of Ghaṭikala Sudarśana. He composed the play with a view to establish the supremacy of Rāmānuja system. Vedamauli, the hero of the play, is accompanied by characters like Sumati and Sunitā, who personify the epics, Dharmaśāstra and other Śāstras.

Dāsacaritam of Śrīśailasuri is a poem in sixteen cantos dealing with the Viśiṣṭādvaita philosophy, particularly the Vaiṣṇava tradition. The protagonist, Rāmānujadāsa, is initiated into Vaiṣṇavism by Śrīraṅgalakṣmaṇa Muni along with his wife. The poem describes his spiritual journey and inner quest as well as his pilgrimage to 108 holy places. The fifth canto has discourses on two systems for their refutation. Rāmānujadāsa is first inclined to join the Cārvāka system, but gives up the idea after exploring the system; then he is also influenced by the Śaiva sect. Finally he approaches Śrīraṅgalakṣmaṇa Muni.

There are a number of other plays and poems that also have a structure of debate. A new genre in dramatic writings was created and plays with exclusive theme of a philosophical or religious debate were produced. *Mudritakumudacandra*, a *prakaraṇa* by Muni Yaśovijaya, is based on the debate between two Jaina preceptors of diverse sects.

The theme of this play revolves around the debate between Devasūri and Kumudacandra, a Digambara monk. Kumudacandra, the opponent, is described as *jalpa-kelīśraddhāluḥ* (devoted to the sport of debate) here[45] and also *nirvyūḍhanaikavādivijayakelidur-lalitaḥ* (having developed arrogance after winning several debates

---

[45] *Nāṭyasāhityamālā*, vol. IV, p. 8.

like sports).[46] The protagonist, after learning that Kumudacandra has been abusing the Śvetāmbara sect, sends a letter challenging him to have a debate. Before the start of the debate, Kumudacandra describes his victories over Mīmāṁsakas, Sāṁkhyas, Vedāntins, etc. in a very boastful way. Yaśaścandra used the term *jalpotsava* (festival of debate) for this event.[47]

The play presents the scene of debate with the king on chair. The debate however is presented by giving hints of discourse between the opponent and the respondent and the details of the deliberations are not given.

Viśvaguṇādarśacampū of Veṅkaṭādhvarin is a poem in mixed form of prose and verse using the techniques of debate for describing the merits and demerits of various regions, places, cities and religious sects and ideologies in a melody of poetic diction and most subtle imageries. The poet was the grandson of Appayya Dīkṣita, a great philosopher and poet of seventeenth century. With exquisite literary style, Veṅkaṭādhvarin describes here a mega debate between Kṛśānu and Viśvāvasu — two *gandharvas* viewing the earth from above and discussing its surroundings. Kṛśānu presents the prima-facie view and the latter offers resolutions to his remonstrations as well as his deconstructions. Kṛśānu is not only destructive in his attitude, he is very sarcastic and constantly keeps on hammering his punches. He does not hesitate in employing abusive and derogatory language for gods and sacred places — like Badarikāśrama; deities like the Sun or Śaṅkara; rivers like Gaṅgā or Kāverī; and cities like Ayodhyā or Kāśī. In a novel delineation of the techniques of debate, Veṅkaṭādhvarin has introduced moments of theatrical tension. There are dramatic directions like *sārdhāṅgīkāram* (accepting half heartedly). Kṛśānu is very bitter in describing the hypocrisy of the brāhmaṇas of Kāśī and the Maharashtrian brāhmaṇas are also not spared. About the *paṇḍits*

46 *Nāṭyasāhityamālā*, p. 12.

47 *Mudritakumudacandra* III.77.

of Kāśī, he says:

> No one makes studies here. Even if one pursues learning out of hundreds and thousands, he will rest in fallacious arguments and avoid genuine arguments based on Śruti and Smṛti.[48]

Revealing stark realities of his times, the poet gives a voice to the materialist view through his antagonist — Kṛśānu. Kṛśānu goes even to the extent of saying that God functions on the fear psychosis of the poor people, so that the act of worship becomes a give and take business (v. 196). On the other hand, his critiques at some places exemplify the genre of *vyājastuti* (praise disguised as condemnation). About the presiding deity of Ekāmreśvara (Śiva) in south, he says:

> O friend why are you talking of Rudra, his actions are all strange. We find people trying to cool their eyes. Here is he, in accordance with his names Paśupati (god of animals) and Sthāṇu (wood, dumb wit), he has inflicted (one of his) his eyes with fire.[49]

Viśvāvasu's rebuttal is equally interesting:

> He is Hara, he bears fire in His eye as a *hasantī* (hearth) to protect his limbs from the cold caused by moon and Gaṅges.[50]

Kṛśānu who agrees in the end that he was deliberately postulating the *pūrva-pakṣa*, with a view to reaffirm the *siddhānta-pakṣa* (v. 593). Therefore he sometimes presents the prima-facie view with inherent suggestions of the *siddhānta-pakṣa*. This is particularly

---

[48] नाधीतेऽत्र जनो यदि कश्चिदधीते शते सहस्रे वा।
दुस्तर्केषु श्राम्यति दूरीकुरुते श्रुतिस्मृतिसुतर्कान्।।
— *Viśvaguṇādarśa*, p. 81, v. 93

[49] वयस्य किं वर्णयसि विश्वविलक्षणचारित्रं रुद्रम्; लोके हि लोचनशैत्यसम्पिपादयिषया यतमानान् जनानेव पश्यामः। अयं तु पशुपतिः स्थाणुरिति स्वाह्वयमन्वर्थयन्निव आशुशुक्षणिमक्ष्णि निक्षिप्तवान्। — Ibid., p. 247, prose 128

[50] अङ्गानुषङ्गोदितशीतबाधामिन्दोर्द्युसिन्धोश्च समन्वयेन।
हर्तुं वहत्यग्निमयीं तृतीयां हरो हसन्तीमिव हन्त दृष्टिम्।।
— Ibid., p. 248, v. 321

true in his condemnation of the Rāmānuja sect.[51]

As the aerial view rotates from cities, rivers and sacred places to sects and the discussions also turn around the ideas and schools of philosophy. Kṛśānu criticizes Vedāntins, the astrologers, *vaidyas*, *kavis* and *tārkikas*. Replying to Kṛśānu's repudiation of the *tārkikas*, Viśvāvasu emphasizes over the need for cultivation of Tarkaśāstra (logic). A man may spend his life studying the *kāvyas*, he may cross the vast sea of Śāstras, but look at his pathetic condition if he has not studied the Nyāyaśāstra! His tongue would become still when he tries to say something in the assembly where a *vāda* is going on! Enough of these scholars who have not made inquiries into the Pramāṇaśāstra, have not considered the categories and have not delved deep into the logic, and have not studied the *tarkavidyā*![52]

Veṅkaṭādhvarin cites the names of some of the greatest philosophers who displayed their debating skills.[53] Mīmāṁsā of

---

51 हत्वा मार्गे द्विजादीनखिलमपि धनं हन्त हृत्वाऽतिदृप्ता
दुर्वृत्तास्तस्करा ये वनगिरिविलया ये च नीचा इहान्ये।
कृत्वा चक्राङ्कमेषां झटिति विदधतः किञ्च मन्त्रोपदेशं
तैर्दत्तैरेव वित्तैर्दधति तनुममी वंशपारम्परीभिः।।

जारांश्चौरान् जनपददमनान् राजपाशान्महीशान्
शिष्यान् कृत्वाऽतिदृप्ताः श्रुतिपथविधुराः श्रोत्रियैर्ब्रह्मनिष्ठैः।
साकं नो भुञ्जतेऽमी सकृदपि विनतिं कुर्वतेऽग्रे न तेषां
सङ्केतेनैव सिद्धं तदिदमविदुषां श्लाघ्यमाचार्यपुंस्त्वम्।।

— *Viśvaguṇādarśa*, pp. 198-99, vv. 249-50

52 प्रायः काव्यैर्गमितवयसः शासनीयाम्बुराशेः
पारज्ञस्याप्यपरिकलितन्यायशास्त्रस्य पुंसः।
वादारम्भे वदितुमनसो वाक्यमेकं सभायां
प्रह्वा जिह्वा भवति कियतीं पश्य कष्टामवस्थाम्।।
अपरीक्षितलक्षणप्रमाणैरपरामृष्टपदार्थसार्थतत्त्वैः।
अवशीकृतचैत्रयुक्तिजालैरलमेतैरनधीततर्कविद्यैः ।।

— Ibid., pp. 412-13, vv. 557-58

53 ज्ञानाब्धिरक्षचरणः कणभक्षकश्च
श्रीपक्षिलोऽप्युदयनः स च वर्धमानः।
गङ्गेश्वरः शशधरो बहवश्च नव्या

→

Jaimini receives applause for his ability to silence all the *vādīs* belonging to other systems of philosophy.[54]

He refers to diverse sects and their practices. Kṛśānu's tone becomes more aggressive even as Viśvāvasu appears more defensive, pacifying and soothing. Veṅkaṭādhvarin is very sympathetic towards Mādhvas, but he does not hesitate in recording most ruthless statements against them from the mouth of Kṛśānu (vv. 177-82). More elaborate is Viśvāvasu's fervent plea for the Mādhvas (vv. 183-90). But his faith finds full expression in advocating Rāmānuja and his sect. Fierce debates describing bitterness between Śaivas and Vaiṣṇavas are alluded (vv. 337-40). Veṅkaṭādhvarin's approach is for harmony and understanding. He also points out the form of Harihara which is represented in the city of Kāñcī (v. 341).

The descriptions assume a more authentic tone as the poet moves from Bhūloka and Kāśī towards south — he rejoices in presenting the scenario Āndhra and Karnataka. He appears to be better equipped with the knowledge of ground realities in these areas. Kṛśānu severely criticizes Rāmānuja and his followers for making use of dialects, especially Tamil (v. 230). It is here that Veṅkaṭādhvarin makes pronouncements of most sublime and generous ideologue in favour of using Tamil. Kṛśānu makes very strong and bitter pronouncements about some religious sects and Viśvāvasu matches him in defence with equal brilliance.[55]

With his tendency to condemn everything, Kṛśānu unearths

← ग्रन्थैर्निरुन्धत इमे हृदयान्धकारम् ।। — *Viśvaguṇādarśa*, p. 414, v. 560

54 नैयायिका वा ननु शाब्दिका वा त्रयीशिरस्सु श्रमशालिनो वा।
वादाहवे बिभ्रति जैमिनीयन्यायोपरोधे सति मौनमुद्राम्।।
— Ibid., pp. 417-18, v. 564

55 वेदवैदिकविद्वेषदूषिता भस्मरूषिताः।
चण्डाः सन्त्यत्र पाखण्डा लिङ्गालिङ्गितवक्षसः।। — Ibid., p. 137, v. 168
शिरः पुरारेर्द्विजराजपाददिव्यामृतैः सिक्तमितीर्ष्ययेव।
शूद्रा इमे लिङ्गधराः स्वयं तत्स्वपादतोयैः स्नपयन्ति कष्टम्।। — Ibid., p. 138, v. 169

the dark sides and uses the method of *vitaṇḍā*. Kṛṣṇa to him is *corajāraśikhāmaṇi* (crown of thieves and paramours) and *jagadatisandhātā* (deceiver of the world).[56] The section on Maharashtra is particularly damaging. Veṅkaṭādhvarin takes note of the compromises that the brāhmaṇas made with the Muslim rulers.[57]

Veṅkaṭādhvarin is enamoured by the variety of *tīrtha*s in south and sings in their praise with an abandon. The text became so popular that it was discussed for its documentation of various religious sects. It was examined for its debate on various issues. The adherents of Tengle, a religious sect, were not satisfied with the defence that the author of *Viśvaguṇādarśacampū* gave and some supporter inserted ten verses eulogizing this sect. These verses are found even in very old manuscripts of the text.[58]

---

[56] *Viśvaguṇādarśa*, p. 105.

[57] कुक्षेः पूर्त्यै यवननृपतेर्भृत्यकृत्यानि कर्तुं
विक्रीणीते वपुरपि निजं वेतनैरेतदास्ताम्।
विप्रो भूत्वाऽप्यहह गणनानैपुणैर्वञ्चयित्वा
स्वर्णस्तेयं रचयति जनः स्वामिनां पोषकाणाम्।। — Ibid., p. 115, v. 136

[58] *Viśvaguṇādarśacampū*, com. by Bal Krishna Shastri, p. 190.

7

Vāda in Modern Age

THE colonial perspective has remained looming largely over the whole pursuits of the Oriental learning during the past two centuries. In India, this led to contradictions and dichotomies, as the British throughout their rule remained "strangers" in a sharp contrast to the Muslim rulers. They failed to be enlightened by the previous forms of governance, and had to sustain by the means of political ideas from West and their own history. This "intervention upon the actions of Indians whose conduct was determined by the autonomous economic, cultural and or religious regularities of social life" created distances between the British and Indians and chasms in Indian mind.[1] As the gap between political administration by the foreign rulers and indigenous social institutions widened, "the intellectuals began to think that they belonged to the communities united by common forms of social conduct that existed in a sphere distinct from the realm of political action". This produced tendencies of self-defence and revivalism, but also invigorated the debates on Indian customs, traditions and culture. Raja Rammohun Roy spoke of "the social institution of the Hindu community of Bengal" as an entity which needed to be protected.[2] The dichotomy between the state and the society on one hand and the interference of the political actors in social orders and lifestyles on the other led to opposition, sharp reactions and

---

1 Jone E. Wilson, 2010, *Anxieties of Distance: An Intellectual History of India*, p. 1.

2 Ibid., p. 2.

debates amongst Indian intellectuals. Discussions and debates on India's own social body were taken up. As a result, the concepts of *swadeshi* and *svarāj* emerged.

Sanskrit *pāṭhaśālās* and *tols* functioned as sources for knowledge systems and produced *paṇḍits*. François Bernier, who resided in the court of Aurangzeb during 1659-69, described such institutions thriving profusely in the city of Banaras.[3]

The eighteenth and nineteenth centuries form one of the most fertile periods in the history of Indian intellectual discourses. Raja Rammohun Roy[4] (1774–1833), Swami Nārāyaṇa (1781–1830), Debendranath Tagore (1817–1905), Swami Dayananda Saraswati (1824-83), Sri Ramakrishna Paramahansa (1834-86), Keshub Chandra Sen (1838-84), Chattambi Swamikal (1854–1924), Sri Narayana Guru (1857–1928), Swami Vivekananda (1862–1902), Rabindranath Tagore (1861–1941), Mahatma Gandhi (1869–1948), Sri Aurobindo (1872–1951) and Bhim Rao Ambedkar (1891–1956) are some of the names known for revolutionizing the vision and thought processes of the country.

The translations of *Gītā* by Charles Wilkins and *Abhijñānaśākuntala* by Sir William Jones strengthened the spirit of renaissance and awareness of world civilizations. *Gītā* was the first work directly translated from Sanskrit into English by Wilkins, followed by William Jones' translation of *Manusmṛti* under the title *Law Book of Manu* published in 1794 and *Hitopadeśa*, again by Wilkins (1795).

In 1823 August Wilhelm von Schlegel published an edition of

---

[3] Michael S. Dodson, 2011, *Orientalism, Empire and National Culture, Foundation,* p. 43.

[4] There is a controversy about his date of birth. His family as well as in the tradition of Brahmo Samaj have been holding 1772 as the year of Rammohun's birth. Ramesh Chandra Majumdar (1972/2009: 17) has made a detailed analysis of the whole problem and concludes by saying that "based on the reasonable assessment of all the evidences, available to me, the date of Rammohun's birth is 1774 and not 1772".

Bhagavadgītā with Latin translation. This caught the attention of philosophers and linguists like Humboldt and Hegel. Humboldt wrote: "It is perhaps the most profound and the most sublime that the world has on record."[5] German version of Manu's law book was created from Jones's translation.

Debates on India's Identity: Relocating Her Global Image

With the advent of the missionaries, there were rising controversies and debates between the upholders of Christianity and Hinduism. Both sides had to be prepared with the knowledge of textual material juxtaposing the two diverse traditions. The endeavours of Roborto Nobilii in seventeenth century provided further stimulus together with the contributions from W. Carry and W.H. Mill. But it was J. Muir who opened a way for conciliation and "adaptation".[6] The self-assertion by the advocates of Hinduism also received a boost.

Dara Shikoh's translations of the Upaniṣads in Persian were translated into Latin in the beginning of the nineteenth century by a French Scholar Anquetil-Duperron under the title *Oupnekhat* and published from Paris in 1801-02 in two volumes. Duperon's work created ripples that lasted for a century. It was also meant as an appeal to the "followers and opponents of profound Kant" to study the teachings of the *Oupanekhat* from a philosophical angle. These volumes were partly translated into German in 1808 by Th.A. Rixner.[7] Through the Latin translation and the German renderings, German philosophers like Schelling and Schopenhauer were drawn to the Upaniṣads. Schopenhauer declared them as "the product of the highest human wisdom". He used to worship the book of *Oupnekhat* before going to bed. He said:

> There is no other book in the whole world, the reading of which

---

[5] Winternitz, 2003, *History of Indian Literature,* vol. I, Introduction, p. 15.

[6] Wilhelm Halbfass, 1988, *India and Europe*, p. 50.

[7] Ibid., pp. 66-68.

> is as rewarding and solemn, as that of this book, it has comforted me in my life and it will also comfort me while dying.

Winternitz says:

> Starting from the mystic teachings of the Upaniṣads a thought current reaches the mysticism of the Persian Sufism, and the mystic theosophical logos-doctrine of Non-Platonists and the Alexandrian Christians right up to the teachings of Christian mystics Eckhart and Tauber and finally to the philosophy of great German mystic of nineteenth century — Schopenhauer.[8]

Discussions and debates on the philosophy of Upaniṣads were carried on amongst a number of German and French philosophers. A sharp division of opinion between Hegel and Schopenhauer surfaced. India may have been the cradle of civilization and a land where most spiritual practices at the most sublime level were cultivated, but it lacks real philosophy — this was one stand; whereas there was a group of romantics who believed that Europe should return to Indian origins to emerge out of the chaos of modern civilization.[9] The rift between a Euro-centric discourse and a revivalist discourse with romantic fascination towards the East kept on widening.

The remarks of I.A. Richards continue to echo as a stern warning

> . . . to us the Western world is still the World (or part of the World that counts); but an impartial observer would perhaps say that such provincialism is dangerous. We are not yet so happy in the West that we can be sure that we are not suffering from its effects.[10]

There were attempts at reconciliation and creating bridges. *The Philosophy of Mythology* by Hegel considered Indian traditions with a view to an intercultural and interreligious encounter. References

---

[8] Winternitz, *HIL*, vol. I, p. 246.

[9] Wilhelm Halbfass, 1988, op. cit., pp. 73-75.

[10] Quoted in Edward Said, 1985, op. cit., p. 254.

to Kant in these discussions kept the possibilities of hermeneutics alive. B.K. Matilal continues to argue for Indian thought as scientific and analytical and truly "philosophical".

Back in India, the responses of Schelling and Schopenhauer became helpful in the search for a new identity by the Indians like Raja Rammohun Roy and Keshub Chandra Sen. They were drawn to Christianity but found a ground on the Upaniṣadic soil itself for their faith.

In order to convince the Christian missionaries that the best of their teachings is already contained in Upaniṣads, Raja Rammohun Roy himself translated a large number of Upaniṣads and also edited the original Upaniṣadic texts.

The debates between the followers of Advaita Vedānta and other schools of Vedānta have continued with the same vigour till now. Swami Chaitanya Bharati wrote a text *Darśanasarvasvam* in refutation of Śūnyādvaita, Vijñānādvaita and Svatantrādvaita (Śaivamonism) upholding the Śaṅkarācārya's philosophy.[11]

The Role of the Paṇḍit: Vāda Reformulated

The Western subjugation generated a new kind of *vāda* between the *paṇḍits* as informants and the colonizers as rulers. Even though this could not be carried out on an equal footing, the officers of the East India Company and the British judges in the law courts at Calcutta had to depend on the *paṇḍits* for understanding the social institutions under Hinduism.

But then the Company started getting manuals of Hindu law prepared with the very help of these *paṇḍits* to break their monopoly. In fact, the attempts at compiling the legel digests from Sanskrit sources and getting them translated into English; or even preparing translations of philosophical and literary Sanskrit texts

---

[11] Ambikadatta Sharma, 2012, "Advaitavādī Darśanoṅ kā Prasthānamūlaka Vaiśiṣṭya — Eka Samasāmayika Vimarśa", *Unmīlana*, 26(1), p. 7.

formed a part of the strategy of Orientalists to "out" the *paṇḍits*.[12] The origins of one of the most passionate and prolonged debates which the trial of Hastings involved are rooted in the image of India in the seventeenth century.[13]

Hastings could not find any scholar to translate *Vivādārṇavasetu* (A Bridge on the Sea of Litigation) from Sanskrit into English. It was first translated into Persian and then was translated from the Persian translation into English. The translation was printed in 1770 during Hasting's regime under the title *A Code of Gentoo Law*.[14] A German translation of the English rendering of the Persian version appeared in 1778.

Winternitz names two different translators of *Vivādārṇavasetu* from Persian into English — Nathaniel Brassey Halhed and Rud Eric Raspe.

Soon there was a flood of new texts on Dharmaśāstra by the *paṇḍits*. *Vivādabhaṅgārṇava* was authored by Jagannātha Paṇḍita during 1792-94, while Śrīdhara composed *Vyavahāradaśaślokī*. Paṇḍit Durgaprasad wrote a commentary on this work (1825) and A.C. Burnell translated it into English.[15]

It seems that the Company was availing the services of several *paṇḍits* for preparing the manuals like *Vivādārṇavasetu* and *Vivādabhaṅgārṇavasetu*. Michael Dodson refers to the employment of the well-known *paṇḍit* Bāṇeśvara Vidyālaṁkāra in 1773 to work for Company's first legal digest, the *Vivādārṇavasetu*. He was hired from Maharaja Nabakrishna, a prominent merchant and bania to Lord Clive. Nabakrishna maintained a *sabhā* of *paṇḍits* and poets. Later

---

[12] Ambikadatta Sharma, op. cit., 52.

[13] Kate Teltscher, 1995, *India Inscribed: European and British Writing on India 1600–1800*, p. 2.

[14] The word *gentoo* is derived from the Portuguese *gentio*, meaning the Indians as distinct from the Mohammadans (Winternitz, vol. I, Introduction, p. 8).

[15] K. Satchidananda Murty, 1985, *Philosophy in India*, p. 116.

Radhakanta Tarkavagish and Jagananth Tarkapanchanan were hired to prepare the second legal digest. Radhakanta Tarkavagish also composed *Purāṇārthaprakāśa* for Hastings.[16]

Warren Hastings also deputed Charles Wilkins to go to Banaras and learn Sanskrit from the *paṇḍits*. This resulted into the translation of *Bhagavadgītā* by Wilkins which was published in 1785.

The debates on property laws with reference to ancient texts on Dharmaśāstra continued and also led to creation of new texts. Raja Rammohun Roy wrote his "Essay on the Rights of Hindoos over Ancestral Property".[17] William Jones started translating *Vivādabhaṅgārṇavasetu* under the title *A Digest of Hindu Law* which was completed by H.T. Colebrooke after his death and printed from Calcutta in 1798. The whole text is based on the commentary of Jagannātha Pañcānana, "the most widely respected Hindu jurist in eastern India during the late eighteenth century".[18] Distilling rules from the Dharmaśāstra a number of other texts were brought out.[19]

The *paṇḍits* also served as Hindu law officers to interpret the rules. Bharat Bhatta, one such officer in the case of Bhola Dhami vs. Nawaju, consulted and cited the prescriptions from *Vīramitrodaya*. There have been debates over the right of widows to inherit the property of their husband, and also over their right to adopt a child. Bhola Dhami was the adopted son of Nawaju, the widow of Krishna Chandra Dhami in 1780. After a few years, there were disputes between her and the adopted son. She disinherited him and went for a second adoption. Bhola Dhami sued her. The case was taken up in 1800 in Gaya court. On the basis of his consultations with local officers, the judge dismissed Bhola Dhami's claim and upheld the second adoption by Nawaju. But the dispute continued for over

---

[16] Michael S. Dodson, 2011, op. cit., pp. 49-50.

[17] *The English Works of Raja Ram Mohan Roy*, in 6 vols., Calcutta, 1945-58, vol. II.

[18] Jon E. Wilson, 2010, *Anxieties of Distance*, p. 10.

[19] Ibid., pp. 12-13.

twenty years. On the basis of commentaries on *Vīramitrodaya*, Līlādhara who was engaged as law officer this time from Gayā gave the *vyavasthā* (opinion) that the husband's consent is inferred automatically.[20] The case was finally heard in the highest Bengal appeal court (*Sadr Diwani Adalat*) in 1831. This time the *paṇḍits* took a different stand and reversed the whole verdict.

The concept of *vyavasthā* as discussed earlier (see Chap. 5) generated more debates. Convention and precedence played greater role than the textual rules for reaching at the *vyavasthā*.

It was at Bengal that the East India Company first settled and it was in Calcutta that the Asiatic Society was founded by Sir William Jones. Bengal and particularly the city of Calcutta provided platforms for the new dialogues between the traditional scholarship and the Western scientific orientations. There was a section of Sanskit *paṇḍits* who wanted a new educational institution to be established at Calcutta for providing teaching in English and sciences. They held a meeting at the house of Hyde East, magistrate of the Supreme Court of Calcutta on 14 May 1816 for establishing this kind of institution "conceived by the orthodox Hindus and established by the orthodox Hindus, for the orthodox Hindus". R.C. Majumdar has shown that Raja Rammohun Roy had least to do with the establishment of Hindu College which came into inception as a consequence of this meeting. Rather, the persons assembled in the meeting insisted that the Raja will not be involved in starting this institution and no donation from him will be accepted. The participants of the meeting started collecting donations on the spot itself and were able to raise a handsome amount of one lakh rupees then and there. Majumdar concludes that associating Raja Rammohun Roy with the inception of this college was a fabrication and a part of the sustained process of making him a mythical figure.[21]

---

20 Jon E. Wilson, 2010, op. cit., p. 13.

21 Majumdar, 2009, *On Rammohun Roy*, p. 39.

The process of dialogue with literary traditions of Sanskrit classics was accelerated during the beginning of the nineteenth century and more and more translations of Sanskrit classics were appearing. In Bengal, Mrityunjaya Vidyalankar Bhattacharya published *Batris Simhasan* in 1802, *Hitopadeśa* and *Rājā Bali* (both in 1808) in Bengali.

Even the Western scholars and missionaries started preparing new texts in Sanskrit. Revd William Yate's *Elements of Natural Philosophy and Natural History* was rendered into Sanskrit under the title *Padārthavidyāsāra* and was published by the Calcutta School Book Society in 1828.[22]

With the continuity of pre-colonial knowledge systems and institutions in colonial period, the *paṇḍits* serving as native informants also participated in the administrative process, and even served as advisers and philsophers for the East India Company and the British rulers later. They actively contributed to building bridges between diverse polarities and creating knowledge systems.[23]

The emphasis in the new writings during 1850–1947 in Sanskrit was shifted to the presentation and the interpretation of history and contemporary society with a global perspective. Vasudev Sharma Latkar wrote the biography of Shahu Rajaram (1874–1922) in *Śāhucaritam* (1939). Madhusudan Tarkalankar wrote a grammar book of English in Sanskrit — *Iṅglaiṇḍīyavyākaraṇasāraḥ* (1835). Pt. Vinayak Bhatta in *Aṅgrejacandrikā* (Madras, 1801) and *Itihāsatamomaṇiḥ* produced books of history in the modern sense of the term. Attempts to create an understanding of European wisdom were made by the *paṇḍits*. One Sanskrit *paṇḍit* translated Bacon's book under the title *Bekanīyaśāstravyākhyānam*. *Principles of Human Knowledge* by Burkley was translated under the title *Jñānasiddhāntacandrikā*;

---

22 Majumdar, 2009, op. cit., p. 76

23 For more details, see Dodson, 2011, op. cit., pp. 8-10.

Locke's *Essays Concerning Human Understanding* was translated under the title *Mānavīyajñānaviṣayakaśāstram*. Even the English missionaries started writing in Sanskrit for the propagation of Christianity. Rozario published a monograph on dialogue between a brāhmaṇa and a Catholic entitled *Brāhmaṇaromanakai tholikasaṁvādaḥ*. Ram Roy Basu vehemently criticized Hinduism in his *Īśāīvivaraṇāmṛtam* and *Jñānodaya*. Around two dozens of translations or adaptations of Bible came out during the nineteenth century.

The missionaries in India attempted the early translations in Sanskrit. These translations were obviously from the religious texts. Thus in the first decade of the nineteenth century, William Carry, attached to the Baptist church in Shrirampur in Bengal, rendered the Bible in Sanskrit in three parts which was brought out between 1808-11. K.P. Urmis translated the *Sermons on Mountain* under the title *Girigītā*.

The Shift in the Debates

The very purpose of legal institutions became a bone of contention for debates. But then these exercises stimulated a dialogue between traditions and modern civilization. The view of law as "a rule prescribed by superior power" was challenged by William Jones who wanted the law to discern the people's will through local customs and traditions.[24]

Rani of Jhansi, Rulers of Mysore as well as several other princes and kings of various states fought legal battles regarding disputes on the inheritance and property from 1770 till the end of British rule in India. These legal fights created a political consciousness together with an awareness of civil rights.

A celebration on the occasion of the second anniversary of the proclamation of constitutional government in Portugal was organized in Calcutta Town Hall in August 1822. The event was

[24] Jone E. Wilson, 2010, op. cit., p. 8.

reported in two newspapers — *Bengal Hurkaru* and the *Calcutta Journal*. Raja Rammohun Roy attended this event.[25] Speakers referred to struggles for liberty in other places. Roy hosted similar celebrations in Calcutta Town Hall for the Spanish, Portuguese and Latin American Revolutions between CE 1820-23.[26] He learned Vedānta and Upaniṣads from good *paṇḍits* like Mrityunjaya Vidyalankar Bhattacharya (1762–1814) who was well known for his all-round scholarship of Śāstras. Mrityunjaya Vidyalankar however became one of the staunch opponents of Roy and it is believed that he had authored the *Vedāntacandrikā* – a text in refutation of Roy's propositions on Hinduism and Upaniṣadic philosophy.[27]

Anti-*satī* movement was already getting momentum. when Rammohun Roy took up its cause. In fact, before Roy brought out his first tract against the practice of *satī* in 1818, Mrityunjaya Vidyalankar had already recorded his views on *satī* in his official capacity as a *paṇḍit* in the Supreme Court. He had "anticipated most of the arguments later advanced by Raja Rammohun Roy".[28]

In 1822, Rammohun Roy published *Modern Encroachments on the Ancient Rights of Females according to the Hindu Law of Inheritance* showing that "it was the corrupt and defective understanding of Bengal's Dāyabhāga (laws of inheritance) that resulted in the practice of widow burning". He also argued that "India had a constitution and it was the decline of this constitution and its checks and balances that had sunk India into backwardness".[29] "Locating Indian history within the wider realm of international

---

[25] C.A. Bayly, 2010, *Rammohun Roy and the Advent of Constitutional Liberalism: An Intellectual History of India*, p. 19.

[26] Ibid.

[27] Bruce Carlisle Robertson, 1995, *Raja Rammohun Roy:* The *Father of Modern India*, p. 16.

[28] Quoted by R.C. Majumdar in *On Rammohun Roy* (p. 43) from *The Indian Awakening and Bengal* of *N.S. Bose* (2nd edn, 1969, p. 171).

[29] C.A. Bayly, op. cit., p. 23.

constitutional liberalism",[30] he further argued in favour of the reform of Parliament and for switching over to the medium of Indian languages for official and judicial purposes.[31] He employed the term "separation" to suggest the end of British rule and also demanded equal status of Indians in the international fraternity, demanding change in regulation to allow his countrymen to serve in high offices.

It was time when Spencer was launching his protest against British imperialism in England itself. He was also being jeered as unpatriotic. A decade later Spencer was commemorated by the radical Indian nationalist Shyamji Krishnavarma, who instituted the first Herbert Spencer Lectureship at the University of Oxford in 1904.

Shyamji Krishnavarma had already made up his mind to fight againt British imperialism when he arrived in London in 1897. He served as a Sanskrit assistant to Monier-Williams. Before going to Britain, he had worked ceaselessly under the reform movement of Swami Dayananda, and served as Swamiji's "literary legatee". He then joined with Michael Davitt in support for the movement of the Irish Home Rule Ideologues and also stood in support of Mustafa Kamal Pasha. He edited *Indian Sociologist* and in one of his papers paid tributes to Spencer with a staunch criticism of British imperialism.

In this scenario, the idea of *svarāj* emerged as a dynamic conceptual framework. The prefix "sva" indicated the self and *rāj* got linked with the idea of freedom at political, social and psychological levels. After Shyamji Krishna Varma, the idea of *svarāj* was to unfold in Gandhi's criticism of Spencer and liberation of the inner soul of man. *Ātmano mokṣārthaṁ jagad hitāya ca* (for one's own liberation and for the welfare of the world) this saying of Vivekananda became a central principle of Subhas Chandra Bose.

---

30 C.A. Bayly, op. cit., p. 24.

31 Ibid.

This was the time when India was re-emerging and redefining herself in the wake of global debates. Berhamji Malabari approached Spencer for an opinion on the age of consent in marriage. Spencer refused to join the controversy. [32] Berhamji Malabari then sought the support of Max Müller which the later willingly provided.

After the British defeated the Mysore ruler in 1799, constitutional debates raged. Ram Raz assaulted British misrepresentations of Indian history in *An Essay on the Architecture of Hindus* published from London in 1834.[33] He used the term *panchayat* which was taken up as a symbol in Gandhi's idea of "Panchayati Raj".

Rammohun Roy is regarded as "the father of modern India" who produced the first identifiable "canon" of modern Indian political thought.[34] Silk Buckimgham was a co-proprietor of the *Calcutta Journal* started by him. Buckimgham was against British despotism and fought with the East India Company. After his deportation to England, he continued supporting the *Calcutta Journal* and its movement.[35]

In his formative years Rammohun Roy was greatly influenced by the eighth-century group of Arabian thinkers — the Mutazilas. Mutazilas was a rationalist movement founded by Wasil Ata and Amir Ubaid who lived in Basra and Baghdad. They believed in monotheism, denied any resemblance between god and man and human actions resulted out of man's free will.[36] Rammohun Roy wrote and published *Tuhfat-ul-Muwahhiddin* (Gift to Monotheists) in Persian with Preface in Arabian in 1803.

---

[32] Shruti Kapila (ed.), 2010, *Self Spencer and Svaraj: Nationalist Throught and Critique of Liberalism, 1890-1920: An Intellectual History of India*, p. 104.

[33] C.A. Bayly, op. cit., p. 29.

[34] Ibid., p. 33.

[35] Ibid., pp. 29-30.

[36] Saumyendranath Tagore, 1975, *Rammohun Roy: His Role in Indian Renaissance*, p. 8.

In the process of finally abolishing *satī* by legislation, Governor-General Lord William Bentinck "consulted several persons, one of whom was naturally Rammohun Roy who was known to be a great fighter against the evil. But to Bentinck's utter surprise Rammohun opposed the proposal to stop the evil by legislation".[37] Roy perhaps did so because he was confident in the inherent capability of Hinduism to resuscitate and reform itself.

Orientalism

Orientalist discourse had two faces right from the beginning. Edward Said has rightly portrayed its one face:

> If the knowledge of Orientalism has any meaning, it is being a reminder of the seductive degradation of knowledge, of any knowledge, anywhere, at any time. Now perhaps more than before.[38]

But then, Said's analysis, reveals only one side of Orientalism, and his "concept of Orientalist discourse is too monolithic and homogeneous".[39]

On the other hand, the contributions of Orientalist like William Jones and Max Müller helped in the process of a national reawakening. This was the view the intellectuals in India were holding during the last decades of the nineteenth century projected by nationalist journals like the *Indian Mirror*:

> The advent of the English found us a nation low sunk in the mire of superstition, ignorance and political servitude. The advent of scholars like Sir William Jones found us fully established in a rank above that of every nation as that from modern civilization could be distinctly traced. It would be interesting to contemplate what would have been our position if the science of philology had not been discovered.

---

[37] Majumdar, 2009, op. cit., p. 43.

[38] Edward Said, 1985, op. cit., p. 328.

[39] Kate Teltscher, 1995, op. cit., p. 6.

> We should know that it is to the study of the roots and inflexions of Sanskrit that we owe our national salvation. . . . Within a few years after the discovery of Sanskrit, a revolution took place in the history of comparative science. Never were so many discoveries made at once, and from the speculations of learned scholars like Max Müller, the dawning of many truths are even now visible to the world. . . . Comparative Mythology and Comparative Religion are now terms altogether in the world.[40]

During the eighteenth-nineteenth centuries, Orientalism was griping the West, particularly Germany. Raymond Schwab gave an encyclopaedic description of this sweeping impact from 1765 to 1850 in his *La Renaissance Orientale*: "there was a virtual epidemic of *orientalia* affecting every major poet, essayist and philosopher of the period". Schwab's notion that

> Oriental identifies an amateur or professional enthusiasm for everything Asiatic, which was wonderfully synonymous with exotic, the mysterious, the profound, the seminal was a later transposition eastwards of a similar enthusiasm in Europe for Greek and Latin antiquity during High Renaissance.[41]

West moved beyond the "Biblical orient". The first initiative was by Abraham Hyacinthe Anqueil-Duperron (1731–1805), who was

> an eccentric theoretician of egalitarianism, a man who managed his head to reconcile Jansenism with orthodox Catholicism and Brāhmanism, and who travelled to Asia in order to prove the actual primitive existence of a chosen people and the Biblical genealogies. Instead he overshot his early goal and travelled as far as Surat, there to find a cache of Avestan texts, there also to complete his translation of Avesta.[42]

---

[40] From an article published in *Indian Mirror* in 1874, quoted in Nirad C. Chaudhury, 1974, *Scholar Extraordinary: The Life of Professor the Rt. Hon. Friedrich Max Müller P.C.*, p. 318.

[41] Edward Said, 1985, op. cit., p. 51.

[42] Ibid., p. 76.

He finished the translation of Avesta in Surat in 1759 and the translation of Upaniṣads in Paris in 1786. "He has dug a channel between the hemispheres of human genius, correcting and expanding the old humanism of the Mediterranean basin."[43] He started comparative studies between Greek and Persian.

Friedrich Schlegel declared even before he learnt Sanskrit that it was in the East that the Europeans must look for the highest Romanticism. He stated his conviction more emphatically after having learnt Sanskrit in his *Uber die Sprache und Weisheit der Indier* (On the Language and Wisdom of the Indians) in 1808. Nirad C. Chaudhury called it a manifesto of a new Renaissance for Europe from India.[44]

An awareness about the intellectual and cultural India was dawning in the West. The renderings of the Upaniṣads from their Persian translation had also come out before Max Müller started his work. The German philosophers like Schelling and Schopenhauer were attracted to the Upaniṣads. Schlegel's edition and translation of *Bhagavadgītā* attracted linguists and philosophers like Humboldt and Hegel.[45] The responses of Schelling and Schopenhauer became helpful in the search for a new identity by the Indians like Raja Rammohun Roy and Keshub Chandra Sen. They were drawn to Christianity but found a ground on the Upaniṣadic soil itself for their faith.

It is true that Orientalism initially served the colonial masters, but it is also true that the Orientalists in Germany, England and other European countries tried to establish contacts with the *paṇḍits* in India and quite often also depended on them for original

---

[43] Edward Said, 1985, op. cit., p. 51.

[44] Nirad C. Chaudhury, 1974, op. cit., p. 126.

[45] In 1823 August Wilhelm von Schlegel published his edition of *Bhagavadgīta* with Latin translation. Humboldt wrote: "It is perhaps the most profound and the most sublime that the world has on record" (Winternitz, vol. I, Introduction, p. 15).

sources. This also led to a process of dialogue and sometimes debates between the Orientalists and the *paṇḍits*. William Jones appreciated "the superior accuracy of their scholarship" and accuracy and authenticity with which they helped.[46] The Orientalist scholars from the West to a large extent worked for the empowerment of colonial rule, but their correspondences with Indian scholars and Sanskrit *paṇḍits* gave an opportunity to the *paṇḍits* to develop their own vision to compete with the Orientalist discourse.

Like William Jones, H.H. Wilson also learned Sanskrit from the *paṇḍits*. He had forged relationships with Indian scholars. It was with their help that he could produce a translation of *Meghadūta* in 1814. Wilson was an influencial figure; he served as a secretary to the Asiatic Society in Calcutta from 1811, and in 1823 became the secretary to the Government's Central Committee of Public Instruction, where he was a leading advocate for the promotion of Sanskrit education in India. He wanted to encourage Sanskrit learning for uplifting of the Indian society. He pleaded for encouraging Sanskrit studies, to enable the Indians to better understand their own culture and literature. He utilized his stay at the Banaras Sanskrit College during 1819-20 to prepare for the Bodon Professorship and also acknowledged that the Oriental *paṇḍits* of the city "afforded him valuable opportunities for improving (his) knowledge of Sanskrit". Wilson's *Dictionary of Sanskrit and English* was translated and amended and an enlarged version of the original compilation prepared by "Learned Natives for the College of Fort William", under the supervision of Pt. Raghumani Bhattacharya.

It was because of Sanskrit and the intrinsic values which it imbibed, the Orientalist carried with them a feeling of illumination amounting sometimes to euphoria.

In 1867 Max Müller had published an advertisement in *The*

---

[46] William Jones, 1775 , "The Tenth Anniversary Discourse, 28 February", *Asiatik Researches*, no. 4.

Pundit of Banaras inviting subscriptions to his edition of *Ṛgveda* with an explanation of the whole scheme of translation. The advertisement drew sharp reactions from traditional scholars. Responses from several *paṇḍits*, including the rejoinder by Pt. Shiv Prasad in Sanskrit were subsequently published in *The Pundit*.[47]

During the last decades of the nineteenth century, Kāśī and Calcutta became centres of vigorous intellectual exercises provoked by the onslaught of Orientalism. Pramadādāsa Mitra was one of the most vocal members of these groups. He came from a Bengali merchant family settled at Banaras and had served as Assistant Anglo-Sanskrit Professor in Banaras College teaching English through the medium of Sanskrit to the traditional students there. Working in close association with R.T.H. Griffith, the Principal of the college and other European scholars there, he was instrumental in revising the English translation of *Sāhityadarpaṇa* by J.R. Ballantyne. However, he developed sharp differences with the European Orientalists later much to their chagrin. When George Thibaut proposed to introduce the techniques of modern Orientalism for improvement of Sanskrit studies in the college, by introducing the works of John Muir, Max Müller and H.T. Colebrooke in the syllabus, Mitra launched an angry protest. He wrote that "even a most confident and learned European Sanskritist will not deny that he has yet to learn a good deal about the numerous philosophical systems of India" and for a deep understanding of texts these scholars were still dependent upon the *paṇḍits* of "the true India type", [48] Thibaut criticized Pramadādāsa for being overly partial to the *paṇḍits*. Mitra also refuted the view of Āryanization and European scholars view of Vedic deities in his letter to the editor of *The Pundit* (November 1876).

---

47 Shiv Prasad, 1869, "Mokṣamūlarakṛtaṛgvedānuvādaḥ", *The Pundit*, October, 4(41): 110-14.

48 Letter of Pramadādāsa Mitra to the Director of Public Instruction, dated 2 April, 1884 in UP State Archive Lucknow cited in *Orientalism, Empire and National Culture* by Michael S. Dodson, p. 45.

Romantic Shifts in the Debate

Sir William Jones (1746-94) came to India in 1783 to assume the charge of a superior judge in Fort William. Jones was a poet, jurist, polyhistoric classicist and indefatigable scholar "whose powers would recommend him to such as Benjamin Franklin, Edmund Burke, William Pitt and Samuel Johnson."[49] Before Jones left for India in 1783, he had mastered Arabic, Hebrew and Persian. "The figure of Jones functioned – and continues to function – as a reassuring vindication of British rule."[50]

He completed the translation of Kālidāsa's play *Abhijñānaśākuntala* on 17 August 1788; and in 1789 his edition of *Abhijñānaśākuntala* (*Sacontala or The Fatal Ring: An Indian Drama*) with an English translation was published. The publication heralded the dawn of a new era termed as the "Śakuntalā era" by a French writer, Raymond Schwab in his *Oriental Rennaissance.* It created a furore all over the world and had to be reprinted in five impressions immediately. It is with reference to Jone's *Sacontala* that Herder wrote to one of his friends:

> Do you not wish with me that instead of these endless religious books of the Vedas, Upavedas, and Upāṅgas, they should give us the more useful and more agreeable works of the Indians, and especially their best poetry of every kind? It is here that the mind and character of a nation is best brought to life before us, and I gladly admit that I have received a truer and more real notion of the manner of thinking among the ancient Indians from this one Śakuntalā, than from their Upāṅgas and Upavedas.[51]

Forster, a political activist, who created the German version of *Abhijñānaśākuntala* on the basis of William Jone's translation was visualizing a hidden bond between *Śakuntalā* and Europe through his rendering.

---

[49] Edward Said, 1985, op. cit., p. 77.

[50] Kate Teltscher, 1995, op. cit., p. 192.

[51] Quoted in Nirad C. Chaudhury, 1974, op. cit., p. 127.

Kālidāsa reached Goethe via William Jones and Forster. Goethe's enchantment with *Śakuntalā* remained undiminished throughout his life. Forty years after the composition of his poetic tribute to *Śakuntalā*, when the French scholar Chézy sent him his *Editio Princeps of Śakuntalā* (1830) with translation and notes and bearing the citation of Goethe's poem also, Goethe thanked Chézy and wrote back to him that "*Śakuntalā* has been a start for him that made night more pleasant than day and it had marked an epoch in his life". *Abhijñānaśākuntala* became an exemplification of new human values and romanticism in France.

In India, this rediscovery of Kālidāsa did cast an impact on her socio-political fabric. During the one hundred years after the publication of William Jones' translation of Kālidāsa's play, the image of Śakuntalā as a lady seeking freedom from age-old inhibitions gets somehow connected to the idea of freedom. On the other hand, performances of *Abhijñānaśākuntala* on Parsi theatre were catering to popular taste. The vulgarity and uncouth nature of these performances generated debates on Indian identity in theatre and performing arts. In northern India, a very significant role in these debates was played by Bharatendu and Jai Shankar Prasad, two eminent figures in India's literacy history.[52]

Sixty years after the publication of *Abhijñānaśākuntala* by Jones, Max Müller started publishing *Ṛgveda* with *Sāyaṇabhāṣya* in four volumes (1849-75). Both Jones and Max Müller were drawn towards India with their love for Sanskrit and helped to create a romantic image of India in West and also to stimulate the spirit of Renaissance. Both of them could address the mindset of traditional as well as the modern scholars of Sanskrit in India. If the discovery of Śakuntalā by Jones paved the way for neo-romanticism and

---

[52] For details of the performances and translations of *Abhijñānaśākuntala* during 150 years after the publication of its first English translation by William Jones and their impact in global scenario, see my article "Abhijñānaśākuntala on Modern Stage" in *Nāṭyaśāstra in the Modern World* edited by me.

Renaissance in India and abroad, the publication of Max Müller's *Ṛgveda* was an event of much more far-reaching consequences. It has been one of the most significant events in the world history of ideas for having initiated a meaningful dialogue between the East and the West.

Even traditional Sanskrit *paṇḍits* and *veda-pāṭhins* in India could not remain unaffected by the phenomenon that was Max Müller. In Maharashtra, S.P. Pandit was one of the first savants who appreciated Max Müller's work. Not only this, he also followed Max Müller's model when he took up the work of preparing a critical edition of *Atharvaveda*. But S.P. Pandit could achieve something which Max Müller could only dream about — besides manuscripts, he had access to the notice of oral textual traditions and took due notice thereof.

After Max Müller, Raja Ram Shastri Bodas and Shivaram Shastri Gore also brought out *Ṛgveda* with *Sāyaṇabhāṣya*. They followed Max Müller's edition but also utilized fresh manuscript material. When the Bombay edition of *Ṛgveda* by Raja Ram Shastri Bodas and Shivaram Shastri Gore came out, Max Müller had already issued three volumes of the second edition of his *Ṛgveda*. Hence he could consult this Indian edition only for the last volume of his second edition. But Max Müller thoroughly checked the Indian edition and accepted its readings at four places in the last volume of his second edition of *Ṛgveda*. In this way it was the beginning of an era of correspondence between Sanskrit scholars of India and Europe. The episode of Max Müller's *Ṛgveda* taken up for correction of its manuscripts by the brāhmaṇas of Pune, but untouched by them and read by a non-brāhmaṇa in an assembly has been recorded by Nirad C. Chaudhury and other biographers of Max Müller. Chaudhury also records that Martin Hague had written a letter to Max Müller apprising him of the proceedings of this assembly. Another assembly was called to pass a resolution of thanks in favour of Max Müller.

Alfred Ludwig produced a complete German translation of *Ṛgveda* from Prague in six volumes published during 1876-88. Max

Müller and Oldenburg also translated selected hymns in Sacred Books of East. The whole discourse of Orientalism found its footing with the publication of *Ṛgveda* with these translations. Debates on translating Vedic texts and discussions on the principles of textual criticism were initiated.

More than all these, the publication of *Ṛgveda* revolutionized the whole concept of the growth of civilization, the world history and the culture demanding a revision of the prevailing notions and changing perceptions. The concepts of the families of languages such as the Indo-Aryan languages, Indo-Europeans languages and Indo-Iranian language emerged. In their romantic enthusiasm for that was foreign, unfamiliar and distant, the Germans were particularly attracted to India. India also became synonymous to Oriental wisdom. Some of the Orientalists started using terms like "Indian wisdom". Friedrich Schlegal became the founder of Indian philology in Germany due to his work *On the Language and Wisdom of Indians: Contributions to the Foundation of Archaeology* published in 1803. (Winternitz, 2003 vol. I: 13). Through the kinship between languages, the world of Orientalists was thrilled at discovering the new facets of relationships between nations and societies in prehistoric times. This also gave rise to the fictitious notion of an "Indo-Germanic race" having far-reaching consequences in world history of nineteenth and early twentieth century. An Indo-Germanic mind started working, leading to a plethora of presumptions. In the manuscript meant to be read out as an academic lecture, Schopenhauer wrote in the beginning:

> The results of what I propose to deliver before you are in agreement with the oldest of all world-views, namely the Vedas.[53]

Theological and Religious Debates

The row of debate between *Nyāyāmṛtaṁ* and *Advaitasiddhi* led to a series of texts like *Taraṅgiṇī, Āmoda* and *Kaṇṭakoddhāra* from the side

[53] Winternitz, 2003, *A History of Indian Literature*, vol. I, p. 248.

of Dvaita Vedānta, whereas texts like *Gurucandrikā*, *Laghucandrikā*, *Viṭṭhaleśī* and *Gauḍabrahmānandī* came out in their rebuttal from the adherents of Advaita Vedānta. The series of debates have continued during nineteenth, twentieth and twenty-first centuries with almost the same vigour and zeal even though their range and social appeal have considerably shrunk. The works of Jālihāla Śrīnivāsācārya and Ananthakrishna Shastri further took up the issues. The debates between Advaita and Viśiṣṭādvaita that were initiated by Vedāntadeśika's *Śatadūṣaṇī* and Anantakṛṣṇa Shastri's *Śatabhūṣaṇī* were given fresh stimulus by the advent of works by Bellamkoṇḍa Rāmārāyakavi and Parvate Raghunāthācārya who were converted to Advaita and stood up for its defence in the beginning of the twentieth century. The staunch proponents of Advaita like Karapatri Swami, Kāśīkananda Giri, Suri Ramachandra Shastri on one hand and the adherents of Dvaita like Satyadhyānatīrtha, Vidyāmānyatīrtha, Tāmraparṇi Śrīnivāsācārya joined the line of these serious debates. Works of Tryambaka Shastri from Maharashtra, Raju Shastri and Natesh Shastri from Tamil Nadu, Venkamatya and Kuṇigal Rāma Shastri from Karnataka extended the frontiers of debate between the Advaita and Dvaita schools of Vedānta.

Theological and sectarian debates assumed bitterness during this period. In *Radde-Hanūd* Mohammad Ismail Bokani criticized Hindu ways of life which was published from Mumbai in 1845. More editions of the work from several places were issued. Badridas Chaube wrote *Radde-Musalman* in reply. Maulana Ubedullah wrote *Tohaful-Hind* (Gift of India) in Urdu. Indra Mani gave a reply to it in his *Tohaful-Islam*. This series in the form of attacks and counter-attacks continued.[54] *Satyārthaprakāśa* of Swami Dayananda also became a precursor to such debates. There were texts on unscientific nature of various religious sects. Bachcharaj Singhi wrote *Jaina Śāstroṅ kī Asaṅgat Bāteṅ* (Inconsistencies in Jaina Śāstras).[55]

---

54 *Satyārthaprakāśavimarśa*, p. 14.

55 Ibid., p. 122.

The Debates by Roy

Raja Rammohun Roy composed a text *Tohfatu-'i-muwahiddin* comprising a discourse on monotheism in Persian with Preface in Arabic. This work must have created a wave of protests and disagreements, as another text *Jawab-i-Tuhfat-ul-muwahiddin* in defence of the earlier work came out in 1820. According to Bruce C. Robertson, this second work is falsely attributed to Roy.[56] *Jñānacarcā* was published in refutation to Rammohun's ideas in 1821. Roy was accused of using the Islamic argumentative style to refute Islam.[57]

He was challenged for a face to face debate by Subrahmanya Shastri of Madras. The meeting was held during December 1816. Rammohun was able to silence his opponent "by the great cogency of his reasoning, as well as by long array of scriptural authorities that he quoted in favour of his views".[58] The dispute was reported widely and was attended by a large audience.[59] *Vedāntacandrikā* by an anonymous author was a public censure for Rammohun. Perhaps the ghost author was Mrityunjaya Vidyalankar.[60] Radhakanta Dev Bahadur was the man behind the whole campaign against Rammohun. An English translation of *Vedāntacandrikā* entitled *An Apology for the Present State of Hindoo Worship* was also published. Roy was criticized by Christian mercenaries for reducing the Christ to a human being. Rammohun gave a strong refutation to *Vedāntavandrikā* in his *Bhaṭṭācārya Sahit Bicār* (in Bengali).[61]

In order to convince the Christian missionaries that the best of their teachings is already contained in Upaniṣads, Raja Rammohun Roy himself translated a large number of Upaniṣads and also edited

---

56 Bruce Carlisle Robertson, 1995, op. cit., p. 25.

57 Ibid., p. 27.

58 Ibid., p. 32.

59 Ibid., p. 33.

60 Ibid.

61 Ibid., pp. 158-59.

the original Upaniṣadic texts.[62]

Consulted by the authorities, the *paṇḍits* upheld the custom of *satī* with the rider that permission for "suttee" is not to be allowed in case of the pregnant women and a lady having very small children, or if she is in a tender age herself. After this, the government issued a directive to magistrates and police officers in 1817 to allow the "suttee". As a result between 1815 to 1818, as many as 2,365 widows were burnt alive. Alarmed by the enormous number the government issued regulations to place restriction against the practice of *satī*, the orthodox *paṇḍits* opposed these regulations and submitted a petition to the government to repeal the regulations.[63] During 1818-19 Rammohun Roy wrote a series of tracts in Bengali and English to show that the practice of *satī* was not approved by Hindu Śāstras. The leaders of Dharma Sabha engaged an attorney of the Calcutta Supreme Court to carry the appeal to England. Roy also finalized his plans to visit England. The appeal of the *paṇḍits* was rejected as Rammohun Roy has been a regular attendant in the Privy Council where it was heard.

In the *Brief Remarks Regarding Modern Encroachments on the Ancient Rights of Females: According to Hindoo Law of Inheritance* (1822) Roy pleaded how the plight of Hindu women has become precarious due to modern interferences and that even the *satī* cases had multiplied.[64]

Dharma Sabha founded by Radha Kant Deb tried to arrest the progressive movement of Brahmo Samaj. It also started a weekly called *Samācāracandrikā* to give a boost to its opposition to the movements of progressive thinkers like Roy. *Samācāracandrikā* criticized Rammohun Roy for travelling to England for personal gains.

Debendranath Tagore, son of Dwarkanath Tagore, was a

[62] Winternitz, 2003, op. cit., Introduction, p. 17.

[63] Saumyendranath Tagore, 1975, op. cit., p. 88.

[64] Mary Carpenter, 1977, *Last Days of Rajah Rammohun Roy*, p. 61.

friend of Rammohun Roy. Debendranath Tagore was drawn to Upaniṣadic philosophy and founded Tattvabodhini Sabha, which was later merged with the Brahmo Samaj in 1842. He also started a monthly journal *Tattvabodhini Patrika*. He also sent five students to Banaras for the study of Veda. Then he drifted from the Vedic and Upaniṣadic lore as well to formulate his own philosophy of intuition.

Keshub Chandra Sen joined the Brahmo Samaj at the age of nineteen in 1857. He fell apart from the Brahmo Samaj when Debendranath disallowed some members from wearing the sacred thread and formed the Brahmo Samaj of India. His opposers then formed a third Brahmo Samaj known as the Sādhāraṇa Brahma Samāja. Mahadev Govind Ranade came in contact with him and as an offshoot of the Brahmo Samaj, a Prārthanā Samāj in Maharashtra came into inception.

The Vilification and Its Aftermath

In 1835 Sylvain Lévi wrote:

> These peoples are inheritors of a long tradition of history, of art, and of religion, the sense of which they have not entirely lost and which they are probably anxious to prolong. We have assumed the responsibility of intervening in their development, sometimes without consulting them, sometimes in answer to their request. . . . We claim, rightly or wrongly, to represent a superior civilization, and because of the right given to us by the virtue of this superiority, which we regularly affirm with such assurance as makes it seem incontestable to the natives, we have called in question all their traditions.[65]

The whole scenario in India had changed after the departure of Warren Hastings. William Jones was even subjected to an overt and abject criticism by James Mill. For Mill, Kālidāsa's magnum opus was "a story which was above the powers of imagination in an uncultivated language". Sir William Jones was regretfully rejected:

---

[65] Quoted in Edward Said, 1985, op. cit., p. 249.

> It was unfortunate that a mind so pure, so warm in pursuits of truth, and so devoted to oriental learning, as that of Sir William Jones, should have adopted a hypothesis of a high state of civilization in the principal countries of Asia.[66]

The History of British India by Mill is in fact an example of a *vitaṇḍā* text, ridden with futile rejoinders or *jātis*, an attempt at deconstructing all that the constructive Orientalism had created. In fact, it was the most eloquent expression of the magisterial and utilitarian view of the British rulers leading to a denouncement of Hindu ways of life. It served as a guideline to the British policy makers for ruling India. Mill contemptuously dismissed all the claims of India's achievements in the fields of science and culture. In the subsequent editions of this book, H.H. Wilson made attempts at correcting his wild and sweeping generalizations and over-reactions. Mill was extremely ruthless in demolishing whatever glory invested by Jones and the Orientalists to Sanskrit literary traditions.

Mill's work also provided a footing to Macaulay, who in his famous minute on education summarily dismissed the value of Sanskrit literature in his most decrying terms:

> I am quite ready to take the oriental learning at the valuation of the orientalists themselves. I have never found one amongst them who could deny that a single shelf of a good European library was worth the whole native literature of India and Arabia.[67]

However, his condemnations of Indian culture and Sanskrit literature generated another kind of debate. Lord Bentinck appointed William Adam for investigating the state of education in Bengal. Adam in his reports voiced the concerns of traditional *paṇḍits*; he also collected the signatures of several *paṇḍits* from Calcutta Sanskrit College, as a confirmation of the *vyavasthā* (opinion) on the continuance of the employment of Sanskrit for

---

[66] Quoted by Nirad C. Chaudhury, 1974, op. cit., p. 133.

[67] Ibid.

translating Western knowledge texts in it.[68]

Lancelot Wilkinson was carrying on his experiments at the *pāṭhaśālā* in the small town of Sehore near Bhopal in central India. He utilized astronomical texts like *Sūryasiddhānta* with their scientific perspective.[69] Paṇḍit Bapudev was his protégé. John Muir was appointed Superintendent of Banaras Sanskrit College. A Christian polemicist, he had already authored a tract in Sanskrit *Mataparīkṣā* denouncing principal tenets of Hinduism. Before that, he had also announced a prize of Rs. 50 for the best essay in Sankrit verse on the design and power of God, which should not refer to Hinduism. He advocated Sanskrit medium and authored several other texts also in Sanskrit.[70] Ballantyne also published Sanskrit translation of the three chapters of *Genesis,* titled *The Bible for Pundits* along with the original, to invoke the *paṇḍits* to testify and search their validity through their scriptures.[71] Ballantyne's *Christianity Contrasted with Hindu Philosophy* led to a series of debates. Devout Christians could not tolerate his comparison of Vedāntic *Nirguṇa Brahman* with the God of Christianity. He was accused of presenting "too favourable" a characterization of Vedānta. His detractors understood *nirguṇa* as devoid of not only physical attributes, but of intellectual and moral characteristics as well. Byllantyne had to approach the *paṇḍits* for substantiation of his view of *nirguṇa*. The *vyavasthā* (opinion) given by the *paṇḍits*, including the savants like Vitthal Shastri and Bapudev Shastri, was published along with the signatures of sixteen others by Byllantyne in his *Bible for Pundits*.[72]

Rajendralal Mitra became an icon in the whole intellectual and political movement that was struggling hard to establish an Indian identity and challenging the Euro-centric interpretations

[68] Michael S. Dodson, 2011, op. cit., p. 85.

[69] Ibid., p. 84.

[70] Ibid., p. 92.

[71] Ibid., p. 113.

[72] Ibid., p. 116.

of Indian culture. Mitra criticized the Weber's view that *Rāmāyaṇa* was composed under the influence of Homer's *Iliad* and wrote sarcastically:

> Alexander during his three week's stay in Punjab taught the Indians according to different authors, the art of preparing male dresses, the mode of piling bricks and stones for buildings, the principles of architecture, the plan of harnessing horses, writing, drama, astronomy, philosophy and all and everything that convert a race of naked savages into civilized men, and it would be preposterous to suppose that he would not leave behind him a copy of the old Homer for the edification of the Indians.
>
> — Rajendralal Mitra 1872: 53.[73]

With his firm protest of the idea of ancient India's indebtedness to Greece in respect of learning the constructions by stone, Mitra was embroiled in a controversy with James Fergusson, even though he acknowledged that Fergusson was the "highest authority on Indian architecture".[74]

Debates on Social Issues

During eighteenth, nineteenth and twentieth centuries debates focused around social issues, emerging in the new political situation. One such issue was widow marriage. The Brahmo Samaj of Bengal, Prārthanā Samāj of Maharashtra and the Arya Samaj advocated in favour of widow remarriage.

In Maharashtra, Pandit Vishnu Parashuram Shastri launched a vigorous movement for remarriage of widows with Justice Mahadev Govind Ranade as his active supporter. Narayan Chandavarkar in his speech at the Bombay Provincial Social Conference in 1901 is reported to have remarked:

> The movement created a stir in those times, and those identified

---

[73] Quoted by Andrew Sartori, 2010, *Beyond Cultural Contact and Colonial Discourse: Intellectual History of India*, p. 72.

[74] Ibid.

> with it held a formal discussion at Poona on the question of validity of widow remarriage according to Śāstras with His Holiness Śaṅkarācārya in the seventies of the last century. . . . Of course it was a foregone conclusion that His Holiness would decide against the combatants, but the discussion had one good effect, it drew pointed attention to the condition of Hindu child widow and several widow remarriages took place. All honours to late Shri Vishnu Shastri, the late Madhavdas Raghunathdas and to late Karsanadas Mulji for the courage with which they led the movement.[75]

Around 1850, the Brahmana Sabha of Bengal referred the issue of widow marriage to Pt. Rajaram Shastri of Kāśī. He issued a detailed document in refutation to widow marriage. The statements of some other *paṇḍits* were also included in this document and it was circulated along with these statements all around the country and was received with protests from several corners. The document was also published in book form entitled *Vidhavodvāhaśaṅkāsamādhiḥ* (Resolving Doubts on Widow Marriage). Rajaram Shastri obtained the consent of fifty-two well-known *paṇḍits* of Kāśī on his document. Baldev Upadhyaya (1994: 178) has produced the list of these *paṇḍits*. A point by point rejoinder against this document was issued from Mumbai. Upon this, Paṇḍit Bal Shastri of legendary fame, reissued the document of his *guru* Paṇḍit Rajaram Shastri with his detailed Sanskrit commentary incorporating his replies to the counter-arguments presented by the reformists (Baldev Upadhyaya 1994: 147-48). It was in this series of debates that Ishwara Chandra Vidyasagara wrote a treatise in Sanskrit in support of widow remarriage. Rākhaldas Nyāyaratna (1829–1914) also wrote a treatise against widow remarriage (Baldev Upadhyaya 1994: 331). There were similar treatises for and against sea voyage. In his *Pratyantaprasthānamīmāṁsā*, Pt. Madhusudhan Ojha discussed the validity of sea voyage for trips to other countries.

After the death of the father of Rai Krishnadas, his widow was

[75] Quoted by Indulal Yajnik, 1950, *Shyamji Krishnavarma*. p. 13.

trying hard to marry her daughters. The marriage of the younger daughter was being solemnized, on the question whether the Dharmaśāstra would allow her to marry the younger daughter before the marriage of the elder one, Shiv Kumar Shastri gave ruling against it. He also returned the golden coin which the widow offered him. Lakshmi Chandra Agrawal, a young man of Kāśī was sent to London and study chemistry. After his return he wanted to launch an industry, but Agrawal Sabha of Kāśī started opposing him for his sea voyage. An assembly of *paṇḍits* was called, Shiv Kumar Shastri was invited, but he refused to come, saying that he will not agree to any decision in favour of sea voyage which the assembly is expected to make.

Young scholar Shyamji Krishna Varma gave a number of lectures in Sanskrit on the reformist movement during 1875-77 before his departure to England.[76]

Dayananda in his *Satyārthaprakāśa* explicitly advocated widow marriage and favoured marriage between young boys and girls by mutual consent, and went to the extent of suggesting that the young boys and girls may marry on their own. Marrying them without their consent is behaving like animals.[77] There were debates related to moral dilemmas in literature too. *Śāstrārtha* has been leading to hermeneutics and emergence of cross-cultural perspectives.

Inculcation of democratic values and spread of education amongst the lower castes led to an awakening and several socio-spiritual movements. Swami Nārāyaṇa was born in Ayodhya on 3 April 1781. He used to have discussions with local *paṇḍits* before

---

[76] Quoted by Indulal Yajnik, 1950, op. cit., pp. 19-35.

[77] "वरकन्या की दोनों को परस्पर प्रसन्नता होय, फिर माता, पिता वा बन्धु विवाह कर दैंवे, अथवा आप ही दोनों विवाह कर लेवें, पशुवत् विवाह का व्यवहार करना उचित नहीं, जैसे कि गाय वा चेरी (बकरी) को पकड़ के दूसरे के हाथ में दे देते हैं, वे ले के चले जाते हैं जैसी इच्छा होय वैसा करते हैं इस प्रकार का व्यवहार मनुष्यों को कभी न करना चाहिये . . .।" — *Satyārthaprakāśa*, 1st edn, chap. IV, p. 100 quoted in *Satyārthaprakāśavimarśa*, p. 15

migrating on his *kalyāṇa-yātrā* and is said to have convinced them of the practical soundness of Viśiṣṭādvaita philosophy. He visited as many as 187 sacred shrines during his journey for the spiritual quest and had discussions with several religious *gurus*. He received convincing answers to his queries from Swami Muktanand in 1799 at the Ramanand Swami Ashram at Loj, southern Saurashtra and was initiated by the Swami.[78] Chattambi Swamikal (1853–1924), a mystic and scholar, was born in a Nair family. He is known as *vidyādhirāja* (king of knowledge). He fought against the caste hierarchy and brāhmaṇa monopoly. He composed *Vedādhikāranirūpaṇam* — a treatise on examining the question — who are authorized to study Vedas. This and other books as well as the speeches by him led to the revival of self-respect amongst the lower castes.

The lineage of saints and seers continued and there were re-visits to settled social and ethical norms. Sri Narayana Guru was born in a family of untouchables called Chaovan-Ezhava in 1856 in Kerala. He died in 1928. He wrote several works in Sanskrit and Malayalam. He was an Advaitin and initiated several meaningful reforms. In his *Nārāyaṇasmṛtiḥ*, he offers alternate views on the rigidity of caste and female education, etc.

In 1911, the government proposed to issue an ordinance authorizing the lower-caste people to officially designate themselves as non-Hindus. This created a furor in Kāśī leading to a series of debates. A big conference was organized in Kāśī. Shiv Kumar Shastri was requested to preside over it. He gave a verdict that the untouchables will remain an indivisible part of Hindu society. [79]

---

[78] T.P. Shankarankutty Nair, 2013, "Swami Narayan to Swami Chinmayanand", *Dhīmahi*, p. 125.

[79] The verdict of Shiv Kumar Shastri is reported as follows: "अछूत होने से ही व्यक्ति हिंदू धर्म के क्षेत्र से बहिष्कृत नहीं किया जा सकता। वह उतनी ही मात्रा में हिंदू है जितनी मात्रा में कोई सवर्ण व्यक्ति अछूत हिंदू समाज का अविभाज्य अंग है।" — Baldev Upadhyaya 1994: 150

Debates of Arya Samaj

Arya Samaj was founded in Bombay in 1875 and revised in 1877 at Lahore.

Gurudatta Vidyarthi became a flag holder for the reformist movement of Arya Samaj. He was a think-tank for the tirade against the European Sanskrit scholars — Muir, Max Müller and Monier-Williams. He studied in Government College at Lahore and later on became Professor of Science in the same institution. In his essay "The Terminology of Veda and European Scholars" published in *Vedic Magazine* in 1889, he pointed out the deficiencies of European scholars in their understanding of Veda and their lack of knowledge of Vedāṅgas.

Satyārthaprakāśa: A Text on Debate

Swami Dayananda Saraswati (1824-83) was definitely one of the savants of modern age who resuscitated the *vāda* tradition. Despite the abusives that he hurled at his opponents[80] and many a time his failure to appreciate their points of view, he remained open to debates and dialogues. He also provoked and challenged the clergy and heads of other religions to enter into debate with them. After Paṇḍitarāja Jagannātha, who has been referred in the previous chapter, none of the traditional *paṇḍit*s bothered to have scholarly debates with the followers of alien religions and traditions, even though the infighting between various sects under Vedānta very much continued.

Dayānand used the trics of *vāda* (*vāk-chala* and *jāti*s) to build up a strategy for his reformist movement. Maulana Mohammad

[80] The opposite parties on occasions felt aggrieved by his use of derogatory adjectives. The *paṇḍit*s of Mirzapur gave a notice to him for holding a *śāstrārtha* (debate) with the following rider — you often use harsh words like fool, wicked, etc. If you speak about us in such terms, you will be punished. *Dayananda Saraswati ko Likhe gaye Patra aur Vigyapan,* ed. Yudhir Mimamsaka, part III, quoted by Harsha Narayan 2010, *Dayananda: Eka Punarviśleṣaṇa*, p. 13.

Kasim Nanotavi wrote to him a letter on 14 August 1878 pointing out the inconsistencies in his stands. At one stage he accepted the authority of twenty-one Śāstras and circulated their list. Another time he upheld the authority of only four Vedas. Swamiji replied to Maulana in the letter dated 15 August 1878 — "you should first understand the meaning of *śāstra*".[81]

Unfortunately the accounts of Swami Dayananda's debates are either shrouded in a hazy mass of legends built up by his devotees, or they have been coloured with the spirit of glorifying his *digviyaya* (over-all victory). No authentic biography on him is available. The accounts presented by his rivals (*sanātanīs*) are equally unreliable. One thing about him is certain. The course of his postulations and precepts continued to change because of discussions, dialogues and debates with the followers of diverse faiths, he revised his opinions and stands through *vāda.*

He was not against idol worship till he faced the *paṇḍits* of Kāśī in a historical debate. In the same way he was also not through and through against the Purāṇas. At one stage, he refused to accept the authority of *Bhāgavata Purāṇa*, but held *Devībhāgavata Purāṇa* in high respect. He had written a text on refutation of *Bhāgavata*, entitled *Bhagavatakhaṇḍanaṃ*. Here he extoled *Devibhāgavata Purāṇa*. It was perhaps in reaction to the attacks from his rivals that subsequently in 1969 he declared that all Purāṇas are fraudulous.[82]

Swami Dayananda is known for settling the disputes in debates by unusual methods. Madam Blavatsky in her homage to Dayananda has narratated an incident with regard to his dispute with some fanatics. One of whom is said to have hurled a cobra at him, saying "Let this Viṣṇu decide which of us is right!" Swami Dayananda caught the cobra and with a single vigorous movement crushed the head of the reptile, saying "Let him do so . . . your god has been too

---

[81] Harsha Narayan, 2010, op. cit., p. 17.

[82] Ibid., p. 3.

slow. It is I who have decided the dispute. Now go."[83]

He wrote *Satyārthaprakāśa* also with a spirit to provoke debates. He revised many of his postulations in the second edition of the text, viz. recommending non-vegetarian food for certain rituals, sanction against the śūdras to study Veda and against the ladies for *yajñopavīta* (sacred thread), the concept of salvation as eternal and unending, etc.

Swami Dayananda advocated Advaitic view when he entered into a *vāda* (debate) with a clergy John Robton in 1866. But after one year he changed his position to embrace dualism.[84]

In his Preface to *Satyārthaprakāśa*, Swamiji says:[85]

> My purpose for creating this text is to bring out the *satya* — that which is true — to spell out *satya* as *satya* and falsehood as falsehood. This I understand as the light of *satya*. Telling lies as *satya* and *satya* as lies is not *satya*. To describe something as it really is in writing and to believe in it — is *satya*. A prejudiced person justifies his *asatya* as *satya* and *satya* of other's as *asatya*. Thus he cannot attain the tenet of *satya*. Therefore this is the duty of reliable scholars that in their discourse as well as in writings they should deliver the real nature of *satya* and *asatya* to the society. After that having understood their own good and bad they will accept *satya* and give up *asatya* and remain happy.[86]

---

[83] Harsha Narayan, 2010, op. cit., p. 24.

[84] Ibid., p. 8.

[85] Quoted in *Satyārthaprakāśavimarśa*, Preface.

[86] मेरा इस ग्रन्थ को बनाने का मुख्य प्रयोजन सत्य — सत्य अर्थ का प्रकाश करना है, अर्थात् जो सत्य है, उसको सत्य और जो मिथ्या है, उसको मिथ्या ही प्रतिपादित करना है। वह सत्य नहीं कहाता, जो सत्य के स्थान में असत्य और असत्य के स्थान में सत्य का प्रकाश किया जाए। किन्तु जो पदार्थ जैसा है, उसको वैसा ही कहकर लिखना और मानना सत्य कहाता है। जो मनुष्य पक्षपाती होता है, वह अपने असत्य को भी सत्य और दूसरे विरोधी मत वाले सत्य को भी असत्य सिद्ध करने में प्रवृत्त होता है, इसलिए वह सत्य मत को प्राप्त नहीं हो सकता। इसीलिए विद्वान् आप्तों का यही मुख्य काम है कि उपदेश व लेख द्वारा सब मनुष्यों के सामने सत्यासत्य का स्वरूप समर्पित कर दें, →

Swami Dayananda again and again proclaimed his impartiality and his engagement with a fair debate.[87] He was open to discussion and amendments. He revised some of his concepts and postulations in the second edition of *Satyārthaprakāśa* — specially about eating of meat and the concept of liberation.

Commenting on *Yajurveda* XXVI.2 (*yathā imāṁ vācaṁ kalyāṇīm āvadāni janebhyaḥ brahmarājanyābhyāṁ śūdrāya ca āryāya ca . . .*) he says: Just as the Almighty God has breathed the earth, waters, fire, air, moon, and the sun and crops, etc. for all, in the same way, He has created the Vedas also for all. If there is a restriction (for anyone to study Veda), it is for the specific purpose, i.e. a person who is unable to learn even after being taught, being devoid of intelligence, he is a śūdra. It is of no use to teach him and make him study. And if you impose a ban on women from studying Veda, it is the effect of your foolishness, vested interest and lack of wisdom. See, there is proof of women studying Veda in Veda itself — *brahnacaryeṇa kanyā yuvānaṁ vindate patiṁ.*

Question: So, shall the ladies study Veda then?

← पश्चात् वे अपना हिताहित समझकर सत्यार्थ का ग्रहण और मिथ्यार्थ का परित्याग कर के सदा आनंद में रहें। — *Satyārthaprakāśa*, Preface, p. 2, vs 2050, Sarvadeshik Arya Pratinidhi Sabha, New Delhi

[87] यद्यपि मैं आर्यावर्त देश में उत्पन्न हुआ और बसता हूँ तथापि जैसे इस देश के मतमतान्तरों की झूठी बातों का पक्षपात न कर यथातथ्य प्रकाश करता हूँ, वैसे ही दूसरे देशस्थ व मत वालों के साथ भी वर्तता हूँ। जैसा स्वदेश वालों के साथ मनुष्योन्नति के विषय में वर्तता हूँ, वैसा ही विदेशियों के साथ भी, तथा सब सज्जनों को भी वर्तनायोग्य है। — Ibid.

जो जो सर्वमान्य सत्य विषय हैं, वे तो सब में एक से हैं, झगड़ा झूठे विषयों में होता है। अथवा एक सच्चा और एक झूठा हो तो भी कुछ थोड़ा-सा विवाद चलता है। यदि वादी-प्रतिवादी सत्यासत्य निश्चय के लिए वाद-प्रतिवाद करें तो अवश्य निश्चय हो जाए। — Ibid., *anubhūmikā*, p. 3

जब तक वादी-प्रतिवादी होकर प्रीति से वाद वा लेख न किया जाए, तब तक सत्यासत्य का निर्णय नहीं हो सकता। जब विद्वान् लोगों में सत्यासत्य का निश्चय नहीं होता, तभी अविद्वानों को महाअंधकार में पड़कर बहुत दुःख उठाना पड़ता है, इसलिए सत्य के जय और असत्य के क्षय के अर्थ मित्रता से वाद व लेख करना हमारी मनुष्य जाति का मुख्य कार्य है। यदि ऐसा न हो, तो मनुष्यों की उन्नति कभी न हो। — Ibid., *anubhūmikā*, p. 2

Answer: Definitely they should. See, in Śrautasūtras it is said: *strī mantraṁ paṭhet* (the lady will recite the *mantra*). If the lady has not studied Vedas and Śāstras, how can she recite *mantra* with proper pronunciation? Amongst the ladies of Bhāratavarṣa, there have been gems like Gārgī, who after studying Vedas and Śāstras became scholars. This explicitly said in *Śatapatha Brāhmaṇa* (Kāṇḍa 14).[88]

Citing Kaikeyī's example that she accompanied her husband to battlefield, he again argues that a brāhmaṇa lady should be taught all *vidyās*, a kṣatriya lady should also be taught all *vidyās*, but she should be specially trained in martial arts and governance; a vaiśya lady should be specially trained in management and a śūdra women in cooking, etc. But all ladies should be educated at least in *vyākaraṇa, dharma, vaidyaka, gaṇita* and *śilpavidyā* (*Satyārthaprakāśa*, p. 74).

He adopted a novel method of debating taking recourse of *jāti* and *vitaṇḍā*. This is explicit in his advocacy of refutation of child marriage. After deciphering the best age for marriage of a girl is between 16 to 24 years and for a boy between 25 to 48 years, he produces the opponent's views citing the Smṛti texts which recommend the marriageable age at 8 years for girls. In refutation of these, he produces citations from *Brahma Purāṇa*, which has just been composed (*sadyonirmita*) and challenges his opponents how

---

88 जैसे परमात्मा ने पृथिवी, जल, अग्नि, वायु, चन्द्र, सूर्य और अन्नादि पदार्थ सबके लिए बनाए हैं, वैसे ही वेद भी सबके लिए प्रकाशित किए हैं, और जहाँ-जहाँ निषेध किया है उसका अभिप्राय यह है कि जिसको पढ़ने-पढ़ाने से कुछ भी न आवे, वह निर्बुद्धि और मूर्ख होने से शूद्र कहाता है। उसका पढ़ना-पढ़ाना व्यर्थ है। और जो स्त्रियों को पढ़ने का निषेध करते हों, वह तुम्हारी मूर्खता, स्वार्थता और निर्बुद्धिता का प्रभाव है। देखो! वेद में कन्याओं के पढ़ने का कारण

ब्रह्मचर्येण कन्या युवानं विन्दते पतिम्। — अथर्व., अनु 3, प्र. 24, कां. 11, मं 18

प्रश्न - क्या स्त्री लोग भी वेदों को पढें?

उत्तर - अवश्य। देखो - श्रौतसूत्रादि में - इमं मन्त्रं पत्नी पठेत्। . . . जो वेद शास्त्रादि को न पढ़ी होवे, तो यज्ञ में स्वरसहित मन्त्र का उच्चारण और संस्कृतभाषण कैसे कर सके? भारतवर्ष की स्त्रियों में भूषणरूप गार्गी आदि वेदादि शास्त्र को पढ़ कर पूर्ण विदुषी हुई यह शतपथ ब्राह्मण (कांड 14) में स्पष्ट लिखा है। — *Satyārthaprakāśa*, p. 73

do they dare to overrule the authority of Brahmā (ibid., p. 79). The opponent draws his attention to the impossible situation which the so-called verses from the so-called *Brahma Purāṇa* describe, Swami Dayananda retorts by saying that if our excerpts present an impossible situation, your citations equally present an impossible situation. Then he shows the impropriety of marrying a girl at the age of eight through scientific notions of modern age — that physically and mentally she is quite unfit for marriage.

Here Dayananda in a novel way makes use of *sāmānya-chala* and *jāti* to silence the opponent. He advocates the marriage by mutual consent, seeing the photographs of each other.[89]

He construes *mantras* for his purpose. For example: *daśa asyaṁ putrān ādhehi patim ekādaśaṁ kṛdhi* (*Ṛgveda* X.85.45) says that ten sons should be born from a lawful wife and let her husband become her eleventh son. Dayananda interprets this line as a message that a man should not produce more than ten issues.

He views that phenomenal world is a reality. The serpent seen in the rope is also a reality and dreams are also a reality (ibid., p. 290).

Refutations of Satyārthaprakāśa and Rejoinders

Satyārthaprakāśa provoked strong reactions and a prolonged series of refutations and rejoinders from the supporters and detractors of Swami Dayananda.

The chain of debates was initiated as early as 1848 when one Anantaram converted to Islam and authored a work entitled *Tohaful-Hind* in condemnation of Hinduism. Munshi Indramani, who had worked with Dayananda had debated with him but was unable to vanquish him.[90]

Vaidika Satyārthaprakāśa by Akhilanand Sharma, *Dayānandatimirabhāskara* by Pt. Jwala Prasad, *Dayananda-Saraswati-*

---

[89] *Satyārthaprakāśa*, p. 90.

[90] Harsha Narayan, 2010, op. cit., p. 28.

mukha-capeṭika (A Slap on the Face of Dayananda Saraswati) by Thakar Das Jaini and *Dayananda-chala-kapaṭa-darpaṇa* (A Mirror of Conceit and Deception of Dayananda) were some of the books in Hindi where Dayananda was bitterly attacked. The attacks in response were equally intensive. Tulasi Ram wrote and published a rejoinder of Pt. Jwala Prasad's book in his *Bhāskaraprakāśa arthāt Paṇḍita Jwala Prasad-kṛta Dayanandtimirabhāskara kā Uttara* (1897). Baldev Prasad, a brother of Jwala Prasad, replied to it in his *Dharmadivākara*, and this led Pt. Tulasi Ram to come out with *Divākaraprakāśa*.[91]

Pt. Jwala Prasad, the author of *Dayānandatimirabhāskara* has been challenging Dayananda on public platforms. Tulasi Ram wrote *Bhāskārābhāsa* as a strong rejoinder to *Dayānandatimirabhāskara.* Bhavani Prasad Nambaradar of Devarikalan, a village in Sagar district of Madhya Pradesh issued a critique of *Bhāskārābhāsa* in his *Bhāskarābhāsanivāraṇa* (1901).[92] Pt. Bhimsen carried the tirade of *sanātanī*s further. Nityanand Brahmachari used to enter into debates with Pt. Jwala Prasad. Several sessions of *śāstrārtha* by Pt. Bhimsen with Nityanand and other Arya Samajis were organized at Madhav Bagh, Mumbai between 1901-10: at Delhi (1900), Agra (1901), Alipur (Punjab) in 1902 and Munger in 1904.[93]

The magnum opus of Umapati Dwivedi, *Sanātanadharmoddhāraḥ* is an answer to Dayananda's *Satyārthaprakāśa*. Divided into several sections and running in more than 1,500 pages, the second part of the first volume of *Sanātanadharmoddhāraḥ* refutes the view of Naiyāyikas who do not believe in *svataḥ prāmāṇya* of Veda, and seventy-four pages are devoted under

---

91 *Satyārthaprakāśavimarśa*, Ramprakash, p. 31.

92 The first edition of *Bhāskārābhāsanivāraṇa* was published by the author himself in 1901 and he again brought out a second edition in 1914 from his village. The first page of the volume gives a list of donors whose munificence provided for the cost of printing.

93 Purnasingh Verma, 1918, *Paṇḍita Bhimasena Sharma kā Jīvan Carit*, pp. 62-66.

kṣudropadravavidrāvaṇaprakaraṇa (a chapter on repealing the mischief of petty people) the views of Weber and Max Müller are criticized. Around 200 pages are devoted to an encounter with Dayananda and his views on Veda.[94] Another voluminous work of similar nature is *Mahāmohavidrāvaṇa* (A Repealing of the Illusions) against the views of Dayananda by Vedantacharya Mohanlal was published in 1883. Pt. Giridhar Sharma Chaturvedi was supposed to be another apostle standing to stall Dyananda's movement through debates.

Some other works written in opposition to Dayananda and his movement were *Yathārthaprakāśa* by Anand Swaroop, *Satyārthadarpaṇa* by Ajit Kumar Shastri, *Satyārthaprakāśa kī Chīchāledar* by Kalu Ram Shastri, and another work of the same name by Premacharya Shastri, *Satyārthaprakāśasamīkṣā* by Jagannatha Das, *A Refutation of the Satyartha Prakash of Pt. Dayananda Saraswati* by Gulam Mohamad (Hazi Hanif Sadiq), *Haque Prakasha* in Urdu by Sanaullah Amritsari. This has continued till very recent times when Veer Bharat Talwar in his book *On the Critique of Satyārthaprakāśa* and Dr Namvar Singh have expressed strong resentment over some of the postulations of Dayananda. There were critiques from a number of Western scholars also.[95] Talwar called Dayananda illogical/irrational for his adherence to Vedas.

Dayānanda's Debates on Public Platforms

Swami Dayananda became a votary of debates and assiduously perused *śāstrarthas* throughout northern India for more than thirty years of his life.[96] His *śāstrārthas* were held in *darbārs* (royal courts),

---

94 Baldev Upadhyaya, 1994, *Kāśī kī Pāṇḍitya Paramparā*, pp. 383-84.

95 Ibid., p. 72.

96 Some of the places where the *śāstrarthas* of Dayananda were carried were – at Agra, Anupashahar with Pt. Ambadatta, at Soron with Pt. Angad Shastri, at Meerut with Pt. Harigopal Shastri, at Farrukhabad, Kanpur, Mumbai, Danapur, Chandapur, etc. (Yaduvansha Sahay, 2,000 *Maharshi Dayananda*, pp. 85-286).

assembly halls in different towns, public parks or open grounds. He challenged the *maulavīs* and Christian missionaries. The strategy involved in distributing pamphlets, booklets, advertisements and provocative announcements. The issues were child marriage, widow remarriage and refutation of blind beliefs. The *sanātanī*s were outraged. There were outcries and disruptions during the *śāstrārtha*s. That the onslaught of Ārya Samaj led to communal clashes between his followers and the *sanātanī*s, there are instances of attacks on dalits who joined the Samaj.[97]

Swami Dayananda worked with a mission and missionary zeal. He and his followers sometimes committed extremities in their over enthusiasm for reform and national awakening. Lala Lajpat Rai, himself a follower of the Arya Samaj movement gives a balanced assessment of the strength and limitations of this movement and its great savant.[98]

Dayānanda was a man of dialogue. His meeting with Monier-Williams lasted in a friendly discussion and the latter's appreciation of Dayananda's scholarship.[99] The debate with Siddhakarana, a Jaina monk, was held at Mahooda.[100]

---

[97] *Satyārthaprakāśavimarśa*, Ramprakash, p. 102.

[98] "Dayanand's attitude towards the other religions was a necessity of the times in which he lived, and partly due also to his ignorance of the languages in which the best literature of these religions is found. But, in our opinion, there is no justification for his followers to continue to hold that attitude, and the sooner the Arya Samajists come to this conclusion, the better for them and for their cause. The other religions of the world, including those of India must be studied in the writings of their best exponents, and always spoken of in terms of respect and consideration, even if one is unable to accept them as true in their entirety." — Lala Lajpat Rai, 1967, *History of the Arya Samaj*, New Delhi: Orient Longmans.

[99] Yaduvansha Sahay, 2000, op. cit., p. 314.

[100] Ibid., p. 307.

One of the most controversial of his *śāstrārthas* was held on 16 November 1869 at Anand Bagh of Kāśī (which belonged to the king of Amethi) near Durgakund. Swami Vishuddhanand was one of the most revered saints who led this *śāstrārtha*. Maharaja Ishwari Narayan Prasad Singh, aged 48, the ruler of Kāśī, presided over the event and his 14 year-old son Yuvaraj Prabhu Narayan Singh occupied the seat next to him. Pt. Taracharan Tarkaratna, the chief *Sabha paṇḍit* of the Maharaja, remained present at his orders in the *śāstrārtha* with Swami Dayananda.[101] The *paṇḍits* of Kāśī selected two representatives to confront Dayananda – Swami Vishuddhanand and Pt. Bal Shastri.

The *sanātanīs* have been claiming that Swami Dayananda who in other cities had always been a champion in the *śāstrārthas* was defeated here. The Arya Samajis however tell a different story altogether.

Dayānanda's fiery speeches against idolatry and orthodoxy created furor and they also led the *sanātanīs* to unite and re-organize themselves. When idols of gods were being thrown in rivers,[102] Shraddharam Phullori with the help of several others established a society called Sanatan Dharm Rakshini Sabha. The Sabha organized itself on the lines of Arya Samaj — with schools, newspapers and magazines and *upadeśakas* (preachers). This led to a debate. The main discourse of the *sanātanīs* states that *Satyārthaprakāśa* is full of glaring mistakes, Dayananda's interpretation of Vedas is defective, the Arya Samaj itself is un-Vedic, several of its teaching are opposed to the Vedas, Dayananda and his followers are atheists, his teachings are harmful for the cause of Hindu unity and nationalism.

---

101 Beldeva Upadhyaya, 1991, op. cit., p. 123.

102 At Lahore people threw the idols in Rāvī, Lala Balakram Khatri threw away them in Bazar. — Pushpa Suri, 1997, Arya Samaj Movement with special Reference to Punjab", in *Dissent, Protest and Reform in Indian Civilisation*, ed. S.C. Malik, Simla: Indian Institute of Advanced Study, p. 221

Swami Dayānanda went to the extent of advocating *niyoga* (levirate) for the widows, since he believed motherhood a natural function of woman. But he was rediculed in this by many reformers — like Mahadev Govind Ranade. His own followers were sceptical about the propriety of *niyoga*. After Swamiji's demise, the idea of *niyoga* was totally discarded, but widow marriage was taken up with a missionary zeal. Vidhava Vivah Sabha of Lahore opened five of its branches in Rajasthan in 1815.

Ramabai

Paṇḍitā Ramabai was born one year after the Sepoy Mutiny, i.e. in 1858. Her father Anant Shastri Dongre was a Koṅkanastha "Chitpavan" brāhmaṇa and himself a great *paṇḍit*. He was subjected to condemnation for his attempts at women's education. He tried to teach Sanskrit to his first wife and did not succeed in the attempt. His second wife along with her two daughters used to learn Sanskrit with him. Anant Shastri was severely criticized for this, but he dared to challenge the orthodox *paṇḍits*. A *dharmasabhā* was held to take him to task. During the course of a prolonged debate he silenced the opponents by citing 300 references from the Dharmaśāstras to prove that teaching Veda to women is permitted in the law books. Even though the fundamentalists were defeated in the debate, Anant Shastri was cast out by the society.

He became a recluse, found shelter in Gaṅgāmūla forest (near Mangalore) and ran a Sanskrit *pāṭhaśālā* over there. He was forced to quit this place also and became a life-long pilgrim with his wife and three children, youngest of them was Ramabai, a few months of age. Sitting on her mother's lap, Ramabai learnt *Aṣṭādhyāyī* and some thousands of Sanskrit verses including *Gītā* from her father. Anant Shastri won instant admiration of the folk because of his saintly life and command over Sanskrit texts, but had to run from pillar to post as people were antagonized due to his progressive outlook in teaching women.

Ramabai came into contact with Swami Dayananda, studied

Vaiśeṣika philosophy with him. Swamiji wanted her to work for the Arya Samaj movement. She however could not come in terms with him. Brahmo Samaj inducted her into the efforts to popularize women's education through public lectures. She also worked for Prārthanā Samāj in Mumbai.

In her book *The High Caste Hindu Women* Ramabai herself initiated a debate on the predicament and suffering a Hindu women undergoes. Ramabai draws a sharp contrast with Anandibai Joshi, who was related to her. Ramabai, Anandibai Joshi and Rakhmabai are three faces of Hindu women of nineteenth/early twentieth century.

Ramabai was honoured and the titles of Paṇḍitā and Sarasvatī. She was given the title of Paṇḍitā in a ceremony by Maharaja Jyotindra Moha Thakur in Bengal, and the title of Sarasvatī was conferred upon her by a progressive society of Bengal. *Morals for Women* was the English translation of her first book *Strīdharmanīti* in Marathi (1882). *The High Caste Hindu Women* was published in June 1887. On 29 September 1883 Ramabai was baptized along with her daughter Manorama. She was severely criticized in India and several periodicals like *Induprakash, Subodhpatrika* and *Marahatla,* condemned her. Only Jyotiba Phule stood with her.

> The *Maharatta,* western India's socially conservative English language weekly, sought to negate Ramabai's achievements through patriarchal strategy. It installed Anandibai Joshi as an alternative role model and the real icon of Indian womenhood, a conventional wife, submissive to her husband despite her huge professional education, and more importantly still formally within the Hindu fold, even after spending some years in USA (*Maharatta*, 2 July 1886).[103]

The greatest support to Ramabai came from social reformers like Deshmukh, Ranade, Bhandarkar, Telang — they were also

---

[103] Meera Kosambi (ed.), 2003, *Returning the American Gaze: Pandita Ramabai's "The People of the United States, 1889"*, p. 7.

on the Advisory Board of Sharda Sadan, opened in 1889. Agarkar championed her cause through his journalistic writings. But Jyotiba Phule was the only person amongst her Indian supporters who also endorsed her conversion.[104]

The Śāstrārtha Continues

In Kāśī, scholarly debates between the *paṇḍits* continued to be carried with vigour during the eighteenth and nineteenth centuries. Nāgeśa Bhaṭṭa (CE 1650–1730) and his disciple Vaidyanātha Pāyguṇḍe (CE 1690–1780) engaged in a number of serious debates.

This is the richest period in the history of traditional Sanskrit scholarship and it is also a period of most pathetic degeneration of the *paṇḍit*. During the ninteenth and the early twentieth century the most celebrated savants of traditional Sanskrit scholarship — the Mahāmahopāddhyāyas — Bal Shastri, Shiv Kumar Shastri, Gangadhar Shastri, Damodar Shastri, Ramakrishna Shastri (Tatya Shastri), etc. registered their presence in regular *śāstrārthas* that were held at Kāśī. Mahāmahopādhyāya Pt. Ramavatar Sharma entered into debate on Western philosophy with Dr Venice, a well-known European Sanskritist. A team from Australia is reported to have some recording of this occasion.[105] Ramavatar Sharma is said to have defeated two of his *gurus* in *śāstrārtha* during this time. Sharma quit the service at the Hindu College as he dissented against the orders of a dress code for the teachers. He was appointed at Patna University where Rajendra Prasad, who would become the first President of India, was his student.

During the regime of Ballantyne's administration of Banaras Sanskrit College, the *paṇḍits* debated on Aristotle's concepts of existence.[106]

One of the biggest events in the history of *śāstrārtha* during

---

[104] Meera Kosambi (ed.), 2003, op. cit., p. 11.

[105] Baldeva Upadhyaya, 1994, op. cit., p. 273.

[106] Michael S. Dodson, 2011, op. cit., p. 106.

nineteenth-twentieth century was related to two stalwarts – Damodar Shastri and Bachcha Jha. Baldeva Upadhyaya (1994: 137) says that thousands of people had gathered to witness this *śāstrārtha*. In another event of similar magnitude, Paṇḍit Gangadhar Shastri is said to have defeated Paṇḍit Gattulal Shastri who was an adherent of the Vallabha sect.[107] This *śāstrārtha* was held at the Gopal Mandir.

Those who are reported to have been the well-known practitioners of *Śāstrārtha* amongst the *paṇḍits* of Kāśī were patronized by Kāśī Nareśa. A *paṇḍit-sabhā* was founded at Kāśī during this time. It functioned under the state of Kāśī and the King of Kāśī had ordered for its regular meetings every month. The meetings comprised discussions and *vāda* in Sanskrit. A *samasyā* or problem was taken up in every sitting of the *paṇḍit-sabhā*. Some temples also organized similar *Sabhas*.[108]

The *śāstrārtha* between Pt. Shiv Kumar Shastri and Pt. Ramdhan Panchanan was held having Mahāmahopādhyāya Pt. Kailash Chandra as the jury. The former gave a point by point refutation of the Dvaita *mata* of his opponent and won the debate. Pt. Shiv Kumar Shastri also defeated Pt. Ras Mohan Sarvabhauma, a protégé of the ruler of Kashmir in the debate.[109]

Paramārthadarśanam

Paramārthadarśanam of Mahāmahopādhyāya Ramavatar Sharma (1887–1928), one of the most remarkable texts in the history of Indian philosophy and *vāda* tradition, came out in the first decade of the twentieth century. Surprisingly Wilhelm Halbfass who made a very exhaustive survey of recent philosophical works from India in his *India and Europe* nowhere mentions *Paramārthadarśanam* nor does he take any notice of great *paṇḍits*

---

[107] Michael S. Dodson, 2011, op. cit., p. 137.

[108] Ibid., p. 136.

[109] Ibid., p. 231.

like Ramavatar Sharma. G.C. Pande calls Ramavatar Sharma "an original critical and modern philosopher" who "certainly produced a new and original system of philosophy which in part developed through the criticism and interpretation of traditional Indian schools. In this sense perhaps the system can be called a new Indian system."[110] (Wilhelm Halbfass is also not referring to G.C. Pande also, who raised fresh questions in Indian philosophy and aesthetics through his works like *Bhakridarśanavimarśaḥ* and *Saundaryadarśanavimarśaḥ*.)

Aspiring to establish the seventh philosophical system, Ramavatar Sharma wrote the whole text including the aphorisms, *kārikās, bhāṣya* and *vārttikas* — all by himself. He accepts a reality that is Supreme Consciousness, but it is not Absolute, it is *sākṣī* (observer) and the world is observed by it. The observer and the object make one indivisible unity. He refutes the theory of *vivarta* (unreal effect), because the world to him is neither negated nor dissolved. Refuting the world-view of the rest of the philosophies, the author of *Paramārthadarśanam* presents his own system and conceptual framework with new definitions of *jīva, ātman* and *viśva* (world). He propounds the theory of Dehāntaravāda — accepting an inherent relationship between body and soul — but his propositions are neither akin to the Cārvāka philosophy nor Marxism, because he proposes distinct theories of a *viśvātmakacaitanya* (Universal Consciousness) and Viśvavaicitryavāda (queerness of the world). A *jīva* is like a bubble on the vast sea of the Universal Consciousness. The Universal Consciousness is both knowable and unknowable. It partially reflects itself in the limited psyche of the individual soul.

Debating with traditional systems and orthodox philosophies, Sharma introduces some new concepts here. His idea of life involves dynamic concepts. Life to him has three levels — individual, social and universal.

---

[110] *Paramārthadarśanam*, Introduction by G.C. Pande, p. v.

Creating Hermeneutics

B.K. Matilal initiated dialogues between Indian and Western philosophies on one hand and also between diverse philosophical systems of Indian philosophy on the other.

Dayakrishna tried to initiate dialogues between the teachers of Philosophy Department of Rajasthan University and the *paṇḍits* of Sanskrit College, Jaipur. They became sterile and drab. But in the dialogues at Pune, Varanasi and Calcutta the *paṇḍits* responded creatively.

The paradigm that the West is strong in materialist gains and India in spirituality was instituted by the British to legitimize the colonial project, says Edward Said. The mystical aura of the so-called Indian spirituality provided an escape to the educated Indian and a cover for the inferiority before the superior technology of the West.

Pt. Badarinath Shukla (1898–1988) was an outstanding Naiyāyika of Kāśī. Known for his original works *Ārambhavādaḥ and Śataślokī* on Nyāya-Vaiśeṣika system, he had proposed a new concept of *mokṣa* in Nyāya philosophy by defining it as *sukhātmaka* (imbued with pleasure). He was first introduced to the world of modern philosophers perhaps in 1982 when Dayakrishna convened a seminar at Sārnāth on Nyāya philosophy. He created quite a sensation amongst the traditional *paṇḍits* as well as the modern scholars of philosophy by his presentation on *nyāyaśāstrīyavicārapaddhatyā dehātmavādasambhāvanā* (the possibility to accept body as self according to Nyāya methodology). The event raised a new debate. Pt. Shukla argued that *ātman* (the self) need not be accepted as an additional category, its purpose is served by the body and the mind only. He clearly had a vision of modern democratic values that have been emerging.

Pt. Shukla argued for *ātman* as a body substance according to the tenets of Nyāya-Vaiśeṣika systems. The individual self carries nine *viśeṣa guṇas* (special qualities), which are *jñana, icchā, dveṣa, prayatna, dharma, adharma, bhāvanā, sukha* and *duḥkha* and five *sāmanya guṇas* (general qualities), i.e. *saṁkhyā, parimāṇa, pṛthaktva, saṁyoga* and *vibhāga*. These fourteen qualities exist in the individual self and it can be accepted to be an indivisible part of the body. Thus the individual self is not a separate substance, as the body and the mind (*manas*) joined together would serve all the purposes of the existence of a human being. The combination of body with mind can be accepted as the individual self, as all the *viśeṣa guṇas* of individual self — *buddhi, sukha, duḥkha, icchā, dveṣa* and *prayatna* — will exist in the body and remaining other *dharma, adharma, bhāvanā* will remain only in the *manas*. Through this bifurcation of the qualities, Pt. Shukla revised the concept of *viśeṣa guṇas* and redefined some of them as *sāmānya guṇas*. He located these *sāmānya guṇas* in the body. The distribution of *sāmānya* and *viśeṣa guṇas* in the body and mind respectively satisfies all the requirements of an individual self, therefore the need to consider the self as a separate entity from the body and the mind is nullified, and there is no need to accept the self as the ninth substance.

Considering all possible objections to the theory of Dehātmavāda, Pt. Shukla refutes them one by one. When we accept body as an individual self, then the question arises how one would remember the experiences of childhood in old age when the body is totally different in both ages? Theoretically it would require the existence of a consciousness aware of that experience which remains unchanged in old age. In orthodox Nyāya, the individual self meets this requirement. Shukla attributes this function to *manas*, which always remains connected with body. The acceptance of a substance apart from *manas* and the body would lead to *gaurava-doṣa*. Concluding his arguments, Shukla cites a number of social objections that occur if an additional ninth substance like the individual self is accepted. The acceptance of soul as a ninth substance leads to the belief in rebirth. People think that their suffering is a result of the actions of the previous birth, and they tolerate injustice and oppression. The theory of *ātman* and rebirth helps in maintaining status quo and serves the interest of the oppressors. Dehātmavāda on the other hand would make the people confident and enable them to create better conditions in this life. Those who accept body as self may be more disciplined and alert to make their life more beautiful and fruitful. With this view in mind, Shukla has argued as a Naiyāyika in favour of the theory of Dehātmavāda which belongs to Cārvāka philosophy keeping in view the outlook of a common man. He was misunderstood by traditional scholars who severely criticized him for supporting atheism.

The Dialogue Renewed

Pt. Vidya Niwas Mishra exhibited a remarkable capacity for entering into dialogue with nations and cultures. On one hand he advocates *varṇāśrama* system, on the other he has opposed the whole concept of racial purity. *From the Ganges to the Mediterranean* edited by Oscar Pujol Riembau comprises a series of discussions between Vidya Niwas Mishra and Rafael Dieste, a Spanish writer and philosopher. This kind of bilateral dialogue between intellectuals, each representing distinct culture and philosophy, happens on very rare occasions. The whole experiment incorporates the best of human intellect where both the discussants look into the inner recesses of the minds of each other, and they are able to look beyond as well. Oscar Pujol, himself a well-known scholar of Sanskrit and Indian philosophy, has taken up a unique initiative by the way of becoming instrumental in arranging the whole series of discourses and discussions. He has made genuine efforts for the realization of an idea which has immense possibilities and as he himself puts it, which could result into a dialogue between "a representative of critical modernity and a representative of genuine traditions". This dialogue — very much revealing in itself — has led to the rediscovery of several traditions, and also a revisit to all that is known by the terms the East and the West; it has also resulted in creating bridges and better understandings. Mishra and Rafael have enlightened each other, have helped each other for introspections and investigations, and shunning all pretensions and prejudices, both have come out with admittances of strong and weak points of two distinct cultures. Mishra admits that a tendency towards "self-closure" has surfaced on occasions in the tradition of Indian culture, whereas Rafael's deliberations lead to an understanding of the dilemmas and inner contradictions of the West; of the disasters and dangers that lie ahead in the race against time and nature. He is able to show how the abundance of technology is leading to an amnesia and erosion of values. The havoc created by colonization of the nature and colonization of human world, the futility of greed and desire for possession, and value of polyphony — find a convincing footing in Rafael's discourse.

These dialogues are marked with a frank admittance of differences between the interlocutors. The basic differences between the East and the West remain. Both have imbibed the experience of loneliness, but in a different way. Mishra aptly puts it:

> You arrive at loneliness through all your actions and achievements. We start from loneliness, but we do not want to remain lonely, we want to see ourselves in the other.

While Rafael overrules the possibility of a dialogue between two diverse cultures, Mishra believes that it is possible to create dialogue across cultures, the very continuity of Indian traditions and their relevance in modern world would lead to the viability of this kind of a dialogue. Despite distinctive outlooks, this discussion between them leads to the conclusion that "basically human kind is the same all over. Human kind is the same in India or in the West".

These dialogues have turned out to be critiques of our times and without taking recourse to the post-modern techniques, they deconstruct several ancient and modern myths. The myth of progress, the myth of golden age or locating paradise in the past — together with some of the modern myths like the myth of science and the myth of social equality have been deconstructed through the edge of these discussions. Mishra unravels the double standards of the notions of secularism, democracy and many others. It is here that both Mishra and Rafael present a joint memorandum by the way of offering the critique of modern civilization and a warning note on its tending to become Faustian.

Mishra's Concept of Reality "as an incommensurable vibration" assumes a new significance in the context of modern scientific perspectives and the primordial vibration or *spanda* comes to be viewed in the context of complementariness and interconnectivity in the universe, and the vertical and horizontal hierarchies in social order. He suggests a new perspective to the whole concept of *varṇa-dharma* by visualizing the connections between four castes and four types of consciousness — *manas* (mind), *buddhi* (intellect), *citta* (conscience) and *ahaṁkāra* (ego). The interactions with Rafael enable him to review his concepts in contrast to the Western idea of the individual and to project the non-anthropocentric view of Indian culture. It is due to the insight of Mishra that Rafael has also been able to rediscover some of the basic notions from the Western world-view and reinvest them with a new perspective. This intensive exchange of ideas between two creative minds has also resulted in the expansion of definitions of a number of established categories like knowledge, time, space and Reality. The Concept of Reality and the time–space framework have been viewed in all their multiple nature, and new dimensions have been added therein with the reference to the Nyāya-Vaiśeṣika which views the *avayava* (part) different from the *avayavī* (the whole). In the discussion on various notions of time — objective, spiral, experiential, psychological, etc. — Mishra spells out the subtle difference between the experiential time and the psychological time, taking into consideration the aesthetic frame that the former involves in. Rafael explains the anarchies of sleeping time and the legislations of time in memory.

This vigorous exchange of ideas has enabled both interlocutors to redefine some of the known categories. Rituals lead to the recharging of man through the re-enactment of the primordial act of creation. A deity is not what he or she appears to be, "it is that which has been invoked through incantations, according to a particular process". To Rafael "man is a nostalgic animal — with an awareness of scarcity, having the consciousness of separation, of being an alien, an expatriate from a country that is not the one where he was born".

Mishra has created new illustrations, metaphors and parables. He explains the relation between the micro, and the macro, and between human body and the cosmos by the illustration of the leaf and tree, unfolding the view of a bio-centric universe. His discourse contrasts the Western unilinear view with a vision of plurality. There are several gods, several centres are perceived, with every centre having several gods in its periphery. There is a continuous shift of centres and peripheries. He spells out the concept of "cosmic movement" through this idea of moving centres and moving peripheries.

Being Different: An Indian Challenge to Western Universalism by Rajiv Malhotra is a study in failures and possibilities of East–West dialogue. Authored by a person from non-academic background, it offers fresh insights on the dichotomies in cross-cultural contacts. Rajiv repositions and reverses the gaze, instead of being observed by the West, he becomes the observer.

> I am simply using the dharmic perspective to reverse the analytical gaze which normally goes from West to East and unconsciously privileges the former.

He instigates a debate on the cultural and spiritual matrix of *dharma* civilizations as distinct from the Western culture.

> This distinctiveness is under siege, not only from unsustainable and inequitable development but also from something more insidious: the widespread dismantling, rearrangement and digestion of dharmic culture into Western frameworks, disingenuously characterized as "universal". — Malhotra 2011: 12

In the context of this distinctiveness and the spiritual value he makes an attempt to evaluate the cultural chauvinism of much Western thought in its encounters with other cultures. further remarks:

> .... people from dharmic cultures tend to be more accepting of difference, unpredictability and uncertainty than Westerners. The dharmic view is that so-called "chaos" is natural and normal; it needs, of course, to be balanced by order, but there is no compelling need to control or eliminate it entirely nor to force cohesion from outside. The West, conversely, sees chaos as a profound threat that needs to be eradicated either by destruction or by complete assimilation. — Ibid., p. 168

Malhotra proclaims further (p. 177) with pride and confidence that:

> Western scholars find it difficult to acknowledge fully the merits of Indian systems of thought, even when the influence of these systems on West is irrefutable.

Chaos arises when one experiences phenomena which do not lie within one's psychological and cultural comfort zones. Malhotra contrasts the opposite polarities in the light of Indian creativity, adaptability and ability to absorb as well as the non-translatability of certain terms involving the key concepts.

Malhotra insists on preserving difference with mutual respect — not with mere "tolerance". The book addresses the challenge on differences and talks about unexamined beliefs that both sides hold about themselves and each other.

Epilogue

THE theories and practices of *vāda* as described in this book belong to antiquity, but they have not been treated as antique or mummified. The issues generated by the changing socio-political situations were taken up in traditional *vāda* discourses. This has led to paradigm shifts. For example, the consideration for *mokṣa* (salvation) has been unique in Indian intellectual discourses. In the past two centuries, the discourse on *mokṣa* did not remain confined to individual aspirations; it was also considered at social and global levels. Paṇḍit Baljinnath, a traditional scholar of Śaivism from Kashmir of twentieth century, redefines the concept of *mukti* with its varieties, and he includes *rāṣṭramukti* (liberation of the nation) as one of them in his *Svātantryadarpaṇaḥ* — an original treatise on Śaiva philosophy.

Vāda served as a means for seeking democratic rights and justice. The debate of Draupadī, Vidura and Vikarṇa on one side and Duryodhana, Karṇa, etc. on the other; or the most heated debate between Śakuntalā and Duṣṣanta as described in the second chapter of this work can be cited as examples.

The practice of Vibhajyavāda adopted by Buddha provided the framework for Anekānta — "the theory of non-one-sidedness" or "the theory of many-sidedness of reality". It helped in nourishing the plurality in *vāda* traditions. The history of intellectual debate between the orthodox schools of Indian philosophy on one hand and the schools of Buddhist philosophy on the other created awareness and brilliance in intellection.

The *vāda* traditions re-emerged with a wider and far more

consequential outreach during the nineteenth and the twentieth centuries. Swami Dayananda restructured them with all the potentiality of public debates. He also became an architect of the democracy of *vāda* in our times.

In this scenario, the idea of *svarāj* was evolved with a dynamic conceptual framework. The prefix *sva* indicated the self and *rāj* got linked with the idea of freedom at political, social and psychological levels. The last chapter refers to Shyamji Krishna Varma, an unsung hero raising his voice against the totalitarian approaches of West and coming close to Spencer in this process. The idea of *svarāj* was to unfold in Gandhi's criticism of Spencer and liberation of the inner soul of man. *Ātmano mokṣārthaṁ jagad hitāya ca* (for one's own liberation and for the welfare of the world) this saying of Swami Vivekananda became a central principle of Subhas Chandra Bose.

In his *Svaraj in Ideas,*[1] K.C. Bhattacharyya called for developing indigenous systems of thinking and warned against blind adherence to Western thoughts and systems. It is to be noted that in recent decades discussions have been revolved again and again around this lecture by Bhattacharyya and philosophers like Kalidasa Bhattacharyya, Dayakrishna, Rajendra Prasad, Ramchandra Gandhi and S.P. Gautam commented on it. The Hindi translation of this lecture was published in *Pratiman* – a journal of the Centre for Study of Developing Societies (New Delhi) with critical comments. A seminar on it was conducted at the IIAS in 2014.

Bhagwan Das, one of the modern Indian philosophers, had emphasized the need to understand the idea of *svarāj* in the context of social, moral and organizational frameworks. Ambikadatta Sharma rightly suggests that Bhattacharyya's postulations should be considered in the context of the hermeneutics of the idea of *svarāj* presented by Bhagwan Das (1869–1958) and R.D. Ranade (1886–1957) as well as its linkage with Vedic concept of *svarāñjyam* and *vairājyam.*

[1] Delivered as a lecture in 1929, published in *Vishvabharati Journal,* XX: 103-14 in 1954, and reprinted in 1984 in *Indian Philosophical Quarterly* XI.4.

Appendix

Selected List of Vādas Referred in This Work

Debates on Public Platforms

- Anant Shatri Dongre's debate with fundamentalists (p. 324).
- Assembly to pass a resolution of thanks in favour of Max Müller (p. 302).
- Aśvaghoṣa's debate with Pārśva (pp. 96-97).
- Brāhmaṇas of Pune holding an assembly for correction of *Ṛgveda* manuscripts (p. 302).
- *Brahmodyas* as described in *Śatapatha Brāhmaṇa* (pp. 44-45).
- *Brahmodyas* desctribed in the Upaniṣads (pp. 47-51).
- *Brahmodyas* organized during the performance of Aśvamedha ceremony as described in *Yajurveda* (pp. 45-46).
- Buddha's debate with Saccaka (p. 86).
- Buddha's debate with Saccaka *Dhammakathā* (discussion of *Dhamma*) techniques of *kathā* in *Kathāvatthu* (p. 86).
- Dayanand's Debates (pp. 304, 312, 314-24)
- Debate between Aṣṭāvakra and Vandin in Janaka's court as described in *Mahābhārata* (pp. 76-77).
- Debate between Māṇikyasūrin and Śaṅkara as described in *Jalpakalpalatā* (pp. 125-26).
- Debate between Nāgasena and Milinda as described in *Milindapañho* (pp. 94-96).
- Debate between Raṅgojibhaṭṭa and Vidyādhīśa (pp. 136-37).
- Debate conducted in the assembly of 6,000 sages in Himalayan region (p. 698).

- Debate of Draupadī with Bhīṣma and others (pp. 70-75).
- Debate on split of the Saṁgha (Buddhist order) (pp. 90-94).
- Debates between the followers of Mahāvīra with Buddha or his disciples (pp. 87-89).
- Debates by Bal Shastri, Shiv Kumar Shastri, Gangadhar Shastri, Damodar Shastri, Ramakrishna Shastri (Tatya Shastri), etc. (pp. 326-27).
- Debates by Kuṇḍalakeśī (p. 94).
- Debates in Buddhist councils *saṅgītis* (pp. 90-94).
- Debates of Lokāyatikas in the hermitage of Kaṇva (p. 55).
- Debates of Nīlakeśī (pp. 104-05).
- Debates of other sages with Yājñavalkya (pp. 48-50).
- Debates of Udayana (pp. 111-12, 116, 118-20).
- Debates of Vādirāja (p. 122).
- Discussion and debate between Rāma, Bharata, Jābāli and Vasiṣṭha on nullification of Rāma's banishment (pp. 55-62).
- Gārgī's debate with Yājñavalkya (pp. 48-50, 117).
- Jagannātha vs. a Maulavī at Jaipur (p. 136).
- Jāratkārava Ārtabhāga's debate with Yājñavalkya (pp. 48-50).
- Paṇḍitā Ramabai's debates (pp. 324-26).
- Raja Rammohun Roy in debate with Subrahmanya Shastri (p. 305).
- Rāmānuja and Rāmānanda and several medieval saints preaching their philosophy and standing against the caste system (p. 10).
- Raṅgojībhaṭṭa (Raṅgojī) vs. Vidyādhīśa (pp. 136-38).
- Śakuntalā's debate with Duṣṣanta (p. 75).
- Sañjaya Kātyāyana, Pūraṇa Kaśyapa, Makkaliputta Gosāla (Maṅkhaliputra Gośāla), Ajita Keśakambalin, Kakuda Kaccāyana (p. 83).
- Śaṅkara's conquests (pp. 115-18).
- Śāstraparīkṣās organized in city of Pāṭaliputra (p. 7).
- *Śāstrārthas* in marriage (p. 4, 4 fn).
- *Śāstrasabhās* (p. 7 fn).

- Sulabhā's debate with King Janaka (pp. 21-22, 32, 53-54).
- Śvetaketu — his dialogues with the King Pravahaṇa Jaivāli and Janaka (pp. 50-51).
- Śvetaketu's *vāda* against sexual exploitation of women (p. 51).
- Uddālaka Āruṇi's participation in a *brahmodya* (pp. 44-45).
- Uṣastā's debate with Yājñavalkya (p. 49).
- *Vākyārthasabhās* (p. 7).
- Vāseṭṭha and Bhāradvāja (p. 86).
- Veṅkaṭanātha's debates (pp. 127-31).

Dialogues and Discussions

- Dialogue between Sītā and Rāma in Daṇḍakāraṇya on the vulnerability of violence and practice of non-violence (pp. 55, 62-63).
- Kausalyā's conversation with her husband Janaka on the question of action vs. asceticism (p. 68).
- Sitā's conversation with Rāma on his disowning of her after Rāvaṇa is vanquished (pp. 63-65).
- Śvetaketu's conversations with his wife Suvarcalā (pp. 52-53, 68)
- The *saṁvāda* between Kṛṣṇa and Nārada on various questions of diplomacy (p. 70).
- Viśvāmitra's debate with a *cāṇḍāla* on *dharma* (p. 77).
- Yudhiṣṭhira asks Bhīṣma on the choice between violence and non-violence (p. 68).
- Yudhiṣṭhira's dilemma on *karma* (action) and *jñāna* (knowledge) and his debate with Draupadī, Bhīma and others (p. 67).

Philosophical Debates in Texts

- Akalaṅka (pp. 106-07, 111).
- Al-Biruni (pp. 122-24).
- Appayya Dīkṣita vs. Mādhvavedānta (pp. 135-36).
- *Arthaśāstra* as a text of debates (pp. 42, 88-89).
- Bādarāyaṇa and Śaṅkarācārya (pp. 9-10, 32).

- *Bhaṭṭojikuṭṭanam* (p. 138).
- Buddha's condemnation of debates (pp. 19-20).
- Critique of Cārvāka philosophies by other systems (pp. 79-80, 190-96).
- *Dabistān-e-mazahib* (pp. 34, 143-46).
- Debate between *Nyāyāmṛtam* and *Advaitasiddhi* (p. 132).
- Debate described in the Vedic Saṁhitās (pp. 42-44)
- Debate in *Nirukta* (pp. 77-78).
- Debates between Buddhist Logicians and Naiyāyikas (pp. 98-101).
- Debates between Idealism and Materialism (pp. 190-96).
- Debates by the Lokāyatikas or the Cārvākas (pp. 10, 12).
- Debates of Nāgārjuna in *Vigrahavyāvartinī* and *Mādhyamikakārikā* with Nyāya, Vedānta (pp. 97-100).
- Debates on Orientalism (pp. 295-99).
- Debates on Philosophy of Language (pp. 114-15).
- Debates on Scriptural Authority (pp. 208-09).
- Debates on the Absolute and God as Creator (pp. 213-19).
- Debates on the nature of Reality (pp. 196-208).
- Debates on the theory of knowledge (pp. 209-12).
- Debates within Buddhist schools (pp. 97-98).
- Debates within Orthodox systems of philosophy Jñānakarmsamuccayavāda vs. Kevalajñānavāda (pp. 188-89).
- Dharmakīrti vs. Nyāya (pp. 23-26, 107-12).
- Dharmakīrti's disagreements on *vyāpti, nigrahasthānas* and *hetu* (with Diṅnāga and Gautama) (pp. 108-83).
- Dialogue hymns of *Ṛgveda* (p. 44).
- Diṅnāga vs. Bhartṛhari's philosophy of Śabdabrahmavāda (p. 107).
- Friedrich Schlegal, Schopenhauer (pp. 284-86, 297, 303).
- Haribhadra (pp. 87, 105-06, 111).
- *Kāmasūtra* of Vātsyāyana (pp. 52, 90, 106).
- Madhusūdana vs. Rāmārya (pp. 134-35).

- Madhva and Trivikrama (pp. 125).
- *Mahānirvāṇatantra* (pp. 149-50).
- *Manoramākucamardanī* (p. 138).
- *Mubahisa-e-Hudusa-e-duniya* (p. 34).
- Nandaka's discussions on *kathā* in *Anumānasutta* and *Upālisutta* (p. 86).
- *Raṅgojibhaṭṭadhikkāra* (p. 137).
- Refutation of other systems by Devasūri in his *Syādvādamañjarī* (p. 122, 125).
- Rejoinders to Appayya Dīkṣita (pp. 135-36).
- S. Radhakrishnan's critique of Albert Switzer's view (p. xiii).
- *Samaṇasutta, Svarājyaśāstra,* commentaries on *Gītā* and *Japuji* (p. xiii).
- *Samudrasaṅgama* (pp. 146-48).
- Śaṅkara's disagreement with Manu on *kāma* and the dignity of *gṛhasthāśrama* (pp. 188-89).
- Sarahapā's disagreements with Buddhism and other systems (pp. 193-94).
- *Sarvadarśanasaṁgraha* (pp. 81, 101-02, 130).
- *Śatadūṣaṇī* (pp. 128, 130).
- *Tarkatāṇḍava* of Vyāsatīrtha (pp. 126, 132).
- *Tattvopaplavasiṁha* (pp. 112-14).
- The *Mahābhāṣya* of Patañjali (pp. 80, 90).
- Vijñānabhikṣu's reformulation of classical Sāṁkhya and his disagreement with Vedānta on concept of *dṛṣyatva* (p. 190).
- Vyākaraṇa Setumādhavācārya's *Tattvakaustubha* as critique of Bhaṭṭoji under the title *Tattvakaustubhakuliśa* (p. 138).
- Zalāluddin Dāvānī — his *Akhlaque Nāsirī* (p. 34).

Debates on Legal and Socio-political Matters in the Texts

- Bādarāyaṇa's views in his *Apaśūdrādhikaraṇa* countered by the other philosophers like Bhāguri, the *Mahābhārata* or *Gītā* (p. 222).
- Bādarāyaṇa's views on the rights of śūdras to study Veda in his

Apaśūdrādhikaraṇa of *Brahmasūtra*, Pūrva-Mīmāṁsā supporting his views (p. 221).

- *Bhaṭṭācārya Sahit Bicār* (p. 305).
- Critique of *varṇāśrama*-centric culture by tāntric systems (pp. 222-24).
- Debate on the coronation ceremony of Shivaji (pp. 237-38).
- Debates in Dharmaśāstras on laws of inheritance, women's rights and marriage (pp. 227-36).
- Debates of Ārya Samaj (p. 314).
- Debates on caste system (p. 236).
- Debates on Polity and Governance (p. 227).
- Debates on *satī* (pp. 292, 295, 306).
- Debates on the provision of divorce in marriage (pp. 230-32).
- Debates on widow marriage: *Vidhavodvāhaśaṅkāsamādhih* (pp. 310-11).
- Edicts of King Aśoka (p. 11).
- *Laghuṭaṅka* a rejoinder to *Vajrasūcī* (pp. 226-27).
- Mritjunjaya Vidyalankar *Vedāntacandrikā* (pp. 292, 305).
- Refutations of *Satyārthaprakāśa* and rejoinders (pp. 319-24).
- Rejection of caste system by Dharmakīrti and other Buddhist philosophers (p. 224).
- *Satyārthaprakāśa* as a text in *vāda* (pp. 315-19).
- The debates on property laws (pp. 288-89).
- *Vajrasūcī* and the Debate on the Caste System (p. 226).
- *Vajrasūcyopaniṣad* (p. 226).
- *Vivādabhaṅgārṇava* (p. 287).
- *Vivādārṇavasetu* (pp. 287-88).
- *Vyavahāradaśaślokī* (p. 287).

Debates on Literary Theory, Aesthetics and Literature

- *Āgamadambaraprahasana* of Jayantabhaṭṭa (pp. 269-71).
- Bhavabhūti's plays as *vāda* texts (pp. 262-65).
- *Bṛhattrayī*: as a *vāda* discourse (pp. 266-69).

- Concepts and categories of *vāda* in literary theory (pp. 245-46).
- Debates on the theory of *alaṁkāra* (pp. 256-57).
- *Dhuttakkhāṇa* (*Dhūrtākhyāna*): Debates by Rogues (p. 269).
- Kālidāsa's *kāvyas* as Debates (pp. 259-62).
- *Kāvyamīmāṁsā* as a *vāda* text (pp. 247-48)
- Major debates in literary theory (pp. 246-47).
- *Naṭāṅkuśa*: a *vāda* with the Cākyārs (pp. 257-59).
- *Nāṭyaśāstra* as a *saṁvāda* text (pp. 239-40).
- *Rasa* discourse: debates and diversities (pp. 248-56).
- *Vāda* in *kāvya* and *kāvya* in *vāda* (pp. 271-81).
- *Vāda* reflected in the conceptual framework of *Nāṭyaśāstra* (pp. 241-45).
- *Vādas* in Kāvya-literature (p. 259).

Debates Within

- Hanumān's debate with his own self during his search for Sītā in Laṅkā (p. 32).
- Hymn of Dīrghatamas as a debate with the self (p. 44).
- *Vāda* going on within the poet-seer (p. 43).

Bibliography

Primary Sources

Abhidharmakośabhāṣya of Vasubandhu, ed. Prahlad Pradhan, Patna: K.P. Jayasawal Research Institute, 1967.

Abhidharmakośakārikā, ed. Rahul Sankrityayana, Kāśī Vidyapeeth, 1931.

Abhinavakāvyālaṁkārasūtram of Radhavallabh, Varanasi: SSVV, 2005.

Abhirājayaśobhūṣaṇam of Rajendra Mishra, Allahabad: Vaijayant Prakashan, 2006.

Advaitasiddhiḥ of Madhusūdana Sarasvatī, tr. and ed. Karuna Bhattacharya, Delhi: ICPR, 1992.

Āgamadambaraprahasana of Jayantabhaṭṭa, ed. V. Raghavan, Darbhanga: Mithila Institute Series, 1974.

Ākhyātavādaḥ of Raghunāthaśiromaṇi, with comm. of Rāmabhadra Sārvabhauma, ed. Prabal Kumar Sen, Calcutta: Sanskrit Pustak Bhandar, 1979.

Anekāntajayapatākā of Haribhadra, ed. H.R. Kapadia, Baroda: BOS, 1940.

Apohasiddhiḥ of Ratnakīrti, ed. Har Prasad Shastri, *Bibliothica Indica*, Calcutta: Asiatic Society, 1910.

Arthaśāstra with comm. *Śrīmūla* of T. Ganapati Shastri and tr. and intro. N.P. Unni, New Delhi: Bharatiya Book Corporation, 3 vols., 2006.

Atharvaveda, Delhi: Nag Publishers, 1994.

Ātmatattaviveka of Udayana, Varanasi: Chowkhambha Sanskrit Series Office, 1940.

Bodhicittavivaraṇa of Ācārya Nāgārjuna and *Bodhicittabhāvanā* of Ācārya Kamalaśīla, tr. and ed. Gyaltsen Mandol, Sarnath, Varanasi: Central Institute of Higher Tibetan Studies, 1991.

Brahmasūtra with *Śāṅkarabhāṣya*, *Śrīśaṅkarācārya-granthāvalī*, vol. III, Delhi: Motilal Banarsidass.

Buddhacaritam of Aśvaghoṣa, ed. E.H. Johnston, Calcutta, Baptist Mission Press, 1935.

Buddhacaritam of Aśvaghoṣa, ed. Surya Narayan Chowdhury, Varanasi, 1943.

Caraka Saṁhitā: Agniveśa revised by Caraka and Dṛḍhabala, with *Āyurvedadīpikā* of Cakrapāṇidatta, ed. Vaidya Jadavji Trivikramji Acharya, Bombay: Nirnaya Sagar Press, 1941.

Caraka Saṁhitā, vol. I, ed. Gangasahaya Pandeya, Kāśī Sanskrit Series No. 194, Varanasi: Chowkhambha Sanskrit Series Office, 1970.

Catuḥśatakam, Āryadeva, with Candrakīrti's *Vṛtti*, ed. Bhagchandra Jain "Bhaskar", Nagpur, 2007.

Dāsacaritam, ed. T. Anantanarayana, Tirupati: Oriental Research Institute, 1989.

Daśapadārthī of Candra, ed. Uma Raman Jha, Jammu: Ranvir Kendriya Sanskrit Vidyapeeth, 1977.

Dharmottarapradīpa of Durveka, ed. Dalsukhabhai Malvania, Patna: Kashi Prasad Jayaswal Research Institute, 1971.

Dhuttakkhāṇa (*Dhūrtākhyāna*) of Haribhadrasūrin, Bombay: Singhi Jain Granthamala, 1944.

Dhvanyāloka, ed. and tr. K. Krishnamurti, Delhi: Motilal Banarsidass, 1982.

Dhvanyāloka, with *Locana* of Abhinavagupta and Kerala Commentaries, vols. I-II, ed. C.M. Neelkanthan, Tripunithura Ernakulam: Centre for Heritage Studies, 2011.

Hetubindu of Dharmakīrti, ed. P.P. Gokhale, Delhi: Sri Satguru Publications, 1997.

Hetubinduṭīkā of Bhaṭṭa Arcaṭa with Āloka of Durveka Miśra, ed. Pandit Sukhlalji Sangvi and Muni Jinavijaya, Ahmedabad: Saraswati Pustak Bhandar, 2011-12.

Hetubinduṭīkā, Gaekwar Oriental Series, Vadodara: Oriental Institute, 1949.

Isibhāsiyāin (*Ṛṣibhāṣitāni*), ed. Samani Kusum Prajna, Ladnun, Rajasthan: Jain Vishva Bharati, 2011.

Jalpakalpalatā of Ratnamaṇḍana, Sheth Devachand Lalbhai Jain Pustakoddhar Fund Series-11, Bombay, 1912.

Jñānaśrīmitranibandhāvaliḥ of Jñānaśrīmitra, ed. Anant Lal Thakkur, Tibetan Sanskrit Series, Patna: KJRI, 1961.

Kālidāsagranthāvalī (complete works of Kālidāsa), ed. Rewa Prasad Dwivedi, Ujjain: Kalidasa Academy, 2008.

Kāvyālaṁkārakārikā of Rewa Prasad Dwivedi, Varanasi: Kalidasa Samsthana, 1977.

Kāvyamīmāṁsā of Rājaśekhara, with *Madhusūdanī*, Varanasi: Chowkhambha Sanskrit Series Office, 1991.

Kāvyaprakāśa of Mammaṭa, ed. with English tr. Ganganatha Jha, Varanasi: Bharatiya Vidya Prakashan, 1885.

Khaṇḍanakhaṇḍakhādya of Śrīharṣa, Hindi tr. Hanumat Prasad Shastri, Varanasi: Chowkhambha Sanskrit Series Office, 1970.

Kirātārjunīyam of Bhāravi, with *Ghaṇṭāpatha* and *Prakāśa* commentaries, Varanasi: Chowkhambha Sanskrit Series Office.

Laghuṭaṅka, published in *Vajrasūcī of Aśvaghoṣa and the Concept of Varṇa-Jāti Through the Ages* by Ramesh Bharadwaj, Delhi: Vidyanidhi Prakashan, 2007.

Mādhyamakaśāstram with comm. *Prasannapadā* of Candrakīrti, ed. P.L. Vaidya, Darbhanga: Mithila Institute, 1960.

Mahābhārata, 19 vols., 1933-66, Pune: BORI.

Mahābhārata, 5 vols., 1955-69, Gorakhpur: Gita Press.

Mahābhārata, 5 vols., Delhi: Satguru Publications.

Mahānirvāṇatantra with English tr. M.N. Datta, ed. J.L. Gupta, Delhi: Chowkhambha Sanskrit Pratishthan, 2003.

Mahiṣaśatakam of Vāñchānātha, ed. Radhavallabh Tripathi, Delhi: Bharatiya Book Corporation, 2011.

Manusmṛtiḥ with com. *Manvarthamuktāvalī*, Delhi: Motilal Banarsidass, 2000.

Milindapañho, Bauddhabhāratīgranthamālā 13, ed. Swami Dwarakadas Shastri, Varanasi, 1998.

Mūlamādhyamakakārikā with com. of Candrakīrti, St. Petersburg: *Bibliotheca Buddhica*-IV, 1903-13.

Mūlamādhyamikakārikā, ed. Kenneth K. Inada, Tokyo: The Hokusedo Press, 1970.

Naiṣkarmyasiddiḥ of Sureśvarācārya, ed. Premavallabha Tripathi, Chowkhambha Sanskrit Series, 2009.

Nāradasmṛti, ed. Heramba Chaterjee Shastri, Calcutta: Sanskrit College, 1988.

Nārāyaṇasmṛtiḥ, Sree Narayana Guru, New Delhi: D.K. Printworld, 2007.

Naṭāṅkuśa (anonymous), ed. K.G. Paulose, Tripunithura: Government Sanskrit College Committee, 1993.

Nāṭyaśāstra of Bharata, with comm. *Abhinavabhāratī*, GOS, Vadodara: Oriental Institute, vol. I, 4th edn, 1992; vol. IV, 1964.

Nāṭyaśāstra, vol. II, Delhi: Parimal Publications, 1988.

Navyanyāyavādagranthāḥ, critically edited with an introduction in English by Sweta Prajapati, Vadodara, 2008.

Nīlakeśī (*Neelakesi*), Tamil text, English version by A. Chakravati, Jaipur: Prakrit Bharati Academy, 1994.

Nirukta of Yāska, with Durgācārya's *Vṛtti*, ed. Vaijnath Kāśīnātha Rajwade, Anandasrama Sanskrit Granthavali 88, part I, 1921, part II, Ananda Sharma, Pune, 1926.

Nyāyabindu with com. of Dharmottarācārya, ed. and tr. Chandra Shekhara Shastri, Kashi Sanskrit Series No. 22, 2nd edn, Varanasi: Chawkhambha, 1954.

Nyāyadarśanam, vol. 1, chap. 1 (with the *Bhāṣya* of Vātsyāyana, the *Vārtika* of Udyotakara, the *Tātparyaṭīkā* of Vācaspati and the *Pariśuddhi* of Udayana), ed. Anantalal Thakur, Mithila Institute Series No. 20, Vaishali, Muzaffarpur: Prakrit Jain Institute, 1967.

Nyāyadarśanam, Varanasi edn with Hindi comm. by Swami Dwarkadas, Varanasi: Bauddha Bharati, 1976.

Nyāyadarśanam, Varanasi edn with Hindi comm. by Sachchidanand Mishra, Varanasi: Bharatiya Vidya Prakashan 1999.

Nyāyakusumāñjaliḥ of Udayana, with Hindi tr. Vishveshvar Siddhāntaśiromaṇi, Varanasi: Chowkhambha Vidya Bhawan, 1978.

Nyāyakusumāñjaliḥ with four commentaries, Chowkhambha Sanskrit Series, Varanasi: Chowkhambha, 2013.

Nyāyamukha of Diṅnāga, ed. Guiseppe Tucci, Chinese and Tibetan Translation Series, Heidelberg: Materialen Zür kunde des Buddhismus, 1930.

Nyāyapariśiṣṭaṁ, with *Pañjikā* of Vāmkeśvaradhavaja, ed. S.N. Ramadeshika, Tirupati: Kendriya Sanskrit Vidyapeetham, 1978.

Nyāyapraveśa of Diṅnāga, *Bibliotheca Indo Buddhica*, No. 41, ed. with notes A.B. Dhruva, repr., Delhi: Sri Satguru Publications, 1987.

Nyāyapraveśa of Diṅnāga, ed. B.J. Sandesara, Gaekwad's Oriental Series, No. 38, Baroda: Oriental Institute, 1968.

Nyāyapraveśa, with *Nyāyapraveśavṛtti* of Haribhadra and *Nyāyapraveśavṛttipañjikā* of Pārśvadeva, ed. with notes and introduction by A.B. Dhruva, 1st edn, Bibliotheca Indo Buddhica, No. 41; 1930, Delhi: Sri Satguru Publications, 1987.

Nyāyapraveśakasūtram, with *Nyāyapraveśavṛtti* of Haribhadra and *Nyāyapraveśavṛttipañjikā* of Pārśvadeva, ed. with Hindi tr. by Ranjan Kumar Sharma, Sarnath: Central Institute of Tibbetan Studies, 1999 (ref. in this work from this edition).

Nyāyasudhā of Jayatīrtha, ed. Raja S. Giri Acharya, Mantralaya Sri Guru Sarvabhuma Sanskrit Vidyapith, 2003.

Paramārthadarśanam, Ramavatar Sharma, New Delhi: Motilal Banarsidass, 1994.

Pātañjalayogadarśanam with *Tattavavaiśāradī, Yogavārtikabhāṣya and Vyāsabhāṣya*, Delhi: Bharatiya Vidya Prakashan, 1981.

Pātañjalayogasūtram, ed. Ramshankar Bhattacharya and Amaldhari Singh, Delhi: Bharatiya Vidya Prakashan, 1979.

Prabodhacandrodaya of Kṛṣṇamiśra, with comm. *Candrikā* and *Prakāśa*, ed. Vasudev Panashikar, Bombay: Nirnaya Sagar Press, 1935.

Pramāṇapaddhatiḥ of Jayatīrtha, Eng. tr. Shrinivas Verkhedy, Manipal, Karnataka: Manipal University Press, 2011.

Pramāṇasamuccaya of Diṅnāga, ed. H.R. Rangaswamy Iyengar, Mysore: Mysore University Publication, 1930.

Pramāṇavārtikam of Dharmakīrti, with self-*Vṛtti* and comm. of Manorathanandin, ed. (?) Ramchandra Pandeya, Delhi: Motilal Benarsidass, 1989.

Pramāṇavārtikam, ed. Rahula Sankrityayan, Appendix to the *Journal of the Bihar and Orissa Research Society*, No. 24, 1938.

Pramāṇavārtikam, ed. Rahula Sankrityayana with the comm. of Manorathanandi, Patna: Bihar and Orissa Research Society, 1940.

Pramāṇavāritikam, ed. Rahul Sankrityayana, with comm. of Prajñākaragupta, Patna: Kāśī Prasad Jayaswal Research Institute, 1953.

Pratītyasamutpādakārikā: V.S. Apte Commomeration Volume, ed. V.V. Gokhale and M.G. Dhadphale, Pune: D.E. Society, Furguson College, 1978.

Pratītyasamutpādakārikāvyākhyānam (Sanskrit translation from Tibetan), ed. Ven Samdhong Rinpoche & Ramshankar Tripathi, Sarnath: Central Tibetan Institute, 1986, Raniero: Gnoli, 1960.

Pūrvamīmāṁsāsūtras of Jaimini, with English comm. of Ganganath Jha, Varanasi: Bharatiya Publishing House, 1979.

Rāmāyaṇa of Vālmīki (text as constituted in its Critical Edn), Gen. ed. Ramakrishna T. Vyas, Vadodara: Oriental Institute, 1992.

R̥gveda (in five vols.), with Sāyaṇa's *bhāṣya*, Pune: Vaidik Samshodhan Mandal.

Ṣaḍdarśanasamuccaya of Haribhadrasūri, tr. K. Sacthchidananda Murty, Delhi: Eastern Books Linkers, 1957, 2nd edn, 1986.

Saduktikarṇāmṛta of Śrīdhara, ed. S.C. Banerjee, Calcutta: Firma KLM, 1964.

Sambandhaparīkṣā, ed. Swami Dwarikadas Shastri, Varanasi: Bauddha Bharati, 1972.

Sāṁkhyasāra of Vijñānabhikṣu, ed. Shivkumar, Delhi: Eastern Book Linkers, 1988.

Saṅkalpasūryodaya of Veṅkaṭanātha (Vedāntadeśika), ed. Pandit V. Krishnamacharya, part III, Madras: Adyar Library, 1948.

Santānantarasiddhi, tr. Hidenori Kitagawa, The *Journal of Greater India Society*, vol. XIV (1 & 2), 1955.

Sarvadarśanasaṁgraha of Mādhavācārya, by Ishvara Chandra Vidyasagar, *Bibliotheca Indica*, 21, Calcutta, 1853-58.

Sarvadarśanasaṁgraha, tr. E.B. Cowell and A.E. Gough, London: Trübner and Co. 1892, 1894 repr., CSS, vol. X, Varanasi, 1978.

Sarvadarśanasamanvayaḥ of Gopala Shastri Darshanakesari, ed. Madan Mishra, New Delhi: Shri Lal Bahadur Shastri Rashtriya Sanskrit Institute of Indology 1981.

Śāstradīpikā of Pārthasārathimiśra (Tarkapāda), with *Vivṛti* of R. Mani Dravid, ed. with notes Sharda Narayanan, Chennai: Ambika Akshravali, 2015.

Śāstrārthavārtāsamuccaya of Haribhadarsūri, Hindi tr. Notes and Introduction by K.K. Dixit, Ahmedabad: LD Institute of Indology, 1969.

Satyārthaprakāśa of Dayānand, New Delhi: Sarvadeshik Arya Pratinidhi Sabha, vs 2050 (1993).

Saundaryadarśanavimarśaḥ of Govinda Chandra Pandey, Varanasi: Sampurnanand Sanskrit University, 1965.

Śrīmacchaṅkaradigvijayaḥ by Madhva, Shringeri: Akhil Bharat Shankar Seva Samiti, 1972.

Śrīśaṅkaravijayamakaranda, compiled from all *Śaṅkaravijayas* and other sources by Vaidya S.V. Ramkrushna Shastri, New Delhi: Meharchand Lachchmandas, 1984.

Śṛṅgāraprakāśa of Bhoja, ed. Rewa Prasad Dwivedi vols. I-II, New Delhi: IGNCA, 2011.

Subhāṣitaratnabhāṇḍāgāra, Narayanram Acharya, 1986, Varanasi, Chowkhamba Sanskrit Series Office.

Subhāṣitaratnakośa, compiled by Vidyākara, ed. D.D. Kosambi and V.V. Gokhale, Cambridge, MA: Havvard University Press, 1957.

Subhāṣitāvalī compiled by Vallabhadeva, ed. Peterson, Pune: Bhandarkar Oriental Institute, 1961.

Śuklayajurveda, ed. Ravi Prakash Arya, New Delhi: Parimal Publications, 1st edn 1997, 2nd edn 1999.

Svārthānumānapariccheda, ed. Dalsukha Malvaniya, Varanasi: Banaras Hindu University, 1959.

Svātantryadarpaṇaḥ of Pundit Baljinnath, Jammu: Jammu Vidyapeeth.

Tarkāmṛtaṁ of Jagadīśa Tarkālaṁkāra, with the *vivṛti* of Jīvanakṛṣṇatīrtha, ed. Vishnupada Mahapatra, Delhi: Manyata Prakashan, 2009.

Tantrāloka of Abhinavagupta, ed. Madhusudan Kaul, Kashmir Sanskrit Series, Srinagar: Government of Jammu and Kashmir.

Tārkikarakṣā of Varadarāja, ed. Mallinga, Varanasi: Varanasi Rajakiya Sanskrit Pathshala, 1903.

Tattavasaṁgraha of Śāntarakṣita, GOS No. LXXXIII, Vadodara: Oriental Research Institute, 1939.

Tattvopaplavasiṁha of Jayarāśi, with Hindi tr. and ed. Pt. Sukhalalji Sanghvi and Rasiklal Parekh, Varanasi: Bauddha Bharati, 1987.

Tattvopaplavasiṁha, ed. with Hindi tr. Kashinath Naupane and Ambikadatta Sharma, New Delhi: D.K. Printworld, 2015.

Udayanagranthāvaliḥ, works of Udayanācārya, ed. Kishor Nath Jha, 2011.

Vādanyāya of Dharmakīrti, ed. P. P. Gokhale, Delhi: Sri Satguru Publications, 1993.

Vādanyāya with *Sambandhaparīkṣā* and *Vipañcitārtha* of Śāntarakṣita, ed. Dvarikadasa Shastri, Bauddha Bharati Series No. 8, Varanasi: Bauddha Bharati, 1972.

Vajrasūcī of Aśvaghoṣa, published in *Vajrasūcī of Aśvaghaṣa and the Concept of Varṇa-Jāti Through the Ages* by Ramesh Bharadwaj, Delhi: Vidyanidhi Prakashan, 2007.

Viṣṇusmṛti, with comm. Keśavavaijayantī of Nandapaṇḍita, ed. V. Krishnamacharya, Adyar Library Series 93, Madras: Adayai Library 1964, repr. 1996.

Viśvaguṇādarśacampū of Veṅkaṭādhvarin, with comm. *Padārthacandrikā* of Balkrishna Shastri and Hindi translation of Jatashankar Pathak, ed. Surendra Nath Shatri, Varanasi: Chowkhambha Vidya Bhawan, 1963.

Yājñyavalkyasmṛti, with *Mitākṣarā* of Vijñāneśvara, ed. Narayan Ram Acharya, Bombay: Nirnaya Sagar Press, 1949.

Yajurvedasaṁhitā (see *Śuklayajurveda*).

Yaśodharacarita of Vādirāja, ed. K. Krishnamoorthy, Dharwad: Karnatak University, 1963.

Secondary Sources

Aggrawal, V.S., 2015, General President's Address on the 22nd Session of the All Indian Oriental Conference, reprinted in *Saumārajyotiḥ*, Souvenir of AIOC, 47th Session, Gauhati University, 2-4 January.

Ahmed, Zahiruddin, 2007, *Introduction to Buddhist Philosophy in India and Tibet*, Delhi: Aditya Prakashan.

Altekar, A.S., 1953, "Idea and Position of Indian Women in Social Life", in *Great Women of India*, ed. Madhavanand Swami and Majumdar Rameshchandra, Howrah: The Holy Mother Birth Centenary Executive Committee, Belur Math.

Athawale, Sadashiv, 1997, *Cārvāka: Itihāsa āṇi Tattavajñāna* (in Marathi), Wai: Prajñā Pathashala Mandal, 3rd edn.

Aurobindo, Sri, 2001, *The Upanishads*, part II, *Kena and Other Upanishads*, Pondicherry: Sri Aurobindo Ashram.

Bandyopadhyaya, Nandita, 1977, *The Concept of Logical Fallacies*, Calcutta: Sanskrit Pustak Bhandar.

Banerji, Sures Chandra, 2004, *Sanskrit Culture of Bengal*, Delhi: Sharada Publishing House.

Bapat, P.V., 1956, *2500 Years of Buddhism*, New Delhi: The Publications Division, Govt. of India.

Barlingay, S.S., 1976, *A Modern Introduction to Indian Logic*, Delhi: National Publishing House.

Bayly, C.A., 2010, "Rammohun Roy and the Advent of Contributional Liberalism", in *An Intellectual History of India*, ed. Kapila Shruti, Cambridge: Cambridge University Press.

Bharadwaj, Ramesh, 2007, *Vajrasūcī of Aśvaghaṣa and the Concept of Varṇa-Jāti Through the Ages*, Delhi: Vidyanidhi Prakashan.

Carpenter, Mary, 1997, *Last Days of Rajah Rammohun Roy*, Calcutta: Rammohun Library & Free Reading Room, 4th edn.

Chakrabarti, Arindam, 2014, "Just Words: An Ethics of Conversation in the Mahābhārata", in *Mahābhārata Now*, ed. Arindam Chakrabarti and Sibaji Bandyopadhyay, New Delhi: Routledge, Taylor & Francis.

Chakrabarti, Arindam and Sibaji Bandyopadhyay (eds.), 2014, *Mahābhārata Now*, New Delhi: Routledge, Taylor & Francis.

Chakrabarti, Samiran Chandra, 2013, *Tattvabodha,* monograph, Kolkata: School of Vedic Studies, Rabindra Bharati University.

Chatterjee, A.K., 1975, *The Yogācāra Idealism,* Delhi: Motilal Banarsidass, 2nd edn.

Chattopadhyaya, Debiprasad, 1981, *Lokāyata*, New Delhi: People's Publishing House.

Chaudhury, Nirad C., 1974, *Scholar Extraordinary: The Life of Professor Rt. Hon. Friedrich Max Muller P.C.*, Delhi: Oxford University Press.

Dasgupta, S.N., 1957, *A History of Indian Philosophy,* 5 vols., Cambridge: Cambridge University Press.

Datta, D.M. and S.C. Chatterjee, 1960, *An Introduction to Indian Philosophy,* Calcutta: University of Calcutta, 6th edn.

Deo, Acharya Narendra, 1971, *Baudha-Dharma-Darśana,* Patna: Bihar Rashtra Bhasha Parishad, 2nd edn.

Deshpande, Madhav M., 2010, "Kṣatriyas in Kali Age?: Gāgābhaṭṭa and His Opponents", *Indo-Iranian Journal: Brill IIJ*, 53: 95-120.

———, 2011, "Will the Winner Please Stand Up: Conflicting Narratives of a Seventeenth–Century Philosophical Debate from Karnataka", in *Knowing India: Colonial and Modern Constructions of the Past — Essays in honour of T.R. Trautmann*, ed. Cynthia Talbol, New Delhi: Yoda Press, pp. 366-67.

Dharmavir, 2010, *Kāmasūtra kī Santāneṅ* (Hindi), Delhi: Vani Prakashan.

Dodson, Michael S., 2011, *Orientalism, Empire and National Culture,* New Delhi: Foundation Books.

Figueira, Dorothy Matilda, 1991, *Translating the Orient: Reception of Śakuntalā in Ninteenth Cenetury Europe*, Albany, NY: State University of New York Press.

Ganguli, Kisari Mohan (tr.), 1997, *The Mahābhārata*, vol. I, Delhi: Munshiram Manoharlal.

Giri, Gagandeo, 1982, *Cārvākaṣaṣṭi*, Ranchi: Jyoti Publications.

Gokhale, P.P., 1992, *Inference and Fallacies Discussed in Ancient Indian Logic,*

Delhi: Sri Satguru Publications.

Halbfass, Wilhelm, 1988, *India and Europe: An Essay in Understanding*, Albany, NY: State University of New York Press.

———, 1991, *Tradition and Reflection*, Albany, NY: State University of New York Press.

Ingalls, D.H.H., 1988, *Matertials for the Study of Navyanyāya Logic* (Harvard Oriental Series, No. 40, Cambridge, MA: Harvard University Press, 1951), Indian repr. Delhi: Motilal Banarsidass.

Jain, Phool Chand and Ramashankar Tripathi (eds.), 2007, *Sanskrit Vāṅmaya kā Bṛhat Itihāsa* (vol. XII: *Jaina, Bauddha and Cārvāka Philosophies*), Lucknow: Uttara Pradesh Sanskrit Sansthan.

John, D. Dunne, 2004, *Foundations of Dharmakirti's Philosophy*, Boston: Wisdom Publications.

Kannan, Sushma, 2014, *Indian Literature*, Sep.-Oct.

Kapila, Shruti (ed.), 2010, *An Intellectual History of India,* Cambridge: Cambridge University Press.

Kumar, Ujjawal, 2014, "Grounds of Saṅghabheda: Division or Split in the Saṅgha", *Pāli-Prākṛt-Anuśilanaṁ*, I(2): 60-66.

Macdonell, A.A. and A.B. Keith, 1995, *Vedic Index of Names and Subjects,* vols. I and II (1st edn, London: John Murray, 1912), repr., Delhi: Motilal Banarsidass.

MacEvilley, Thomas, 2002, *The Shape of Ancient Thought: Comparative Studies in Greek and Indian Philosophies*, Delhi: Motilal Banarsidass.

Madhvanand, Swami and R.C. Majumdar, 2001, *Great Women of India*, Los Angeles: Advaita Ashrama.

Majumdar, Ramesh Chandra, 2009, *On Rammohun Roy*, Calcutta: Asiatic Society, 1972, repr.

Malhotra, Rajiv, 2011, *Being Different: An Indian Challenge to Western Universalism*, New Delhi: HarperCollins.

Mani, Vettam, 1975, *Puranic Encyclopaedia: A comprehensive Dictionary with Special Reference to the Epic and Puranic Literature*, Delhi: Motilal Banarsidass.

Matilal, B.K., 1968, *The Navya-Nyāya Doctrine of Negation*, Harvard Oriental

Series No. 46, Cambridge, MA: Harvard University Press.

———, 1981, *The Central Philosophy of Jainism (Anekāntavāda)*, Ahmedabad L.D. Institute of Indology.

——— , 2005, *Epistemology, Logic and Grammar in Indian Philosophical Analysis*, New Delhi: Oxford University Press.

Michael, Axel (ed.), 2001, *The Pandit: Traditional Scholarship in India*, Delhi: Manohar.

Mishra, Vidya Niwas, 2009, *From Ganges to Mediterranean,* Varanasi: Shubhi Publications.

Müller, Max, 1919, *Six Systems of Indian Philosophy*, London: Longmans, Green and Co.

Murty, K. Satchidananda, 1985, *Philosophy in India*, Delhi: Motilal Banarsidass and ICPR.

———, 2007, *Evolution of Indian Philosophy,* New Delhi: D.K. Printworld, 2nd edn.

Murti, T.R.V., 1968, *The Central Philosophy of Buddhism,* London: George Allen & Unwin (2nd edn).

Musalgaonkar, Gajanan Shastri (ed.), 1999, *Sanskrit Vāṅmaya kā Bṛhat Itihāsa*, (vol. IX: *Nyāya*), Lucknow: Uttar Pradesh Sanskrit Sansthan.

Nair, T.P. Shankarankutty, 2013, "Swami Narayan to Swami Chinmayanand: A Look at Indian Spiritual Legacy", *Dhīmahi, Journal of CIFSS*, IV: 116-35.

Narain, K., 1986, *Critique of Mādhva Refutation of Śaṅkara School of Vedānta*, Delhi: Munshiram Manoharlal.

Narayan, Harsha, 2010, *Dayanand: Eka Punarviśleṣaṇa* (in Hindi), Lucknow: Akhil Bharatiya Sanskrit Parishad.

Narsalay, Madhavi, 2015, "The King with One Kingdom but Two Coronations: Analysing Śrī Śrīśivarājyābhiṣekaprayoga and Śrīśivarājyābhiṣekakalpataru two Coronation texts for Chatrapati Śivājī Mahārāja", abstract published in the Book of Abstracts, 16th World Sanskrit Conference, Bangkok, Delhi: Pragun Publication.

Numbardār, Bhavānī Prasād, 1911, *Bhāskarābhāsanivāraṇa: Tulasīrām Rachit Bhāskaraprakāśa kā Yuktiyuktakhaṇḍana* (Hindi), published by the author from Devarikalan, Sagar.

Pande, G.C., 1957, *Studies in the Origin of Buddhism*, Allahabad: University of Allahabad.

———, 1998, *Life and Thought of Śaṅkarācārya,* Delhi: Motilal Banarsidass (1st edn 1994), repr.

Pratap Chandra, 1977, "Study of Ideological Discord in Ancient India: Search for a Suitable Model", in *Dissent, Protest and Reform in Indian Civilization*, ed. S.C. Malik, Shimla: Indian Institute of Advance Study.

Prebish, Charles S. (ed.), 1995, *Historical Dictionary of Buddhism*, Delhi: Sri Satguru Publications.

Radhakrishnan, S., 2013, *Indian Philosophy*, 2 vols., New Delhi: Oxford University Press.

Raghuramaraju, A., 2006, *Debates in Indian Philosophy: Classical Colonial and Contemporary*, New Delhi: Oxford University Press.

Rai, Lajpat (Lala), 1967, *History of the Arya Samaj*, New Delhi: Orient Longman.

Rajesh, K., 2015, "Intellectual Discourses in Medieval India: Historical Tracts of Śāstrasabhās", 47th Session of AIOC, Guwahati, 2-4 January 2015, Summaries of Papers.

Ramabai, 2003, *Returning the American Gaze: Pandita Ramabai's "The People of the United States" (1889)*, ed. Meera Kosambi, Delhi: Permanent Black.

Randle, H.N., 1976, *Indian Logic in the Early Schools* (OUP, 1930), Indian Edition, Delhi: Munshiram Manoharlal.

Rastogi, Navjivan, 2012, "Tantric Thought of Kashmir: A Framework of Humanistic Culture", *Sanskrit Vimarśaḥ*, New Series 5, New Delhi: Rashtriya Sanskrit Sansthan.

Richards, I. A., 1950, *The Philosophy of Rhetorics,* New York: Oxford University Press (2nd edn).

Robertson, Bruce Carlisle, 1995, *Raja Rammohun Roy: The Father of Modern India*, New Delhi: Oxford University Press.

Robinson, R., 1969, "Early Buddhist Theory of Knowledge", *Philosophy: East and West,* 19: 69-82.

Rothermund, Dietmar, 1986, *The German Intellectual Quest for India*, Delhi: Manohar.

Sahay, Yaduvansha, 2000, *Maharshi Dayanand* (Hindi), Allahabad:

Lokabharati Prakashan.

Said, Edward, 1985, *Orientalism*, Harmondsworth, Middlesex: Penguine Books.

Sarkar, Anil Kumar, 1998, *Dynamic Facets of Indian Thought: Western Impact on Indian Thought*, New Delhi: South Asian Publishers.

Sartori, Andrew, 2010, *Beyond Cultural Contact and Colonial Discoursed: Intellectual History of India*, ed. Kapila Shruti, Cambridge: Cambridge University Press.

Sen, Amartya, 2005, *The Argumentative Indian*, London: Allen Lane.

Shanbhag, D.N., 1996, *Vādirāja, the Dvaita Poet: Great but Ignored*, Dharwad: Sri Rama Prakashan.

Sharma, Ambikadatta, 2012, "Advaitavādī Darśanoṅ kā Prasthānamūlaka Vaiśiṣṭya — Eka Samasāmayika Vimarśa", *Unmīlana*, 26(1).

Sharma, Dhirendra, 1974, *The Negative Dialectics*, New Delhi: Sterling Publishers.

Shastri, D.N., 1976, *The Philosophy of Nyāya-Vaiśesika and Its Conflict with the Buddhist Diṅnāga School (Critique of Indian Realism)*, New Delhi: Bharatiya Vidya Prakashan (2nd edn).

Shastri, Hari Prasad, *The Rāmāyaṇa of Vālmīki*, vol. I (1952, 3rd edn 1976), vol. II (1957, 3rd edn 1976), vol. III (1959, 3rd edn 1976), Shanti Sadan, 29, Chepstow Villas, London.

Siddheshwar, Chitrav (ed.), 1964, *Prācīnacaritrakosha* (Marathi), Pune: Bharatiya Charitra Kosha Mandala.

Solomon, A. Esther, *Indian Dialectics* (2 vols.), Ahmedabad: B.J. Institute of Learning and Research, vol. I, 1976; vol. II, 1978.

Stcherbatsky, T., 1962, *Buddhist Logic*, vols. 1 and 2, New York: Dover Publications.

Sundaram, C.S., 1999, *Contribution of Tamilnadu to Sanskrit*, Chennai: Institute of Asian Studies.

Suzuki, D.T., 1970, *Outline of Mahāyāna Buddhism*, New York: The Schocken Books (4th edn).

Swain, B.K., 2003, *Dharmaśāstra: A Link Between Tradition and Modernity*, Varanasi: Chowkhambha Sanskrit Bhawan.

Tagore, Saumyendranath, 1975, *Rammohun Roy: His Role in Indian Renaissance*, Kolkata: The Asiatic Society.

Teltscher, Kate, 1995, *India Inscribed: European and British Writing on India 1600–1800*, Delhi: Oxford University Press.

Thomas, E.J., 1951, *History of Buddhist Thought*, London: Routledge and Kegan Paul (2nd edn).

Tom, J.F. Tillemans, 1999, *Scripture, Logic, Language: Essays on Dharmakīrti and His Tibetan Successors*, Wisdom Publications.

Tripathi, Radhavallabh, 1991, *Lectures on Nāṭyaśāstra*, Pune: CASS, University of Poona.

———, 2005, *Kāmaśūtra of Vātsyāyana*, ed. with English translation, New Delhi: Pratibha Prakashan.

———, (ed.), 2008, *Glory of Sanskrit Tradition*, 2 vols., New Delhi: Pratibha Prakashan.

———, 2012, "Dhruvasvāminī: Eka ṭīkā" (Hindi), *Naṭaraṅga Quarterly*, 92, April-June.

———, 2012, *Nayā Sāhitya, Nayā Sāhityaśāstra*, New Delhi: Rajkamal Prakashan.

———, 2014, *Dharmakīrti*, monograph under makers of Indian Literature Series, New Delhi: Sahitya Akademi.

——— (ed.), 2014, *Nāṭyaśāstra in the Modern World*, New Delhi: D.K. Printworld.

———, Mahāvīracarita kā Paraśurāmaprasaṅga", *Nāṭyam*, 56: 141-43.

Upadhyaya, Baldev, 1963, *Śrī Śaṅkarācārya* (Hindi), Allahabad: Hindustani Academy (1st edn 1950).

———, 1994, *Kāśī kī Pāṇḍityaparamparā*, Varanai: Vishvavidyalaya Prakashan (1st edn, 1983).

Vattanky, John S.J., 2011, *Gaṅgeśa's Philosophy of God*, Chennai: The Adyar Library and Research Institute.

Verma, Purnasingh, 1918, *Pandit Bhimsen Sharma kā Jīvan Charit* (Hindi), Itawa: Brahma Press.

Viswesvari Amma, K., 1985, *Udayana and His Philosophy*, Delhi: Nag Publishers.

Wayman, A., 1958, "The Rules of Debate according to Asanga", *Journal of American Oriental Society*, 78: 29-40.

Wilson, Jon E., 2010, "Anxieties of Distance" in *An Intellectual History of India*, ed. Shruti Kapila, Cambridge: Cambridge University Press.

Winternitz, 2003, *History of Indian Literature*, vol. I, tr. Subhadra Jha, Delhi: Motilal Banarsidass.

Yagnick, Indulal, 1950, *Shyamji Krishnavarma: Life and Times of an Indian Revolutionary*, Bombay: Lakshmi Publication.

Zelliot, Elleanor, 1982, "A Medieval Encounter between Hindu and Muslim: Eknath's Drama-poem 'Hindu-Turk-Saṁvāda'", in *Images of Man: Religion and Historical Process in South Asia*, ed. F.W. Clothey, Madras: New Era Publications.

Journals

Journal of American Oriental Society, vol. 78 (1958).

Indo-Iranian Journal, Brill, 53.2010.

Naṭaraṅga-92, April-June, 2012.

Nāṭyam 56, Natya Parishad, Dr. Hari Singh Gour University, Sagar.

Pāli-Prākṛt-Anuśīlanam: Journal of Pāli Adhyayana Kendra of The Rashtriya Sanskrit Sansthan, Lucknow Campus.

Sanskrit-Vimarśaḥ (New Series), Rashtriya Sanskrit Sansthan, New Delhi.

Unmīlana, 26(1), Jan.-June 2012, Darshan Pratishthan, Jaipur.

Index

84,000, *yonis*, thesis of 83
A Code of Gentoo Law 287
a dialogue between two diverse cultures, possibility of 332
A Refutation of the Satyartha Prakash of Pt. Dayanand Saraswati, 321
abhāva, nature of ix
Abhidhammapiṭaka 93
Abhidharmakośa 198
Abhidharmakośabhāṣya 84
Abhidharmasamuccaya 178
Abhijñānaśākuntala 13, 283, 300-01
Abhinavabhāratī 243, 248
Abhinavagadā 135
Abhinavagupta 115, 224, 242-43, 248-49
abhinaya, three types of 249
abhiṣeka of Chatrapati Shivaji 237
abhyanujñā 178
abhyupagama siddhānta 159
Ācārya
    Dharmapāla 109
    Viśveśvara 118
Ācāryakula xiii
Acyuasa-a-am (*Avyutaśatakam*) 131
Acyutadevarāya 133
Adam, William 308
adharma 18
adhika 178, 184
Adhikaraṇa 130
adhikaraṇa siddhānta 159
Adhikaraṇadarpaṇa 130
Adhikaraṇanāmāvalī 133
Adhikaraṇasāra 149
ādhipateya-pratyaya 100
adhvaryu
    is liberation 49
    priest 49
Ādhyakṣikas 102
adhyātmavidyā 3
Ādi Brahma Samāj 149
Ādipurāṇa 12
Āditya 49
adoṣodbhāvana 183
Advaita 121
    system, refutation of 128
    tradition of Vedānta 132

Vedānta 34, 36, 121, 127, 133, 199, 201, 208, 214, 286, 304
Vedāntin 205
vs. Dvaita 127

Advaitakālānala 135

Advaitasiddhi 134, 202

Advaitavāda, theories of 130

Advaitavādin 204, 275

Advaitin 188, 203, 313

Āgama 150, 266
texts 5, 239
of Jaina tradition 191
tradition 223

Āgamaḍambaraprahasana xi, 269-70

Āgamic
and Śramaṇic traditions 221
traditions 225

Agarkar, Gopal Ganesh 325

Agastya 63, 259

Aggrawal, V.S. 47-48

Agni 268

Agrawal, Lakshmi Chandra 312

Agrawal Sabha of Kāśī 312

ahetu, three types 175, 177-78

ahiṁsā, moral doctrine of 87

Ahīndranagaram 131

Ahmed, Zahiruddin 198

Aikātmyavādins 147

Aitareya Brāhmaṇa 238

aitihāsikas 41

Aja 61

Ajitakeśakambalin 83, 85, 193

Ājīvaka Gosāla 87

Ājīvaka(s) 7, 10, 67, 78, 83, 224
sect 8, 85, 191

Ajñānavāda 8

Akalaṅka 106, 111

Akbar (Emperor) 34, 143-45

ākhyānavida 41

Akkā Mahādevī 140

Akṣapāda Gautama 112

Ākulavāda (theory of accepting opposites) 87

ālambana-pratyaya 100

alaṁkāra as the quintessence in literature 257

Alaṁkāraśāstra 239, 245
ācārya of 14
history of 246

Ālāra Kālāma 85

ālaya-vijñāna 119

Al-Beruni viii, xi, 122-24, 209

Al-Beruni's India 123-24, 209

Alexander, the Great 310

alfazari 123

All India Oriental Conference 7

Altekar, A.S. 234

Amaruka, a great poet 272

Ambaṭṭhasutta 195

Ambedkar, B.R. 10, 283

Āmbhīyāḥ 88

Ambikadatta 286-87, 337

Amir Ubaid 294

Amita 139, 193

Amma, K. Vishweshvari 37, 197

Āmoda 303

Amritsari, Sanaullah 321

Amṛtarañjanīrahasya 130

Amṛtavādinīrahasya 130

amūlyadānakrayin 26

anaikāntika 163

Anand Swaroop 321

Ānandavāda 248

Ānandavardhana xii

Anantaram 319

ānantyadoṣa 109

ananuyojya 177

ananuyojyānuyogaḥ 178

Anasūyā 265

anātman 190

ancient Indian knowledge systems vii

Āṇḍāla 140

anekāṁśikas 84

Anekānta 86-87
- as Saṁhāravāda, theory of 87
- framework for 336
- theory as "inclusive middle" 84
- theory of 86, 113, 270

Anekāntajayapatākā 105

Anekāntavāda 85
- methodology of 87

Anekāntavijayapatākā 87

Aṅgrejacandrikā 290

anirvacanīyatākhyāti 201

Anirvacanīyatāvāda 201

Aṇṇagarācārya 13

Anquetil-Duperron, Abraham Hyacinthe 284, 296

ānṛśaṁsya 18

antaḥkaraṇas, four types of 147

Antarvyāptivāda 181

Anti-*satī* movement 292

anuloma sambhāṣā 170

anumāna 16, 111, 113, 182, 197, 214
- is crucial for sustaining any conversation or debate 157
- theory(ies) of 36-37, 109, 112
- three essential categories for the validity of an 211

Anumānasutta 86

Anumitivādin 246

anupalabdhi 25
- is a *pramāṇa* 211

anupalambha 120

anusandhāna vyāpāra 250

anuyoga 86, 177

anuyojya 177

anuyojyasya ananuyogaḥ 178

Ānvīkṣikī vii, 2, 41-42, 55, 66, 81, 83, 88, 193

anyārthaṁ 184, 229

aparigraha 194

Āpastamba 229

Āpastamba-Dharmasūtra 51, 230

Apaśūdrādhikaraṇa 10, 221

apavarga, state of 219

Appayyakapolacapeṭikā 135
Aprāptanāṭyaśāstrīya Grantha 249
āptopadeśa 168
Ārabhyārambhakavāda 205
Ārambhavāda 8, 81, 205
Ārambhavādaḥ 329
Āraṇyakas 152
Arcaṭa 110-11
argument age of, 40
argumentative
  design of *vāda* 75
  philosophies 247
Aristotle 2
ariyapariyesana 85
Arjuna 16
Arkacandra 104
artha and *kāma* 154
arthahīnaṁ 184, 229
arthāntara 178
arthaśāstra 225, 227
Arthaśāstra x, 21, 42, 88-90, 166, 184, 186-87, 195, 230-32, 247, 270
arthī 228
Āruṇa 50
Arundhati 265
Arya Samaj 310, 314, 323
  movement 322, 325
  onslaught of 322
Arya Samajis 320, 323
Āryabhaṭṭa, propositions of 124
Āryadeva 101, 195, 205
Āryanization 299
asādhanāṅga-vacana 183
Asadvāda 27, 169
Asaṅga 13, 35, 101, 178, 180
  defined six kinds of *vāda*, 178
Asatkāraṇavāda 27
āśaya 16
Āścaryacūḍāmaṇi 258
Asiatic Society 289, 298
āśramasamuccaya 189
Aṣṭādhyāyī 324
Aṣṭasahasrī 114
Aṣṭāvakra 51, 76-77
āstika philosophers 102
Āsuri of *asura* descent 80
Aśvaghoṣa 94, 96, 226
Aśvala 48-49
Aśvamedha
  ceremony 45
  yajña 21, 44
Ata, Wasil 294
Atharvaveda 11, 43-44, 47, 238, 302
Athawale, S. x, 79-80
ātmamanaḥ saṁyoga, theory of 218
ātman 118, 190
  as *acetana* and *dravya* 200
  and *rebirth*, theory of 330
Ātmatattvaviveka 3, 118, 120
atomistic cosmology, fundamental theory of 212
Atri 223
Aurangzeb 283

Aurobindo, Sri xiv 283
Auśanasas 88
avadhūtas 150
avaidika darśanas 208
avara type of priest 51
Avesta 138
  translation of 296-97
Avestan texts 296
Awasthi, Bachchulal xiv
Ayoda Dhaumya 50
Āyurveda x, 8, 34, 152, 166-67, 169
  epistemology for, 168
Āyurvedic debates, 177

Bābā Lāldās Bairāgī 147
Bachcha 327
Bacon, Sir Francis 290
Bādarāyaṇa 102, 212, 221-22
  injunctions of 10
Bahadur, Radhakanta Dev 305
Bāhudantīputra 88
Balabhadra 124
Balarāma 267
Bali, Rājā 290
Baljinnath, Paṇḍit 336
Ballantyne, J.R. 299, 309, 326
Bāṇa 102, 115
Bandhyopadhyaya, S. 28, 32, 53, 152, 155
Banerji, Sures Chandra 134, 141, 149-50
Bapu, Paṇḍit Subaji 226
Bapudev, Paṇḍit 309
Bārhaspatyas 88, 271
Bārhaspatyasūtra 192
Basaveśvara 140
Basu, Ram Roy 291
Batris Simhasan 290
bauddhabandhuḥ ix
Bauddhācārya 119
Bauddhadhikkāra 118
bauddhika-vimarda 248
Baudhāyana 80
Bayly, C.A. 44, 292-94
Bekanīyaśāstravyākhyānam 290
Bengal Hurkaru 291
Bentinck, Lord William (Governor-General) 236, 295
Bernier, François 136
Bhadrā, Kuṇḍalakeśī 94, 104
Bhagavadgītā 284, 288, 297
Bhāgavata schools of religious order 223
Bhāgavata Purāṇa 134, 143, 315
Bhagavatakhaṇḍanaṁ 315
Bhagavatīsūtra 88
Bhagavatpādābhyudaya 30
Bhāguri 80, 222
Bhakridarśanavimarśaḥ 328
bhakti
  and *śṛṅgāra*, confluence of 131
  leads to *mokṣa* 219
Bhakti movement, onslaught of 121

Bhaktimāhātmya 118

Bhāmaha 246

Bhaṇḍālekhyanyāya 26

Bhandarkar, Ramakrishna Gopal 325

Bharadvāja 80, 86

Bhāradvājas 88

Bharadwaj, Ramesh 97, 227

Bharata 12, 55-58, 62, 64, 72, 225

Bharata Muni 22-23, 239-42, 244, 248, 250, 260

Bhāratavarṣa 223

Bharatendu 301

Bhāravi 16, 266-67

Bhartṛhari 10, 108, 113-15

Bhartṛhari's philosophy of Śabdabrahmavāda 107

Bhāruci 189

Bhāsa 258, 262

Bhāsarvajña 112, 180

Bhāskara 101, 130-31

Bhāskārābhāsa 320

Bhāskarābhāsanivāraṇa 320

Bhāskarācārya 195

Bhāṣya 12, 48, 117

bhāṣyakāra 32

Bhat, G.K. 263

Bhāṭṭa 274

Bhaṭṭa Bhāskara 116

Bhatta, Bharat 288

Bhaṭṭa, Kamalākara 236

Bhaṭṭa, Nāgeśa 236, 326

Bhatta, Pt. Vinayak 290

Bhaṭṭa, Raṅgoji 136-38

Bhaṭṭācārya Sahit Bicār 305

Bhaṭṭācārya, Gadādhara 8, 134

Bhattacharya, Chiranjib 194

Bhattacharya, Karuna 202

Bhattacharya, Mrityunjaya Vidyalankar 290, 292, 305

Bhattacharya, Pt. Raghumani 298

Bhattacharyya, K.C. 337

Bhāṭṭa-Mīmāṁsā 275

Bhaṭṭoji Dīkṣita 136, 138

Bhaṭṭojikuṭṭanam 138

Bhavabhūti (Umveka) 10, 32, 262-64

Bhavadeva 274

Bhavanātha 274

Bhāvaviveka 98, 103-04

Bhave, Vinoba xii-xiii

Bhaviṣya Purāṇa Pariśiṣṭa 119

Bhedadhikkāra 135

Bhedavidyāvilāsa 135

Bhīma 16, 266-67

Bhīma and Suyodhana, *gadā-yuddha* between 135

Bhīmācārya 208

Bhimsen, Pt. 320

Bhīṣma 18, 53, 68, 71-72

Bhogavāda 259

Bhoja 245, 249

Bhonsale, Shahuji 238

bhraṣṭaṁ 184, 229

Bhūgolanirṇaya 134

Bhupendra, Walkhaede 146

Bhūtacaitanyavādins 191

Bhūtavāda (materialism) 80
  teacher of 105

Bhūtavādins 47, 191

Bhūtika 105

Bible for Pundits, The 309

Biblical
  genealogies 296
  orient 296

Bilhaṇa 10

Biographies of Śaṅkarācārya 117

Blavatsky, Madam 315

Bloomfield, Maurice 47

Bodas, Raja Ram Shastri 302, 311

Bodhasiddhi 120

Bokani, Radde-Hanūd
  Mohammad Ismail 304

Bombay Provincial Social
  Conference 310

Bose, Subhas Chandra 293, 337

Brahma Purāṇa 318-19

Brahmā 61, 148, 261, 269
  authority of 319
  eulogy to 262

brahmacārins 51

brahmacarya 80

Brahmachari, Nityanand 320

Brahmagupta 123-24

brahma-jijñāsā 188

Brahman 41, 46, 49, 81, 126, 188-90, 200, 205, 219
  denying the knowledge of 10
  is *sadrūpa* 203
  knowledge of 221
  true knowledge of 188

Brahman, Chandrabhan 147

Brahmana Sabha 311

Brāhmaṇaromanakaitholikasaṁvādaḥ 291

Brāhmaṇas 152

Brāhmanical and Śramanic
  traditions 189

Brāhmanism 208, 296
  reinvigorated 101
  tenets of 25

Brahmapariṇāmavāda 205

brahma-ratha 7

brahma-sabhā 7

brahma-saṁsad 7

Brahmasūtra 10, 33, 80, 82, 130, 133, 188, 195, 212, 221
  bhāṣya on 200

Brahmavāda 47

brahmavādin 47-48

brahmavādinī 47, 54

brahmavadya and *brahmavādya*, other terms for *brahmodya* 47

brahmavidyā 50-51

Brahmo Samaj 283, 306-07, 310, 325

brahmodya 6-7, 45-46, 48-49

Brahmotsava 131

Bṛhacchaṅkaravijaya 30

Bṛhadāraṇyaka Upaniṣad 3, 6, 48-49, 51, 117, 148, 190

Bṛhadvyākaraṇabhūṣaṇa 137

Bṛhaspati 80, 112-13, 184, 191-92, 229, 233-34, 275
  identity of 192

Bṛhaspati's disguise as Cārvāka 192

Bṛhaspatismṛti 184, 228, 233

British imperialism 293

Buddha 19-20, 60, 83-85, 87, 91-92, 97, 99, 104-05
  disciples of, 93

Buddha's
  concept of *pratītyasamutpāda* 199
  contemporaries 85
  debate with Saccaka 86
  discourse on *dhamma* 86
  discourses 93
  mahāparinirvāṇa 93
  way as exclusive middle 84

Buddhacaryā 20

Buddhaghoṣa 191

Buddhapālita 98, 103

buddha-vacanas 90, 196

Buddhism ix, 3, 10, 42, 78, 81, 85, 94, 101, 113, 118, 131, 198, 221-22

Buddhist 182, 198, 204, 214
  epistemology 109
  in disguise (*pracchannabaudha*) ix
  logicians 98, 104, 107
  monastery 270
  monks 11
  philosopher Jñānaśrī 118
  philosophers 182, 214, 224
  philosophy(ies) ix, 8, 110-11, 139, 193-94, 274, 336
  schools 112
    of Śūnyavāda and Vijñānavāda 81
    of Yogācāra and Vijñānavāda 219
  systems 58
  theory of causality 213
  traditions 7

Buddhists 110, 124, 180-81, 190, 195-97, 203, 208-09, 223-24, 270, 275

buddhyastra 21

Burgsan, critique of xiii

Burke, Edmund 300

Burkley, George 290

Burnell, A.C. 287

Caitanya, 121, 139, 141

caitanyasvarūpa-jñānamūrti 147

Cakārasamartham 130

cākyārs, theatre practices of 257

Calcutta Journal 291, 294

Calcutta School Book Society 290

Calcutta Supreme Court 306

Campakeśācārya 132

Cāṇakya 31

Caṇḍīdāsa 194

Candrakīrti 101

Candrasenīya Kāyasthas as kṣatriyas, status of 238

Candrikā 274

Caraka 8, 166-70, 172, 175-78, 209
  produces a long list of technical terms 174

Caraka Saṁhitā 166-78

Caritakāvyas 31

Cāritravardhana 120

Carpenter, Mary 306

Carry, W. 284, 291

Cārvāka 2-3, 7, 42, 58, 78-80, 190, 193, 195, 200, 218, 273
  genesis of 79
  philosophy of 193, 268
  system 26, 81, 103, 112, 270, 276

Cārvāka philosophy x, 192, 275, 328, 331
  critiques of 195

Cārvāka: Itihāsa āṇi Tattavajñāna x

cārvākamata 193

Cārvākas xi, 9, 12, 54, 83, 143, 191, 196, 224, 271

Cārvākaṣaṣṭi 193-94

Caryāgītikośa 139

categories of *vāda* 261
  in literary theory 245

categories of *vāk-pāruṣya* 21

categorizations related to *vāda* 155

Catholicism, orthodox 296

Catuḥśataka 101

Catuḥśatī 110

caturāśramya 189

Cāturmatasāmarasya works 148

cāturvarṇya 226

Chaitanya Bharati, Swami 286

Chakrabarti, Arindam 28, 32, 53, 152, 155

chala 101
  conceptual framework of, 271

Chand Boddhale 141

Chandavarkar, Narayan 310

Chāndogya Upaniṣad 81, 83

Chaovan-Ezhava 313

Chaturvedi, Pt. Giridhar Sharma 321

Chaube, Badridas 304

Chaudhury, Nirad C. 297, 300, 302, 308

Chézy, Antoine Léonard de 301

Chhāndogya Upaniṣad 6

child marriage 322

Chinese sources 96

Chishti, Khwaja Moinuddin 146

Chitrav, Siddheshwar 5

Christian missionaries 286

Christianity 144-45, 291

Christianity Contrasted with Hindu Philosophy 309

Cicero, Marcus Tullius 155

citra rasas, eleven types of 249

Citrakūṭa, debate in 62

Citsukhācārya 122, 262

Citsukhī 122

civilization, cradle of 285

Clive, Lord 287

Clothy, E.W. 141

codes
- for conducting the debate 184
- of conduct 237

Codvila 115

Colebrooke, H.T. 288, 299

Comparative
- Mythology 296
- Religion 296

concept(s) of
- *adoṣodbhāvana* 183
- *ajñāna* 201
- *ākāśa* 148
- *ānanda* 219
- *anumāna* and *pañcāvayava vākya* 242
- *ānvīkṣikī* 3
- *āpta* 168, 181
- *Ātman* and God in Nyāya-Vaiśeṣika systems 103
- *bhakti* 68
- *brahmodya* 44
- creation 147
- *dṛṣyatva* 190
- *ekajñānasaṁsarga* 211
- families of languages 303
- growth of civilization 303
- hearsay 209
- *Īśvara* and *Ātman* 106
- *jāti* 269
- *jīvātman* and *paramātman* 148
- jury 185
- liberation 317
- light 147
- *mokṣa* 113, 147, 219
- *mukti* 336
- *nigrahasthāna* 165, 182
- *nyāsa* or *prapatti* 130
- *pañcāvayava-vākya* 156, 181
- *paramārtha* 103
- Para-Vāsudeva 121
- *pralaya* 147
- *pramāṇa* 113
- *pratītyasamutpāda* 97
  - and *kṣaṇabhaṅga* 203
- *puruṣa* and *prakṛti* 206
- *pūrva-raṅga* 241
- *putrikā* 235
- reality 333
- *sabhā* 13
- *sādhārṇīkaraṇa* 250
- *sākṣī* 121
- salvation in *darśanas* xiv
- *siddhas* 147
- sixfold probans 180
- soul 147
- *swadeshi* and *svarāj* 283
- *tadutpatti* 211
- time and space 147
- *upacāra* 53
- *vāda* 245
  - and its techniques 166
  - in poetics 245
- *varṇa-dharma* 333
- *vidyās* 42
- *vijñāna* ix
- *vyavasthā* 289

conceptual framework
- for Vādaśāstra 35
- of *chala* 271
- of *Nāṭyaśāstra* 241

conceptual universe of Vādaśāstra 152

consciousness, theory of 270

controversy on Śiva's acceptability in the Vedic pantheon as a God 261

conversation, delineation qualities of 155

Coomarswamy, Ananda K. xiv
corajāraśikhāmaṇi 281
criticism of
  Mādhva system 135
  Madhva 134
cross-cultural perspectives, emergence of 312
Cūlavyūhasutta of *Suttanipāta* 19
Cullavagga of *Vinayapiṭaka* 91
cultural chauvinism 334
Dabistān-e-mazahib viii, 34, 143
Dādū 139
Daivavāda (fatalism) 106, 227
Damayantī 268
Damiḍopaniṣat-tātparyaratnāvalī 130
Damiḍopaniṣattātsārah 130
Daṇḍanīti, scholar of 271
Daṇḍin 115, 250
Daneshmund Khan 136
Dara Shikoh viii, 124, 136, 146-48, 284
darbārs 321
darśana(s) 2, 101, 223
  and *dharmaśāstra*, nexus between 222
  concept vii
  purpose of 115
Darśanasarvasvam 286
Darśapūrṇamāsa sacrifice 45
Das, Bhagwan 337
Das, Jagannatha 321
Das, Ray Jadhav 147
Dāsabodha 238
Dāsacaritam of Śrīśailasuri 276
Daśaratha 55, 57, 59, 61, 264
Daśarātra *yajñas* 44
Daśarūpaka 243
Dasgupta, S.N. 167
Dāvānī, Zalāluddin 34
Dave, Prashant xii
Davitt, Michael 293
Dāyabhāga 292
Dayakrishna 312, 329, 337
Dayananda, Swami 31, 283, 293, 304, 314-17, 319-24, 337
Dayānandadigvijaya 31
Dayānandatimirabhāskara 319-20
Dayanand-chala-kapaṭa-darpaṇa 320
Dayanand-Saraswati-mukha-capeṭika 319
Deussen, Paul 4
Deb, Radha Kant 306
debate(s) between
  Advaita and Dvaita schools of Vedānta 304
  Advaita and Viśiṣṭādvaita 304
  Advaitins and Mādhvas 201
  Arjuna and Indra 267
  atheism and theistic schools 268
  Bādarāyaṇa and Śaṅkarācārya 32
  Devasūri and Kumudacandra 276
  Draupadī, Bhīma and Yudhiṣṭhira 16

Idealism and Materialism 190
Jaina *ācāryas* and Buddhists 125
Janaka and Sulabhā 21, 32
Kṛśānu and Viśvāvasu 277
Pārvatī and Śiva 272
practitioners of Āyurveda 168
Raṅgoji Bhaṭṭa and Vidyādhīśa 137
Śaivites and Vaiṣṇavites 132
Śakuntalā and Duṣṣanta 336
Śiva disguised as a *brahmacārī* and Pārvatī 260-61
two Jaina preceptors of diverse sects 276
upholders of Christianity and Hinduism 284
Vedic and non-Vedic philosophical systems 224

debate(s)
amongst Indian intellectuals 283
concepts and categories of 178
constitutional 294
describing bitterness between Śaivas and Vaiṣṇavas 280
ethics of 17, 19
history of 38
in India, history of 40
in-depth analysis of the techniques and methodology of 228
new techniques and methodologics for 184
of Draupadī, Vidura and Vikarṇa 336
on harsh treatment to ladies 264
on predicament and suffering a Hindu woman 325
on the cultural and spiritual matrix of *dharma* civilizations 334
on the dilemma of Śṛī Kṛṣṇa 267
techniques of 81
theory of 34, 156, 169, 182
votary of 321
with Draupadī and Bhīma 67

debating with himself 65

Dedamari, Muhammad Azam 141

Dehalvi, Ajhamad 146

Dehātmavāda 330
theory of 330-31

democratic values, inculcation of 312

Deshmukh, Gopal Hari 325

Deshpande, Madhav M. 136-38, 236-38

Devasūrin 27, 34, 37, 122, 125

Devībhāgavata Purāṇa 315

dhammakathā, genre of 86

Dhanañjaya 243

dharma of *vanavāsa* 62

Dharma Sabha 306

dharma 15, 17-19, 34, 42, 56-57, 60-63, 70-73, 130, 152
last criterion of xiv
loss of 77
path of 268
rigour of 58
rules of 17

dharma–dharmī relationship 213

Dharmadivākara 320

dharma-jijñāsā, non-essentiality of 188

Dharmakīrti, ix 13, 23-26, 35, 37, 102-03, 107-13, 180-83, 203, 206-13, 216, 224
opponents of 112
rejects *chala* and *jātis* as parts of *vāda* 183
terminology of 178

Dharmakīrti's
contemptuous behaviour, stories of 108
idea of *tādātmya* 211

Dharmakīrtian framework of inferential knowledge 210

dharma-mahāmātras 11

dharmārthakarmasattvā 14

dharmārthakuśala-śramaṇabrāhmaṇa-vāsa 14

dharmasabhā 237, 324

dharmaśāstra over *arthaśāstra*, prominence of 228

Dharmaśāstra 38, 60, 88, 166, 227 276, 287-88, 312
for Āryāvarta 223

Dharmaśāstras 15, 59, 189, 222, 230, 233, 235-36, 324
principal 56
students of 103

dharma-sthāna 184

Dharmavir 230

dharmayuga 53

Dharmottara 270

Dharmottarapradīpa 110

Dhṛtarāṣṭra 73

dhūrtapravivāda 244

Dhuttakkhāṇa (*Dhūrtākhyāna*), xi 269

Dhyānalokas 128

dialectical demolition of all theories 98

dialogue between
a brāhmaṇa and a Catholic 291
a brāhmaṇa and a *mahār* 143
Dyumatsena and Satyavān 68
Rāma and Sitā before Sitā's *agniparīkṣā* 55
Śaṅkarācārya and a *cāṇḍāla* 30
Śauceya and Uddālaka Āruṇi 44
Sītā and Rāma in Daṇḍakāraṇya 55
Śiva and Pārvatī 5
Suvarcalā and Śvetaketu 68

dialogues and discussions, tradition of 1

dialogues of
Agastya and Lopāmudrā, 259
guru and *śiṣya* 5
Purūravas and Urvaśī 259
Yama and Yamī 259

dichotomy between *pravṛtti* and *nivṛtti* 222

Dictionary of Sanskrit and English 298

Diels, Hermann 160

Dieste, Rafael 332-34

difference between
dharma and *dharmin* 203
jīva and *Paramātman* 201
Paṇḍitavāda and Rājavāda 95
Sautrāntika and Vaibhāṣika 197
Sunnīs and Śiyās 144

Digest of Hindu Law 288

digvijaya 115
Dikshit, Shrinivas x
Dīkṣita, Appayya 135-36, 148, 277
Dīkṣita, Rājacūḍāmaṇi 115
Dīkṣita, Tirumala 115
Dilīpa and Kumbhodara,
  discussion between 261
ḍiṇḍikarāga 26
Ḍiṇḍikas 26
Diṇḍimakavi, ego of 129
Dīn-e-Ilāhī 144
Diṅnāga 2, 37, 102-03, 105, 107-08, 181-82, 184, 206, 210
  aphorisms of, 105
  school 109
Diṅnāga and Dharmakīrti
  idea of inference in 110
  theory of 110
Diṅnāga–Dharmakīrti 203
  school 206
Dīpāṅkarajñānaśrī 110
Dīpaśikhā 273
Dīrghatamas, seer of
  Asyavāmīyasūkta 44
discussions
  and *vāda* in Sanskrit 327
  between, Vidya Niwas Mishra
    and Rafael Dieste 331
  new techniques and
    methodologies for 184
Divākara, Siddhasena 12
Divākaramitra 102
Divākaraprakāśa 320
diverse
  knowledge systems x
  schools of Vedānta 121
diversification, age of 40
Divyaprabandha 130
Dodson, Michael S. 283, 288, 299, 309, 326-27
Dohākośa 194
Dongre, Anant Shastri 324
drama, ten major forms of 243
Draupadī 15, 17, 29-30, 70, 73-74, 76, 267
  question of 71
Dravid, Rajeshwar Shastri 36, 161-62
Draviḍa Āmnāya 131
Drāviḍagāthās or
  Deśikaprabandhas 131
Droṇa 72
dṛṣṭānta 100
Duḥkhavāda 248
Duḥśāsana 70
Durgā, cult of 150
Durgaprasad, Paṇḍit 287
durnaya 87
durvaitaṇḍikas 160
Duryodhana 16, 29-30, 74, 79
  and Yudhiṣṭhira's dice game
    between 70
  court of 72
dūṣaṇa texts 128
Duṣṣanta 75
Duṣyanta 13
Dvādaśadvāraśāstra 98
Dvaita 121

philosophy 133
Vedānta 133, 304
Dvaitādvaita 121
Dvaitavādins 190
Dvaitin Vidyādhīśa 137
Dvāpara 268
Dwivedi, Umapati 320
dynamic
concepts 328
conceptual framework 337

East, Hyde 289
East India Company 151, 286-87, 289-90, 294
East–West dialogue, possibilities of 334
Eckhart, Meister 285
Editio Princeps of Śakuntalā 301
egalitarianism, eccentric theoretician of 296
ekacitta 111
Ekāmreśvara (Śiva) 278
ekāṁśa-vyākaraṇīya 84
ekāṁśikas 84
Ekanātha 139, 142-43
ekānta 90
Ekāntavādin 84
ekavākyatā 147
Epicureanism 196, 259
Epicurus 196
eternal *dharma* is greater than *rājadharma* 58
ethics of debate 17, 19
evanescence, theory of 270

fake debate 243
Farrukh, Mardan 139
female education 313
Fergusson, James 310
fierce debate between, Māṇikya Sūri and a Naiyāyika from Varanasi 125
five qualities of interlocutors' statements 153
five-member syllogism 75, 160, 175, 181, 200
Forster, Georg 301
Franklin, Benjamin 300
fundamentalism 237

Gāgā Bhaṭṭa 237-38
gāndharva-vivāha 75
Gandhi, Mahatma 283, 294
Gandhi, Ramchandra 337
Gandhi's criticism of Spencer 293, 337
Ganesh, Shatavadhani R. 28
Gaṅgā 265
Gaṅges 278
Gaṅgeśa 120-21, 218
Gārgī 21, 48-50, 54, 117, 318
Garuḍa 128
Gāthāpatiputra Taruṇa, *gāthās* of 8
Gauḍabrahmānandī 304

Gauḍapāda, ix 200-01

Gautam, S.P. 337

Gautama 2-3, 33, 35, 42, 50, 80, 98, 100, 107, 112, 120, 130, 156, 158, 160, 162, 174, 176, 178, 180, 182-83, 203, 214-15, 269, 271
  has described twenty-four *jātis* 163

Gautama's system of Nyāya 8

Gautamīya Nyāya 111-12, 165, 182-83

Gautamīyas 107

Gāyatrī 192

Geldner K.F. 6, 47

Ghaṭikala Sudarśana 276

Giri, Anantānanda 115

Giri, Gagandeo 193

Giri, Kāśīkananda 304

Girigītā 291

Gītā xiii, 123, 189, 221-22, 283, 324

Gītābhāṣya of Rāmānuja 130

Gītārthasaṁgraharakṣā 130

God, realization of 147

Goethe, Johann Wolfgang von 301

Gopatha Brāhmaṇa 50

Gore, Shivaram Shastri 302

Govinda Dīkṣita, descendant of 10

Govindanātha 115

grāmyadharmaka 240

Great Trinity of Sanskrit epics 266

Greek thought 124

Greeks and Hindus, knowledge systems of 122

gṛhasthāśrama 80, 116, 189

Gṛhyasūtram 78

Griffith, R.T.H. 299

gross consciousness 198

Gulam Mohamad 321

Guṇaguṇibhedabhaṅgavāda 120

guṇas 148

Gurucandrikā 304

Gurvāvalī 125

Habbā Khātūn 140

haitukas 195

Halbfass, Wilhelm xiii-xiv, 284-85, 327-28

Halhed, Nathaniel Brassey 287

Hanumān 32, 56, 64-66

Haque Prakasha 321

Haribhadra Sūri ix, 37, 105-06, 111, 160, 185, 192, 195-96, 206, 218

Harihara 129, 280

Hariharānandanātha 149

Harṣa 102

Harṣacaritam 103

Hastings, Warren 222, 287-88, 307

Hastinīmāhātmya 131

hāsyacitra 249

hāsyavāda 244

hatred of reason 1

Hegel, Georg Wilhelm Friedrich, 284, 297

Hemacandra 80

Herbert Spencer Lectureship 293

Herder, Johann Gottfried von 300

hetu 100
- employment of 37
- five categories of 180

Hetubindu 24, 26, 109-10, 207, 211

hetu-pratyaya 100

hetuvādas 55

Hetuviḍambanopāya 36, 122

hetuvidyā for logic 178

hetvābhāsa 174, 176

hetvābhāsas 162
- as *asiddha* 163

hetvantara 178

Hevajratantra 194

High Caste Hindu Woman, The 325

High Renaissance 296

hīnādhikaṁ 229

Hīnayāna 96, 196-97

Hind Tattvajñāna no Itihāsa xii

Hindu *avatāras* 146

Hindu community, legal and social practices of 222

Hindu Śāstras 306

Hinduism 145, 292
- advocates of 284
- Hinduism, principal tenets of 309

Hindu-Turk-Saṁvāda 142

Hindutva 10

Hīra, a *paṇḍit* in the court of King Vijayacandra 119

History of British India, The 308

Hitopadeśa 283, 290

Homer, 310

hostile debate 172-73

Humboldt, Wilhelm von 284, 297

idealism vs. realism 127

identity vs. difference 127

ideologues, age of dialectic of 55

ignorance, philosophy of 8

IIAS 337

Iliad 310

Inada, Kenneth K. 99-100

India in West, romantic image of 301

Indian
- architecture, highest authority on 310
- astronomers 123
- culture and Sanskrit literature, condemnations of 308
- debate has a rich history of three millennia 7
- intellectual discourses 124
  - history of 239, 283
- philosophical systems, non-orthodox 33
- philosophy,
  - history of xii, 327
  - orthodox schools of 336

six systems of 192
tradition
of *vāda* 2
power of xiii
of intellectual discourse xiii
wisdom 303
world-view, genesis of 5
Indian Mirror 295
Indian Sociologist 293

Indo-Germanic
mind 303
race 303

Indo-Greek cultures 122

Indra 16, 43, 59, 248, 260, 268

Indramani, Munshi 319

indriyārthasannikarṣa 109

Induprakash 325

inference, logistics of 112

Ingalls, Daniel H.H. 121

Iṅglaiṇḍīyavyākaraṇasāraḥ 290

intellectual
debate,
history of 98, 108
theory and practice of vii
discussions and debates 68

interfaith dialogues and syncretic approaches to philosophical and religious issues 121

Iranshah 138

Irish Home Rule 293

Īśādidaśopaniṣadaḥ 51

Īśāīvivaraṇāmṛtam 291

Īsarāphīla 148

Īśāvāsyopaniṣat 130

Ishwari Narayan Prasad Singh, Maharaja 323

Isibhāsiyāin (*Ṛṣibhāṣitāni*) viii, 7, 83

Islam 144-45

Islamic
argumentative style to refute Islam 305
perspective 34
traditions 148

Ismāilīs 144

Īśvarakṛṣṇa 122

Īśvarānumāna 120

Īśvarasiddhi 214

Īśvaravāda 213-14, 219

itihāsa 8, 70, 125

Itihāsatamomaṇiḥ 290

Jābāli 55, 58-61, 85

jadaviteṣṭitaṁ 26

jagadatisandhātā 281

Jagadekamalla Jayasiṁha, Cāḷukya king 122

Jagannātha, Paṇḍitarāja 136, 138, 147, 314

Jagannātha Temple 119

Jaimini 4, 78, 80, 82, 115, 280

Jain, Sagar Mal 83

Jaina
Āgamas 88
Anekānta doctrine 84
monks 102, 114
naked 26
philosophers 104
philosophy 87, 194

tradition 7, 36
Jaina Śāstroṅ kī Asaṅgat Bāteṅ 304
Jainas 103, 223-24, 270, 275
Jainatattvaślokavārttika 36
Jaini, Thakar Das 320
Jainism 3, 8, 10, 42, 78, 81, 222
jalpa 8, 12, 81, 101, 159, 186, 243
jalpa and *vitaṇḍā* 160, 175
as types of *kathā* 175
Jalpakalpalatā 34, 36, 125
jalpa-kelīśraddhāluḥ 276
jalpotsava 277
Jamadagni Bhārgava 42
Janaka 48, 51, 53-54, 64-65, 264-65
wife of 68
Janārdana 137, 141
Jaṅgamaliṅga 140
Jansenism 296
Japujī xiii
Jāratkārava Ārtabhāga 49
jāti 82, 101, 112, 163, 319
and *vitaṇḍā*, recourse of 318
Jātukarṇya 51
Jawab-i-Tohfatu-'i-muwahiddin 305
Jayanta Bhaṭṭa 27, 111-12, 122, 180, 195, 269-71
Jayarāśi 26, 34, 36, 112-14, 191-92
Jayatīrtha 126, 201, 262
commentaries of, 134
Jha, Ganganath 214, 248
Jibariāla 148
jijñāsā 177
Jinarakṣita 270
Jitāri, head of Vikramaśilā University 110
jīvas 126
jīvātman at par with *Paramātman* 201
Jñānasambandhar, a Naynār and a Śaiva saint 106, 122
jñāna 68
Jñānacarcā 305
jñānakarmasamuccaya 189, 219
Jñānakarmasamuccayavāda 188-89
Jñānasiddhāntacandrikā 290
Jñānaśrī, Buddhist philosopher 118
Jñānaśrīmitra 111
Jñāneśvara 139
Jñānodaya 291
Johnson, Samuel 300
Jones, Sir William 283, 288-89, 291, 295, 298, 300-01, 307-08
Joshi, Anandibai 325
Judaism 143, 145
Judge Viśvarūpa 270
Jyotindra Moha Thakur Maharaja 325

Kabīr 10, 139
Kahoḍa 76

Kaikeyī 58, 61, 318

Kakuda Kaccāyana 83, 85

Kāla 106

kalaha 19

Kalahavivādasutta of *Suttanipāta* 19

Kālapriyanātha, *yātrā* of 263

Kālāśoka 92

kālātītavacana 178

kālātyayāpadiṣṭa or *bādhita* 163

Kālavāda (pessimism) 106, 227

Kālavādins 47

Kali,
  age of 150, 268
  entourage of 268

Kālidāsa 13, 75, 120, 259-61, 300-01, 307
  rediscovery of 301

Kālidāsa's poetic fancies 262

Kalpalatā 133

kalpanā, alternatives for 113

kalpavṛkṣa 139, 194

kalyāṇa-yātrā 313

Kāmagītā of *Mahābhārata* 28

Kamalaśīla 103-04, 195

Kāmandakī, Buddhist nun 264

Kāmaśāstra 52

Kāmasūtra x, 22, 52, 90, 195, 230, 262

Kāmasūtra kī Santāneṅ 230

Kambalāśvatara 193

Kaṇāda 80, 146, 203
  followers of 103

Kaṇādarahasyam 146

Kāṇadeva 101

Kaniṣka 93

Kannan, Sushma 140

Kant, Immanuel 284, 286

Kaṇṭakoddhāra 303

Kaṇva, Sage 75
  hermitage of 54, 75

Kapila 68, 80, 105
  followers of 103

Kapila, Shruti 294

Karāvatī sect 143

Karkaṭī 54

karma and *jñāna*
  conflict between x, 188
  doctrine of cumulative pursuit of x, 101
  relationship between 189

karma 68, 106
  theories of 83

karma-prakṛti, part of *pndgala-jagat* 206

Karmavāda 106

Karṇa 73, 336

Karṇakagomin 208

kārṣāpaṇa 21

kāryāvasthā 126

Kashmir Śaivism 139

Kaśyapa 18

Kaṭha Upaniṣad 200

kathā 6, 8, 29, 86, 159, 161, 186
  nature of 186
  seven regulations of 161
  techniques of 86

three forms of 12

kathābhāsa 186

Kathaka 162

kathāsāda 180

kathāsallāpa 161

kathātyaya 180

Kathāvatthu in *Abhidhamma Piṭaka* 86, 91, 93

Kaṭhopaniṣad 7, 134, 188

Kātyāyana 184, 223, 229-30, 233-34

Kātyāyanasmṛti 233

Kaumārila 131

Kauṇapadanta 88

Kauṇḍa Bhaṭṭa 137

Kauravas 17, 71-73

Kausalyā 68, 265

Kauṣītaki Brāhmaṇa 46, 50

Kauṭilya 2, 21, 41-42, 88-89, 184, 186, 193, 230-32, 247

Kautsa 77-78

Kavitārkikacakravartī 13, 131

kāvya lakṣaṇas, thirty-six 242

kāvyagoṣṭhī 125

kāvyakāra-parīkṣās 14

Kāvyamīmāṁsā 3, 7, 15, 38-39, 42, 81, 89, 246-48

kāvyānumiti, theory of xii

Kāvyaprakāśa 245, 271

Kāyasthadharmapradīpa 237

Keith, A.B. 6, 47, 50, 221

Kevalajñānavāda 188

kevalānvayī hetu-adṛṣṭa 210

Ḳhalīftullāh, Akbar is described as 144

khaṇḍana, Jaina tradition of 34

khaṇḍana-granthas 138

Khaṇḍanakhaṇḍakhādya 27, 31, 34, 36, 114-15, 119, 160, 165, 186, 195

Khatri, Lala Balakram 323

King
- Aśoka 93
  - edicts of 11
- Bimbisāra 92
- Daśaratha 58
- Devanātha 131
- Dhṛtarāṣṭra 17, 72
- Harṣa 92
- Janaka 49, 68, 76
- Madanajit 105
- Mahāpadma Nanda 93
- Milinda 95-96, 161
- Pravahaṇa Jaivāli 50-51
- Priyadarśī Devānam Priya 11
- Rāmagupta 233
- Śaṅkaravarman 270
- Siddharāj 125
- Udayana 120
- Vattagmaṇī 93
- Veṅkaṭadevarāya 133

Kiraṇāvalī 118, 120

Kirātārjunīyam xiv, 16-17, 266

Kosambi, Meera 325-26

Krishna Varma, Shyamji 293, 337

Krishnadas, Rai 311

Krishnamurti, J. xii

kriyāpāda 184, 228

Kṛśānu 127

Kṛśāśva 127

Kṛṣṇa 12, 29, 47, 123, 127, 141, 146, 268, 281
followers of 102

Kṛṣṇadevarāya 133

Kṣaṇabhaṅgavāda (theory of momentariness) 120, 206

Kṣṇabhaṅgasiddhiḥ 110

Kubjavardhana, Pāṇḍyarāja 106

kula-dharma 61

Kulārka Paṇḍita 158

Kulārṇava Tantra 224

Kumar, Ujjawal 91-92

Kumārajīva 96

Kumārapāla 234

Kumārasambhava 259-62

Kumārila Bhaṭṭa ix, 27, 102-03, 108-10, 117, 122, 193, 204, 208

Kumārila's philosophy 273

Kumbhāsi Maṭha 133

Kumudacandra, a Digambara ascetic 125, 277

Kuṇḍalakeśī 94

Kuntaka 271

Kuru dynasty 75

kūṭiyāṭṭam 257-58
theatre, popularity of 259

La Renaissance Orientale 296

Laghucandrikā 202-04

Laghurahasyas 131

Laghuṭaṅka 226

Lakṣaṇāvalī 120

Lakṣmaṇa 64

Lakṣmī 150

Lal-Dêd 139, 141

Laṅkāvatārasūtra 99

Latkar, Vasudev Sharma 290

laukika language 78

laukika nyāyas 26

Laukya Bṛhaspati 79

Law Book of Manu 283

learning, four branches of 67

Lévi, Sylvain 307

Li Rong XI 97

liberties and improvisational techniques, condemnation of 257

Likhita 223

Līlādhara 289

Liṅgāyata sect 140

Locke, John 290

Lokatattvanirṇaya 105

lokavyavahāras 222

Lokāyata 41, 55, 131, 190, 193, 195
Vitaṇḍāvādaśāstra 191
philosophy 80
originator of 79

lokāyatas x

Lokāyatasūtra 80

Lokāyatikas 10, 12, 54-56, 103, 193

Lollaṭa 250

Lord

Jagannātha 12, 120
Veṅkaṭeśa 128
Viṣṇu 276

Ludwig, Alfred 47, 302

Macaulay, Thomas Babington 308

Macdonell, A.A. 6, 47, 50, 221

Mādhava 29-30, 32, 108, 115, 130

Mādhavācārya 37, 101

Madhavanand Swami 234

Madhavdas Raghunathdas 311

Madhavi Narsalaya 238

Mādhavīyaśaṅkaradigvijaya 115

Madhusūdana's critique of Madhva 135

Madhva 10, 121, 125-26, 131, 136, 219, 224

Mādhva
scholar Vijayīndra 135
school, epistemology of 35
system 134, 201
tradition 135-36
Vedānta 82, 132
Vedāntin 81

Madhvācārya 132

Madhvādhvakaṇṭakoddhāra 135

Madhvamatavidhvaṁsana 135

Madhvanand, Swami 230, 238

Mādhvas 280

Mādhvasiddhāntabhañjanī 137

Madhvatantramukhamardana 135

madhyamā pratipad 84
idea of 97

madhyamā, idea of 198

Mādhyamika 103, 199, 203
system or Śūnyavāda 98

Mādhyamikakārikā 100

Mādhyamikas 104

Mādhyamikaśāstra 98, 101
essence of 199

madhyastha 117, 185

Māgha 266-67

Mahābhārata 8-9, 15, 17-18, 21, 30, 35, 50-55, 66-77, 79-80, 83, 134, 155, 177, 188, 192, 195, 221-22, 269
crucial debates in 77

Mahābhāṣya 39, 80, 90

Mahādeva 91

mahāgraha 224

Mahāmahopādhyāya
Pt. Kailash Chandra 327
Pt. Ramavatar Sharma 326-27

Mahāmahopādhyāyas 326

Mahāmohavidrāvaṇa 321

Mahānirvāṇatantra 149-51

Maharatta 325

mahāsaṁgha 93

Mahāvibhāṣā 94

Mahāvidyā 150
syllogisms 158

Mahāvidyāviḍambana 158

Mahāvihāra of Anurādhapuram 93

Mahāvīra viii, 87-88, 105

Mahāvīracaritam 263-64

Mahāvyūhasutta 19-20
Mahāyāna 97, 99, 196
Mahendrasiṁha 125
Mahima Bhaṭṭa xii, 246
Mahiṣaśatakam xi, 10
Mahodadhi 274
Maitrāyaṇī Upaniṣad 192
Maitreyī 54
Majjhimanikāya 84
major philosophical systems, tenets of 55
Majumdar, R.C. 230, 234, 283, 289-90, 292, 295
makāras, five 150
Makkaliputta Gosāla (Maṅkhaliputra Gośāla) 83, 85
Malabari, Berhamji 294
Mālatīmādhavam 263-64
Mālavikāgnimitram 262
male-dominated world-view 223
Malhotra, Rajiv 334-35
Malik, S.C. 323
Mallinātha xiv, 186
Malvania, Dalsukhabhai 87
Mammaṭa 271
Mānavas 88
Mānavīyajñānaviṣayakaśāstram 291
Māṇḍūkyakārikā ix
Mangādiyasuttanta 20
Mani, Indra 304
Mani, Vettam 51
Māṇikya Sūri 125
Māṇikyamuni 125-26
Maṇipravāḷam 128
Manīṣāpañcakam 30
Maṅkhali Ghosāla 8
Maṅki 83
Manoramā 138
Manoramākucamardanī 138
mantra-kāla 42
Manu xiv, 21, 41, 189, 192, 222-23, 230, 235
Manusmṛti 21, 230, 234-36, 283
many-sidedness of reality, theory of 86, 336
Marahatla 325
Marxism 328
maryādā puruṣottama 56
Mataparīkṣā 309
Matilal, B.K. 84, 86-87, 210, 286, 329
Mātṛceṭa 101
Mātṛgupta 249
Maurya, Candragupta 88
Mayūra 115
Mazm-ul-Baharain 146, 148
Medhātithi 59
Meghadūta 120, 298
Mehta, Narmada Shankar xii
Mikaila 148
Milindapañho 7, 13, 91, 94-96, 161
Mill, James 307-08
Mill, W.H. 284

Mīmāṁsā 82, 111, 113, 177, 210, 214, 217, 219, 279
  philosophy 4
  postulates the theory of *śakti* 213
  system 81, 215
  would hold the *svataḥ prāmāṇya* 208

Mīmāṁsādarśana 115

Mīmāṁsaka 27, 82, 211, 217

Mīmāṁsāpādukā 130

Mīmāṁsāsūtra 4, 78, 80, 82-83

Mīrābāī 139-40

Mishqati, Dawood 141

Mishra, Jayakrishna 236

Mishra, Madhusudan 39

Mishra, Vidya Niwas 331-34

Miśra, Bhāratī 28, 116-17

Miśra, Durveka 110

Miśra, Kṛṣṇa 191, 273-74

Miśra, Maṇḍana 28, 115-17, 122

Miśra, Padmanābha 146

Miśra, Śaṅkara 36, 161

Miśra, Śivāditya 204

Miśra, Vācaspati 103, 109, 111, 180, 195, 205, 216-17, 273

Mitākṣarā 3

Mitra 42

Mitra, Pramadādāsa 299

Mitra, Rajendralal 309-10

modern
  age 40
  civilization,
    chaos of 285
    critique of 333
  Indian political thought 294
  scholars of Sanskrit 301

Moggaliputta Tissa alias Upagupta 93

Mohammad,
  miracle of 145
  tragic episode of 144

Mohanlal, Vedantacharya 321

Mokkala 104

mokṣa 2, 115, 123, 222
  four categories of 219
  idea of 266
  in Nyāya philosophy new, concept of 329

momentariness, theory of 199

Monier-Williams, M. 5-6, 293, 314, 322

monotheism, discourse on 305

Mubahisa-e-Hudusa-e-duniya 34

Mudrārākṣasa 31, 272

Mudritakumudacandra xi, 27, 125, 276-77

Muhammad Tughlak, Sultan 141

Muir, John 284, 299, 309, 314

Muktanand, Swami 313

Muktivāda 8

Mūladeva 269

Mūlamādhyamikakārikā 98-100, 103

Mulji, Karsanadas 311

Müller, Max 192, 195, 294-99, 301-02, 314, 321

Muni, Śrīraṅgalakṣmaṇa 276

Mutazilas 294

myth of
- golden age 332
- progress 332

myth of Sanakādi brothers 5

Nabakrishna, Maharaja 287

Nābhāga 234

Nāgārjuna 20, 97-100, 102-04, 107, 114, 198
- disciples of 101

Nāgārjuna's philosophy, foundation of 103, 203

Nāgasena, Monk 13, 91, 96, 161

Nahuṣa 234

Nair, T.P. Shankarankutty 313

nairātmya 92

Naiṣadhacaritam 195, 268

Naiṣadhīyacarita 119

Naiyāyikas 8, 82, 98, 109, 112-13, 118, 120, 197, 200, 202, 205, 208, 210, 211-14, 216, 269, 320, 331
- of Gautamīya tradition 209
- orthodox 23, 26, 111, 180-82, 207, 210-11

Naiyāyika's
- concept of Reality 204
- proposition of *apavarga* 219

Nala 268

Nālandā 101, 109

Nālandā University 102

Nāmadeva 139

Nambaradar, Bhavani Prasad 320

Nānak 139

Nanda, rule of 92

Nandaka 86

Nandakavāda Sutta of *Majjhimanikāya* 86

Nandapaṇḍita 235

nāndī and *bharatavākya*, contemporary debates on philosophy through 261

Nandin 127

Nandīratna 125

Nanotavi, Maulana Mohammad Kasim 314

Nārada 15, 17, 21, 69, 223, 228, 231-33

Nāradasmṛti 15, 18, 228, 231-32, 234

Narahariśeṣa, Paṇḍit Kṛṣṇa 237

Narain, K. 202

Narayan, Harsha 315-16, 319

Narayana Guru, Sri 283, 313

Nārāyaṇa, Swami 283, 312

Nārāyaṇabhaṭṭa 37

Nārāyaṇācārya 135

Nārāyaṇasmṛtiḥ 313

Naryosang viii, 138-39

Nāsirī, Akhlaque 34

Nasr-ud-Dīn, Sheikh Baba 141

nāstika 79

nāstika-darśanas 208

nāstikas 67, 102

Naṭāṅkuśa 257-59

Naṭaraṅga 233

nāṭya, nature of 240

nāṭya rasa 249

Nāṭyasāhityamālā 276-77

Nāṭyaśāstra vii, 22, 240, 243-44, 248, 258, 262
  as a Saṁvāda Text 239
  conceptual framework of 241

Nāṭyaśāstraviśvakośa 249

Nāṭyaveda 22, 240

Navya-Nyāya 121, 204

Nayā Sāhitya Nayā Sāhityaśāstra 257

Nāyaka king Veṅkaṭappā, court of 136

Nayamaṇimālā 148

Nayamañjarī 148

Nayamayūkhamālā 148

Nayamuktāvalī 148

Nayavāda 87

Neelkantha, K.N. 120

Nibandhana 273-74

Nigamaparimala 130-31

niggaha 86

niggama 86

nigrahasthāna 50, 101, 159, 174
  called *apratibhā* 50
  called *avācyavacana* 50
  framework of 183, 283
  twenty-two 165

niḥsvabhāva 98

nikṛti 66

Nikṣeparakṣā 130

Nīlakaṇṭha 21

Nīlakeśī, a Jaina nun 37, 104-05

Nīlāmbara sect 270

Nimbārka 224

nimitta kāraṇa, God as 214, 216

Nirgrantha
  order 94
  sect 8

Nirguṇātmavādins 102

nirṇaya 159, 184, 228

Nirṇayasindhu 236

Nirukta 40, 77

nirvāṇa is structured on negative dialecticism 219

Nirvāṇatantra 149

nirvyūḍhanaika-vādivijayakelidurlalitaḥ 276

Niścalapurī 238

Niṣkaṇṭaka 186

nivṛtti and *pravṛtti*, clash between 66

niyatānupūrvī 78

niyati 106

Niyativāda 47
  philosophy of 83

Niyativādins 47, 261

Nobilii, Roborto 284

non-one-sidedness, theory of 86, 336

non-Platonists, mystic theosophical logos-doctrine of 285

non-Vedic sects 269

Nṛsiṁhāśrama 132, 135

Nūranāmā 141

Nur-ud-Dīn Sheikh (Nund Rishi) 141

Nyāsaviṁśatiḥ 130

Nyāya 3, 42, 81-82, 113, 131, 163, 176, 200, 210
  and Vaiśeṣika, synthesis of 120
  as *tarkavidyā* 3
  epistemological categories of 112
  orthodox 110, 330
  philosophy 16, 35, 156, 162, 242, 245
  system 83, 166, 176
    refutation of 113
  traditions 180
  terminology of 50

Nyāyabhāṣya 100

Nyāyabhūṣaṇa 112

Nyāyabindu 35, 113, 182

Nyāyadarśana 3, 42, 67, 160, 174, 242

Nyāyakandalī 118

Nyāyakośa 208

Nyāyakusumāñjali 33, 118, 196, 217-18

Nyāyamañjarī 112, 195, 270

Nyāyāmṛtam 132, 134
  and *Advaitasiddhi*, row of debate between 303

Nyāyāmṛtataraṅgiṇī 134

Nyāyapariśuddhi 36, 130

Nyāyapraveśakasūtram 2, 15, 105, 185

Nyāyapraveśavṛtti 185

Nyāyaratna, Rākhaldas 311

Nyāyaratnākara 193

Nyāyaratnāvalī 133

Nyāyaśāstra 279

Nyāyasiddhāntadīpa 218

Nyāyasudhā 134, 263

Nyāyasūtra 2, 3, 8, 33, 35, 42, 80, 98, 100, 107, 112, 120, 130, 156-60, 163-65, 179, 203-04, 214-15, 269, 271

Nyāya-Vaiśeṣika 81-82, 109, 118, 203-04, 213, 333
  school 203
  system 205, 329
    later 211
  tenets of 197, 329
  theorists of 197

Nyāyavārttika 107

Nyāyavārttikatātparyaṭīkā 112

Nyāyavārttikatātparyaṭīkāpariśuddhi 112

Nyāyaviniścayavivaraṇa 122

Nyāyaysiddhāñjana 130

nyūna 178

ohabrahmaṇaḥ 41

Ojha, Pt. Madhusudhan 311

Oldenburg, Hermann 303

On the Critique of Satyārthaprakāśa 321

opponents, buffoonery of 26

Orient and Occident relationship between, xiv

Oriental
- Rennaissance 300
- studies 151

orientalia, virtual epidemic of 296

Orientalism 296, 303
- constructive 308
- onslaught of 299

Orientalist discourse 295, 298

Orientalists, strategy of 287

orthodox
- Catholicism 296
- Naiyāyikas 23, 26, 111, 180-82, 207, 210-11
- Nyāya 110, 330
- philosophies, apostles of 108
- schools of Indian philosophy 336

Oupnekhat 284

Padārthadharmasaṁgraha 120

Padārthamaṇḍana 204

padārthas,
- fourteen 156
- sixteen 35

Padārthatattavanirūpaṇa 204

Padārthavidyāsāra 290

padavākya-pramāṇajña 262

Padma Purāṇa 195

Padmapāda 115, 118

Padmapādacaritam 117

Pādukāsahasram 129

pakṣa 116, 159

Pallava
- court 107
- Renaissance ix

Pañcamatabhañjana 132

Pañcānana, Jagannātha 288

Pañcapādikā 118, 134

Pāñcarātra 208, 275
- system 131
  - of Āgama 103

Pāñcarātrarakṣā 130

Pañcaśikha 68

Pañcatantra 272

pañcāvayava-vākya 26, 54, 67, 157, 179, 273
- structure of 181

Panchayati Raj 294

Pāṇḍavas 17, 66, 72

Pande, G.C. 30-31, 85, 115, 122, 189, 198, 221, 327-28

Pandey, Ramesh Kumar 5

Pandit, S.P. 302

Paṇḍita, Caṇḍu 119

Paṇḍita, Jagannātha 287

Paṇḍita, Trivikrama 125

Paṇḍita, Viśveśvara 237

Paṇḍitavāda 95

paṇḍits, assemblies of 4

paṇḍit-sabhā 327

Pāṇḍya, Kūna 106

Pāṇḍya, Sundara 106

Pāṇḍya rulers of Mathurā 122

Pāṇini, *sūtras* of 39

Pāṇinian
- system of grammar 138
- tradition 182

parājayādhikaraṇa 183
parājayavastu 183
paramāṇus, yoga of 206
Paramapadasopāna 131
paramārtha and *vyavahāra*, nexus between 222
Paramārthadarśanam 327-28
paramārthasat 206
paramārtha-satya 103, 111, 203
Paramatabhaṅga 130-31
parārthānumāna 35, 157
  theory of 182
  three constituents of 182
Parāśara 104, 223, 231, 233
Pārāśaras 88
Pāraskara 78
Paraśurāma 236, 263-64
  contempt of 264
  onslaught of 264
parataḥ pramāṇa,
  principle of 82
  theory of 208
paravādas 95
pariṇāma, theory of 212-14
Pariṇāmavāda 205, 212
paripūrṇa vaidikas 147
Pariśiṣṭa 120
parṣatsattvā 14
Pārśva 96-97
parvabrāhmaṇa 25-26
parvakārin 25
Pārvatī 5, 259, 261
Pāṣaṇḍimatakhaṇḍana 133
Pasha, Mustafa Kamal 293
Pāśupata 131, 208, 270, 275
Pātañjala Yoga 37
Patañjali 80, 115, 182
Patel, M. 138
path of renunciation 267
paṭiññā 86
paṭipucchā kathā 86
paura-jānapadas, counsel of 62
Payasisuttanta 195
Pāyguṇḍe, Vaidyanātha 326
perception, definition of 113
Persian Sufism, mysticism of 285
Perumāḷ, Cheramān ix
philosophical
  debate 48
  thought, essence of 79
philosophy of
  action and *dharma* 261
  Cārvāka 193, 268
  grammar 113
  individual salvation 267
  intuition 307
  language 115
  materialism 190
  Niyativāda 83
  Saptabhaṅgīnaya 87
  Śūnyavāda 97, 199
  Tantra 140
  Viśiṣṭādvaita 126
Philosophy of Mythology, The 285
Phule, Jyotiba 325-26
Phullori, Shraddharam 34, 323
pīrs 141
Piśācaka 105

Piśuna 88

Piṭakas 86, 94

Pitt, William 300

Plato 1

Portuguese and Latin American Revolutions 292

post-Śaṅkara Advaitins 132

Prabhācandrasūri 125

Prabhākara ix, 27, 102, 131, 204
- school of Mīmāṁsā 204

Prabhāvakacarita 125

Prabodhacandrodaya 191, 195, 273-74, 276

Prabodhasiddhi 120

Pracchannatārkikas 102

Prācīnacaritrakośa 5

Prahlāda, tale of 18

Prajāpati (the Lord of Creation) 5

prajāpati 43

Prajñāvāda 47

Prajñāvādin 48

Prakaraṇapañcikā 111

prakaraṇasama 163

Prakāśa 274

Prakṛti 132

pramāṇa 2, 82, 111, 168, 191
- tradition 1
- definitions of 113

Pramāṇadvitvasiddhiḥ 110

pramāṇāgamavarjitaṁ 184, 229

pramāṇālaṁkāras, treatment of 245

Pramāṇanirṇaya 134

Pramāṇapaddhati 35

pramāṇas 81, 116
- from *Nyāyasūtra* 113
- four 67
- treatment of 109

Pramāṇasamuccaya 107

Pramāṇaśāstra 3, 279

Pramāṇavārtika 107, 181, 203, 207-08, 216

Prāmāṇyavāda 8

praṇipatya jineśvaram 105

Prārthanā Samāj 307, 310, 325

Prasad, Baldev 320

Prasad, Jai Shankar 233, 248, 301

Prasad, Pt. Jwala 319-20

Prasad, Pt. Shiv 299

Prasad, Rajendra 326, 337

Prāsaṅgika school of Mādhyamika philosophy 103

Prāsaṅgikābharaṇa 133

Praśastapāda 120, 122

Praśna Upaniṣad 185

prāśnika 15, 184

Pratapchandra xiv, 9-10, 85

pratijñā 26, 100, 116, 228

pratijñāhaniḥ 178

Pratijñāyaugandharāyaṇa 258

pratikāmin 70

Pratiman 337

pratipakṣa 159

pratipraśnena-vyākaraṇīya 84
pratipṛcchā kathā 86
pratiṣṭhāpanā 176
pratitantra siddhānta 159
prativādī 164-65, 185, 228
prativādibhayaṁkara 12-13
prativādin 15, 69, 102
pratyakṣa 111, 113, 126
Pratyantaprasthānamīmāṁsā 311
pratyanuyoga 177
pratyarthī 228
pratyavaskandana 184
Prauḍhamanoramā 136
Prauḍhamanoramākucamardinī 136
pravṛtti and *nivṛtti*,
  clash between x, 66
  opposite ways of 188
  tussle between 68
pravṛtti mārga and *nivṛtti mārga*, realignment between 222
pravṛtti-vijñāna 119
Pṛthivī 265
public debates, potentiality of 337
pudgala-jagat 206
punarbhūs, three types of 231
punarukta 178
Pundit, The 298
Purāṇa 113
Purāṇakaśyapa 83, 85, 193
Purāṇārthaprakāśa 288
Purāṇas 195, 269
  students of 103
Purandara 193
Purūravas and Urvaśī, hymn on 44
Puruṣa 46, 190
  is *vibhu* and *nitya* 206
  represents the *Jīva* 275
Puruṣakāravāda 106, 227
Pūrva-Mīmāṁsā 203, 221
pūrva-pakṣa 13, 42, 66, 90, 184, 228, 258, 264, 266, 268, 273, 278
pūrvavyavahāravidhi 184
Putreṣṭiyajña 55
putrikā, context of a 235

Radde-Musalman 304
Rādhā 141
Radhakrishnan, S. xiii, 1
Rāghavabhaṭṭa 249
Raghu 234
Raghunāthācārya, Parvate 304
Raghuramaraju, A. viii, xiv
Raghuvaṁśa 261-62
Rahasyarakṣā 130
Rahasyatrayasāra 131
Rahasyopadeśa 141
Rai, Lala Lajpat 236, 322
rājadharma 62
rājakula 13
Rājapraśnīya 88
Rajaram, Shahu 290

Rājaśekhara 3, 7, 14, 39, 42, 81, 89, 247-48
Rājavāda 95
Rajesh, K. 7
Rājyaśrī, Harṣa's sister, was a Sammatīya 92
Rakhmabai 325
Rāma 12, 32, 55-63, 66, 85, 135, 146, 225-26, 264-65
  devotees of 135
  genealogy of 61
Ramabai, Paṇḍitā 324-25
Rāmacaritamānasa 135
Rāmācārya 132
Ramakrishna Paramahansa, Sri 283
Ramana Maharshi xii
Ramanand Swami Ashram 313
Rāmānanda 10, 224
Rāmānuja ix, 10, 23, 27, 121, 126-28, 130, 201, 219, 224, 280
  Darśana 201
  sect 279
  system, supremacy of 276
Rāmānuja's philosophy through debates 275
Rāmānujadāsa 276
Rāmārāyakavi, Bellamkoṇḍa 304
Rāmārya 134-35, 202
Rāmāyaṇa 55, 58, 60-63, 85, 193, 195, 225-26, 264, 269, 310
  theme, *prabandha* on 132
  characters of 55
Rāmāyaṇa II 57
Rāmdās, Saint 238
raṇachoḍanīti xiii
Ranade, Mahadev Govind 307, 310, 324-25
Ranade, R.D. 337
Raṅganātha, God 131
Raṅgojibhaṭṭadhikkāra 137-38
Rani of Jhansi 291
rasa
  is *anumiti*, realization of 246
  theory of 248
Raspe, Rud Eric 287
Rastogi, Navjivan 222, 224
rāṣṭramukti 336
Rati 273
Ratnākara 161
Ratnakīrti 110-12
Ratnamaṇḍana 34, 36, 125
Ratnaprabha 125
Rāvaṇa 63-64
Raz, Ram 294
remarriage of women 231
Renaissance 302
  and awareness, spirit of 283
  spirit of 301
revelation, age of 40
Ṛgveda 41, 43-44, 47, 79, 134, 192, 221, 299, 301-03, 319
  with *Sāyaṇabhāṣya* 302
  dialogue hymns of 44
Richards, I.A. 285
Riembau, Oscar Pujol 331
Rixner, Th.A. 284

Ṛjuvimalā 273

Robertson, Bruce C. 292, 305

Roth, Rundolf von 47

Roy, Raja Rammohun 44, 149, 236, 282-83, 286, 288-89, 292, 294-95, 297, 305-07

Rozario 291

Ṛṣināmā 141

ṛṣis 50

Ṛṣyaśṛṅga, Sage 55

Rūha-e-Azam 148

Rumi 139

Rupa Bhavani 141

Śābarabhāṣya 273

Śabarasvāmin 78, 204

śabdānuvedha, theory of 210

śabda-pramāṇa 176

sabhā 15, 43-44
    is called *nariṣṭhā* 43
    of *paṇḍits* and poets 287

sabhāpati 186

sabhāsada 43

sabhya 15

Saccharitrarakṣā 130

Sachan, Edward C. xi, 123-24

Sacontala 300

Sacred Books of East 303

Sadānanda 121

sadasattva-anadhikaraṇarūpaṁ 201

sadasi anuvidheyasamvaraṇa, two
    types of 162

sadasya 116-17, 184-86

Ṣaḍdarśanasaṁgraha 160

Ṣaḍdarśanasamuccaya 37, 105, 195

saddhi 95

sādhanā 222

sādhanābhāsas 182

Sādhāraṇa Brahma Samāja 307

sādhya 109

sādhyasama 163

Sādiks 144

Sadr Diwani Adalat 289

sadvāda 27, 169

Saguṇātmavādins 102

sahaja, idea of 139

Sahajīyā sect 193

Sahajīyās 139, 194, 270

Sāhityadarpaṇa 299

Sāhityaśāstra vii

Śāhucaritam 290

Said, Edward 285, 295-97, 300, 307, 329

Śaiva 270-71
    philosophy 336
    sect 276

Śaivism 106, 139, 262

Śaivite philosophy 140

Sakalāyatanapaddhati xiii

Śakaṭāsura 127

sākṣī 122

Śākta monotheism 150

Śāktas 143

Śaktibhadra 258
Śaktivāda 8
Śakuni 66
Śakuntalā 75, 301
    and Duṣṣanta, war of words between 76
    and Europe, hidden bond between 300
    tale of 54
Śākuntalopākhyāna 75
Śākyabuddhi 208
Śālikanātha 111
Salunkhe, A.H. x
Samācāracandrikā 306
samānāntara-pratyaya 100
Samaṇasutta xiii
Samantaphalasutta 195
sāmānya 82, 111
    lakṣaṇa 109-10
    chala 163, 319
Samarāṅgaṇasūtradhāra 250
sāmarthya, idea of 181
sambhava 177
saṁgha 91, 93
    split of 92
    split in 91
saṁghabheda 92
saṁgharāji 92
Saṁgraha text 101
samiti 43-44
Sāṁkhya 2-3, 41-42, 80-82, 113, 131-32, 143, 191, 194, 200, 205-06, 208, 213-15, 217, 262, 275
    classical 190
    concept of *prakṛti* 206
    philosophers 25
    stands as a *pradhānamalla* 189
    system 25, 68
    theories of *Prakṛti* and *Puruṣa*, critique of 103
    view of *rasa* 248
Sāṁkhyas 277
Sāṁkhyasāra 190
Sāṁkhyasūtra 80
Sāmmatīyas 92
saṁnyāsa 116, 194
sampṛcchā 42
Samrāiccakahā 80
saṁskāras 143
Saṁskṛtasūtrārtha 133
Samudramanthana 22, 240
Samudrasaṅgama 146-48
saṁvāda 8, 42, 69-70
    between Kṛṣṇa and Nārada 70
    contours of 124
saṁvāda-prakaraṇa 48
saṁvṛti-satya 81, 103, 111, 203
Sanatan Dharm Rakshini Sabha 323
Sanātana Dharma 221
Sanātanadharmoddhāraḥ 320
Sanaullah Maulawi 34
sandhāya saṁbhāṣā 170, 178
sandhi 23
saṅgītis 90
Sañjaya Kātyāyana 83, 85

Saṅkalpasūryodaya 128-29, 274, 276
Śaṅkara ix-x, 9, 101, 108, 125, 130, 133, 185, 200
  and Rāmānuja, fundamental difference between 126
Śaṅkara's
  Advaita 131
  concept of Reality 202
  concepts of *ajñāna* and the world as *vivarta* 202
  monism, critics of 126
Śāṅkarabhāṣya 32
  of *Brahmasūtra* 195
  on *Kena Upaniṣad* 200
Śaṅkarābhyudayaḥ 115
Śaṅkarābhyudayam 115
Śaṅkarācārya ix, 12, 28, 30-31, 37, 48, 102, 106, 115-16, 122, 188-89, 195, 311
Śaṅkarācārya's
  dialectic method 117
  philosophy 286
Śaṅkarācāryacaritam 115
Śaṅkarācārya-granthāvalī 51
Śaṅkaradigvijaya 29-30, 32, 108-09, 115-17
Śāṅkara-Vedānta 37, 81, 134, 201
Śaṅkaravijayam 115
Śaṅkaravijayamakaranda 30
Śaṅkaravijayavilāsaḥ 115
Saṅkarṣaṇa 270-71
Śaṅkha 223
Śāṅkhāyana Brāhmaṇa 50
Saṅkīravāda 87
Śaṅkuka 246, 250
Sanskrit
  literary traditions 308
  pāṭhaśālā 324
Santānāntaradūsaṇa 110
Santānāntarasiddhi 110
Śāntarakṣita 103-04, 111, 195, 205
sapiṇḍa relatives 233
Saptabhaṅgīnaya 134
  philosophy of 87
Saptapadārthī 204
Sarahapā, 139 193-94
Sarasvatī, Goddess 12, 127
Sarasvatī, Madhusūdana 126, 134, 149, 201-02
Sarasvatīkaṇṭhābharaṇa 245
Sarayū 13
sārdhāṅgīkāram 23
Śārika 273
Śārikanātha 274
Śāriputra 94
Sartori, Andrew 310
Sārvabhauma, Diṇḍimakavi 128
Sarvabhauma, Pt. Ras Mohan 327
Sarvadarśanasaṁgraha 27, 34, 37, 81, 101, 130, 191, 201
Sarvajña Siṁhabhūpāla 129
Sarvajñātman 118
Sarvamatasaṁgraha 37
Sarvasevāsaṅgha xiii
Sarvasiddhāntasaṁgraha 195

Sarvāstivādin 94, 197
sarvatantra siddhānta 159
sarvātmanā yoga 206
Sarva-vastu-śabala-vāda 87
Śaśadhara 218
śāstrakāra-parikṣās 14
śāstrakāvya 268
śāstra-parīkṣās 7
śāstrārtha 5, 312, 321-23, 326-27
  between Pt. Shiv Kumar Shastri and Pt. Ramdhan Panchanan 327
  history of 326
Śāstrārthavārtāsamuccaya 106, 195-96, 199, 206, 218
Śāstrārthavicārapaddhati 36, 161-62, 185
Śāstras 69, 136, 182, 276, 279, 292, 318
śāstra-sabhā 7, 236, 238
Śāstravārtāsamuccaya viii, 105
Śāstric knowledge, bombardment of 258
Śatabhūṣaṇī 304
Śatadūṣaṇī 128, 130, 304
Śatānanda 264
Śatapatha Brāhmaṇa 44-45, 50, 318
Śataślokī 329
Satchidananda Murty, K. vii, x, 4, 6, 126, 287
Śaṭhakopasūri 130
satī, practice of 236, 306
Satkāryavāda 212
ṣaṭpakṣī 164
satpratipakṣa 163
Śatrughna 64
satsaṅga 140
sattā 27
sattva-viśiṣṭa sattvābhāva 202
Satyadhyānatīrtha 304
Satyaikātmatāvāda (true monism) 147
Satyārthadarpaṇa 321
Satyārthaprakāśa 304, 312, 314, 316-20, 323
Satyārthaprakāśa kī Chīchāledar 321
Satyārthaprakāśasamīkṣā 321
Satyārthaprakāśavimarśa 312, 322
Saundaryadarśanavimarśaḥ 328
Sautrāntika 97, 196, 198
Sāyaṇa 43, 78
Sāyaṇabhāṣya 301
Schelling, Friedrich Wilhelm Joseph 284, 286, 297
Schlegel, Friedrich 297, 303
Schopenhauer, Arthur 284-86, 297, 303
Schwab, Raymond 296, 300
Sen, Amartya viii, 13, 60
Sen, Keshub Chandra 283, 286, 297, 307
Sepoy Mutiny 324
Sermons on Mountain 291

Śeṣakṛṣṇa 136
Seśvara Sāṁkhya 190
Seśvaramīmāṁsā 130
Shah-e-Jahan (Emperor) 146
Shahjahan, court of 136
Shanbhag, D.N. 133
Sharma, Akhilanand 319
Sharma, Dhirendra ix, 204
Sharma, Ramavatar 328
Shastri, Ramakrishna (Tatya Shastri) 326
Shastri, Ajit Kumar 321
Shastri, Anantakṛṣṇa 304
Shastri, Bal 326
Shastri, Bapudev 309
Shastri, D.N. 109-10
Shastri, Dakshina Ranjan 194
Shastri, Damodar 326-27
Shastri, Gangadhar 326-27
Shastri, Hari Prasad 64
Shastri, Kalu Ram 321
Shastri, Kuṇigal Rāma 304
Shastri, Natesh 304
Shastri, Paṇḍit Bal 311, 323
Shastri, Paṇḍit Gattulal 327
Shastri, Paṇḍit Rajaram 311
Shastri, Pandit Vishnu Parashuram 310
Shastri, Polaga Rama 149
Shastri, Premacharya 321
Shastri, Pt. Harigopal 321
Shastri, Raju 304
Shastri, Shiv Kumar 312-13, 326
Shastri, Shri Vishnu 311
Shastri, Subrahmanya 305
Shastri, Suri Ramachandra 304
Shastri, Tryambaka 304
Shastri, Vitthal 309
Shekh Mohammad 141
Shekh, Miran 146
Shivaji,
  abhiṣeka of 237
  fictitious genealogy of 237
Shrinivasacharya, Lakshmipuram 149
Shukla, Balram 139
Shukla, Pt. Badarinath 5, 329-30
Siddhakarana 322
siddhānta-pakṣa 66, 160, 266, 273, 278
Siddhāntarahasya 274
*siddhānta*s 101
Sikh *gurus* 10
Silk Buckimgham 294
*śilpaka*s of rustic nature (*grāmyadharmaka*) 22
Singh, Namvar 321
Singhavi, Muni Sukhalalji 34, 36-37, 109-10, 113-14, 122, 191
Singhi, Bachcharaj 304
Śiromaṇi, Raghunātha 204
Sirr-e-Akbar 146-47
Śiśupāla 267-68

Śiśupālavadham 267

Sītā 32, 56, 62-63, 65-66, 265

Śiva 148, 259, 269
    source of birth of 261
    subtle image of, 261

Śivadigvijaya 237

Śivadṛṣṭi 114

sixty-three Nāyanārs 106

Śiyā 144

Skanda-Gumanig-vizar 138

Ślokavārttika 193

Smārta
    karmas 143
    view 143

Smṛtis 150, 225, 227, 234

socio-cultural framework 224

Socratics 155

Solomon, E.A. xv, 2, 20, 35, 86-88, 90, 125, 152, 158, 167

Somadeva 80

Somānanda 114

sound probans, six characteristics of 24

Spaṣṭatārkikas 102

speech,
    eighteen blemishes of 152
    qualities of 16

Spencer, Herbert 293-94
    Gandhi's criticism of 293, 337

śrāddha ritual 25

śramaṇic traditions 86

Śrautasūtras 318

Śrāvastī 94

Śrībhāṣya 130

Śrīdhara 112, 118, 204, 287

Śrīharṣa 12, 27, 34, 36, 114-15, 119, 122, 165, 186, 195, 266, 268

Śrīkṛṣṇa 79

Śrīmadbhagavadgītā 151

Śrīnivāsācārya, Jālihāla 304

Śrīnivāsācārya, Tāmraparṇi 304

Srinivasan, V.V. 274

Śrīśivarājyābhiṣekakalpataru 238

Śrīśivarājyābhiṣekaprayoga 238

Śrīvādirāja Maṭha 133

Śrīvidyādhīśavijaya 137

Śrīyatirājavijayam or *Vedāntavilāsa* 276

śṛṅgāracitra 249

Śṛṅgāraprakāśa 245

Śruti 200, 208-09

Śrutitattvaprakāśikā 133

Stcherbatsky, Theodor/Fyodor ix, 102

sthāpanā 176

sthāpanīya 84

Sthavira Vatsa 92

sthaviras 93

strīdhana 235

Strīdharmanīti 325

Subhāṣitanīvī 130

Subhāṣitaratnabhāṇḍāgāra 272

Subhāṣitaratnakośa 272

Śubhatuṅga or Kṛṣṇa I,

Rāṣṭrakūṭa king 107
Subodhpatrika 325
subtle consciousness is mind consciousness 198
Sudarśanasūrya 131
Śuddhādvaita 121
Sudhanvan 18, 225
Śūdrācāraśiromaṇi 237
Śūdrāhnikapaddhatiḥ 236
Śūdrakamalākara 236
Sudurjaya 102
Sufi saint Miyan Mir Dehalvi and Bābā Lāldās Bairāgī, discourses of 146
Sufi traditions of Islam and Upaniṣadic philosophy, synthesis of 146
Sufism 139, 146
Sugrīva 64
Śukla Yajurveda 43, 46
Śukra 184, 229
Śukra and *Mānava Dharmaśāstra* 226
Śukrācārya 192
Śukranīti 141
Śukrasmṛti 228
Sulabhā 54, 155, 177
  discourse of 152
  story of 9, 53
Sultanpuri, Latif 146
Sundara Pāṇḍya, a philosopher of Advaita Vedānta 106
Sundaram, C.S. 13, 104, 117, 131
Śūnyādvaita 286
śūnyatā 100
Śūnyavāda 97-98, 196
  philosophy of 97, 199
Śūnyavādin 114, 199
Supreme Court 292
Supreme Court of Calcutta 289
Sureśvara 118, 189
Sūryasiddhānta 309
Sūtra text 82
sūtradhāra 241
Sūtras 79
Suttanipāta 19-20
Suttapiṭaka 93
Suvarcalā 52, 54
svabhāva 106
svabhāva hetu 24
Svabhāvavāda 106, 193, 227
Svabhāvavādins 47, 193, 261
svairiṇīs, four types of 231
svarāj, idea of 337
Svaraj in Ideas 337
Svarājyaśāstra xiii
svārthānumāna 157
Svarūpaprakāśa 121-22
svataḥ prāmāṇya 82
  of Veda 320
Svatantrādvaita 286
Svātantrika school under Mādhyamika Buddhism 103
Svātantryadarpaṇaḥ 336
Svayūthyavicāra 110

Svedāyana 45
Śvetaketu 9, 50-53, 76
Śvetāmbara sect 277
Śvetāśvatara Upaniṣad 6, 47
Swain, B.K. 230, 236
Swami, Karapatri 304
Swamikal, Chattambi 283, 313
Switzer, Albert xiii
Syādvāda 103, 122, 134
Syādvādamañjarī 27
Syādvādaratnākara 34, 37

tad bālavilasitam 26
tādrūpyānusandhāna 250
Tagore, Debendranath 283, 306-07
Tagore, Dwarkanath 306
Tagore, Rabindranath 151, 283
Tagore, Saumyendranath 294, 306
Taittirīya Āraṇyaka 221
Taittirīya Brāhmaṇa 81
Taittirīya Saṁhitā 44, 46
Taittirīya Upaniṣad 134, 188
Talbot, Cynthia 136
Talvakāropaniṣad, *bhāṣya* of Madhva on 134
Talwar, Veer Bharat 321
Tamil *kāvya* 104
tan mugdhavilasitaṁ 26
tanmātras 148
Tantra 139, 149-50
    philosophy of 140
tantra-yuktis 89-90
Tantric cults 223-24
Tāntrikas 223
Taraṅgiṇī 202-03
tarka 66, 59
    five types of blemishes of 159
tarkābhāsa 159
tarka-kāla 78
Tarkalankar, Madhusudan 290
Tarkapanchanan, Jagananth 288
Tarkaratna, Pt. Taracharan 323
Tarkaśāstra 66
    cultivation of 279
Tarkatāṇḍava 132
Tarkavāgīśa, Harirāma 134
Tarkavagish, Radhakanta 288
tarkavidyā 279
Tārkikarakṣā 160-61
Tārkikas 102
Tātadeśika or Tātārya 132
tathāgata 60, 91
    eulogy of 108
Tātparyacandrikā 130
Tātparyapariśuddhi 111
tattvabodha, idea of 2
Tattvabodhini Patrika 307
Tattvabodhini Sabha 307
tattvabubhutsuvāda 161, 178
Tattvakaustubha 136, 138
Tattvakaustubhakuliśa 138

Tattvamuktākalāpaḥ 130
Tattvapradīpa 262
Tattvaprakāśikā 134
Tattvasaṁgraha 103, 195
Tattvasaṁgrahapañjikā 195
Tattvasandeśa 130
Tattvaṭīkā 130, 195
Tattvopaplavasiṁha 26, 34, 36-37, 112-14, 191-92
Tauber 285
Telang, K.T. 325
Teltscher, Kate 287, 295, 300
Tengle, adherents of 281
Theravāda tradition 93
thesis of 84,000 *yonis* 83
Thibaut, George 299
Tibetan traditions 108
time–space framework 333
Tohaful-Hind 304, 319
Tohaful-Islam 304
tradition of
  Nyāyadarśana 3
  vāda envisages pluralism viii
  Vedānta 9
traditional
  knowledge systems vii
  Nyāya system 107
  vāda discourses 336
Traikālyaparīkṣā 107
trigata 241
Tripathi, G.C. 121
Triṣaṣṭiśalākāpuruṣacarita 80
truth is the greatest *dharma* 58
Tuhfat-ul-Muwahhiddin 294, 305
Tukārāma 121, 139
Tulasi Ram 320
Tulasīdāsa 135
tyāgīs, sect of 143

Ubedullah, Maulana 304
Uber die Sprache und Weisheit der Indier 297
Ubhayābhisārikā 242
Ucchedavādins 193
udāharaṇa 86
Udayana 3, 12, 27, 33, 35, 102, 111-12, 116, 118-22, 164, 196-97, 204-05, 211, 213, 217-18
Udayana's theories of Nyāya 119
Udayanamāhātmya 119
Uddaka Rāmaputta 85
Uddālaka Āruṇi 45, 50, 83
  hermitage of 51
Uddhava 267
Udyotakara 103, 107-08, 205
ūhabrahmāṇaḥ 41
Ultimate Reality ix, 2, 148, 188
Umveka 115, 262
universal consciousness 328
untouchability, caste notion of 30
upacāra-chala 163
upādāna kāraṇa, God as 214
Upadhyaya, Baldeva 108-09, 134-35, 237, 311, 321, 323, 326-27

Upāli 91

Upālisutta 86

upanayana 86

Upaniṣad 48, 200

Upaniṣadic
- debates 47
- philosophy 150, 292
- style 226
- texts, original 306
- thought 190

Upaniṣads 21, 40, 50, 152, 284, 292, 297
- use the term *brahmodya* for *vāda* 38
- followers of 103
- mystic teachings of 285
- translation of 297

Upanyāsaratnamālā 134

upapatti 16

uparūpaka 240

Upāyahṛdaya 20

Urmis, K.P. 291

Uṣastā 49

uttara 184

Uttarādi Maṭha 136

uttara-pakṣa 42, 81, 90, 228, 267

Uttararāmacaritam 32, 263-65

Vacanas of medieval saints 140

vācika abhinaya, theory of 241

vāda 12, 81, 115, 159, 186
- argumentative design of 75
- as a *digvijaya* 31
- Asaṅga defined six kinds of 178
- between
  - Māṇikyamuni and Śaṅkara 125
  - *paṇḍits* as informants and the colonizers as rulers 286
  - Śaṅkara and Umveka 117
- *brahmodya* for 40
- categories of 261
- categorizations related to 155
- correct method of 87
- culture of xi
- dynamics of 9
- efficacy of 19
- envisages a culture of pluralism and democratic values 1
- essential for protecting his message 20
- four pillars of 15
- *granthas* 8, 127
- has a wider connotation 6
- history of 38
- in
  - *kāvya* 271
  - literary theory, categories of 245
  - *Mahābhārata*, theory of 152
- Indian tradition of 2
- intellectual refinement through 108
- is a pervasive concept 160
- Jayarāśi became a model for the practitioners of 114
- journey for 115
- *kāvya* in 271
- Mahāvīra's tradition of 87
- manifestations of xiii
- manifests in some of the hymns of *Ṛgveda* 259
- of intrinsic nature 179
- of particular nature 179
- or *vyavahāra* recording of 184

potential nature of xiii
practice of 36
practitioners of 12
process of 8
ramifications of xi
saddhi for 7
saṁvāda and *vivāda* are two faces of viii
Sanskrit traditions of viii
served as a means for seeking democratic rights and justice 336
six types of court rooms for holding 13
techniques 272
formulation of 271
techniques of 54, 66, 123, 228, 242, 245, 269
theoretical
aspects of 35
discussion on 34, 152
theories and practices of vii-viii, 166, 336
theory of 23, 34-36, 90, 166, 168
tradition 314, 327, 336
essence of 90
plurality in 336
tradition of 1, 39
trics of 314
types of 175
utility of 20
vitality of vii
was a means of propagation of Buddha's message 102
with a clergy John Robton 316
with social institutions and oppressive systems xi
worked for erasing boundaries 10
world history of 95
vāda, *jalpa* and *vitanda* 160
is named as *kathā*, gamut of 160
Vādadvātriṁśikā 37
vādāhava(s) 31, 128
vādakathā 116
vādālaṁkāra 179
five types of 179
Vādanyāya 25-26, 35, 212
Vādārtharatnamālā 132
Vādaśāstra, conceptual framework for 35
conceptual universe of 152
vāda-text, genres of creating a 38
vāda-tradition, progress of 15
Vādavāridhi 8, 36
Vādavidhi 35
vāda–vivāda 20
vādī 164, 185, 228
and *prativādī*, questions and objections of 184
vādībhasiṁhasūrin 12
vādikesarin 13
vādin(s) 15, 30, 69, 102
team of 88
Vādīndra 158
vādinigraha 180
vādiprativādiniyama, two types of 162
vādipuṅgava 107
Vādirāja 122, 132-34
Vāditrayakhaṇḍana 128, 130
Vādivinoda 161

vādivṛṣabha 107
vāg-vijñapti 180
Vāhidiyā and Vāyajīd, tenets of 144
Vaibhāṣika 97, 196
vaidalavratikas 195
Vaidalyasūtra 98
Vaidika Satyārthaprakāśa 319
Vaiśālī, monks of 93
Vaiśeṣika 3, 26, 42, 81-82, 131, 175, 191, 200, 205, 219, 275
  cosmology 212
  philosophy 111, 120, 212, 243, 324
    universal categories of 175
  system 81, 120
    theories of 146
  teacher Lokajit 105
Vaiśeṣika's
  concept of *ātman* 200
  conceptual framework for reality 204
Vaiśeṣikasūtra 80, 146, 203
Vaiśikācala 243
Vaiṣṇava
  Pāñcarātra system 121
  schools of religions order 223
  tradition 276
Vaiṣṇavas 143
Vaiṣṇavism 269
  onslaught of 121
  opponents of 268
  tenets of 130, 132
Vājasaneya 50
Vajrasūcī 96, 226
Vajrasūcyopaniṣad 226-27
vāk-chala 163
Vakh of Lal-Dêd 140
vākovākya 6, 245
  alaṁkāra 133
vāk-pāruṣya 21
  categories of 21
vakrokti 271
vākyābhinaya, twelve types of 241
vākya-doṣas, five 177
Vākyapadīyam 113
vākyaprasaṁśās, five 177
vākyārtha-sabhās 7
validity of
  "hearsay" 209
  sea voyage 311
  Shivaji's coronation 238
Vālin, cave of 133
Vallabha sect 327
Vallabhācārya 121
Vālmīki 85, 265
Vālmīki Rāmāyaṇa 65-66, 263
vāma mārga 225
Vāmana 250
vānaprastha 80
Vāñchānātha xi, 10
Vāñcheśvara 10
Vandin 76-77
Varadācārya alias Alagiya Maṇavala 12
Varadācārya, Śrīvātsya 276
Varadarāja 128, 195
Varāhamihira 123

Varma, Shyamji Krishna 312

varṇāśrama system 270

varṇāśrama-centric
- culture 224
- world-view 223

vārttikas 80
- formulated by Kātyāyana 39

Varuṇa 18, 42, 248, 268

vāsanāsaṁkrama 196

Vāsantī 265

Vasava 10

Vāseṭṭha 86

Vasiṣṭha, Sage 55, 61, 69, 265

Vasiṣṭha 69

Vasubandhu 35-36, 84, 101, 215

Vasumitra 94

vātaraśanā munis 221

vātaraśanās 221

Vātavyādhi 88

Vatsīputrīyas 92

Vātsyāyana x, 22, 52, 90, 100, 102-03, 106-07, 163, 204, 214-15, 231

Vattanky, John S.J. 120, 214-18

Vazirchandra, editor of *Arya Musafir* 34

Veda 56-57, 80, 82, 208, 314, 321
- having three functions 78
- authenticity of 112
- authority of 106
- *mantras* of 77

Vedādhikāranirūpaṇam 313

Vedāṅgas 314

Vedānta 80, 82, 127, 134, 190, 194, 203, 205, 214, 262, 273, 286, 292
- and Islam, equations between 148
- system 274
- absolutism of 203
- Bhāskara school of 205

Vedāntacandrikā 292, 305

Vedāntācārya 131

Vedāntadeśika (Veṅkaṭanātha) ix, 13, 127-28, 130-31, 304

Vedāntakaṇṭakoddhāra 132

Vedāntaratna-mañjūṣā 148

Vedāntic
- and Śaivite world-views 150
- concepts 146
- idea of spiritual unity 30
- *Nirguṇa Brahman* 309
- of monist system 190
- Śaṅkara 270
- view is unfolded through dialogues and discussions 273

Vedāntins x, 114, 219, 268, 273, 277, 279

Vedārthasaṁgrahavyākhyāna 130

Vedas 41, 143, 318
- people, life and culture of 43
- philosophies 85
- philosophy, six systems of 78
- ritual 103, 221, 236
  - exegesis of 4
- sacrifices 21
- Saṁhitās 38, 40, 130
- Smṛtis 130
- study 117
- system, demolition of 108
- traditions 221

Vedic 7
and non-Vedic Āgamas 270
concept of *svarāñjyam* and *vairājyam* 337
darśanas 82, 208
dharma 56
learning, Kaṭha and Kalāpa branches of 57
literature 47
Magazine 314
Veṇābāī 238
Venice, Dr 326
Veṇidatta 204
Venkamatya 304
Veṅkaṭādhvarin 4, 23, 31, 127, 277, 279-81
Veṅkaṭanātha 36, 127-31, 274
Verkhedy, Shrinivas 35
Verma Purnasingh 320
Vetravatī 13
Vibhajyavāda,
practice of 86-87, 336
technique of 85
vibhajyavādena-vyākaraṇīya 84
Vibhajyavādin 84
Vibhīṣaṇa 64
vibhūtis 12
Vicāraśāstra 81
viḍambana 23, 240
Vidhava Vivah Sabha 324
Vidhavodvāhaśaṅkāsamādhiḥ 311
Vidhivāda 8
Vidura 17-18, 71, 73-74, 336
Vidvanmodataraṅgiṇī 194
vidyādhirāja 313
Vidyādhīśa 136-37
Vidyālaṁkāra, Bāṇeśvara 287
Vidyāmānyatīrtha 304
Vidyānanda 114
Vidyāraṇya 129-30
Vidyarthi, Gurudatta 314
Vidyasagara, Ishwara Chandra 311
Vigrahavyāvartanī 98-99
vigrāhya saṁbhāṣā 170, 178
Vijayīndra 135
vijigīṣuvāda 178
vijñāna,
diverse nature of six
pursuit of 114
Vijñānabhikṣu reformulates the whole system of Sāṁkhya 190
Vijñānādvaita 286
Vijñānavāda 97-98, 113, 196, 199
Vijñānavādin ix, 119, 197, 200-01
Vijñāneśvara 3, 19, 234
vikarmastha 195
Vikarṇa 71, 73-74
village panchayats 44
Vinaya
and Abhidhamma 94
texts 93
violence and non-violence, choice between x
vipakṣa 116
vipratipatti 161

Vīramitrodaya 289
Virdi, P.K. 230
Virocana and Sudhanvan, quarrel between 18
viruddha 163, 178
Virūpākṣa 240
Viśākhadatta 31, 272
Viśākhila 88
viṣayabhoga 139
Viṣayatāvāda 8
Viśeṣākhyāna 110
Vishuddhanand, Swami 323
Viśiṣṭādvaita
  philosophy 130, 276
    practical soundness of 313
  philosophy of 126
  propounder of 128
  system 132
  votary of 127
Viṣṇu 148, 234, 261-62, 268-69
  incarnation of 85, 118, 264
Viṣṇu Purāṇa 5, 195
Viṣṇudharmottara Purāṇa 238, 249
Viṣṇusmṛti 223, 225, 233, 235
Viṣṇutīrtha 133
vistāra-kāla 120
Viśvaguṇādarśa 278-81
Viśvaguṇādarśacampū 4, 23, 31, 127-28, 277, 281
Viśvāmitra 77
viśvātmakacaitanya, theories of 328
Viśvavaicitryavāda 328
Viśvāvasu 23, 127
Viśveśvara Paṇḍita (Gāgā Bhaṭṭa) 237
vitaṇḍā 8, 12, 34, 81, 101, 112, 114, 159, 186, 191
  is destructive debate 160
  text 308
  method of 99
  tactics of 34
  theory of a different kind of 161
vīthyaṅgas, thirteen 244
Viṭṭhaleśī 304
vivāda 19
Vivādabhaṅgārṇava 287
Vivādabhaṅgārṇavasetu 287-88
Vivādārṇavasetu 287
Vivādatāṇḍava 236
Vivaraṇaprameyasaṁgraha 195
Vivaraṇārṇava 134
vivarta 126
Vivartavāda 205
Vivasvān 61
Vivekananda, Swami 236, 283, 293, 337
von Schlegel, Wilhelm 283, 297
Vrātyaprāyaścittavinirṇaya 236
Vṛddhāmbhi 270-71
vyājastuti, genre of 278
Vyākaraṇa Setumādhavācārya 138
Vyākaraṇa 113-15, 131
  as a philosophy 114
  as *darśana* 114
  idea of 114

Vyākaraṇa-mahābhāṣya 39
Vyaktiviveka xii, 246
vyaṅgyakaraṇa 23, 240
Vyañjanāvāda 246
vyāpti 209
vyartha 178
Vyāsa 66-68, 75, 266
Vyāsatīrtha 126, 132, 201-02
vyavahāra 15
Vyavahāradaśaślokī 287
Vyavahārādhyāya 235
vyavahāras, kinds of 228
vyāvahārika sattā 81
Vyomaśiva 111-12
Vyutpattivāda 8

Wayman, A. 35, 178, 180
Weber, Max 10, 321
Western dialecticism 2
widow remarriage 310-12, 322, 324
    treatise against 311
Wilkins, Charles 283, 288
Wilkinson, Lancelot 227, 309
Wilson, H.H. 298, 308
Wilson, Jon E. 282, 288-89, 291
Winternitz, Moriz 284-85, 287, 303, 306
woman's defence in a cruel society of men 64

Yādava 130-31
Yādavābhyudaya 129
Yadusena 142
yajña 78
    ritual 185
    cosmic view of 46
Yājñavalkya 3, 6, 19, 21, 48-50, 96, 106, 117, 223-35
Yājñavalkyasmṛti 3, 6, 19, 21, 227-28, 233, 235
Yajnik, Indulal 312
Yājñika-Mīmāṁsakas, school of 167
Yajurveda 43, 45-46, 317
Yakṣa, 54
Yama 268
    and Yamī, hymn of 44
Yaśaścandra 277
Yaśastilakacampūḥ 80
Yāska 40-41, 77-78
Yaśodhara 52
Yaśovijaya, Muni 276
Yate, Revd William 290
Yathārthaprakāśa 321
Yati, Prakāśātma 134
Yati, Satyanātha 135
Yatin, Durgāprasāda 117
Yatirāja 128
Yavanadarśana 141
Yoga 2, 41, 80, 82, 131, 143, 208
Yogācāra schools of Buddhist philosophy 203
Yogācārabhūmi 178
Yogācāra-Mādhyamika 103

Yogasūtra 80

Yogavāsiṣṭha 54, 148

Yudhiṣṭhira 16, 66-68, 71, 73-74, 79
  and Duryodhana, game of dice between 76
  and Vyāsa 266
  Rājasūya ceremony of 267

yuktakula 13

Yuktimallikā 133

Yuvaraj Prabhu Narayan Singh 323

Zelliot, Elleanor 141-43

Zoroastrianism 34, 138, 143

Zudaism, scripture of 144